Library of
Davidson College

THE DEVELOPMENT AND OPERATION OF MONETARY POLICY
1960–1983

The Development and Operation of Monetary Policy 1960–1983

A selection of material from the
Quarterly Bulletin
of the
BANK OF ENGLAND

CLARENDON PRESS · OXFORD
1984

Oxford University Press, Walton Street, Oxford OX2 6DP
London New York Toronto
Delhi Bombay Calcutta Madras Karachi
Kuala Lumpur Singapore Hong Kong Tokyo
Nairobi Dar es Salaam Cape Town
Melbourne Auckland
and associated companies in
Beirut Berlin Ibadan Mexico City Nicosia

Oxford is a trade mark of Oxford University Press

Published in the United States
by Oxford University Press, New York

Editorial matter and selection
© Bank of England 1984

All rights reserved. No part of this publication may be reproduced, stored in a retrieval system, or transmitted, in any form or by any means, electronic, mechanical, photocopying, recording, or otherwise, without the prior permission of Oxford University Press

British Library Cataloguing in Publication Data
Development and operation of monetary policy 1960-1983.
1. Monetary policy—Great Britain—History —20th century
I. Quarterly bulletin: Bank of England
332.4'941 HG939.5
ISBN 0-19-877234-3
ISBN 0-19-877233-5 Pbk

Printed in Great Britain
at the University Press, Oxford
by David Stanford
Printer to the University

CONTENTS

Introduction	1
1. The changing background to monetary policy	**5**
The operation of monetary policy since the Radcliffe Report (December 1969 *Bulletin*)	7
The importance of money (June 1970 *Bulletin*)	14
2. Competition and Credit Control	**31**
The introduction of Competition and Credit Control	31
Monetary management in the United Kingdom (March 1971 *Bulletin*)	33
Key issues in monetary and credit policy (June 1971 *Bulletin*)	39
The travails of Competition and Credit Control	42
What went wrong?	44
3. Monetary targets	**45**
The choice of monetary aggregate	45
Adoption of a monetary target	45
The operation of monetary targets	47
Speech to the biennial dinner of the Institute of Bankers, Scotland (March 1977 *Bulletin*)	49
Reflections on the conduct of monetary policy (March 1978 *Bulletin*)	51
4. Reflections on the role of monetary targets	**59**
British economic policy over the last decade (June 1983 *Bulletin*)	63
Setting monetary objectives (June 1983 *Bulletin*)	65
5. Operations in the gilt-edged market	**74**
Official transactions in the gilt-edged market (June 1966 *Bulletin*)	75
Sykes Memorial Lecture (December 1971 *Bulletin*)	83
The gilt-edged market (June 1979 *Bulletin*)	86
The Bank's operational procedures for meeting monetary objectives (June 1983 *Bulletin*)	98

CONTENTS

6. Operations in the money market   **105**

Money market operations up to 1971   105

    The management of money day by day (March 1963 *Bulletin*)   107

Competition and Credit Control and after   114

    Competition and Credit Control (June 1971 *Bulletin*)   115

    The supplementary special deposits scheme (March 1982 *Bulletin*)   117

The debate on methods of monetary control   128

    Monetary base control (June 1979 *Bulletin*)   129

    Monetary Control (Chapters 1 and 4, and Annex A of the Green Paper, Cmnd 7858, HMSO, 1980)   137

    Background note on methods of monetary control (December 1980 *Bulletin*)   148

Money market operations since 1981   150

    Monetary control: next steps (March 1981 *Bulletin*)   152

    Monetary control—provisions (September 1981 *Bulletin*)   154

    The role of the Bank of England in the money market (March 1982 *Bulletin*)   156

    'Overfunding' and money market operations (June 1982 *Bulletin*)   165

    Bills of exchange: current issues in a historical perspective (December 1982 *Bulletin*)   166

Econometric Appendix   171

    The demand for money in the United Kingdom: experience since 1971 (September 1974 *Bulletin*)   172

    A transactions demand for money (March 1978 *Bulletin*)   188

Index   193

ACKNOWLEDGEMENTS

Many hands have been involved in the preparation of this volume, as indeed there were in writing the individual papers included, and even more minds contributed to the development of the thought of the Bank on these matters that the book seeks to portray. Authorship is therefore truly of the Bank. Readings and other material in the collection have mostly been taken from issues of the *Bank of England Quarterly Bulletin* spanning a period of 20 years. Introductory and linking passages have been written specifically for this volume and it is proper to acknowledge the contributions of W A Allen, E A J George and C A E Goodhart in this, and in the selection of material for inclusion to which Mrs T M May and J C Townend also contributed. Oxford University Press originally suggested the idea of such a book.

The account would not have been complete without material from the Green Paper on *Monetary Control* (Cmnd 7858) which was prepared jointly by H M Treasury and the Bank of England, and the Bank wishes to thank HMSO for permission to reprint parts of this paper.

Editorial work in preparing the text for the publishers was undertaken by D J Reid who is grateful to Mrs S I Gibbs, Miss E J Gunn, Miss M L Mercer and Mrs G C Rhone for secretarial assistance at various stages in its production.

INTRODUCTION

In August 1959, the Radcliffe Report[1] recommended that the Bank of England should publish a quarterly bulletin. In the Committee's view, the Bank should make 'a more determined effort in its Annual Report, or at more frequent intervals, to illuminate the problems of monetary management which confront the authorities' (para 859). A possibility would be the issue of a quarterly bulletin in which could appear either some of the more technical discussions of monetary issues or signed articles on more controversial matters. We do not suggest such a bulletin merely as a method of promoting informed discussion of the working of the monetary system, since there is already an ample range of technical journals, but in order to allow a fuller and freer exposition by members of the staff of the Bank of issues which they are in a unique position to discuss (para 861).

The Bank accepted this recommendation, and the first issue of its *Quarterly Bulletin*, dated December 1960, was published in January 1961. The *Bulletin*, thenceforward, has provided a platform for the publication of written material, encompassing speeches and articles, ranging from regular commentaries to technical econometric research,[2] on matters of interest to the Bank.

Among the subjects of interest to the Bank, a preeminent concern has been the conduct of monetary policy. This concern has several facets. It is, perhaps, possible to distinguish two of these. The first involves the strategic issues about the overall direction and conduct of monetary policy. The second covers the operational problems, notably of dealing in the key domestic financial markets, in order to achieve those strategic objectives. Although the dividing line between the strategic and the operational is inevitably uncertain, it is possible to characterise papers on monetary issues in terms of this distinction, as being primarily policy-oriented or operational.

This book offers a selection of such papers combining the major papers and pronouncements made by the Bank on the conduct, objectives and operations of British monetary policy. Being a selection of papers, prepared by several different hands over a number of years, it cannot, and does not attempt to, provide the overall coverage of a text book. But no study of domestic finance and monetary policy in the United Kingdom in the period since the end of the 1960s would be complete without a careful appreciation of the views of the Bank.

The material in this book takes several different forms. Most of the papers on the operational aspects of monetary policy are concerned with the management of domestic financial markets and describe the introduction of new methods of operation, or are briefing articles on the working of the bill and gilt-edged markets. The material concerned with policy has, however, been more varied. This has ranged from highly technical econometric studies aimed at elucidating the quantitative relationships between the monetary aggregates, real incomes, prices, and interest rates, to more analytical papers employing both general theory and historical experience in order to review the conduct of monetary policy, through to speeches expounding the view of the Bank on the immediate issues of the time, usually delivered formally by the Governor. Most of these speeches, however, also covered other matters besides domestic monetary policy. In particular, each year in October the Governor addresses the Lord Mayor's dinner at the Mansion House. This generally provides an opportunity for reviewing major policy issues concerning the Bank during the current and coming years, among which monetary policy has usually had a large role. Extracts from these, and certain other speeches, form an important part of the record of the development of the Bank's views. But, since they are extracts, they need to be woven into a wider story of the development of these views, and this has been done by connecting and scene-setting passages.

The contents of the book divide naturally into two main parts along the lines described earlier. The first four chapters deal with more general policy issues and describe the overall development of monetary policy during the last 25 years. Chapter 1 covers the changing background to monetary policy from the time of the Radcliffe Report through to the introduction of Competition and Credit Control in 1971, which forms the subject of Chapter 2. The background to and introduction of monetary targets are described in Chapter 3 while Chapter 4 contains some reflections on the role of monetary targets in the light of experience operating with them.

---

1 *Committee on the Working of the Monetary System*; HMSO, Cmnd 827, 1959.
2 Owing to the increasing volume and technicality of the research work done in the Bank, many of the research papers subsequently were published in the *Discussion Paper* series, which began in October 1978; this was further complemented by a series of *Technical Papers*, which began in August 1982.

INTRODUCTION

The second part of the book consists of two chapters on the Bank's operations in the gilt-edged market (Chapter 5) and the money market (Chapter 6).

Two further papers have been included as an Econometric Appendix. These relate mainly to the policy part of the book, but stand somewhat apart from it. The first describes the breakdown of the demand for money function for broad money after 1971 and the second examines the stability of the demand for narrow money, M1. Econometric techniques have developed considerably since these papers were written and far more econometric work has been undertaken within the Bank than is portrayed in these papers. They have been included more as examples of studies that at the time did influence the formation of views on policy than because they are models of their genre.

A collection such as this also provides an opportunity to assess the development of the Bank's views over the years: to observe those aspects that have remained relatively constant, and those that have changed against the background of rapidly changing external circumstances and shifting theories and views. It has, indeed, been a period of major changes in both circumstances and ideas.

At the start of the period, for most of the 1960s the United Kingdom was on a fixed exchange rate regime with, by international standards, both low real growth and also relatively low inflation. The problems then were mainly seen as how to raise the low growth rate without running into a balance of payments constraint. Meanwhile monetary policy was seen by most commentators and academics in the United Kingdom as a rather minor instrument, which involved two main forms. The first was action on interest rates, which was seen as having some, but uncertain and limited, effect on external capital flows and a, perhaps, weaker impact on domestic expenditures. The second was direct credit rationing, which was thought to have a stronger effect, though subject to ever-increasing erosion and evasion, on domestic expenditure. Such views are clearly represented in the paper prepared jointly with the Treasury in 1969 on *The operation of monetary policy since the Radcliffe Report*,[1] included in Chapter 1.

Already by that time, however, the policy environment had started to change, with inflation becoming an increasingly insistent element in the problem of economic management, and one which was widely perceived to be especially closely associated with specific monetary disturbance. By this time, too, and partly as a result, academic views on the role of monetary policy had started to change under the growing influence of the monetarist school. The resulting debate was naturally of great importance to central banks generally and, accordingly, the Bank was itself concerned to assess the analytical arguments and econometric findings. This was the aim of the second paper in Chapter 1 on *The importance of money*.

Increasing attention to the rate of growth of monetary aggregates was to become one of the major themes in the evolution of monetary policy in the following period. Another was the attempt to dispense with direct credit controls. These had been in operation almost continuously through the 1960s and had become increasingly irksome over time. As they continued to be applied year after year, their structural disadvantages, in suppressing competition and the efficient evolution of the financial system, became even greater: at the same time, their conjunctural use in limiting and controlling domestic expenditure became less compelling over time, as the growing erosion and evasion of such direct controls (disintermediation) made it increasingly difficult to observe what effect, if any, they were having.

This was the background against which the Bank, in 1971, initiated a major change in the operation and conduct of monetary policy, generally known as Competition and Credit Control.[2] The arguments for making this major change were foreshadowed in the Jane Hodge Memorial Lecture entitled *Monetary management in the United Kingdom*, delivered by the Governor in December 1970, and the *modus operandi* of monetary policy under the new system was then described in a speech he gave at Munich in May 1971 on *Key issues in monetary and credit policy*. These form the two main components of Chapter 2.

This new system, launched in September 1971, soon found itself in the middle of a turbulent period. The years 1971–73 witnessed a climactic boom for the whole western industrial world, fuelled in the United Kingdom by expansionary fiscal policies, and ultimately brought to an end by the first oil price shock in 1973–74. The resulting general international pressures caused the final collapse of the Bretton Woods pegged exchange rate system, with the United Kingdom abandoning its own adherence to the pegged exchange rate system in June 1972. Meanwhile, the UK Govern-

---

1 The titles of articles that appear elsewhere in this book have been set in *italics*.

2 The note introducing the new system of Competition and Credit Control, taken from the June 1971 *Bulletin*, is included in Chapter 6. An extract from the *Sykes Memorial Lecture* given by the Chief Cashier on Competition and Credit Control in November 1971, and reproduced in the December 1971 *Bulletin*, is included in Chapter 5. These two papers contain material important in understanding the Bank's market operations but they are also an essential part of the story of Competition and Credit Control told in Chapter 2.

INTRODUCTION

ment was trying to deal with the consequential inflationary pressures by direct measures—incomes policies—to limit increases in prices and wages.

The abandonment of direct credit ceilings and controls, and the adoption of the more market-oriented system, allowed, indeed encouraged, the banks to compete and participate in the aggressive and expansionary atmosphere of those years. They were further enabled to do so by the new techniques, developed in the United States, of liability management, whereby the banks did not have to wait to receive deposits in order to obtain funds to on-lend. Instead, when a lending opportunity was perceived, they could go out into the market to bid for wholesale funds. In addition, there were at times distortions to relative interest rates which artificially inflated the broad monetary aggregates. Taken together, and despite generally rising interest rates during this period which served to constrain the growth of the narrow monetary aggregates from mid-1973 onwards, these factors contributed to a massive and undoubtedly unhealthy expansion of bank credit and bank deposits.

This could not be allowed to continue. In order to prevent it, a form of control over the rate of increase of banks' interest-bearing deposits, known as the supplementary special deposits scheme or 'corset', was introduced at the end of 1973. This represented an undesired, but necessary, withdrawal from the objectives of Competition and Credit Control: a paper describing and reviewing this scheme over the whole period of its operations was published in the March 1982 *Bulletin* and is reprinted in Chapter 6.

Despite this reversion to a degree of direct credit rationing, the need for continuing concern with the rate of growth of the monetary aggregates was felt at this time to be even more essential. Likewise, the need for a financial anchor to replace the exchange rate in order to constrain inflationary pressures was equally strongly felt. From 1973 onwards, objectives were adopted for the monetary aggregate M3 which were initially unpublished. By 1976, however, a combination of foreign example (Germany and the United States had adopted publicly-announced monetary targets) and the collapse of external confidence in sterling led to the adoption of a publicly-announced monetary target for the United Kingdom. In Chapter 3 that experience is reviewed, drawing on material in Governor's speeches. The adoption of publicly-announced monetary targets in 1976 was, perhaps, the second great landmark for domestic monetary policy (the first being the adoption of Competition and Credit Control) during these years.

After 1979 the Government placed even greater emphasis on the announcement and achievement of the monetary target (which now applied to sterling M3), and not just for one year ahead, but over a longer medium-term horizon. The re-affirmation of the importance of monetary targetry, however, coincided with a further period of rapid structural change. The abolition of exchange controls in October 1979 necessitated the removal of the 'corset', since any domestic constraint on financial intermediation brought about by the 'corset' could then be simply and easily avoided by intermediation through banks abroad. As had happened on previous occasions when such direct controls were removed, the pent-up volume of funds that had been shifted to other channels, often unperceived, returned after the abolition of the control to the banks and was larger than had been realised or predicted. Meanwhile, the pressures on the various sectors of the UK economy, caused by conflict between the strongly-entrenched inflationary forces within the economy on the one hand, and the determined counter-inflationary policies of the Government on the other, led to unusual financial needs and pressures for intermediation through the banks; the personal sector was induced to use its massive financial surplus to provide the funds to the banks which companies needed to borrow. Further distorting effects on monetary growth were subsequently caused by the Civil Service strike, which, for several months, reduced the inflow of tax receipts, especially from the company sector. For such various reasons, the relationships between the monetary target, sterling M3, together with its credit counterparts, and nominal incomes became even more uncertain during this period. Although sterling M3 exceeded its target considerably for two years, nevertheless the rate of growth of nominal incomes declined over the same period (and also subsequently) more rapidly than had been expected. Put another way, velocity fell more sharply than had been predicted.

The authorities reacted to this by extending the range of target aggregates, adding an additional broad monetary aggregate, PSL2 (representing the wider definition of private sector liquidity), and adding a narrow monetary target, M1: and they stated explicitly that, in interpreting monetary developments, they would look at other available evidence, including movements in the exchange rate, inflationary expectations, and interest rates.

These changes in the form of policy were necessary to meet changing circumstances, including increasing financial innovation, which made the relationship between any single monetary aggregate and nominal income difficult to interpret in the short term. They

INTRODUCTION

were not regarded as involving any change in the substance or intent of monetary policy.

It is against this background that the contents of the final policy chapter, Chapter 4, including two papers reflecting on the later years of monetary targetry, are presented.

The problems of monetary management during these later years, led, in addition, to a lengthy review of the methods of monetary control, which included the official study published as a Green Paper.[1] Although this official study did not advocate any major change in the methods of monetary control (monetary base control having been the major change most commonly advocated), there were a number of subsequent, more minor, changes, largely intended to reduce the extent of direct intervention by the authorities, eg in setting minimum lending rate by administrative fiat, and *pro tanto* increasing the scope for market determination. These latter changes are described in notes that appeared in the December 1980, March 1981 and September 1981 *Bulletins* and these, together with an earlier paper which examined monetary base control, are included in Chapter 6.

It is clear from this short résumé of events, that the surrounding conjuncture, the received theoretical wisdom, and related policy regimes, have been subject to marked changes during these years. Yet throughout the period the Bank has maintained an underlying consistency of purpose and viewpoint. In its operations, the Bank has the responsibility of acting for the authorities in the domestic financial markets—the money, or bill, market and the gilt-edged market. This practical experience has induced an understanding of what can be achieved in such markets, despite their changing features over time, that is described more fully in the papers on the workings of these markets in Chapters 5 and 6.

Even more important, however, every central bank has a particular responsibility to do all that it can to maintain the value of the currency, both internally and externally. This responsibility makes it particularly sensitive to the damage caused by inflation, and concerned to achieve the implementation of those policies that may help to control inflation. Throughout the period, the Bank has been concerned to prevent undue monetary expansion. Initially this concern arose in part because practical experience in the foreign exchange market indicated that domestic monetary and credit expansion put downward pressure on sterling. But the desire to prevent depreciation of the exchange rate has been simply another facet of the Bank's desire to maintain the value of the currency.

The Bank, however, has never felt that the containment of inflation should, or could, be left to the sole responsibility of monetary policy. Throughout the years the Bank has argued that monetary policy needs to be coherently supported by other policies, notably fiscal policy.

The Bank has consistently felt the need for a financial anchor, whether it be a fixed exchange rate or a monetary target, which needs to be both publicly announced and vigorously defended, in order to give a confident basis for private sector decision-makers to plan forward. But it has never, on the other hand, felt that economic relationships were sufficiently predictable, or the financial system so static, that the conduct of policy could be safely placed on a quasi-automatic basis with the adoption of constant rules.

1 *Monetary control*; HMSO, Cmnd 7858, 1980.

CHAPTER 1
The changing background to monetary policy

Most of the material in this collection was published after 1970, but the scene is set by a retrospective look at monetary policy in the previous decade—*The operation of monetary policy since the Radcliffe Report* (page 7), published in the December 1969 *Bulletin*. This paper, written jointly by the Bank and the Treasury, provides a backdrop against which subsequent developments may be judged. As will be quickly appreciated, the paper restates the general Radcliffe position, approvingly and almost in its entirety; the paper indicates that the authorities generally followed the precepts of Radcliffe through this decade. The problems of economic management, and within that of monetary management, which were accepted to have been considerable, occurred, according to the paper, because circumstances became more difficult, rather than from any inherent defect in the (Radcliffian) policies themselves; indeed it saw monetary policy as having only a minor, and often permissive, role on its own.

In some important respects this paper on post-Radcliffe experience marked a watershed in the Bank's thinking about monetary policy. Even before it was delivered there were signs of an emerging interest—albeit a cautious, pragmatic, interest—in the rate of growth of the money supply as an indicator of monetary conditions and as a guide to policy. This can be seen in the speech given by the Governor (then Mr L K O'Brien) to the Lord Mayor's dinner for the bankers and merchants of the City of London, at the Mansion House, in October 1968.

The level of internal demand still gives cause for concern. I know there are weighty opinions which do not consider that the trend of the money supply has any reliable significance in this context. Maybe it is no foolproof guide, but I for my part believe that we should be more concerned with it, as indeed I know many informed observers overseas feel we should be. The money supply cannot become the be-all and end-all of policy. But when it continues to rise rather fast, and from a level that is high by historical standards, and, above all, when it does this at a time of deficit in overseas payments and when people are uneasily aware that the longer they hold money the less they get for it, then I am sure we must pay attention.

The Governor returned to the same topic at the Mansion House speech in October 1969, linking the importance of monetary control specifically with domestic credit expansion (DCE) and external flows. Referring to his remarks a year earlier he said:

... certainly since then it [the rate of growth of the money supply] has become of increasing concern to the authorities and I believe rightly so. The concept of domestic credit expansion, or DCE, which concentrates on what is happening to the money supply in the context of what is happening to the balance of payments is a useful one. I would not go so far as to describe it as some wonderful new, or rediscovered instrument of policy but I am sure we have benefited, and will continue to benefit, from paying close attention to it.

The Bank has always seen the need for other policies to work in concert with monetary policy, and later in the same speech, the Governor attributed much of the credit for more successful monetary control to the success of fiscal policy in securing a financial surplus.

We have been greatly helped by the extraordinary situation so far as the financing of the public sector is concerned. A substantial surplus in this sector taken as a whole, and a dramatically large one in the narrower context of central government expenditure, is unprecedented. Good though this is, one cannot but regret the heavy additional taxation that has been necessary to produce such a result. As you know, year after year, I have called attention to the urgent need to do something about the other side of the account—government expenditure. ... It is difficult enough to keep expenditure within its planned boundaries even for one year. To keep it within properly planned boundaries year in and year out is even harder, but no less urgent.

In his Mansion House speech the next year the Governor went on to discuss the role that incomes policy might also play in conjunction with monetary policy.

I know that some feel I should limit my public pronouncements to reporting on the movements in the money supply and our efforts to influence it. It is my belief, however, that for a lasting solution to the problem of inflation we must look much wider than the bounds of conventional monetary and fiscal policy. I do not see how we can expect to maintain a fully employed fully informed and increasingly well-off democracy, in which the development of wages and prices is left entirely to the operation of market forces. The bodies on both sides of the bargaining tables, the unions and employers in both the public and private sectors, are too big and too powerful for such a process to yield us the result most likely to contribute to our general welfare and prosperity. If we try to rely on the market place and on the strict operation of fiscal and monetary policies, we shall find, I think, that we can achieve price stability only at the cost of unemployment that might be on a very large scale indeed.

But, despite the Government's adoption of incomes policy, welcomed at that time by the Bank, there was no doubt about the central need to control monetary growth at the same time, as the Governor reaffirmed later in the same speech.

I do not accept either that the monetary authorities can exercise a precise control over the rate of increase in the supply of money from month to month, or that in regulating the course of the economy overwhelming priority should be given to trying to influence movements in this particular magnitude. Real life is too complex and the objectives of policy too many and various for us to be able to rely on any simple rule.

But when all this is said, there is no question in my mind that developments in the money supply and domestic credit are important: and it is clear that whatever the special factors may have been, the rate of increase in the spring and summer was higher than one would wish to see continue.

Against this background, which demonstrates the importance which the Bank increasingly attached to concern with the rate of growth of the monetary aggregates and with influencing such growth, it was natural that there would be a wish for an in-house review of the ferment of economic studies re-appraising the nature of the relationships between the money stock and economic developments more widely. This is the subject of the second paper of this chapter *The importance of money* (page 14) together with its first appendix which comments on the empirical evidence obtained by researchers in several countries on the nature of the relationship. This paper was published in the June 1970 *Bulletin*.

The operation of monetary policy since the Radcliffe Report

A paper prepared in the Bank of England in consultation with H.M. Treasury, as one of a number of papers presented at a conference held at Hove in October on the subject "Radcliffe – ten years after". The paper will be re-printed in a book entitled Money in Britain 1959/69, *to be published by the Clarendon Press in March 1970.*

If the fundamental nature of the economic difficulties confronting the United Kingdom has perhaps not altered over the past decade, the difficulties have certainly become much more severe. There have at the same time been dramatic developments in financial institutions and markets, both domestically and internationally. In these circumstances, and especially as some of the limitations of demand management through fiscal policy have been revealed, there has been considerable evolution in the methods and tactics of monetary policy. Broadly, however, the approach to policy has been similar to that of the Radcliffe Committee in that the authorities have consistently believed that it was right to pay attention to and try to understand the general financial position of all sectors of the economy and insufficient to concentrate exclusively on a single variable such as the quantity of money, however that may be defined.

This paper begins with a brief survey of some of the developments in the general economic context within which monetary policy has had to work. This is followed by a discussion of the actual operation of policy over the period – the broad approach followed, the problems and complications which have been encountered and the responses which have been made in methods and tactics. Finally, there is an attempt to assess the effects of monetary policy, both in itself and in relation to fiscal policy.

I The context of monetary policy
a The economic problems and objectives

During the ten years since 1959 official policy has been particularly concerned to achieve two major economic objectives – the acceleration of the sustainable rate of growth of the economy and the rectification of the balance of payments – without sacrificing the goal of a high level of employment to which all post-war British governments have been committed. Though the Radcliffe Committee discussed both these objectives, they were, perhaps, not as acutely aware as we are today of the difficulty of pursuing both of them at the same time. Nor was the problem of the balance of payments as serious then as it became later. Indeed, the Committee looked back (paragraph 633) to "a substantial surplus on current account over the past ten years" suggesting "no fundamental lack of balance in the United Kingdom's trading position". The repeated exchange crises had, in the Committee's view, been due not "to any failure on the part of the United Kingdom to pay her way but to the volatility of various elements in the balance of payments and to the lack of reserves adequate to withstand the resulting pressure on them".

In the attempts made by successive administrations since 1959 to foster an acceleration of the United Kingdom's growth rate by official policies, monetary policy was seen as having primarily a permissive rôle. In the earlier part of the period, when it was hoped it would be possible to provide a long-term solution to the balance of payments problem through an acceleration of the increase in national productivity, monetary policy therefore occupied a somewhat subsidiary rôle. Monetary measures were largely taken, as had been common in the earlier period, as supporting elements in general 'packages' of measures. Later, as a short-term conflict between the balance of payments and domestic expansion – especially expansion not centred on productive capital expenditures – became increasingly strong, economic policy had increasingly to be directed to the short-term balance of payments problem. The earlier conception of prolonged periods of relatively permissive monetary policy punctuated only occasionally by bouts of short-lived severe measures gave way to the prolonged use of stringent measures of all kinds. Moreover, as the limits of effectiveness of fiscal policies, incomes policies and exchange controls appeared to be more nearly reached, the relative emphasis placed on monetary policy increased.

b International developments
Externally, the Radcliffe Committee looked back on the years of the dollar shortage, inconvertible European currencies and relatively low levels for interest rates throughout the world. Although the United States had by 1959 already moved into the position of substantial external deficit which has been maintained ever since, this major change was not yet widely recognised. The Committee suggest (paragraph 684) that the problem of dollar shortage might be "... more intermittent and less intractable than is sometimes supposed, and that it has already changed in character and is likely to continue to do so"; but they did not believe "... that the rest of the world, including the United Kingdom, can safely dismiss from its calculations any future difficulty in effecting settlements with the United States." Certainly they did not foresee the problem of dollar surplus.

The major European currencies only became fully convertible in 1958 and there were a number of liberalising moves in the next few years. As a result the sixties have seen an international mobility of short-term capital on a scale unprecedented since pre-war days.

The prolonged U.S. deficit and the convertibility of major currencies have had several important consequences for the operation of U.K. monetary policy. One was the enormous growth of the euro-dollar market, which barely existed in 1959 and now amounts to some $40 billion. London is, of course, the major centre for euro-dollar transactions, and the effects of this development on the structure of both financial institutions and financial markets in the United Kingdom are discussed briefly below. A further effect has been that both in 1966–67 and 1968–69 a restrictive U.S. monetary policy has had a substantial influence on short-term flows and on international interest rate levels. Although 'covered margins' have ceased to have the significance they previously had, they obviously remain important.

c The central government borrowing requirement
The period has been marked by a rapid growth in the borrowing requirement of the central government – from a position of approximate balance in 1958/59 to £1,335 million in 1967/68 – and by a similar increase in the borrowing requirement of the public sector as a whole. Implicit in this trend is the problem of ensuring that public expenditure does not pre-empt an excessive share of the growth of real resources. But there are monetary problems, too, in financing a deficit for the public sector; and as the deficit grew, the means of financing it had increasingly severe implications for finance in the private sector. The Radcliffe Committee reported (in paragraph 528) that they could "... find no automatic rule for restricting a Government that is determined to spend." Ten years later we are still without an automatic rule. But much effort has been, and is being, devoted to improving the statistics and the administrative techniques for keeping public spending and borrowing on course. The results are already apparent in a striking reversal since 1967/68: the central government has moved from a deficit of £1,335 million in 1967/68 to a surplus of £273 million in 1968/69. And in 1969/70 not only the central government but the whole public sector should be in a position to make a net repayment of debt. This in turn will have unfamiliar consequences for finance in the rest of the economy.

d Institutional financial developments
In 1959 the deposit banks (the London clearing banks, together with the Scottish and Northern Ireland banks) accounted for 85% of the total sterling deposits of the U.K. banking sector. By 1968 they had increased their deposits by about two thirds; but their share of total sterling deposits had fallen to 75%, as the sterling deposits of the accepting houses, overseas banks and other banks trebled, from about £1,000 million to £3,000 million. Meanwhile the rapid growth of the euro-dollar market has resulted in an increase in foreign currency deposits from a few hundred million in 1959 to about £16,000 million now. Not only has the business of existing banks in London increased, but also many overseas banks have been encouraged by the development of the euro-dollar market to set up new offices or branches in London. The total number of banks in London has risen by more than 50% since 1959. The deposit banks have, however, been inhibited from directly taking in any significant amount of foreign currency deposits by their cash and liquidity ratios which make it difficult for these banks to employ such deposits profitably – though many of them have been able to participate in the business through their subsidiaries. Their share of the U.K. banking sector's total sterling and foreign currency deposits has thus fallen to 50%.

The overall growth of the accepting houses, overseas banks and other U.K. banks has had a number of important consequences for policy. Restriction of the lending of the deposit banks alone would have been increasingly inequitable and ineffective in restricting total bank credit; on the other hand, the structures of the balance sheets of the other banks differ so greatly from those of the deposit banks and from one another, that control over their lending by means of balance sheet ratios poses difficult problems, and the possibility of switching in and out of foreign currency has had implications for the balance of payments, interest rate policy and exchange control.

e Developments of financial markets

As striking as the growth of the accepting houses and overseas banks, and very closely linked with it, has been the growth of new short-term financial markets unknown, or relatively unimportant, when the Radcliffe Report was written. The euro-dollar market has already been mentioned. Domestically the parallel money markets – the market in sterling inter-bank funds and the market for local authority deposits (each attracting about 8% of the assets of the accepting houses, overseas and other banks) – have grown up alongside the Treasury bill market; interest rates in these markets are not in any fixed or conventional relation to Treasury bill rates. More recently, important markets first in dollar, then in sterling certificates of deposit have grown up. There has also been a strong revival of the use of commercial bills over the ten-year period.

f Developments in information

Finally, a very important change has occurred in the information available to the policy-makers. As the magnitude of this change and the extremely short period for which usable statistics have been available are often underrated, it may be worth saying a little about it.

The approach of the Radcliffe Committee to monetary policy, with which, as has already been indicated, the authorities have been broadly in sympathy, could not be realised without a major development in statistical information on the financial positions of all the main sectors of the economy and the flows of funds between them. The Radcliffe Committee remarked that appropriate financial statistics should ". . . be capable of being fitted together so as to show the total movement of funds, not merely the flow through individual financial institutions" (paragraph 865) and this is the aim which has been kept in mind in developing the flow of funds or sector financing accounts.

Six sectors are now distinguished – personal, public, banking, other financial institutions, industrial and commercial companies, and overseas. These accounts have been linked to the capital accounts of the corresponding sectors derived from the national income statistics, with the aim of explaining the financial surplus or deficit of each sector – *i.e.* the residual after setting the sector's capital expenditure against its savings – which is what it is presumed to have lent to, or borrowed from, other sectors. Ideally, within such a framework it should be possible to decide on appropriate measures to influence the flows of funds between sectors and their effects on real expenditures. Considerable progress has in fact been made towards using the statistics, in a rough and ready way, for these purposes. The estimates of the financial surpluses and deficits themselves cannot provide any independent check on the national income estimates and forecasts, since they are derived from them; but the process of completing the sector financing tables can often provide 'plausibility checks' by bringing to light relationships between financial and real magnitudes which are implied in the national income forecasts but look unlikely in relation to past experience (*e.g.* between company profits and fixed investment). More directly related to the conduct of monetary policy is the assessment of the outlook for the flows of funds between sectors. Attempts are made to forecast these flows in the light of past experience, and in particular to assess the sources from which the public sector will derive whatever it will need to borrow – or to which it may be able to repay debt.

In this field, however, although we have come a long way since 1959, it is perhaps more striking how far we have still to go. The figures go back only a very small distance: annual data (with a high degree of estimation) to 1952, quarterly data only to 1963. There are many difficulties in deriving sector figures accurately from the available statistics. There are serious conceptual problems in seasonally adjusting these financial figures, so that it is only within the last year or two that it has been possible to make a sensible attempt to do so: and we are still far from satisfied with the results. Moreover, many of the relationships are likely to vary cyclically, so that in effect four or five years' figures may provide only one set of parameters.

There is considerable delay in collecting the figures: it takes at present up to four months after the end of a quarter to assemble a set of financing accounts for that quarter. But perhaps the most important barrier to intelligent use of the financial statistics lies in the large residual errors. One of the main advantages of the technique is supposed to be that it goes beyond the statistics of financial institutions as such and displays what is happening in the company and personal sectors. Yet it is just in these two sectors that the largest residual discrepancies appear. Thus on average over the four years to 1968 over £500 million a year of net lending or spending by companies remains unexplained and over £600 million a year of net borrowing or receipts by persons is similarly unaccounted for. Discrepancies of this order naturally weaken confidence in the estimates as a whole.

Of course, the errors indicated by these discrepancies may derive at least partly from the national income and expenditure accounts. But there are certain known gaps in the sector financing accounts, outstanding among which are the lack of any adequate figures of trade credit and the lack of any regular reports by companies of their transactions in financial assets/liabilities. Attempts are being made to close these gaps, which are no doubt responsible for swelling the residual discrepancies. Meanwhile, it is useful to have constantly in view a measure of the mismatch of the two sets of data.

Whatever the shortcomings of the data, however, a position has certainly been reached where much useful analysis can be undertaken with a view to determining some of the important relationships – both between financial and real variables and within the financial framework itself. We are stepping up very sharply work of this kind in the Bank and the Treasury; and we hope to learn from work done outside – for example, from the studies on the company sector at present being done at Stirling University. Indeed, we have deliberately extended this section of this paper in the hope of stimulating interest in the academic world in work in conjunction with the authorities on areas important for policy-making.

Even if it could be compiled with reliable estimates in

every box, however, the complete flow-of-funds matrix is not a handy means of communicating running comment on the latest developments, nor therefore a convenient aid to short-term policy reviews. There is a parallel need for prompt and frequent indicators as to how the underlying position is developing. Interest rates and such magnitudes as the government deficit, the level of bank advances, the sale of gilts – and of course the transactions of the Exchange Equalisation Account – have long been watched. More recently, however, an aggregate comprising broadly the growth of the domestic money supply plus or minus any external deficit or surplus and styled "domestic credit expansion" (D.C.E.) which is available relatively quickly has come into use as a helpful additional indicator.

Much work remains to be done on the nature of any causal inter-relationships between D.C.E. and the important real magnitudes; but there is some indication from work already carried out of some statistically significant associations, and charts comparing the movements of D.C.E. and some expenditure series have been published in the Bank's *Quarterly Bulletin*. The stress at present laid on D.C.E. is as a prompt, shorthand supplement to, rather than a replacement of, the regular 'real' and financial forecasts for the economy. Moreover, fully to interpret and draw policy significance from movements in D.C.E. it is necessary to disaggregate it and analyse developments in its constituent parts. For this, of course, the sector financing accounts are useful.

II Policy developments over the last ten years

As has already been emphasised, the official approach to policy has over the whole period laid stress on influencing the cost or availability of credit flows to the various sectors of the economy.

Developments over the last ten years in the means of giving effect to credit policy were a continuation of a process already under way before the Radcliffe Enquiry. Credit controls have gradually become more specific and direct, in that the forms of credit to which restrictions are applied, the priorities to be observed and the exemptions to be allowed have been defined in more detail (though the authorities continue to have a strong aversion to making the banks' individual decisions for them). Moreover, various forms of control have been applied to a widening range of banks and other financial institutions have been covered.

Certain areas have been subject to quite specific control by the authorities. Thus credit extended through finance houses for the purchase of cars or consumer durables has been affected by variations in the regulations concerning down-payments and the terms of repayment. Hire purchase controls were used quite actively in the 1950s and despite the Radcliffe Report's verdict that they were suitable for use only for short periods at times of emergency, they have been employed for quite long periods and the terms have been changed thirteen times since 1959. Controls were reimposed in April 1960, and were tightened progressively in June 1965, February 1966 and July 1966. Following relaxations in 1967, the controls were tightened at the time of devaluation and again in November 1968, when they reached the same level as at July 1966. There has, however, been persistent criticism of this particular weapon both because of its high specificity of effect – though this can also be seen as one of its principal advantages – and also because of a steady increase in avoidance. Official recognition of the problems of controls in this area was underlined by the appointment of the Crowther Committee.

Private housebuilding is another sector which has been subject to quite specific effects from monetary policy, not because of any direct official controls over the flow of credit through the financial intermediaries concerned, but as a result of changes in the general level of interest rates brought about by the authorities. The institutional fact that building society rates are sticky and respond to movements in general rates only partially and with a lag means that raising the general level of interest rates usually produces a marked reduction in the supply of funds available for house purchase, which in turn influences the rate of housebuilding.

Apart from these two specific areas, the authorities have concentrated their efforts in monetary policy largely on influencing lending by the banking system; but they have not attempted to achieve this by acting to reduce the cash base of the system. The authorities are always prepared to deal in Treasury bills and gilt-edged stocks at a price, because they attach importance to the maintenance of an effective market in these instruments. So any holder of such government debt – and indeed of other types of government debt such as national savings – can always switch into or out of cash at will; should the debt instrument be near to maturity, at little cost. To achieve influence over the banks' lending by means of pressure on their cash must involve conscious manipulation of interest rates primarily to that end. But in the short run at least, the market's reaction to interest changes can be perverse in the sense that the public will sell as rates rise – expecting worse to come – and is generally unpredictable. The authorities' stance has generally been to decide on an interest rate policy broadly appropriate to the general aims of economic policy at the time rather than using it to enforce a particular level of cash reserves irrespective of the wider effects of such a policy.

Broadly similar considerations govern action on the liquidity ratios of the clearing banks and Scottish banks, but it has nevertheless been possible to exert some leverage by this means. This pressure has been, on occasions, reinforced by the use of the Special Deposits scheme. Although the first impact of a call for Special Deposits is on the banks' cash position, their normal and expected reaction is to encash enough of their liquid assets to make the payment, so that the impact is immediately transmitted to their liquidity position. Use of the Special Deposits scheme can also cause interest rate variations – if, for example, the banks are induced to sell gilts – which are not entirely to the liking of the authorities, but at least such a response is more calculable and subject to the influence of the authorities. The scheme, which at the time of the Radcliffe Report had been worked out but not used, was first employed in April 1960. Except for a period of about two and a half years between 1962 and 1965, some calls on the clearing banks and Scottish banks have been outstanding even since.

One of the authorities' problems has been that monetary restraint has frequently seemed necessary at times when it would have been difficult to sell large quantities of government debt to the public at any reasonable price. So at such times the banks often obtained additional liquid assets. Moreover in the earlier years of this decade, largely as a consequence of war-time finance, they were still holding very large quantities of liquid assets and short-dated gilts.

One solution to problems of this kind might have been to require the banks to keep their total lending to the private sector within a specified ratio to their deposits (as proposed in paragraph 527 of the Radcliffe Report). A 'private sector lending ratio' may indeed appear to have substantial advantages over a liquidity ratio, because it would be simpler in appearance and because it might be thought to be more certain in its effect. There are several reasons why the device has not been adopted. First, there are, of course, seasonal variations in lending to the private sector, so that the prescribed ratio would either have to look forward to the next seasonal peak — and so look too relaxed for the intervening months — or be varied frequently in an attempt to follow the seasonal pattern. In either case it would be difficult to give the changes any clear and decisive impact. And there would be no safety-valve (such as is provided with a liquidity ratio by sales of gilt-edged). This looks at first sight like an advantage; but the practical result would probably be that the banks would fail to maintain the prescribed lending ratio, because they do not have 'instant' control over their advances and deposits. There are obvious embarrassments in prescribing a minimum ratio between quantities that are liable to large random fluctuations.

In recent years the situation has improved in one respect: the proportion of government debt in the banks' total assets has considerably declined during the past decade leaving the banks less scope for cushioning the impact of restraint by switching their lending from the public to the private sector. The problems of controlling both the credit base and monetary liquidity more generally, on the other hand, have not become significantly easier. The major difficulty is that circumstances which call for the dampening of economic activity tend to be unfavourable to government financing in non-liquid form particularly through sales of gilt-edged. Obviously the task may become more difficult at times when the central government needs to raise large amounts of new finance as it did, for example, during the bulge in public sector capital investment programmes in the middle 1960s. But even with the central government in overall surplus as at present, the position of the authorities remains vulnerable because of the constant need to refinance maturing debt.

With gilt-edged maturities currently at a rate of around £1,500 million a year, a primary official objective must continue to be that described in the Bank of England *Bulletin* in June 1966, that is to maintain market conditions that will maximise, both now and in the future, the desire of investors to hold British government debt. This long-term objective obviously affects the authorities' choice of tactics in a particular short-run situation. Because the market response to a moderate price change for gilt-edged has been found to be unstable and often perverse in the short term, the movement of interest rates required to achieve adequate liquidity absorption through debt operations may be so large that a rapid or seemingly arbitrary adjustment could permanently damage the willingness of investors to hold gilt-edged, compounding the difficulties of monetary management in the future. What can be achieved at any given time is essentially a matter of judgment of the state of market expectations and of the effects upon them of alternative courses of action, both in the long and the short run, and both within and outside the gilt-edged field. This means that there can be no simple code of conduct for debt management but that each situation must be assessed in the light of the complex of circumstances then prevailing and the current aims of policy, including the need to preserve the attractiveness of the market in the longer term.

In some cases official judgment has favoured moderating considerably any movements of interest rates; in other situations, however, where the market was tending to move in a manner considered to be an appropriate adjustment to current conditions, official intervention has been on a very limited scale, allowing market forces to be much more fully reflected in prices. In the last years of the period, as greater weight has been placed on monetary policy, there has been a greater flexibility in policy on interest rates and a greater willingness to allow upward pressures on rates in the market to take effect; and this has given more scope for flexible tactics in debt management.

To allow the authorities to adapt their tactics to market conditions more readily, two changes of technique have recently been introduced in official dealings in the gilt-edged market. In July of this year it was made known that the authorities would no longer announce the price at which they were prepared to sell tap stocks, but would instead consider bids made by the market. Some two months earlier it was announced that the official buying price for stocks within three months of maturity would for the time being not be tied to the Treasury bill rate, but that the Government Broker remained ready to receive offers of such stock.

In practice during the past ten years the level of interest rates has fluctuated considerably, and there is little evidence that a more active approach would have been more effective. For example, even with yields at the historically high levels of the recent past, it was not at all clear that official sales of stock would have been increased in the short term by lowering prices still further, and the long-term effects of such tactics would certainly have been harmful. In short, official operations in gilt-edged continue to be constrained both by the underlying market situation and by long-term concern for the maintenance of a broad market.

For much of the ten-year period the circumstances required more severe restraint on credit than could be achieved by acting on liquidity and ratios. It was therefore necessary to have recourse to direct forms of control — the imposition of lending ceilings. Direct requests to the deposit banks to restrict the level of their advances had been made at times in the 1950s. A similar request was made in July 1961, in association with a call for Special Deposits. However, it was no longer possible, on grounds of either equity or efficiency, to restrict ceilings to deposit banks alone, and on this occasion the request was addressed to all groups of banks and to a wide range of financial institutions. The terms of the request were fairly general (". . . that the recent rate of increase in advances should be greatly reduced"). Lending ceilings were reimposed in 1965 when all banks and hire purchase finance houses were asked to restrict their lending to an annual rate of increase of 5% in the twelve months to March 1966. Specific ceilings of this general kind have been in force for most of the time since then. The quantitative ceilings have been accompanied by qualitative guidance – again, not a new development – on the direction of lending. This guidance has always accorded priority to export finance.

The increased importance of banks other than the deposit banks has made it appropriate to devise a form of control over their lending, analogous to Special Deposits, for use when moderate, rather than severe, restraint is necessary. Because of the wide diversity in the balance sheet structures of the accepting houses, overseas banks, etc. it would have been difficult to devise a mechanism which, like Special Deposits, worked simply by its effect on the banks' liquidity. The Cash Deposits scheme was therefore designed so that it could be made to impinge, if necessary, on the banks' earnings as well as on their liquidity. It provides for the banks to make cash deposits with the Bank of England calculated as a percentage of certain of their deposit liabilities in sterling (together with foreign currency deposits to the extent that they have been switched into sterling). The Bank would normally treat all participating banks alike and would pay a market rate of interest, linked to the Treasury bill rate, on all Cash Deposits. But they reserve a right in exceptional cases to treat banks individually; and also to pay a lower rate of interest than the Treasury bill rate. These penalty aspects of the scheme would not necessarily be invoked; their mere existence should help to reinforce any official guidance to the banks on their lending. However, this scheme has not yet been used because it has continued to be necessary to exercise tighter control through ceilings.

Problems have also arisen of influencing lending by other financial institutions, particularly finance houses. As has been pointed out above, hire purchase terms control, imposed by the Board of Trade, gives some measure of control over parts of the credit. But terms control applies to only certain goods and certain forms of lending and in any case has been subject to increasing avoidance. Direct requests by the Bank of England for the observance of ceilings over lending were therefore extended beyond the banking sector to include the members of the Finance Houses Association and larger non-members in 1965. At present they are being asked to bring their lending down to 98% of its level at end-October 1967. Within this ceiling, the finance houses have been asked not to grant personal loans for the purchase of goods subject to terms control on easier terms than would apply to a hire purchase agreement.

As with the banks, the Bank rely on the voluntary co-operation of the finance houses for the implementation of ceiling control. Again as with the banks, there are obvious objections to ceiling control as a method of restricting credit – such as arbitrary choice of a base date, and curtailment of competition between controlled institutions. There is also the inescapable problem of the borderline (which has to be drawn somewhere) between institutions to which requests for credit restriction are directed and those to which they are not. But although check-traders, small finance houses and other institutions are not at present covered by ceiling controls, the Bank find that limiting their requests to members of the F.H.A. and to larger non-members covers the bulk of finance house lending, while avoiding the complexities that any significant extension of the present coverage would involve. It is also true that institutions not receiving the Bank's requests do not generally finance themselves to any significant extent by taking deposits or borrowing on the capital market, but have to rely on sources of finance already controlled. As noted above, the authorities are aware of the shortcomings of ceiling control for finance houses, and have been considering alternative methods of control for some time. The views of the Crowther Committee on Consumer Credit are expected to be received during 1970.

The Bank send copies of the notices or letters issued to the banks and finance houses on credit restraint to the British Insurance Association, the National Association of Pension Funds, the Building Societies Association, and to institutions such as Industrial and Commercial Finance Corporation and Finance Corporation for Industry. These institutions are asked to bear the Bank's objectives closely in mind, but are not asked to keep to ceilings on their lending.

III The effects of monetary policy

Preceding sections of this paper have attempted to describe briefly the changes in the context in which monetary policy has been operating over the past ten years and developments in the tactics and methods employed. It is reasonable to ask in conclusion what the result has been. What can monetary policy be said to have achieved? In fact, it is very difficult to answer such questions. Even the wider question of the effects of economic policy, comprising fiscal, monetary, incomes, industrial, regional and external policies, cannot be given a simple answer, for these, too, are inseparable from social and foreign policies. In one sense, economic policy may be said quite simply to have failed, in that none of the major economic problems facing the United Kingdom in 1959 can be said to have been solved and some of the most important of them have become more severe. But the explanation cannot be sought wholly in economic events and policies, still less in the narrower range of monetary policies. It would be necessary to analyse and relate the various objectives, not all of them economic and many of them conflicting, which the authorities were aiming to achieve at various times throughout the period. Such a discussion would lead far beyond the bounds of this paper.

When one attempts to measure and distinguish the effects of monetary and other policies the difficulties are even greater. Almost invariably moves in the monetary field have been taken in conjunction with fiscal measures (packages).

Moreover, the rôle of expectations is, in the authorities' view, much greater than is normally assumed in academic and journalistic comment. Changes in the climate of expectations – whether brought about by events outside the United Kingdom, by events within the country but outside the control of the policy-makers, or by the timing and manner of the announcement and implementation of policy measures – can often act either to negate or greatly to reinforce the tactics of the authorities. This is particularly important in relation to sales of government stock, but has much wider application. The winter of 1966/67 provides a striking example. All the indications were that there would be extreme financial stringency at this time when the first impact of selective employment tax (the once-for-all 'forced loan' to H.M. Government) on companies was being felt. In fact, as a result of the package of measures taken in July 1966, augmented by the radical change in expectations that this engendered, there was a marked weakening of demand and financial supply constraints were barely felt.

Certain effects of monetary policy can, however, be fairly clearly demonstrated. A substantial tightening or easing of terms control can be seen to be followed by marked changes in spending on the goods involved. Probably the most striking example of this occurred in 1966. Consumers' expenditure on durable goods fell from £492 million in the second quarter of 1966 to £429 million in the third quarter and £405 million in the fourth quarter. This change in terms was, however, part of the package of measures announced in July, which included higher purchase tax and an increase in Bank rate; the fall in spending cannot be attributed solely to a change in hire purchase terms. Similarly, private house-building has on occasions been severely affected by variations in the available flow of mortgage finance, as occurred, for example, during the mortgage 'famine' in 1965, when lending by the societies was sharply reduced, and the number of houses started for private owners fell from 64,000 in the last quarter of 1964 to 48,000 a year later. On business investment, despite the enormous amount of work that has been done, the evidence remains inconclusive as to the effects of either the cost or the availability of funds, though there is perhaps some support for the *a priori* expectation that investment would be affected. What does seem clear, however, is that the timing of any effect is very uncertain and that the lags as well as being variable tend to be rather long. On consumption, the evidence remains even more sketchy. However, there seem grounds for believing that really tight control of bank lending can, both directly and through its indirect effects on stock market values, exert some effect on consumers' expenditure.

Much will depend on the concurrent severity of fiscal and incomes policy. Following a fiscal year (1968/69) in which the central government was able to make net repayments of debt for the first time for a number of years, it is expected that in 1969/70 the central government surplus will more than offset the borrowing requirements of the local authorities and public corporations, enabling the public sector as a whole to repay debt for the first time certainly since the statistical series began in 1952 and almost certainly since before the War. These surpluses and the current ceilings on credit together form much the most severe monetary restraint that has been imposed for a long time.

In general, it remains the authorities' belief that fiscal and monetary policy work – and must work – jointly. Without monetary restraint, fiscal restraint will either be largely ineffective or – if it is made effective in a conjunctural sense – is likely to have damaging longer-run effects on incentives or the provision of public services. Likewise with a large public sector deficit, monetary restraint to be effective at all will have to be so severe as to risk drastic and unpredictable consequences for the whole financial system. The lesson is perhaps not to expect too much of any one arm of economic policy, especially for 'fine tuning'. As we learn more we should be able to refine our techniques and predict better their effects; but, at least in the present state of our knowledge, it looks unlikely that we shall ever be able to rely primarily on monetary policy for short-term stabilisation of the economy and the balance of payments.

The importance of money

A research paper prepared in the Bank's Economic Section. The paper is largely the work of C. A. E. Goodhart, assisted, particularly in the preparation of the appendices, by A. D. Crockett.

Definition and function

The distinguishing characteristic of that set of assets which may be described as money is that they perform the function of a medium of exchange. This definition does not, however, allow for a clear-cut distinction in practice between those assets which should be regarded as money, and those which cannot be so treated. Cash and cheques drawn on banks are the means of payment for transactions which are generally acceptable in most developed economies, and this fact has led many to conclude that cash and demand deposits in banks are the only real monetary assets. There are, however, certain demand deposits, for example compensating balances held with banks in the United States, which cannot be freely used for transactions purposes. On the other hand possession of a balance on time deposit, or access to overdraft facilities, may allow a purchaser to draw a cheque on his bank account even when he has insufficient demand deposits to meet that cheque. A more fundamental point is that the set of assets which is acceptable as payment for transactions is not immutable over time; it has changed in the past and could do so again in the future. If people should find it economically advantageous to accept, and to proffer, other financial claims in payment for transactions, then the set of assets which is to be described as money will alter.

This difficulty in distinguishing exactly which set of assets most nearly accords with the definition of money, as set out above, has led some to emphasise other characteristics which monetary assets possess, for example 'liquidity' or 'money as a temporary abode of purchasing power'. Such alternative definitions have, in general, proved too indistinct for practical, and more particularly analytical, purposes. Others have argued, on *a priori* grounds, that one or another definition of money, though admittedly imperfect, is the best approximation to the underlying concept of money. Others again have argued that the matter can be determined empirically. If people should regard time deposits with deposit banks, but not time deposits with accepting houses, as close substitutes for demand deposits, then the former asset should be included in the definition of money and the latter asset excluded. To seek a definition in this way implies the expectation of finding a clear division whereby assets to be defined as money are close substitutes for each other, but markedly less close substitutes for all other—non-monetary—financial assets. Whether such a clear division is found in reality is considered later in this paper.

The function of money as a medium of exchange makes it a convenient asset to hold, because it enables the holder to avoid the time and effort which would otherwise have to be involved in synchronising market exchanges (*i.e.* by barter). Convenience, particularly where it involves time saving, is something of a luxury. For this reason one might expect the demand for money, to provide such services, to rise by more than in proportion to the growth of real *per capita* incomes.[1] On the other hand, there are certain economies (of large scale) in cash management that can, in principle, be obtained as transactions get bigger and more frequent. This factor would result in the demand for money increasing by less than in proportion to the growth of real incomes.

The convenience to be enjoyed by holding money balances is only obtained at a cost — the cost, in effect, of not using the funds thereby tied up for purchases of more goods or alternative assets. As a broad principle, holders of money will adjust their holdings of money balances until the extra convenience from holding such balances just offsets the additional costs of having to make do with fewer other goods or assets. In order to bring about this adjustment, the money holder can, in principle, vary his purchases of anything else — financial assets, real capital goods, consumer goods — or of everything equally, in order to bring his money holdings into the desired balance with other possible uses of his funds.

In general, if the additional attraction (utility) of any good or asset does not match its cost, the main weight of the adjustment process falls, at least initially, upon changes in expenditures on close substitutes. If tomato soup seems to be getting rather expensive, the normal response is to buy less tomato soup and more oxtail soup, not less tomato soup and more company securities.

The transmission mechanism, whereby monetary influences affect decisions to spend generally, will be determined by the way in which people adjust their equilibrium portfolio of assets in response to a disturbance initiated, for example, by the intervention of the authorities in financial markets. These reactions, and therefore the transmission mechanism, will depend on which assets people view as particularly close substitutes for money balances.

The distinction between that theoretical approach to monetary analysis which may, perhaps unfairly, be termed 'Keynesian', and that approach which, equally unfairly, may be described as 'neo-quantity' or 'monetarist', turns mainly on divergent *a priori* expectations about the degree of substitution between money and other financial assets, and between financial assets and real assets. These differences are purposely exposed, and perhaps exaggerated, in the following sections, which provide a short résumé of the two approaches. As the points of contention between the two schools of thought can be reduced to issues that are, at least in principle, subject to empirical verification, it is not surprising that the results of the many statistical tests recently undertaken, mainly, however, using U.S. data, have brought many proponents of both views to modify their initial positions.

The transmission mechanism
'Keynesian' analysis
It is the conviction of Keynesian theorists that financial assets, particularly of a short-term liquid nature, are close substitutes for money, whereas goods and real assets are viewed as not being such close substitutes. In support of this position, Keynesians emphasise (a) the difficulty of defining which set of assets actually comprises the stock of money (which implies that such assets are similar in many respects), (b) the ease and simplicity with which a cash position can be adjusted at any given time by arranging the portfolio of financial assets to this end, and (c) the similarity of the character of financial assets adjoining each other in the liquidity spectrum ranging from cash at one end to, say, equities at the other.

If the authorities should bring about an increase in the money stock[1] by open-market operations,[2] for example, the extra convenience which such augmented money balances would provide would, other things being equal, not match the opportunity cost represented by the return available on other assets. Under such circumstances the adjustment back to a position of portfolio equilibrium would, according to Keynesian theory, take place mainly, if not necessarily entirely, by way of purchases of money substitutes, *i.e.* alternative liquid financial assets, rather than directly through purchases of goods and physical assets. This would raise the price and lower the yield on such financial assets, and would cause in turn further purchases of somewhat less liquid assets, further along the liquidity spectrum. The effect of a change in the money supply is seen to be like a ripple passing along the range of financial assets, diminishing in amplitude and in predictability as it proceeds farther away from the initial disturbance. This 'ripple' eventually reaches to the long end of the financial market, causing a change in yields, which will bring about a divergence between the cost of capital and the return on capital.

The effect of changes in the money supply upon expenditure decisions is regarded, by Keynesians, as taking place almost entirely by way of the changes in interest rates on financial assets caused by the monetary disturbance. This analysis, if true, has an immediate and obvious implication for monetary policy. It implies that monetary policy could be undertaken with greater certainty by acting directly to influence and to control interest rates than by seeking to control the money stock.[3]

---

[1] Holding additional money balances, as compared with bonds or equities whose capital value is subject to variation, tends to reduce the risk of unforeseen variation in the capital value of a portfolio of assets taken as a whole. In so far as risk avoidance is also something of a luxury, proportionately more money might be held in portfolios for this reason as people became more affluent. On the other hand, the development of the financial system has led to the introduction of a number of alternative capital-certain assets, in addition to money, which can be encashed at short notice. Therefore one would not expect the demand for money to have been strongly affected, at least in recent years, by the desire to avoid risk, because this motive can be equally well satisfied by holding alternative capital-certain assets yielding a higher return.

[1] As the authorities can, in theory, control the level of the money stock, it is customary in text books to treat the money stock as determined exogenously, that is to say, independently of the rest of the economic system, by the authorities. At a later stage in this paper, this method of treating the authorities' policy actions will be questioned.

[2] Open-market operations are undertaken in financial markets. Actions by the authorities to alter the money stock do not, therefore, affect everyone in the economy equally, but have their initial impact upon people and institutions active in such markets. It is quite possible that those active in such markets could have a higher interest-elasticity of demand for money than the average for the economy as a whole. The possible distributional effects of the particular nature of the authorities' monetary actions have received surprisingly little attention in the literature.

[3] It is, however, the level of real interest rates that influences expenditure decisions, while the authorities can directly observe only nominal interest rates. In order to estimate the real cost of borrowing, the nominal rate of interest has to be adjusted by taking into consideration expectations of the prospective rate of inflation, the possible impact of tax arrangements and expectations of future levels of nominal interest rates themselves.

In addition to the familiar cost-of-capital effect, the impact of changes in interest rates upon expenditures should be understood to include 'availability' effects and 'wealth' effects. Availability effects, in general, result from the presence of rigidities in certain interest rates and the consequent divergence of these rates from the more freely determined market rates (a good example of 'sticky' rates is provided by the Building Societies Association's recommended rates). In such cases a divergence of free market rates from the pegged rate may cause such large changes in the channels through which funds may flow that certain forms of credit may be rationed or entirely cut off. In those markets, such as housing, where credit subject to such effects is of great importance, the impact of availability effects can be considerable. The wealth effect occurs, in the main, because changes in interest rates alter the present value of existing physical assets. For example, if interest rates fall, the present value of physical assets will rise.[1] The ultimate owners of such real assets, very largely the holders of the company securities, will feel better off, and no-one will feel worse off.

Notwithstanding the theoretical argument, it for long seemed doubtful whether changes in interest rates had much effect on expenditure decisions, which appeared in general to be unresponsive to changes in interest rates. This implied, for Keynesians, that monetary policy could have little effect in influencing the level of expenditures; and this appreciation of the situation has been influential in conditioning the conduct of monetary policy in recent decades. In part this finding, of the lack of response to interest rate changes, may have been owing to the coincidence of movements of interest rates and of expectations about the future rate of price inflation, so that variations of real interest rates – even if usually in the same direction, perhaps, as nominal yields – have been much dampened. Indeed in those cases when the main cause of variations in the public's demand for marketable financial assets was changes in expectations of future price inflation, a policy of 'leaning into the wind'[2] by the authorities in, for example, the gilt-edged market would cause divergent but unobservable movements in real and nominal interest rates. If people became fearful of a faster rate of inflation and so began to sell gilts, support for the market by the authorities, who can in practice only observe nominal interest rates, would tend to prevent these rates rising sufficiently to reflect the more pessimistic view being taken of prospective inflation.

In recent years, however, more detailed empirical investigation has suggested the existence of some noticeable interest rate effects – though most of the work has used U.S. data, and the most significant effects have been found on State and local government expenditure, public utilities, and housing,[1] all of which are probably less sensitive to interest rate changes in the United Kingdom. There is, however, need for additional work in this country, to examine how changes in financial conditions affect expenditure decisions. Making use of the improved information that has become available during the last decade or so, further research in this field is being planned in the Bank. One recurrent problem is how to estimate the level of real interest rates, when only nominal rates can be observed.

The less that alternative financial liquid assets were felt to be close substitutes for money balances, the greater would the variation in interest rates on such assets need to be to restore equilibrium between the demand for and supply of money, after an initial disturbance: the larger, therefore, would be the effect on expenditures, *via* changes in interest rates, of open-market operations undertaken by the authorities – given the climate of expectations in the economy. The greater the degree of substitution between money and other financial assets, the less would be the expected effect from any given change in the money supply. In conditions where other financial assets were very close substitutes for money balances, it would be possible, in principle, to envisage adopting a policy of enforcing very large changes in the money supply in order to affect the level of interest rates and thus expenditure decisions. But there would still be severe practical difficulties – for example, in maintaining an efficient and flexible system of financial intermediation – and such a policy would require considerable faith in the stability of the relationship between changes in the volume of money available and in the rate of interest.

If there were a high degree of substitution between money and other financial assets, which could be estimated with confidence, then a change in the money supply would have a small, but predictable, effect on interest rates on substitute financial assets. If financial assets were not good substitutes for money balances, on average, but the relationship seemed subject to considerable variation, then changes in the money supply would have a powerful but erratic effect.

There is, therefore, a close relationship between the view taken of the degree of substitution between money and alternative financial assets, and the stability of that relationship, and the importance and reliance that should be attached to control over the quantity of money. At one pole there is the view expressed in a passage in the *Radcliffe Report* "In a highly developed financial system ... there are many highly liquid assets which are close substitutes for money", so "If there is less money to go round ... rates of interest will rise. But they will not, unaided, rise by much ..." (para. 392). It is only logical that the Committee should then go on to conclude that control over the money supply was not "a critical factor" (para. 397). At the opposite pole there is the monetarist view, of which Professor Friedman is the best known proponent.

---

[1] In some cases there may also be a wealth effect following a fall in interest rates even when the financial asset held is not backed by real capital assets, as for example in the case of dead-weight national debt. In this instance a rise in the present value of these debt instruments – British government securities, etc. – to their holders should in theory be matched by a rise for the generality of taxpayers in the present value of their tax liabilities. In practice this is not likely to happen.

[2] *i.e.* absorbing stock when the gilt-edged market is weak, and selling stock when prices are rising.

[1] One of the most carefully researched studies of monetary effects in recent years came as part of the Federal Reserve – MIT econometric model of the United States. The results of this study, reported by de Leeuw and Gramlich in the *Federal Reserve Bulletin*, June 1969 show a sizable and fairly rapid wealth effect (*via* changes in stock exchange prices) on consumption, and a sizable and fairly rapid cost-of-capital effect on residential construction. There is also a significant, but considerably lagged, cost-of-capital effect on business fixed investment. No evidence that inventory investment is sensitive to such monetary effects was found.

'Monetarist' analysis

In the monetarist view money is not regarded as a close substitute for a small range of paper financial assets. Instead money is regarded as an asset with certain unique characteristics, which cause it to be a substitute, not for any one small class of assets, but more generally for all assets alike, real or financial.

> The crucial issue that corresponds to the distinction between the 'credit' [Keynesian] and 'monetary' [monetarist] effects of monetary policy is not whether changes in the stock of money operate through interest rates but rather the range of interest rates considered. On the 'credit' view, monetary policy impinges on a narrow and well-defined range of capital assets and a correspondingly narrow range of associated expenditures . . . On the 'monetary' view, monetary policy impinges on a much broader range of capital assets and correspondingly broader range of associated expenditures.[1]

In simple terms this means that if someone feels himself to be short of money balances, he is just as likely to adjust to his equilibrium position by forgoing some planned expenditure on goods or services, as by selling some financial asset. In this case the interest-elasticity of demand for money with respect to any one asset, or particular group of assets, is likely to be low, because money is no more, nor less, a substitute for that asset — real or financial — than for any other. More formally, all goods and other assets which are not immediately consumed may be thought of as yielding future services. The relationship between the value of these future services and the present cost of the asset can be regarded as a yield, or rate of return, which is termed the 'own-rate of interest' on the asset concerned. Keynesians and monetarists agree that asset-holders will strive to reach an equilibrium where the services yielded by a stock of money (convenience, liquidity, etc.) are at the margin equal to the own-rate of interest on other assets. Keynesians by and large believe that the relevant own-rate is that on some financial asset, monetarists that it is the generality of own-rates on all other assets. Keynesians, therefore, expect people to buy financial assets when they feel that they have larger money balances than they strictly require (given the pattern, present or prospective, of interest rates), whereas monetarists expect the adjustment to take place through 'direct' purchases of a wider range of assets, including physical assets such as consumer durables.

According to a monetarist's view the impact of monetary policy will be to cause a small, but pervasive, change on all planned expenditures, whether on goods or financial assets. The impact of changes in the quantity of money will be widely spread, rather than working through changes in particular interest rates. A rise in interest rates, say on national savings or on local authority temporary money, would not cause a significant reduction in the demand for money — because these assets are not seen as especially close substitutes for money balances. Such changes in interest rates would rather affect the relative demand for other marketable assets, including real assets. Expenditure on assets, real and financial, is viewed as responding quite sensitively to variations in relative own-rates of interest; indeed monetarists generally regard most expenditure decisions as responding more sensitively to variations in interest rates than Keynesians are prone to believe. The generalised effect of monetary policy in influencing all own-rates of interest will, however, tend to be outweighed in each individual case by factors special to that asset (changes in taste, supply/demand factors particular to that market, etc.), so that no single interest rate can be taken as representing adequately, or indicating, the overall effect of monetary policy. As monetary changes have a pervasive effect, and as their effect is on relative 'real' rates, it is a fruitless quest to look for *the* rate of interest — particularly the rate on any financial asset — to represent the effect of monetary policy.

The crucial distinction between the monetarists and the Keynesians resides in their widely differing view of the degree to which certain alternative financial assets may be close substitutes for money balances; and in particular whether there is a significantly greater degree of substitution between money balances and such financial assets than between money balances and real assets. An example may help to illustrate the importance of this difference of view. Assume that the authorities undertake open-market sales of public sector debt (effectively to the non-bank private sector). The extreme Keynesian would argue that interest rates would be forced upwards by the open-market sales (and by the resulting shortage of cash in relation to the volume of transactions to be financed). Interest rates would not rise by much, however, because an increase in rates on financial assets, such as finance house deposits, which were close substitutes for money, would make people prepared to organise their affairs with smaller money balances. The authorities would, therefore, have reduced the money supply without much effect on financial markets. Because expenditure decisions would be affected, not directly by the fall in the quantity of money, but only by the second round effect of changes in conditions in financial markets, there would be little reason to expect much reduction in expenditures as a result — both because the interest rate changes would be small and because of the apparent insensitivity of many forms of expenditure to such small changes in interest rates.

The extreme monetarist would agree that interest rates on financial assets would be forced upwards by the initial open-market sales. This increase in rates would not, however, tend to restore equilibrium by making people satisfied to maintain a lower ratio of money balances to total incomes, or to wealth. The initial sales of financial assets (as part of the open-market operation), resulting in higher interest rates, would only bring about a short-run partial equilibrium in financial markets. In other words, because of the fall in their price, people would wish to hold more of these financial assets, and this would be achieved through the open-market sales. But the counterpart to the desire to hold more of the cheaper financial assets would not, probably, be to hold smaller money balances, but rather to hold less of other goods. It follows, therefore, that open-market transactions

---

[1] Friedman and Meiselman, "The relative stability of monetary velocity and the investment multiplier in the United States, 1897–1958", Research Study Two in *Stabilization Policies*, Prentice-Hall, 1964, page 217. This section provides an excellent statement of the theoretical basis of the monetarist viewpoint.

enable people to make the desired changes in their portfolio of non-monetary financial assets, but leave them holding too little money. Full equilibrium, in the market for goods as well, would only be re-established when the desired ratio of money balances to incomes was restored. This would be achieved (and could only be achieved) by a reduction in real expenditures. Which expenditures would be cut back would depend on the response to the changing pattern, overall, of prices (yields) on the full range of assets, set in motion by the initial monetary disturbance. In sum, monetary policy, by causing a reduction in the quantity of money, would bring about a nearly proportionate fall in expenditures elsewhere in the economy. In the meantime interest rates, initially forced upwards by the authorities' activities in undertaking open-market sales, would have drifted back down, as the deflationary effect of the restrictive monetary policy spread over the economy, affecting both the demand for capital (borrowing) in the markets and the rate of price inflation.

Thus, if alternative financial assets were very close substitutes for money balances, monetary policy (in the restricted sense of operating on the quantity of money in order to alter rates of interest) would be feeble; if they were not, it could be powerful. The issue is almost as simple as that. Furthermore, as was pointed out earlier, if people appear to treat all liquid, capital-certain, assets as close substitutes for each other, it makes it extremely difficult to attach any useful meaning to that sub-set of such assets which may be arbitrarily defined as money. Thus, the questions of the definition and of the importance of money each hang on the empirical issue of whether it is possible to identify a sub-set of liquid assets with a high degree of substitutability among themselves, but with a much lower degree of substitutability with other alternative liquid financial assets. Whatever the composition of this sub-set, it must include those assets commonly used for making payments, namely cash and demand deposits.

Testing the alternative views
The first stage in any exercise to establish the importance of control over the money stock must, therefore, be an attempt to discover whether money is a unique financial asset, without close substitutes, or is simply at one end of a continuous liquidity spectrum, with a number of very close substitutes. The empirical findings on this matter should help to settle the major difference between the theoretical position of the Keynesians on the one hand and the monetarists on the other. The usual method of estimating the extent of substitution between any two assets is to observe the change in the quantities of the two assets demanded as the relative price (rate of interest) on these assets varies, other things being equal. In the case of money balances, where there is no explicit interest paid on cash and current accounts, the normal procedure, to test whether money is a close substitute for other financial assets, is to examine how much the quantity of money demanded varies in response to changes in the price (rate of interest) of other financial assets, which are thought to be potentially close substitutes. If the demand for money should be shown to vary considerably in response to small changes in the price (rate of interest) of alternative financial assets, this finding would be taken as strong evidence that money was a close substitute for such assets. This relationship is usually described, and measured, in terms of the interest-elasticity of demand for money, which shows the percentage change in the money stock associated with a given percentage change in interest rates on alternative assets. A high interest-elasticity implies that a large percentage fall in money balances would normally accompany a small percentage rise in interest rates on alternative financial assets, and so suggests a high degree of substitution.

There have been in the last decade a large number of statistical investigations designed, *inter alia*, to provide evidence on the degree to which 'money', usually defined as currency and bank demand deposits – M_1 – or as currency plus bank demand and time deposits – M_2 – is a close substitute for other financial assets. A survey of this evidence is presented in Appendix I. Most of these empirical studies are concerned to discover the factors that influence and determine the demand for money. In these studies on the nature of the demand for money, the total of money balances is usually related to the level of money incomes and the rate of interest ruling on some alternative financial asset, for example, on Treasury bills. Alternatively, the ratio of money balances to money incomes (the inverse of the income velocity of money) may be taken in place of the total of money balances, as the variable to be 'explained'. In most important respects, these two methods of approach are interchangeable. There are, however, a considerable number of optional variations in the precise manner in which these equations are specified, which form the subject of fierce debate for the *cognoscenti*.

In particular there is dispute over the form of the income (or wealth) variable which should be related to the demand for money. This issue is, however, peripheral to the question of the extent of substitution between money balances and other financial assets. Evidence on this latter question is deduced from the statistical results of fitting these equations and examining the estimated coefficient measuring the apparent change in money balances associated with a change in interest rates, which is interpreted as the interest-elasticity of demand for money.

Most of the statistical work of this kind has been done using data from the United States,[1] but the results of similar studies using U.K. data[2] give broadly confirmatory results, though there seems, perhaps, some tendency for the estimated stability of the relationships and the statistical significance of the coefficients to be slightly less. Considering, however, that these studies cover a number of differing periods and employ a range of alternative variables, the main results of these exercises show a fair similarity and constancy in both the United States and the United Kingdom.

---
[1] The source of the monetary data used in these studies is shown in each case in the selected survey of empirical results presented in Appendix I.
[2] The results of work using U.K. data are also presented in Appendix I, including some early results of studies under way in the Economic Section of the Bank.

The conclusion seems to be, quite generally, that there is a significant negative relationship between movements in interest rates and money balances (*i.e.* that the higher the interest rate, the lower will be the quantity of money balances associated with any given level of money incomes), but that the interest-elasticity of demand appears to be quite low. The results, as shown in Table A of Appendix I, generally lie within the range −0·1 to −1·0. This range is, however, rather wide. An interest-elasticity of −1 means that an upwards movement in interest rates of 10%, for example from 4·0% to 4·4% (not from 4% to 14%), would be associated with a decline in money balances of 10%. At present levels, this would amount to £1,500 million, which would imply a considerable response of money balances to changing interest rates. On the other hand, an interest-elasticity of −0·1 would imply a much smaller response, of only £150 million. This range, however, exaggerates the diversity of the findings, because the intrinsic nature of the data causes the estimated interest-elasticities to vary depending on the particular form of the relationship tested. If M_2 (money supply defined to include time deposits), rather than M_1 is the dependent variable, the estimated interest-elasticity will be lower, because part of the effect of rising interest rates will be to cause a shift from current to time deposits. If short-term rates rather than long-term rates are used, the estimated elasticity will also be lower because the variations in short-term rates are greater. If the data are estimated quarterly rather than annually, there again appears to be a tendency for the estimated elasticity to fall, probably because full adjustment to the changed financial conditions will not be achieved in as short a period as one quarter. In fact statistical studies using annual data with M_1 as the dependent variable and a long-term rate of interest as an explanatory variable do tend to give an estimate for the interest-elasticity of demand for money nearer to the top end of the range of results, and those with M_2 and a short-term rate of interest will tend to give an estimate nearer the bottom end. Even so, there still remains quite a considerable range of difference in the results estimated on a similar basis, but with data for different periods or for different countries.

The findings, however, do seem sufficiently uniform to provide a conclusive contradiction to the more extreme forms of both the Keynesian and the monetarist theories. The strict monetarist theory incorporated the assumption of a zero interest-elasticity of demand for money, so that adjustment to a (full) equilibrium after a change in money balances would have to take place entirely and directly by way of a change in money incomes (rather than by way of a variation in interest rates). On the other hand, the estimated values of the interest-elasticity are far too low to support the view that the result of even a substantial change in the money supply would be merely to cause a small and ineffectual variation in interest rates.

The area of agreement
The considerable efforts expended upon the statistical analysis of monetary data in recent years have produced empirical results that have limited the range of possible disagreement, and have thus brought about some movement towards consensus. It is no longer possible to aver, without flying in the face of much collected evidence, that the interest-elasticity of demand for money is, on the one hand, so large as to make monetary policy impotent, or, on the other hand, so small that it is sufficient to concentrate entirely on the direct relationship between movements in the money stock and in money incomes, while ignoring inter-relationships in the financial system.

Any summary of the area of agreement must inevitably be subjective. Nevertheless the following propositions would, perhaps, be widely accepted:

(i) The conduct of monetary policy by the authorities will normally take place by way of their actions in financial markets, or through their actions to influence financial intermediaries. To this extent it is really a truism, but nevertheless a useful truism, to state that the initial effects of monetary policy will normally occur in the form of changes in conditions in financial markets.

(ii) Monetary policy, defined narrowly to refer to operations to alter the money stock, will normally have quick and sizable initial effects upon conditions in financial markets. It is not true that operations to alter the money stock would only cause a small change in interest rates without any further effect, nor that the velocity of money will vary without limit.

(iii) Open-market sales of debt by the authorities raise the return, at the margin, both on holdings of money balances and on holdings of financial assets. Any subsequent effect on expenditures, on the demand for real assets, results from the attempt to restore overall portfolio balance, so that rates of return on all possessions are equal at the margin. In this sense monetary policy is always transmitted by an interest rate effect.

(iv) The initial effect of monetary policy upon nominal interest rates may tend to be reversed after a period. For example, any increased demand for physical assets, encouraged by the lower rates of return on financial assets (including money balances), will stimulate additional borrowing in financial markets, thus driving up interest rates again, and the extra money incomes generated by such expenditures will cause an additional demand for money balances. If the increased demand for physical goods leads to a faster expected rate of price inflation, the resulting rise in nominal returns from holding financial assets and money balances will be reduced in real terms, so that the subsequent increase in nominal interest rates will have to be all the greater to achieve equilibrium.

(v) The strength of monetary policy depends mainly on the elasticity of response of economic decision-makers – entrepreneurs, consumers, etc. – to a divergence between the rates of return on financial assets, including the return on money balances, and the rate of return on real assets. Some empirical studies of the elasticity of response of various kinds of expenditures — company fixed investment, stock-building, housebuilding, consumer spending on durable goods, etc. — have found evidence, particularly when working with U.S. data, that demand does respond significantly to variations in nominal interest rates. But these estimated effects, although significant statistically, do not seem to be very large, and they appear to be subject to lengthy time-lags in their operation.

(vi) Although these statistical findings, of the fairly slight effect of variations in nominal interest rates on expenditures, are widely accepted, the inference that monetary policy is relatively impotent is not generally accepted. It is argued, and is becoming widely agreed, that variations in nominal interest rates may be a poor indicator of changes in real rates. As was already suggested in proposition (iv), an expansionary monetary policy is consistent with, and can lead directly to, rising nominal rates of interest, while real rates remain at low levels. If nominal rates of interest do provide a poor index of monetary conditions, many of the studies purporting to estimate the effect of changes in financial variables on expenditures become subject to serious error. This raises the problem of how to measure approximately variations in the real rates of interest facing borrowers and lenders, as these cannot be simply observed from available data.

A qualification

The evidence from the empirical studies shows that there is a statistically significant association between variations in the size of the money stock and in interest rates on alternative financial assets. This relationship is, however, neither particularly strong nor stable.[1] These results are often interpreted as evidence that money balances and such financial assets are not especially close substitutes, and that there may also be a significant degree of substitution between money balances and other assets, including real assets. This, taken together with the much closer statistical association between the money stock and economic activity, induces belief in the importance of controlling the money stock.

The observed loose association between changes in interest rates and in the money stock may, however, be due in part to another cause. It may well be that the relationship between interest rates and the demand for money is obscured by the volatile nature of expectations about the future movement of prices of marketable assets. Most of the statistical studies of the demand for money have related the total of money balances to the calculated yield to redemption of marketable financial assets, e.g. Treasury bills or gilt-edged stocks. This procedure implicitly assumes that the redemption yield is a good guide to the expected yield over the holders' relevant planning period; an assumption which will be generally invalid. People may, at certain times and in certain conditions, expect prices in the market to continue changing in the same direction as in the (recent) past for some (short) time (*i.e.* they hold extrapolative expectations). Or they may expect past price movements to be reversed over some future period, usually when this implies some return to a 'normal' level of prices (*i.e.* they hold regressive expectations).[1]

If people expect a fall in the price of an asset to continue even for a short time, and sell because of that expectation, then the calculated yield to redemption would be rising, while the real yield over the immediate short future could well be falling. This could mean that the effect of rising interest rates in causing some people to economise on money balances was being partly offset, or more than offset, by their effect in causing others to go liquid in anticipation of even higher rates. If market expectations were volatile, one might expect to observe quite large swings in interest rates associated with small changes in the level of money balances, or vice versa, sometimes even in a perverse direction (*i.e.* that rises in interest rates would be associated with increases in desired money balances). This result need not, however, imply that such financial assets were not good substitutes for money, but rather that the calculated yields did not always provide a good unbiased approximation to the true yields on which investors based their portfolio decisions.

There are, therefore, certain complications involved in the use of the yield (to maturity) on any marketable asset, with a varying capital value, as an index of the opportunity cost of holding money. It should, however, be feasible to observe more accurately the true relative return on holding assets with a fixed capital value — for example building society shares and deposits, national savings, local authority temporary money[2] — rather than money, because there is no problem of estimating the expected change in capital values.[3]

---

[1] Although the ratio of the estimated value of the coefficient of the interest-elasticity of demand to the estimated standard error of that value (as measured by the t statistic), is large enough in almost all cases to show that the coefficient is significantly different from zero, the confidence interval frequently covers rather a wide range.

[1] It is quite possible, indeed probably fairly common, to find that expectations of price changes in the near future are generally extrapolative, while expectations for price changes in the more distant future are regressive.

[2] If there are additional penalties imposed for encashment of an asset before some predetermined time period has elapsed, then the alternative yields on such assets cannot be properly estimated without further knowledge of the expected holding periods. Moreover in some cases the rates offered, for example on building society shares and deposits, can be varied at short notice, while in other cases the rates may be fixed over the expected holding period. These are, however, probably lesser complications.

[3] An exercise is under way in the Economic Section of the Bank which attempts to estimate the extent to which persons, and companies, vary their holdings of money, as a proportion of their portfolio of assets whose capital value is certain in money terms, as relative interest rates (on these fixed value assets) change. It is hoped that it will be possible to produce estimates of the elasticity of substitution (for persons and companies separately) between all pairs of capital-certain assets, including money balances. The preliminary results of this exercise have already been reported in a paper on "Substitutions between assets with fixed capital values", read by A. R. Latter and L. D. D. Price at the Association of University Teachers of Economics meeting in April 1970 in Belfast. Only short series of quarterly data are available, going back to 1963, and the sectoral allocation of the various assets is not adequate for the exercise in hand in some respects. For these and other reasons, the preliminary results of this exercise must be treated as extremely tentative. These results, however, suggest an interest-elasticity of demand for current accounts, the main component of M_1, of about 0·5, which is higher than the estimates in some other studies of the demand for money using U.K. data, but which remains well within the range of results obtained in a number of studies using U.S. data, as reported in Appendix I.

It is still, however, difficult to refer to *the* opportunity cost of holding money because, when interest rates are generally increasing – and widely expected to continue increasing – the expected return (over the near future) on holding marketable assets may be falling, at the same time as the return on alternative capital-certain assets is rising.

It might, perhaps, be thought otiose to distinguish between these alternative reasons (volatile expectations or a limited degree of substitution) for finding a low response of the demand for money balances to changes in interest rates. As long as open-market operations cause a significant change in interest rates in financial markets, where the initial effect must occur, it could be argued that the fundamental reason for this reaction, whether it be a low extent of substitution or volatile expectations, was of secondary importance: what mattered was that the change could be foreseen and was large. On the other hand, in so far as market expectations of a volatile nature are regarded as having an important influence on developments in the market, the emphasis of policy under actual working conditions of uncertainty and changing circumstances will be inevitably transferred to market management, away from simple rules of operation on monetary quantities. Furthermore the importance, indeed the existence of any useful definition, of money depends largely on finding a break (of substitution) in the liquidity spectrum between money and other financial assets. If the finding of a fairly low interest-elasticity of demand is not taken as incontrovertible evidence of such a break in the spectrum, the issue of the central importance of the money stock as compared with some wider set of financial assets (even, perhaps, the much maligned concept of liquidity) remains open. It may indeed be questioned whether it is helpful to assign crucial importance to any one single financial variable. The need is to understand the complete adjustment process.

The stability of the income velocity of money

It is not possible to observe with any clarity either the real rates of return on asset holdings, which decision-makers in the economy believe that they face, or the precise process of portfolio adjustment. It is, therefore, difficult to chart and to measure the transmission of the effects of monetary policy. If, however, the sole aim of monetary policy is to affect the level of money incomes, it does not necessarily matter whether it is possible to observe and to understand the transmission mechanism in detail. It is enough to be able to relate the response of a change in money incomes to a prior change in the level of the money stock.

The statistical evidence

So the next stage in the analysis is usually to examine the direct statistical relationship between changes in the money stock and changes in money incomes. As was to be expected – for such a result would be predicted by almost all monetary theorists, irrespective of their particular viewpoint – movements in the money stock and movements in money incomes are closely associated over the long term. Over the last fifty or so years the demand for money appears to have grown at more or less the same rate as the growth of incomes. There have, however, been long spells within this period during which money balances have been growing faster or slower than money incomes. The American evidence suggests that money balances were growing at a faster rate than incomes before 1913, and the reverse has been the case for both the United States and the United Kingdom since about 1947.

The apparent fall in the velocity of circulation of money in the early part of this century in the United States may have been due to higher incomes enabling people to acquire proportionately more of the convenience (mainly in carrying out transactions) which the holding of larger money balances allows. The recent rise in velocity, in both the United Kingdom and the United States, may in turn have been brought about by people, especially company treasurers, seeking to obtain the benefit of economies in monetary management, spurred on by the rise in interest rates.

Alternatively these trends may have been associated with underlying structural changes, for example in the improvement of communications, in the change to a more urban society, in the growth and increasing stability of the banking system, in the emergence of non-bank financial intermediaries issuing alternative liquid assets and competitive services, and in technical developments in the mechanism for transmitting payments. In general it is not possible to ascribe the changing trends in the relative rates of growth of money balances and money incomes to any one, or any group, of these factors with any certainty; nor is it possible to predict when the trend of several years, or decades even, may alter direction. By definition, however, these trend-like movements are slow and quite steady. Only at or near a turning point is the relationship between movements in money incomes and in the stock of money balances likely to be misjudged.

The existence of a significant statistical relationship between these two variables does not of itself provide any indication of the causal mechanism linking the two series. The monetarists, though, usually argue that the money stock has been determined exogenously, meaning that the money supply is determined without regard to the value of the other variables, such as money incomes and interest rates, within the economic system. As the money stock is thus assumed to be determined in such a fashion that changes in money incomes do not influence changes in the money stock, it follows that the existence of a statistical relationship between changes in the money stock and changes in money incomes must be assumed to reflect the influence of changes in the money stock on incomes.[1]

---

[1] In a slightly more sophisticated version of this approach the cash (reserve) base of the monetary system (the cash reserves of the banks, including their deposits with the central bank, together with currency held by the public outside the banking system—high powered money in Professor Friedman's terminology) is taken as exogenously determined while certain functional relationships (*e.g.* the public's desired cash/deposit ratio), which determine the total volume of the money stock consistent with a given cash base, are treated as behavioural relationships influenced by other variables in the system (*i.e.* they are endogenous). This minor variation in the approach makes no fundamental difference to the analysis.

For the moment this basic assumption that the money stock is determined exogenously will be accepted, so that the relationship between changes in the money stock and in money incomes can be treated as cause and effect, running from money to money incomes. On this assumption it is possible to measure both the extent of the effect of a change in the money supply upon money incomes and the extent of variation in this relationship.[1] These results generally show that the residual variation in the relationship between changes in the money stock and in money incomes is large as a proportion of short-run changes in these variables — over one or two quarters — but much smaller as a proportion of longer-run changes, over two or more years.

The interpretation, which has been drawn by monetarists from similar work done in the United States, is that the statistical significance of the relationship between changes in the money stock and in money incomes provides evidence of the importance of monetary policy. But the considerable extent of residual variation in the relationship, especially in the short term, combined with the likely existence of long and possibly variable time-lags in operation, prevents monetary policy — in the restricted sense of control over the money supply — being a suitable tool for 'fine tuning' purposes. From this appreciation of the statistical results comes Professor Friedman's proposal for adopting a rule of maintaining a constant rate of growth in the money stock.

In Keynesian theory changes in the money supply initially affect interest rates on financial assets, and these interest-rate variations subsequently influence the demand for capital goods (investment). Once the level of autonomous expenditure is set,[2] the level of money incomes is determined through the multiplier process. As monetary policy is but one factor affecting the level of autonomous expenditures, in particular fixed investment, one should, perhaps, expect to see a closer relationship between autonomous expenditures and money incomes than between the money stock and money incomes. The monetarists instead believe that expenditures on all goods and assets are pervasively affected by monetary policy (though the transmission process can still be regarded as taking place through interest rate changes in the process of restoring portfolio equilibrium). Thus, if the stock of money remains the same, an increase in demand at one point in the economy ('autonomous' or 'induced'; indeed the monetarists are sceptical about the value of this distinction) will have to be broadly matched by a fall in demand elsewhere in order to maintain equilibrium. Therefore they would expect changes in money incomes to vary more closely with exogenous changes in the money supply than with autonomous expenditures. The next step is usually to see which relationship appears to have a closer statistical fit. A commentary on, and critique of, such exercises is given in Appendix I; it is suggested there that such exercises do not provide a satisfactory method of discriminating between the alternative theories.

The crux of this whole approach, of drawing conclusions from the statistical relationship between movements in the money stock and in money incomes, lies in the assumption that the money supply, or more precisely the monetary base,[1] is exogenously determined. This assumption allows a simple statistical association to be translated into a causal sequence. Is this crucial assumption justified? Clearly some of the factors which result in changes in the money supply/monetary base are endogenous (*i.e.* determined by the contemporaneous value of other variables within the economic system). Thus a large domestic borrowing requirement by the central government or a balance of payments surplus tends to enlarge the money supply. As a large borrowing requirement (fiscal deficit) and balance of payments surplus also result in expansionary pressures in the economy, there are reasons to expect increases in money incomes and in the money stock to be associated, without there being any necessary causal link running from money to money incomes.

But, in theory, a central bank can undertake such open-market operations that, whatever the extent of increase in the money supply/monetary base caused by endogenous, income-associated factors, the final level of the money supply is whatever the central bank wants it to be. In this sense the level of the money supply can be a policy instrument. A policy instrument is not, however, *ipso facto* an exogenous variable; it would only be so if policy were not influenced by the contemporaneous (or anticipated) value of other variables within the system, such as the level of incomes and interest rates. This clearly is not the case.

Obviously, if an increase in incomes causes the authorities to alter the money supply/monetary base, then the existence of a simple statistical association between movements in money incomes and in the money supply does not allow one to distinguish the strength of the intertwined causal mechanisms. In order to investigate whether this raises a serious problem, it is necessary to examine the factors which have apparently led the authorities to cause, or to accept, changes in the money supply/monetary base.

In the United Kingdom a general aim of policy has been to reduce the size of variations in interest rates, while at the same time moving towards a pattern of rates that would seem appropriate in the overall economic context. In so far as a policy of stabilisation of financial markets is pursued, the money supply must tend to vary with money incomes — without necessarily having any causal effect on incomes. An increase in incomes relative to money balances will cause some tightening of liquidity; people will be induced to sell financial assets to restore their liquidity, thus pushing interest rates up; the authorities, to a greater or lesser extent (depending on their view about the preferred pattern of interest rates), will 'lean into the wind' and take up these assets; the money supply increases. There may even be a tendency for changes in market conditions to precede changes in

---

[1] The empirical results of such an exercise are reported in Appendix II.
[2] 'Autonomous' is defined as meaning those expenditures, generally taken to be exports, government expenditures and fixed investment, that are not largely determined by the contemporaneous value of other variables within the economic system.

---

[1] The monetary base includes those assets that either are, or could be, used by the banks as cash reserves. It consists of the cash reserves of the banks, including their deposits with the central bank, together with currency held by the public outside the banking system.

money incomes, in so far as people are able to predict changes in the rate of inflation and activity accurately, and to make their asset dispositions in the light of their expectations. If this were the case an increase in inflationary pressures would be preceded by weakness in financial markets and an increase in the money supply.

There is little doubt that changes in the levels of certain key variables within the system (income levels and interest rates, for example) have brought about changes in the money supply. Therefore the money supply is not exogenous, and the statistical association between changes in the money supply and in money incomes cannot be advanced as evidence in itself of the importance of a quantitative monetary policy. Moreover, as the statistical relationships derived from the past depended on the particular kind of policy aim pursued by the authorities over the period considered, there would be no guarantee of their exact continuation in the future, should that policy be altered. In other words, although velocity has been fairly stable in the past this would be no guarantee of its stability in the future if the authorities chose to alter the rules of the game.

Post hoc, ergo propter hoc ?
There is, therefore, a two-way relationship between movements in the money stock and in money incomes, with causal influences running in both directions. It may, however, still be possible to isolate and to estimate the strength of the causal relationships separately. It will be easiest to do so if the interactions are not simultaneous, but consecutive. Thus, if the money supply responds to changes in money incomes only after a time-lag, or if money incomes respond to changes in the money stock only after a time-lag, it may be possible to distinguish the separate relationships.

In particular, if changes in the money stock cause changes in money incomes, then changes in the money stock would be expected to precede the resulting changes in money incomes with perhaps a rather long lead, depending on the duration of the transmission process. If, however, money stock variations result in part automatically from increases in autonomous expenditures – for example in exports, fiscal expenditures or investment – and in part from the authorities' response to pressures in financial markets, then money incomes would be expected to rise more or less simultaneously with the stock of money. Thus, investigation of the extent to which changes in the money stock lead, or lag, changes in money incomes could be of considerable importance in any attempt to distinguish the main direction of causality.

The preliminary results of research done in the Bank suggest that in the United Kingdom movements in the money stock have preceded movements in money incomes. The pattern of this lead/lag relationship is, however, intriguing, for the relationship between the two series appears to be bimodal, *i.e* to have two peaks. There was a fairly strong correlation between the two series when the monetary series had a very short lead over money incomes, of about two or three months. There seemed to be a further peak in the correlations indicating a much longer time-lag, with changes in the money stock leading changes in money incomes by some four to five quarters. The correlations were generally stronger when the monetary series used was narrowly defined (M_1 rather than M_2).

There have been a fairly large number of other statistical studies attempting to determine whether changes in the money stock do have a significant lead over changes in money incomes. The tests have used different series, from different countries, over different time periods, and the lag relationships have been estimated in different ways. Practically without exception they show that changes in the money stock appear to lead changes in money incomes, but the calculated length of lead has varied quite widely between the various studies, though to some extent this may have been due to the different forms in which the relationship was estimated. Professor Friedman, for example, has claimed that there is evidence of a long and variable time-lag in movements of incomes after variations in the money stock. Other recent statistical work on this subject, both in the United Kingdom and in the United States, has tended rather to suggest that the interval by which the change in the money stock precedes the change in money incomes is quite short, a matter of months rather than of quarters.

A statistically significant lead, therefore, seems to exist even if it is quite short. Does this, then, make it possible to disentangle the causal effects of changes in money supply on money incomes, from those running in the opposite direction? It does not follow that the series which appears to lead always causes the change in the following series. There is a close association between visits to travel agents and tourist bureaux and trips abroad. The visit to the agent precedes the trip abroad, but does not cause it – though it facilitates it. Rather, the desire for travel abroad causes the initial visit to the travel agent. Analogously, desires for increased expenditure may be preceded by an accumulation of cash necessary to finance that expenditure. The demand for such additional money balances will cause pressure on financial markets, and so the authorities, seeking to maintain interest rates within some broad range, may in part accommodate the demand.

It is, however, unlikely that such accumulation of cash would take place far in advance of planned expenditures, for if the balances to be spent were at all sizable it would be generally economic to lend them at interest on higher yielding assets in the meantime. From this source, a lead of money stock over money incomes of only a few weeks might, perhaps, be expected; though rather longer in the United States where the custom of making loans (together with compensating balances), rather than overdrafts, could distort the observed timing between changes in money incomes and money balances.

There are, indeed, a number of other hypotheses which are consistent with a situation in which changes in the money stock precede, but do not cause, subsequent changes in money incomes. However, in the absence of evidence to the contrary, a consistent lead is a prima facie indication of causation.

Most detailed investigations, however, of the effects on expenditures resulting from interest-rate changes (including wealth effects) show quite long average time-lags of the order of one or two years between changes in the monetary base and changes in expenditures.[1] Furthermore, Professor Friedman suggested that changes in monetary conditions affect expenditures only after a long and variable lag. If the duration of the transmission process, whereby changes in monetary conditions affect money incomes, is as long as these studies suggest, it would seem implausible to attribute the finding of a fairly strong relationship between the money stock and money incomes with a very short lead mainly to the impact of monetary changes on money incomes.

The preliminary results of studies made in the Bank which indicated that the lag pattern in the relationship between the money stock and money incomes was a dual one — a very short lead of two to three months and a much longer lead of four to five quarters — further suggested that the relationship between these series might result from the existence of separate causal relationships, each with its own lag pattern, whereby the levels of the money stock and money incomes approached a joint equilibrium.[2]

These findings do not make possible any confident measurement of the relative contributions of the adjustment of the money stock to changes in money incomes, or of the adjustment of money incomes to changes in the money stock, toward the simple overall statistical association between the two series. Even so, some of these results, particularly the observed relationship between bank advances and investment, seem to suggest that changes in monetary conditions do have a significant effect upon expenditures. Equally, other results do not remove scepticism of the view that the simple relationship between movements in the money stock and in money incomes could be interpreted entirely, or even mainly, in terms of the direct impact of monetary conditions upon money incomes.

It follows that these studies of the simple statistical relationship between movements in the money stock and in money incomes can by themselves provide very little information about the strength of monetary policy. The statistical relationship is quite close, but this may reflect to a very large extent the accommodation of movements in the money supply to autonomous changes in money incomes (given the authorities' policy aims and operational techniques). If the authorities should make an abrupt change in their operations (altering the 'rules of the game') the old-established regularities might cease to apply.

Conclusions

The monetary authorities are in a position to alter financial conditions decisively by their operations in certain key financial markets. These market operations can have a considerable influence upon interest rates and also upon the climate of expectations. The existence of financial intermediaries other than banks, which are not so closely controlled, does not, in practice, prevent the authorities from bringing about sharp and considerable changes in financial conditions. Rather the danger is the other way around — namely, that aggressive actions by the authorities in markets subject to volatile reactions could cause exaggerated and excessive fluctuations in financial conditions.

The effect of these operations in financial markets is to cause disequilibria in portfolios. Expansionary monetary policy (narrowly defined to refer to operations to increase the money stock) will cause rates of return on a very wide range of assets, including stocks of all real goods, to be higher, at the margin, than the return available on money balances and other financial assets. In this general sense, monetary policy is transmitted to expenditure decisions via interest rates.

Attempts to measure the effect on expenditures of changes in interest rates on financial assets have on occasions shown these effects to be significant, though relatively small and often subject to long time-lags. There are, however, reasons for believing that these studies may underestimate the strength of monetary policy. In particular, most of these studies use calculated nominal rates of return as an indicator of the impact of monetary policy. Expenditure decisions, however, are affected by relative real interest rates, and these cannot be directly observed. A strongly expansionary monetary policy, which would maintain low real rates of interest, might well be associated, after an initial decline, with rising nominal interest rates.

On the other hand, attempts to measure the effects of monetary policy by correlating changes in the money stock with changes in money incomes probably greatly overestimate the strength of monetary policy. There is a two-way relationship between these variables. It is not correct to regard changes in the money stock as having been determined independently of changes in money incomes; for example, the actions of the authorities in financial markets, which will directly affect the money supply, will usually be strongly influenced by current and expected future developments in the economy. Attempts to disentangle this two-way interaction by considering, for example, the lead/lag relationship, reinforce the view that monetary policy has some causal impact on money incomes, but do not allow this to be clearly isolated and quantified.

---

[1] See, for example, the F.R.B.–M.I.T. model as reported by F. de Leeuw and E. M. Gramlich in "The Channels of Monetary Policy", *Federal Reserve Bulletin*, June 1969. Tables 1 and 2, pages 487–88.

[2] In order to examine this proposition further, the series were disaggregated into their main components to discover whether the estimated relationships between the component series were significantly different from those of the aggregate series. The preliminary results of this exercise, which is still in hand, suggested that this was indeed the case. The relationship between the money stock and consumption appeared to be strongest when the two series were synchronous. The relationship between the money stock and investment suggested that changes in the money stock preceded investment with a long lead of some four to five quarters. When the monetary series was disaggregated into two components – advances to the private sector and other assets (mainly holdings of public sector debt) – movements in bank advances appeared to have a long lead over movements in money incomes, while the relationship between holdings of public sector debt and money incomes was strongest when the two series were synchronous. Indeed the relationship between the two series when bank holdings of public sector debt led money incomes was, perversely, negative. Finally, an examination of the relationship between bank advances and investment suggested the presence of a long (four to five quarters) lead over investment.

Monetary policy is not an easy policy to use. The possibility of exaggerated reactions and discontinuities in application must condition its use. We are not able to estimate the effects of such policy, even in normal circumstances, with any precision. Such effects may well be stronger than some studies undertaken from a Keynesian approach, relating expenditures to changes in nominal interest rates, would suggest, but weaker than some of the monetarist exercises may be interpreted as implying. Furthermore there are probably quite long time-lags in the operation of monetary policy, before it affects most kinds of expenditure. These considerations underline the difficulties of using monetary policy for short-run demand management.

A particular problem, perhaps, is to distinguish what the thrust of monetary policy is at any time. Indeed, it may be harder to decipher what effect monetary policy is having at any moment than to decide what effect should be aimed at. The level of nominal interest rates is not a good indicator of the stance of monetary policy. Rising nominal interest rates are quite consistent with falling real rates of interest. Professor Friedman has argued that the rate of change of the money supply would be a better indicator of the thrust of monetary policy than variations in the level of nominal rates. To the extent that price stability ceases to be an accepted norm, and expectations of inflation, or even accelerating inflation, become widespread, this claim that the rate of growth of the money stock may be a better indicator of the direction of policy than the level of interest rates takes on a certain merit. As, however, there will always be multiple objectives — for example the balance of payments, the level of employment, the distribution of expenditure, etc. — no single statistic can possibly provide an adequate and comprehensive indicator of policy. And basing policy, quasi-automatically, upon the variations in one simple indicator would lead to a hardening of the arteries of judgment.

Appendix I

The evidence of empirical investigations

References in bold type are listed on page 30

Professor Friedman [15] has redefined the Quantity Theory as a theory of the demand for money. Many economists have therefore turned to the estimation of the money demand function (and its analogue, the velocity function) to test the theories advanced by monetarists. These tests have been designed to throw light on a number of issues, some of which — for example, the appropriate definition of money, whether income or wealth is the main determinant of desired money balances, and whether money is a luxury good — are not the really critical issues in the current debate between 'Keynesians' and 'monetarists'.[1] Other questions are, however, vitally important to this debate, and in this review the following are isolated:
  (i) the basic predictability of the demand for money;
  (ii) the role of interest rates in the demand-for-money function; and
  (iii) the relative importance of short-term and long-term interest rates in explaining the demand for money.

Empirical tests have been successful in partially confirming some, at least, of the monetarists' theories. This has encouraged further work designed to compare the stability of Keynesian and monetary relationships. Commentary on, and criticism of, such tests is provided in the final section of this appendix.

The predictability of the demand for money

Although there is nothing in Keynes' work to suggest that the demand for money should be unpredictable (except at very low interest rates), a widespread feeling grew up amongst Keynesians in the post-war period that the availability of money substitutes would render the money–income relationship too volatile to be of much practical use for economic management or forecasting. This was the view that was challenged by the monetarists. Friedman and Schwartz, in their monetary history of the United States[19], demonstrated that real income and real money balances were connected in a reasonably predictable way over the period 1867–1959. Since then, the work of Meltzer[31], Chow[9], Laidler[25] and Courchene and Shapiro[11], among others, have borne out the contention that the demand-for-money function for the United States is fairly well determined over the long period, with coefficients of determination[2] in the range 0·9–0·99. The pioneering long-range study for the United Kingdom carried out by Kavanagh and Walters[24], for the period 1877–1961, established a coefficient of determination of 0·98 in the demand-for-money function.

It is, however, relatively easy to establish an apparently close-fitting relationship when there are strong trends in both dependent and independent (explanatory) variables. A possibly more searching test of the strength of the basic relationship is its predictability when estimated using changes in, rather than levels of, the data. Using changes reduces dramatically the coefficient of determination. For example, in Laidler's very comprehensive study based on U.S. data, the coefficient of determination in a typical equation was lowered from 0·99 to 0·51 when the data were transformed into first differences (*i.e.* changes). For U.K. data, the coefficient of 0·98 by Kavanagh and Walters, noted above, was reduced to 0·49 by first differencing.

The use of lagged dependent variables[3] is another way by which the danger of inferring false relationships from trend-dominated variables can be reduced, though similar dangers are raised in interpreting the lagged term. Most tests using lagged dependent variables (including the models reported in Appendix II) have shown the estimated co-

---

1 As in the main paper, the terms 'Keynesian' and 'monetarist' are used to characterise views that would not necessarily be held by all, or even most, members of each school of thought.

2 The coefficient of determination, or R² statistic, is the proportion of the variance of the dependent variable in an equation which can be associated with, or 'explained' by, changes in the independent variables.

3 Where one of the factors explaining the level of the dependent variable is its level in the previous time period.

efficient of the lagged variable to be highly significant, while the explanatory power of other variables has been correspondingly lower. One explanation of these findings is the presence of time-lags in the process by which a dependent variable adjusts to an equilibrium; but an equally plausible one is the existence of first order serial correlation in the residuals;[1] both influences are probably present to some extent.

The empirical evidence suggests that the demand for money is more predictable than, say, the Radcliffe Committee would have imagined, but probably not predictable enough to be used as an instrument of short-term policy. Furthermore the predictability of the relationship in a period when control of the money supply was not a major feature of policy will not necessarily be a good guide to its predictability under conditions when it was more actively used.

The role of interest rates in the demand-for-money function

The next important point of dispute is the relationship between the level of interest rates and the quantity of money. Many Keynesians have supposed that the interest-elasticity of the demand for money would be relatively high[2] whilst monetarists have believed the elasticity would be low, because money was seen by them as a general substitute for all assets, rather than a specific substitute for interest-bearing financial assets.

In his early writings, Friedman[16] conceded that interest rates might feature in the demand-for-money function but, on the basis of empirical work, contended that in practice they did not. Thus, it was argued that the observed relationship between money and incomes must be a 'direct' one. It has since been shown, however, that interest rates do play a significant role in the demand for money. Of all the studies of this subject published since Friedman's, and which are noted in Table A, only those by Heller[22] for the United States, and by Fisher[13] for the United Kingdom indicate an inability to find a significant role for interest rates.[3] The volume of evidence is now quite widely accepted, at least among Keynesians and some monetarists, as contradicting the view that 'only money matters'. However, the fact that interest rates are significant in the demand-for-money function undermines only the extreme version of the quantity theory, namely that there is a fixed short-term link between the stock of money and money incomes. It leaves open the question of the *relative* importance of income and interest rates in determining desired money holdings.

Nearly all the work that has been done on *levels* of data has shown income to be much more important than interest rates in determining the demand for money. Partial coefficients of correlation[4] are not generally given, but it may reasonably be inferred that incomes are more important from the fact that the margins of error in the estimates of coefficients are relatively much lower for income variables than for interest rates.[5]

That this should be so in the long term is not surprising, because there are long-term trends in both incomes and money. It is in this context more revealing to look at models which are estimated in first difference form (using changes, rather than levels, of data), or with the use of a lagged dependent variable. The study of U.S. data by Laidler[25] showed that the significance of an income variable was much reduced

---

[1] The residuals associated with any estimated relationship are defined as:

$u_t = y_t - \hat{y}_t$ where y_t = the observed value of the dependent variable at time t

$\hat{y}_t$ = the value of the dependent variable at time t calculated from the estimated relationship.

First order serial correlation in the residuals is the correlation between u_t and u_{t-1}.

[2] See for example the *Radcliffe Report* [33].

[3] See footnote *1* on page 27 for a possible explanation of Heller's finding.

[4] The partial coefficient of correlation measures the degree of association between two variables, after allowing for the impact of other variables in the equation. Another means of measuring the relative strength of two separate effects is by beta coefficients (see Goldberger[20]).

[5] It is convenient to compare margins of error by the use of 't' statistics (the ratio of an estimated coefficient to its estimated standard error). In general, the smaller the t statistic, the more subject is the estimated coefficient to sampling fluctuations (random errors), and conversely the higher the t statistic. It is because of sampling fluctuations that a non-zero coefficient may be recorded even though the true value of the coefficient may be zero.

---

when the data were transformed into first differences, though it was still somewhat greater than that of the interest rate variable. Hamburger[21], in a study using logarithmic first differences, found that the coefficient on incomes became insignificant.

Once a role has been conceded to interest rates the question becomes one of how large an interest-elasticity is consistent with according primary importance to money. There is no unambiguous answer to this question, since it hinges on the meaning that is given to words such as 'large', 'primary', etc. This is an example of how the two theories have, partly as a result of empirical testing, drawn together.

The numerical value of the interest-elasticity[1] that has been observed has generally been found to lie in the range -0.1 to -1.0. This is quite a wide band, but part at least of the variation is due to the different forms in which the demand-for-money function has been tested. Some economists, following the letter of Keynes, have used the bond rate in their equations as the opportunity cost of holding money. Others, recognising that Keynes was using a restrictive theoretical model, have suggested that in practice short-term financial assets are more likely to be thought of as substitutes for money, and so have used a short-term rate of interest. Short-term and long-term rates are closely linked as to the direction of movements; but fluctuations in short-term rates are perhaps two to three times larger. Thus, it is to be expected that a higher interest-elasticity will have been observed for long-term rates than for short-term rates.

Another difference lies in the definition of money which has been used. The usual definition in the United States restricts money to currency and demand deposits; but certain monetarists, particularly Friedman, have argued that the definition should be widened to include time deposits, on the grounds that these too are a "temporary abode of purchasing power". It is to be expected that the narrower definition would probably have the greater interest-elasticity, because the wider definition includes assets bearing a yield which moves broadly in line with other market rates.

For these reasons it is, perhaps, to be expected that models using a narrow definition of money and a long-term rate of interest would yield the highest interest-elasticities, and that those with a wide definition and a short-term rate of interest would yield the lowest elasticities. This is broadly the picture which emerges from the empirical results presented in Table A, certainly for those based on annual data. The highest[2] estimates of interest-elasticity are those of Meltzer[31], Brunner and Meltzer[7], Chow[9] and Courchene and Shapiro[11]; all are derived on the basis of the narrow definition of money and a long-term interest rate, and none is below -0.7. Laidler[25] specifically set out to test the relative elasticities using different specifications; and Tobin[35] did much the same thing using a velocity function. Using annual U.S. data from 1892–1960,[3] Laidler produced elasticity estimates ranging from -0.16 using a wide definition of money and short-term interest rates as an argument, to -0.72 using a narrow definition of money and long-term interest rates. Tobin's estimates were much the same, ranging from -0.12 to -0.55.

For the United Kingdom, the only study of note using annual levels of the money stock is that of Kavanagh and Walters[24]. They used a wide definition of money, and a long-term interest rate, and obtained an elasticity of -0.30 for the period 1877–1961; and of -0.50 for the period 1926–61. The relationships between interest-elasticities estimated using U.S. data suggest, perhaps, that had a short-term interest rate been used, the estimated elasticity for the shorter period would have been closer to -0.2.

Thus, despite the superficial appearance of diversity, most of the work done with long runs of annual data produces a fairly consistent

---

[1] The most commonly used measure of interest-elasticity measures approximately the percentage change in money balances resulting from a one per cent change in interest rates, a one per cent change being a change from, say, 4% to 4·04%. To produce equations with constant interest-elasticities, interest rates are usually put directly into logarithmic form. This implies that a change in interest rates from, say, ½% to 1% would have the same effect as a change from 4% to 8%.

[2] In the sense of being furthest from zero.

[3] The data for money on a narrow definition are available only from 1919.

picture. The elasticity of currency and demand deposits with respect to long-term interest rates is probably about -0.7, and with respect to short-term interest rates about -0.25. For a wider definition of money, the relevant figures are slightly lower, and seem to depend more on the particular specification of the model.

Those studies which have used quarterly data have tended to produce lower estimates for the interest-elasticity of the demand for money. Heller[22] was unable to detect any significant influence of long-term interest rates[1] on the demand for money and, when he used short-term rates, the estimated long-run elasticity fell between -0.1 and -0.2. Hamburger[21] used two interest rates (the equity yield and the long-term bond yield) in his study of the demand for money of the household sector, and the sum of their coefficients was about -0.3. Teigen's work[34], undertaken in the framework of a simultaneous equations model, produced long-run elasticities of less than -0.1; though when a similar equation for annual data was estimated, an elasticity of nearly -0.2 was recorded.

The use of quarterly data has presented a number of problems. Chief among these is the existence of time-lags in the adjustment process, the correct specification of which becomes of greater importance when quarterly rather than annual data are used. These time-lags are presumably not due primarily to imperfections in financial markets, because it is relatively easy to move into and out of money balances. It seems more likely that money holders take time to adjust their behaviour after changes in their incomes and in relevant interest rates.

Fisher[13], and Laidler and Parkin[26] found that the results of their quarterly models using U.K. data were much improved by the inclusion of lagged terms.[2] Furthermore, the coefficient of the lagged terms was generally large and significant, indicating quite long adjustment lags. A study using quarterly data for the period 1955-68, which is reported in more detail in Appendix II, bears out these conclusions. On average, around two fifths of the adjustment of money balances towards a new equilibrium seems to take place within the first year.

The existence of time-lags in the demand-for-money function implies that the restoration of equilibrium after an increase in the money supply would require a much greater change in the other variables (income and interest rates) in the short term than in the long term. This is because, at a point in time, the demand for money depends primarily on past values of incomes and interest rates (which by definition cannot be changed) and only to a relatively small extent on current values of these variables. It is, therefore, changes in current values of either income or interest rates which must in the first instance take the strain of adjustment to an exogenous monetary change. If the role of interest rates in the demand for money is considered to be of secondary importance, the response of incomes to a monetary change should be larger in the short run than in the long run, as Friedman[17] acknowledges; however, other evidence which he has produced[19] suggests that in practice changes in the money stock do not appear to affect income until after quite a long and variable time-lag. This inconsistency disappears if a transmission mechanism working via interest rates is postulated. If the demand for money responds slowly to changes in income and interest rates, a change in the stock of money could have a rapid and powerful effect on interest rates, which in turn could have a lagged effect on expenditure, causing income changes to follow an initial change in the money supply. Under these conditions, Burstein[8] has argued that rigid pursuit of a money supply target might lead to unnecessarily wide fluctuations in interest rates and hence in incomes.

The relative importance of long-term and short-term interest rates in the demand-for-money function

If money is simply the most liquid in a spectrum of assets, one would expect the demand for it to be most closely related to the yield on near substitutes, that is to say, on other short-term assets. If, on the other hand, money is an asset that is fundamentally different from other assets there is no reason to expect the demand for it to be any more closely related to the yield on short-term than on long-term assets. These two hypotheses may perhaps be empirically distinguished by testing whether a short-term or a long-term interest rate gives rise to the highest coefficient of determination in a demand-for-money function. Laidler[25] suggests a further test: if the demand function for money is stable, the 'right' interest rate would be expected to show the same relationship to the demand for money in different time periods while the 'wrong' one need not.

Many of the studies noted in this appendix do not provide any direct evidence on this issue. Those that do, however, tend to support the view that in the United States money has been a closer substitute for short-term than for longer-term assets. Laidler finds that using the wide definition of money, the coefficient of determination is much greater for short-term rates than for long-term rates; though in first differences, the superiority of short-term rates is less marked. He also found that when his data were divided into sub-periods, the estimates of interest-elasticity were much more stable with respect to short-term rates than to longer-term rates. Confirmation is provided by the work of Heller[22] who, using quarterly data for the post-war period, detects a significant elasticity for short-term interest rates but not for long-term rates.[1] Lee[29], using differential rather than absolute rates, finds that the yield on savings and loan shares (an asset which may be thought of as being very close to money on the liquidity spectrum) explains the demand for money, under either a narrow or broad definition, better than the yield on longer-term assets.

The results of the study set out in Appendix II, which reports the estimation of demand-for-money equations from data for the United Kingdom, left almost nothing to choose between long-term and short-term rates. Long-term rates were marginally more significant when the definition of money was restricted to currency plus clearing bank deposits; but the short-term (local authority) rate appeared slightly better at explaining changes in money as defined in the Central Statistical Office's *Financial Statistics*. This may result from the deposits of the 'other' banks being more directly competitive with rates in the local authority market. When first differences were used, however, the short rate performed markedly better than the long rate. The estimated values of the coefficients corresponded much better with values recorded using levels, and the significance of the estimates was considerably greater.

Tobin's results[35] (based on Friedman's data) also suggest that there is little to choose between long-term and short-term rates, with long-term rates being marginally more successful in explaining the demand for 'narrow' money, and short rates slightly better for 'wide' money.

The relative stability of Keynesian and monetary multipliers

As noted earlier, a further means of testing the relative importance of Keynesian and monetarist hypotheses of income determination is provided by estimates of the direct relationship between incomes and money on the one hand and between incomes and autonomous expenditures on the other. This approach is open to the objection that it tests only a very simple representation of the underlying models, ignoring the improvements and refinements suggested by theoretical developments. As Johnson[23] has noted this may be defended on the grounds that the "test of a good theory is its ability to predict something large from something small, by means of a simple and stable theoretical relationship"; but it is nevertheless quite possible that the relative explanatory power of simple equations may be a poor guide to the explanatory power of more complex equations derived as reduced forms from a set of interacting relationships.

More specifically, such an approach requires that the explanatory variables introduced should be the main exogenous variables influencing the economy, and that they should not themselves be functionally related to the dependent variables, or else erroneous conclusions may be reached. In general, a single equation model, which is not derived as a reduced form from a full set of structural equations, may be open to question as to whether the explanatory variables included are,

---

[1] These results, however, are partly due to the fact that the estimation period chosen includes the years prior to 1951 when interest rates were pegged. If these years are excluded, both long and short rates become highly significant.

[2] It should be noted, however, that this improvement may owe something to serial correlation in the basic equation, as well as to the existence of time-lags.

[1] Though see footnote 1 to adjacent column.

indeed, truly exogenous. In particular, these tests of the monetarists' hypothesis hang crucially on the assumption that the money supply is exogenously determined, a question which is treated more fully in the main paper.

Quite apart from these problems with the specification of single equations, such equations can only provide information on the behaviour of one variable – albeit a variable of great significance to the economy. No government can possibly be content to rely on a model which only provides a forecast of, say, money income. It is essential to be able to make an informed and consistent judgment on a whole range of other variables, for example, productivity, inflation, unemployment, the balance of payments, the allocation of resources between various kinds of expenditure, etc. Furthermore, the authorities need to have some understanding of the route whereby they affect money incomes by changing their policy instruments. For example, it makes a difference whether monetary policy has its effect overwhelmingly on, say, private housebuilding, or more widely over all forms of expenditure. For this reason a proper test of the adequacy of the alternative models must be whether they can provide information on the behaviour of all the variables which are of concern to the authorities and to economists.

The pioneering comparison of Keynesian and monetary models was that of Friedman and Meiselman[18] in their research study for the Commission on Money and Credit. Using U.S. data for a 62-year period (1897–1958), which was divided into a number of sub-periods, they found that consumers' expenditure was more closely linked with the money stock than with autonomous expenditure in every period except the depression years. For the post-war period, when quarterly data were available, the picture was much the same, though neither hypothesis was at all successful in explaining quarterly *changes* in gross national product (G.N.P.). However, in the long run, velocity appeared to be more stable than at least one definition of the autonomous expenditure multiplier.

But Ando and Modigliani[2], using a definition of autonomous expenditure that was more in line with modern theory, obtained an explanation of consumers' expenditure which was better[1] than the one Friedman and Meiselman had detected using monetary variables. Their main argument, however, was methodological – namely, that to say the average value of the monetary multiplier had been more stable than the autonomous expenditure multiplier over a long run of years did not necessarily make it a particularly useful policy tool. Stabilisation policy would need to take into account a much wider body of knowledge about how economic variables interacted; there was no reason to treat Keynesian and monetary measures as alternatives, nor any justification for picking a single independent variable – which was anyway not always truly independent – to represent each type of policy.

---

[1] As judged by the higher coefficient of determination.

The same criticisms could be applied to a similar study based on U.K. data undertaken by Barrett and Walters[5], which, however, did not produce any very conclusive results. When levels of data were used, there was little to choose between the alternative hypotheses; though both achieved quite high correlation coefficients because of strong trends in all series. When first differences of data were used, the estimated explanatory power (as measured by the coefficient of determination) of both hypotheses was low, though the autonomous expenditure 'explanation' of consumers' expenditure was somewhat better than the monetary explanation for the inter-war years; and the monetary explanation was better before 1914 (when, however, the data are not entirely reliable). Barrett and Walters also showed that when money and autonomous expenditures were jointly considered as predictors of consumers' expenditure, the coefficient of determination was significantly increased, suggesting that, whether or not it is the major determinant, money does play some significant role.

A slightly different approach, followed by Andersen and Jordan[1] compared the impact on G.N.P. of fiscal and of monetary measures respectively. Given the limitations of single-equation models, the tests used were subtle ones. Changes in G.N.P. were separately related to changes in the full-employment budget balance, to changes in the money supply, and also to changes in the money base, which was assumed to be more nearly exogenous than the money supply.

The results obtained by Andersen and Jordan on U.S. data indicated that monetary changes had an impact on G.N.P. which was greater, more certain and more immediate than that of fiscal changes. de Leeuw and Kalchbrenner[30] challenged these conclusions on the grounds that the independent variables had been mis-specified; but although the alternative definitions proposed appeared to re-establish a role for fiscal policy, the case made by Andersen and Jordan for the importance of monetary factors was not refuted. Davis[12], however, showed that if the period to which the tests related was split into two equal sub-periods, the earlier part of the period (1952–60) showed very little relationship between money and incomes; the relationship discovered in the latter period (1960–68) might well have been due to common trends among the variables during these years.

For the United Kingdom, Artis and Nobay[3] have carried out tests very similar to those of Andersen and Jordan. In their study, fiscal policy was found to be more effective than monetary policy; but again little confidence can be attached to the results, because, as the authors themselves point out, these are critically dependent on the assumption that the authorities' fiscal and monetary policy actions are not functionally related to the level of money incomes. As much of the purpose of government action is to reduce deviations of actual incomes from some desired level, these assumptions must be suspect. Thus, if policy is used to offset a change in G.N.P. deriving from another source, it appears as though the policy measure has no effect. Perfect anti-cyclical fiscal policy would produce the *statistical* conclusion that fiscal policy was impotent.

Table A

For reasons of space, this selection of empirical work has had to be extremely compressed. As far as possible, representative equations have been chosen from the work of each author, though often other equations have produced somewhat different coefficients. No reference is made to the other variables, besides interest rates, included in the equations.

Where the equations contain lags, the implied long-run elasticity is given; these equations are marked † and no t statistic is given as its meaning would be ambiguous.

Author	Data used	Definition of money[a]	Interest rate used	Interest-elasticity[b]	t statistic[c]
Demand-for-money equations					
Bronfenbrenner and Mayer [6]	Annual: U.S.: 1919–56	Narrow	Short	−0·33	†
Chow [9]	Annual: U.S.: 1897–1958	Narrow	Long	−0·73	17
Meltzer [31]	Annual: U.S.: 1900–58	Narrow	Long	−0·92	22
,,	,,	Broad	Long	−0·48	10
,,	Annual: U.S.: 1930–58	Narrow	Long	−1·15	12
,,	,,	Broad	Long	−0·70	7
Brunner and Meltzer [7]	Annual: U.S.: 1930–59	Narrow	Long	−1·09	19
,,	,,	Broad	Long	−0·73	15
Laidler [25]	Annual: U.S.: 1919–60	Narrow	Short	−0·21 (−0·11)	12 (3)
,,	,,	Narrow	Long	−0·72 (−0·33)	12 (3)
,,	Annual: U.S.: 1892–1960	Broad	Short	−0·16 (−0·10)	16 (5)
,,	,,	Broad	Long	−0·25 (−0·26)	4 (3)
Lee [29]	Annual: U.S.: 1951–65	Narrow	Short	−0·41	4
,,	,,	Broad	Short	−0·67	3
Motley [32]	Annual: U.S.: 1920–65 (Households only)	Broad	Short	−0·16	5
Courchene and Shapiro [11]	Annual: U.S.: 1900–58	Narrow	Long	−1·00	16
,,	,,	Broad	Long	−0·58	10
Teigen [34]	Quarterly: U.S.: 1946–59	Narrow	Long	−0·07	†
,,	Annual: U.S.: 1924–41	Narrow	Long	−0·20	†
Heller [22]	Quarterly: U.S.: 1947–58	Narrow	Short	−0·12	4
,,	,,	Broad	Short	−0·18	4
,,	,,	Narrow	Long	*	..
,,	,,	Broad	Long	*	..
Hamburger [21]	Quarterly: U.S.: 1952–60 (Households only)	Narrow	Long	−0·16	2
,,	,,	Narrow	Equity yield	−0·13	3
Kavanagh and Walters [24]	Annual: U.K.: 1880–1961	Broad	Long	−0·31 (−0·22)	3 (3)
,,	Annual: U.K.: 1926–61	Broad	Long	−0·50 (−0·25)	6 (3)
Fisher [13]	Quarterly: U.K.: 1955–67	Narrow	Short	−0·11	†
,,	,,	Broad	Short	*	†
,,	,,	Narrow	Long	−0·3	†
,,	,,	Broad	Long	*	†
Laidler and Parkin [26]	Annual: U.K.: 1953–67	Broad	Short	−0·26	†
Bank of England [4]	Quarterly: U.K.: 1955–69	Narrow	Short	−1·05	†
,,	,,	Narrow	Long	−0·80	†
,,	,,	Broad	Short	−0·09	†
,,	,,	Broad	Long	−0·35	†

Author	Data used	Definition of money[a]	Interest rate used	Interest-elasticity[b]	t statistic[c]
Velocity equations					
Latané [27]	Annual: U.S.: 1919–52	Narrow	Long	−0·80	..
Latané [28]	Annual: U.S.: 1909–58	Narrow	Long	−0·77	..
Christ [10]	Annual: U.S.: 1892–1959	Narrow	Long	−0·72	..
Meltzer [31]	Annual: U.S.: 1950–58	Narrow	Long	−1·8	30
"	"	Broad	Long	−1·3	20
Tobin [35]	Annual: U.S.: 1915–59	Broad	Short	−0·12	7
"	"	Narrow	Short	−0·24	9
"	"	Broad	Long	−0·24	6
"	"	Narrow	Long	−0·55	10
Frazer [14]	Quarterly: U.S.: 1948–65	Narrow	Long	−0·8	27
"	"	Broad	Long	−0·37	12
Kavanagh and Walters [24]	Annual: U.K.: 1877–1961	Broad	Long	−0·20 (−0·44)	2 (6)
"	Annual: U.K.: 1923–61	Broad	Long	−0·55	9

* not significant, or wrong sign.
.. not available.
a The 'narrow' definition of money is usually currency plus demand deposits; 'broad' money includes time deposits.
b Values shown in brackets are obtained using first differences.
c The t statistic is the ratio of the estimated coefficient to its estimated standard error.

References

1 Andersen, L. C. and Jordan, J. L.   "Monetary and fiscal actions: a test of their relative importance in economic stabilisation"   *Federal Reserve Bank of St. Louis Monthly Review*, November 1968
2 Ando, Albert and Modigliani, Franco   "The relative stability of monetary velocity and the investment multiplier"   *American Economic Review*, September 1965   pages 693–728. See also other papers on the subject in the same issue
3 Artis, M. J. and Nobay, A. R.   "Two aspects of the monetary debate"   *National Institute Economic Review*, August 1969   pages 33–51
4 Bank of England   Appendix II to this paper
5 Barrett, C. R. and Walters, A. A.   "The stability of Keynesian and monetary multipliers in the United Kingdom"   *Review of Economics and Statistics*, November 1966   pages 395–405
6 Bronfenbrenner, Martin and Mayer, Thomas   "Liquidity functions in the American economy"   *Econometrica*, October 1960   pages 810–34
7 Brunner, Karl and Meltzer, A. H.   "Some further investigations of demand and supply functions for money"   *Journal of Finance*, May 1964   pages 240–83
8 Burstein, M. L.   *Economic theory: equilibrium and change*   Wiley, London 1968   esp. pages 289–326
9 Chow, G. C.   "On the long-run and short-run demand for money"   *Journal of Political Economy*, April 1966   pages 111–31
10 Christ, C. F.   "Interest rates and 'portfolio selection' among liquid assets in the U.S."   *Studies in memory of Yehunda Grunfeld*   Stanford, 1963
11 Courchene, T. J. and Shapiro, H. T.   "The demand for money: a note from the time series"   *Journal of Political Economy*, October 1964   pages 498–503
12 Davis, R. G.   "How much does money matter?"   *Federal Reserve Bank of New York Monthly Review*, June 1969
13 Fisher, Douglas   "The demand for money in Britain: quarterly results 1951–67"   *The Manchester School of Economic and Social Studies*, December 1968   pages 329–44
14 Frazer, W. J.   "The demand for money, statistical results and monetary policy"   *Schweizerische Zeitschrift für Volkswirtschaft und Statistik*, March 1967
15 Friedman, Milton   "The quantity theory of money: a restatement"   *Studies in the quantity theory of money*   M. Friedman, ed.   University of Chicago Press, 1956   pages 3–21
16 Friedman, Milton   "The demand for money: some theoretical and empirical results"   *Journal of Political Economy*, August 1959   pages 327–51
17 Friedman, Milton   "The demand for money: some theoretical and empirical results"   *Journal of Political Economy*, August 1959   page 347
18 Friedman, Milton and Meiselman, David   "The relative stability of monetary velocity and the investment multiplier in the United States, 1897–1958", in "Stabilization policies"   *C.M.C. Research Papers*   Prentice-Hall, 1964   pages 165–268
19 Friedman, Milton and Schwartz, A. J.   *A monetary history of the United States 1867–1960*   Princeton, 1963
20 Goldberger, A. S.   *Econometric theory*   Wiley, New York, 1966   pages 197–200
21 Hamburger, M. J.   "The demand for money by households, money substitutes, and monetary policy"   *Journal of Political Economy*, December 1966   pages 600–23
22 Heller, H. R.   "The demand for money: the evidence from the short-run data"   *Quarterly Journal of Economics*, May 1965   pages 291–303
23 Johnson, H. G.   "Recent developments in monetary theory: a commentary"   *Money in Britain*   D. R. Croome and H. G. Johnson, eds.   Oxford, 1970   pages 83–114
24 Kavanagh, N. J. and Walters, A. A.   "Demand for money in the U.K. 1877–1961: some preliminary findings"   *Bulletin of the Oxford University Institute of Economics and Statistics*, May 1966   pages 93–116
25 Laidler, David   "The rate of interest and the demand for money—some empirical evidence"   *Journal of Political Economy*, December 1966   pages 543–55
26 Laidler, David and Parkin, Michael   "The demand for money in the United Kingdom 1956–67: preliminary estimates"   *University of Essex Discussion Paper* unpublished
27 Latané, H. A.   "Cash balances and the interest rate: a pragmatic approach"   *Review of Economics and Statistics*, November 1954
28 Latané, H. A.   "Income velocity and interest rates: a pragmatic approach"   *Review of Economics and Statistics*, November 1960
29 Lee, T. H.   "Alternative interest rates and the demand for money: the empirical evidence"   *American Economic Review*, December 1967   pages 1168–81
30 Leeuw, Frank de and Kalchbrenner, John   "Monetary and fiscal actions: a test of their relative importance in economic stabilisation—comment"   *Federal Reserve Bank of St. Louis Monthly Review*, April 1969
31 Meltzer, A. H.   "The demand for money: the evidence from time series"   *Journal of Political Economy*, June 1963   pages 219–46
32 Motley, Brian   "A demand-for-money function for the household sector—some preliminary findings"   *Journal of Finance*, December 1967   pages 405–18
33 Radcliffe Report   Committee on the Working of the Monetary System, Cmnd. 827, August 1959   para. 392
34 Teigen, R. L.   "Demand and supply functions for money in the United States: some structural estimates"   *Econometrica*, October 1964   pages 476–509
35 Tobin, James   "The monetary interpretation of history"   *American Economic Review*, June 1965   pages 464–85

CHAPTER 2
Competition and Credit Control

The introduction of Competition and Credit Control

By the end of the 1960s the defects of the post-Radcliffian methods of monetary management were becoming increasingly apparent. There were two main defects. The first was the excessive reliance on direct, or 'ceiling', credit controls, thereby stultifying both competition and efficiency within the banking and financial systems. The second defect lay in the emphasis given to trying to choose an appropriate level of interest rates, rather than using measures of monetary growth as an appropriate guide to financial and monetary conditions; this concern became more acute as inflation and inflationary expectations became higher and more variable.

In view of these defects, the Bank began to plan for a major change of approach, involving scrapping controls and a concomitant abolition of the clearing bank cartel. It intended to replace such direct controls with a market mechanism whereby the total, and the allocation, of credit would be determined by cost. Thus the Bank would vary interest rates in order to influence the total size of banks' sterling books. The earlier work on the demand-for-money function (as noted in Chapter 1) had suggested both how the demand for money might be related to movements in nominal incomes, and how variations in interest rates might be expected to affect the size of the money stock.

By the end of 1970 work on the new system had been taken sufficiently far forward for the Governor to outline current thinking on the problems of the existing system, and to hint at the possible form of the new system to replace it, in the Jane Hodge Memorial Lecture entitled *Monetary management in the United Kingdom* (page 33), delivered on 7 December 1970 and reprinted in the March 1971 *Bulletin*.

The Chancellor foreshadowed the introduction of the new system in his Budget speech in March 1971, and certain confidential discussions with those in the financial system most directly involved took place. A special paper introducing the new system, now entitled *Competition and credit control*, was published in May 1971. This paper, and the subsequent *Sykes Memorial Lecture* given by the Chief Cashier in November 1971, provided detailed accounts of the operational changes involved, for example in the authorities' operations in the domestic financial markets and in the precise form of reserve ratios. They are, therefore, reprinted in Chapters 5 and 6, in the second part of this book dealing with domestic financial operations (pages 115 and 83 respectively).

Since the introductory note had, indeed, to cover operational and technical details, it was not an appropriate vehicle for an exposition of the wider purposes, the economic gestalt, of the new scheme. The Governor took the opportunity of a speech (page 39) to an international bank conference in Munich in May 1971 to describe in more general terms the objectives of this new scheme.

The introduction of Competition and Credit Control was undoubtedly a major step. Although most of the final, detailed, planning was, necessarily, undertaken under the wraps of official secrecy, the outcome reflected a more public debate on the conduct of monetary policy and banking practice, described by the Governor at the Mansion House dinner in October 1971.

The demands that have had to be made upon monetary policy over the past decade and particularly during the very difficult years after the devaluation of 1967 have obliged the Treasury and the Bank, working together, entirely to reappraise their thought and practice in this field. In this task we were greatly assisted by many voices outside. The banking system, and the Committee of London Clearing Bankers in particular, were strongly and rightly critical of many aspects of ceiling controls. There was the vigorous monetary debate in the world of ideas occupied by professional economists, whose messages, for the most part, have been relayed to the rest of the universe by an able corps of financial journalists.

Meanwhile, certain time-honoured practices of the banking system were being critically examined elsewhere. Neither the Prices and Incomes Board nor the Monopolies Commission, in the course of enquiries into bank charges and mergers respectively, found much merit in the so-called interest rate cartel. On the contrary, they argued that however justified it might have been in the past, and however convenient it might be to authority, the cartel was now no less inimical to improvement and innovation than many comparable restrictive practices in other industries. These arguments found much cogent support from individual critics and commentators. For our part, we came to accept their force and their merit—and to recognise that, sooner or later, we would have to modify our own techniques so as to prevent a move towards greater competition in banking from being frustrated by the mechanism of credit control.

On looking back, I consider that this public and official debate about monetary policy and banking practice, in which everyone concerned played a part, served much the same purpose as a full-dress public enquiry, and perhaps the better so for being less formal. Certainly it was a great help to us in our attempts to devise a new approach to credit control. It also meant that when our proposals came along this year, designed to give technical effect to the general objectives of permitting greater competition in banking while preserving effective official control over credit conditions, they were based upon something like a developed consensus. Of course we have not pleased everyone. For many of the theorists we have not gone far enough. There are probably a number of individual practical bankers here tonight who feel that from their point of view, on particular aspects, we have gone too far. In so complex a matter this would not be surprising. However, and this is the important point, I believe that a very wide range of opinion accepts that our moves have been in the right direction and, broadly, along the right lines.

Monetary management in the United Kingdom

The text of the Jane Hodge Memorial Lecture delivered by the Governor at the University of Wales, Institute of Science and Technology, on Monday, 7th December 1970.

Introduction
This evening I want to say something about the operation of monetary policy in Britain and its place in economic management as a whole. Since the war all governments of the United Kingdom have accepted responsibility for aiming to achieve full employment, growth, relatively stable prices and external balance. Monetary policy has an inescapable part to play in pursuit of these aims. Whatever its stance it will have implications of some sort for demand and prices and the balance of payments. However, it is only one of several levers which policy-makers may pull. Policies adopted in other fields – fiscal policy especially – will affect the contribution to be made by monetary policy and can either ease or complicate its task.

The conduct of monetary policy is never a simple matter. Our understanding of the links between the financial world on the one hand and the real world of output and spending on the other is far from perfect. There is a wide divergence of view about how effective monetary policy is in influencing spending and through what particular channels it should primarily aim to operate. A further complication lies in its potentially strong impact on international capital flows, which can undermine the achievement of its own internal objectives as well as make for difficulties in the management of our foreign exchange reserves.

However, whatever may be the possibilities or the difficulties of operating monetary policy, I want to stress one very important point – often neglected or glossed over in abstract discussion. This is that monetary policy is conducted within a particular framework of institutions and markets. This framework provides opportunities, of course, but it also creates constraints. It is an important responsibility of the central bank to foster the growth and efficiency of the financial system as a whole; and its aims in these directions may, from time to time, clash with the immediate goals of monetary policy. From this potential clash there arises a rather wider problem of monetary management.

Deposit banks
For these reasons, I want to begin my survey of monetary management by looking at the institutional structure. To do this thoroughly would, of course, mean casting my net very wide. The range of institutions and activities which can be called financial and which are in one way or another affected by monetary policy is enormous. To avoid making inordinate claims on your time I shall therefore concentrate on the central part of our financial system – and that part over which the Bank of England has most direct influence – the banking system.

It was not so many years ago that domestic banking in this country was conducted virtually entirely by the deposit banks; that is, primarily, the London clearing banks. The asset structure of these banks is largely conditioned by the part that they have historically played in operating the money transmission service of the country; and this has meant that they have developed broadly similar asset portfolios and have come to observe similar minimum ratios for cash and liquid assets. The liquidity ratio was formalised as an aid to credit control when monetary policy entered a more active phase in 1951. In addition the rates which the clearing banks pay on deposit accounts and charge to borrowers vary fairly closely in line with Bank rate.

Cash ratio

These conventions should enable the authorities not only to regulate the cost of the banks' lending but also, in principle, to control its availability by influencing the total of their deposits and of their cash and liquid assets through open-market operations. In practice no attempt has been made to use the cash ratio for this purpose. To do so would have meant making major institutional changes in the system. It would also have been likely to produce large fluctuations in short-term interest rates with unwelcome consequences not merely for the money markets, but for many areas (such as the housing mortgage markets) of wider economic significance. These considerations have led the authorities to continue with the present system under which Treasury bills are always interchangeable with cash through the mechanism of the discount market. In this way dislocations which the uneven pattern of Exchequer spending and receipts might otherwise cause in monetary conditions are smoothed out, while the ready marketability of Treasury bills as the residual source of government finance is ensured. This arrangement, coupled with the use of Bank rate, has given the authorities control over most domestic short-term interest rates.

Liquidity ratio

Nor has the liquid assets ratio been a reliable fulcrum for regulating the expansion of the clearing banks' lending. For many years after the war this was not surprising. The limited outlets for private spending during the war and the pressing need of the Government for finance had made the banks little more than intermediaries for channelling savings into official debt. In 1945 the clearing banks' advances amounted to only 17% of their gross deposits and throughout the fifties there was no choice but direct restrictions when their lending had to be restrained. The real transformation in their balance sheets came during the boom at the end of that decade; and when the economy entered its next phase of expansion in 1963, there was some doubt whether their liquid assets base would be able to support the growth of credit that would be needed. At that time the ratio was lowered from 30% to 28%, still somewhat higher perhaps than would have been necessary on prudential grounds alone. It was then too that the clearers' conventions on interest rates again became a live issue. In the event by the mid-sixties their advances had risen to 50% of deposits while their holdings of gilt-edged had fallen to less than 12%.

This structure has changed little since then and there is no question that at times during the last dozen years the clearing banks' credit base has been under pressure. Even so their holdings of gilt-edged have generally provided them with sufficient latitude to make short-run adjustments. Almost throughout the post-war period, until very recently, the Exchequer was adding, often on a substantial scale, to its domestic borrowing rather than reducing it; and this made it more difficult to contain the banks' lending by debt management alone.

Special Deposits

Because of the difficulty of bearing on the credit base with any precision through open-market operations alone, the possibility of introducing a variable liquidity ratio was explored in the late fifties. The outcome, in 1958, was the Special Deposit scheme, which is essentially similar to a variable liquidity ratio.

While a call for Special Deposits can affect the attitudes of the banks to new lending straight away, there is likely to be some delay before the full effect is seen on the level of advances. In the meantime, and depending on their liquidity position, the banks may sell some investments. But it is open to the authorities – and the banks understand this – to ensure that the whole adjustment by the banks is not completed by such sales of gilts. The initial call for Special Deposits can be supplemented by open-market operations, by action on interest rates or, in due course, by further calls for Special Deposits.

Other banks

So far I have been talking of the deposit banks. Only some dozen years ago the other banks in London accounted for little more than 10% of the deposits held with the banking sector as a whole. Since then – and excluding funds placed among themselves in the inter-bank market – their deposits have increased twenty times to over £17,000 million. This phenomenal expansion came after the widespread move to the convertibility of currencies at the end of 1958 and has been associated with the growth of the euro-dollar market. But, although the bulk of this business is in foreign currencies, these banks have increasingly attracted sterling deposits from British companies and expanded their sterling lending. Their resident sterling deposits, other than on inter-bank account, are now approaching £3,000 million. This represents around 20% of such deposits with the whole banking sector.

These banks are not a homogeneous group. There are the accepting houses, for example; there are head offices of British banks with extensive branch networks abroad; there is an ever-growing number of branches and subsidiaries of foreign banks; and, a most interesting development, there are the subsidiaries of the clearing banks themselves.

I sometimes feel that the clearing banks attract more than their fair share of criticism for being – it is alleged –

unadventurous and slow to react to a changing world. Yet from small beginnings the clearing banks' subsidiaries have grown rapidly to account for well over 10% of deposits with these "other" banks as a whole. If we consider sterling business only, their performance has been even more striking. In the past five years the clearing banks' subsidiaries have increased their sterling resources fivefold; and in the course of doing so they have gained over one third of all the growth in the sterling resources of these "other" banks as a group. I wonder whether those who like to characterise the clearing banks as sleeping giants are really aware of all these developments.

The heavy involvement of the "other" banks in both sterling and foreign currency deposit taking carries implications for the play between domestic and external interest rates and for international capital flows. Local authorities look to these banks for temporary money and the price asked will at times be strongly influenced by euro-dollar rates and by the cost of obtaining forward cover in the foreign exchange market. The relationship between rates in the conventional money market, which are effectively determined by the authorities, and rates in the relatively new parallel markets, where our influence is less direct, is one of the problems currently concerning us.

I have already referred to the common code and liquidity conventions observed by the deposit banks. In general, the growing number of "other" banks observe no such conventions: considerations of banking prudence are largely satisfied by ensuring a broad correspondence between the maturity of assets and the maturity of liabilities. The relatively new and efficient markets in local authority and inter-bank debt, to which I have already referred, enable these banks to adjust their balance sheets to this end very flexibly. The structure of these banks' assets varies very widely, and their liquidity ratios, calculated on almost any basis, range from the very small to the very large indeed.

This diversity of asset structure underlines the problem which has faced us in recent years of devising an effective and reasonably equitable system of credit control, based on liquidity or other asset ratios. In 1967 a scheme of Cash Deposits – analogous to Special Deposits, but designed to bear on earnings as well as liquidity – was worked out for periods of less severe restraint. But circumstances have not yet allowed us to activate this particular scheme. We have been compelled to resort to ceiling controls for relatively prolonged periods – despite their manifest disadvantages.

Lending ceilings
It may seem paradoxical that direct requests should have been used more, rather than less, intensively once the deposit banks' excess liquidity had run off and the Special Deposits scheme had been set up. The reason lies in the circumstances of the sixties, which allowed so little leeway for policy. The external situation was a constant and pressing source of anxiety. Confidence was generally weak, and domestic demand had to be held back both before and after devaluation to encourage the transfer of resources into exports, and to limit imports. Broadly speaking, lending ceilings and guidelines have been in force since 1965. These have applied to lending on commercial bills as well as advances. The leading hire purchase finance houses have been subject to the same restrictions as the banks; and other financial institutions have been asked to bear the objectives of policy closely in mind.

The advantages of ceiling controls are clear enough. They are unequivocal, both for the banks and their customers; their coverage can be extended in equity to competing financial institutions; and they work quickly. But their drawbacks are no less obvious, notably in checking competition and innovation within the banking sector and encouraging the diversion of credit flows through other channels.

All this amounts to saying that quantitative restrictions should be used only when severe restraint is necessary. We are far from happy that we have had to use them so severely and for so long, not only because of their inherent disadvantages but also because of the strain which their prolonged use places upon the very happy co-operative – as distinct from legalistic – relationship which exists in this country between the central bank and the commercial banks. I am a great believer in our system of voluntary co-operation, in which both sides recognise their common interest in the successful development of the economy. And I believe that it is an economical and efficient system in which one side is not continually looking for loopholes in the control and the other side continually trying to plug them. For all that, the longer ceiling restrictions are in force, the greater the strain upon the system. We must all hope that an improvement in our economic conditions such as would permit us to move towards a less restrictive régime will not be too long delayed.

Changing views of monetary policy
From my remarks so far it may be seen that the operation of monetary policy in Britain has developed in a very pragmatic way. The environment conditions policy; and the environment has a habit of changing. So too does opinion about the importance of monetary policy in regulating demand and about the way in which it makes its impact. And recent discussion on these counts has been very lively indeed.

At the end of the war it was widely believed that interest rates should be kept low to finance reconstruction as well as to ease the servicing of a greatly increased national debt; and it was somewhile before it was universally accepted that a slump was not after all inevitable. A fairly comprehensive system of physical controls had been maintained to suppress inflation; and the doctrines of Keynes, at least as interpreted by his followers – it is interesting to speculate on what Keynes himself would have prescribed had he lived to see the shape of the post-war world – had led to a totally new emphasis on fiscal policy. The active drive for cheap money was succeeded by a period in which monetary policy went into limbo. There was general scepticism about its relevance.

The prolongation of controls, however, and the austere budgetary strategy of the time began to generate a reaction in which rising prices and the vulnerability of the reserves also played a part. At the end of 1951 monetary policy again entered an active phase. Having been at 2% almost constantly since 1932, Bank rate was to be varied forty times in the next nineteen years. The changed economic climate and the dismantling of physical controls made it essential to revive monetary policy, but undoubtedly too much was expected of it in the early fifties. Although it has the great advantage over fiscal policy that it can be operated and modified on a day-to-day basis, it is by no means as smooth, speedy or flexible in its effects as is often assumed. As its limitations became more apparent, the need was felt for a reappraisal; and this led to the appointment of the Radcliffe Committee.

You will recall the main lines along which that Committee reported in 1959. They saw changes in interest rates as having a limited and slow effect on capital spending but a potentially significant impact on lending by financial institutions. The money supply was only part of a wider concept of liquidity. People could realise assets, or borrow, as well as run down money balances; and their willingness to do so would be conditioned by prospective income flows. It was on the structure of interest rates therefore that policy should act, chiefly to restrict the availability of credit. In line with this thinking, bank deposits were less important than bank advances. This qualified view of monetary policy, and of the money supply in particular, was to be strongly contested. Even before the Committee was appointed, there had been academic reaction across the Atlantic to the tendency to relegate money to a minor role. In the following years, first in the United States and more recently in this country the monetarist school of thought steadily gained ground.

Monetarist controversy

It is easy to caricature the opposing theories, for some extreme positions have been taken; but it is fair to add that nowadays there are plenty of intermediate positions too. In simplified terms, those who attach only minor importance to the money supply regard financial assets as close substitutes for money, and real assets as a rather different category. On this view a change in the money stock will be associated with only a relatively slight shift in interest rates and people will be content to hold less money in relation to incomes. There will be some effects on spending – through changes in the cost of capital, in the availability of credit and in existing wealth; but the impact will not be pronounced and could more certainly be achieved by acting directly on interest rates in the first place.

On the other hand, those who attach major importance to the money supply see holdings of money as a substitute for a broader range of both financial and real assets, on which the return cannot be generalised. On this view a change in money balances will be associated with erratic movements in interest rates and will then largely be made good by adjustments in spending, for people will be reluctant to hold less money in relation to incomes. In this case policy could exert a strong influence on demand by acting directly on the money supply.

Much work – including some in the Economic Section of the Bank – has been done to test these theories by trying to establish, through associations between the money stock and interest rates, whether or not money and financial assets are in fact close substitutes. One major difficulty is that changes in interest rates are undoubtedly coloured by expectations about the future course both of the rates themselves and of price inflation. The real, as distinct from the nominal, rates of interest that may be in people's minds when they decide to spend or invest cannot be at all closely estimated statistically.

Subject to this qualification, the evidence supports neither extreme. It suggests that changes in the amount of money may have some consequences for money incomes but that in the short run the relationship is neither strong nor predictable. Although the association between changes in money stock and money incomes is undoubtedly strong in the long run, so that movements in the money stock may be useful as an indicator of movements in income, this fact tells us nothing about causation. In particular, since the authorities have not operated in a strictly monetarist way over the past twenty years but have broadly accommodated the rising demand for money balances as incomes rose, statistical associations derived from this period cannot tell us what would happen if policies were radically different.

Official attitudes to monetary policy

Yet, though the argument has not yet been conclusive, it has already served a useful purpose in provoking a general reappraisal of attitudes. The liabilities of the banks have always been significant for policy, of course, since deposits are a key factor in the determination of advances; and it is important that this aspect should not be neglected even if lending ceilings are in force. In recent years, however, we have certainly given more attention than formerly to the growth of monetary aggregates in evaluating policy. These include not only the money supply but also what has come to be known as D.C.E., or domestic credit expansion. Movements in the money supply are influenced among other things by the balance of payments and by inflows and outflows of foreign funds. D.C.E. is some measure – in an arithmetical sense – of the internal factors associated with changes in the money stock, before these are overlaid by external influences. It is thus, in an open economy like ours, sometimes a more useful indicator than the money supply.

But, although there has been some shift of emphasis in recent years, this should be seen in perspective. I certainly accept that such aggregates as the money supply and D.C.E. can be useful indicators of monetary conditions and the impact of policy generally. In particular, it is not a simple matter in an inflationary age to judge the level of interest rates most appropriate to the thrust of policy;

and the growth of the monetary aggregates may offer some guidance in this respect. But to focus solely on the money supply or D.C.E. among the financial, let alone the economic, variables is not enough. It is essential to the understanding of monetary processes and their implications to look much more widely at the stocks of financial assets held throughout the financial sector – and indeed throughout the economy as a whole – and at the financial flows between all the major sectors. We have been concentrating much effort on this in the Bank and shall continue to do so.

Gilt-edged market
In short, while we are keeping a close watch on developments in the monetary aggregates, we are looking at them as guidelines for overall policy rather than as targets. I doubt whether it would be possible to force through a predetermined volume of sales even at the cost of marked instability in interest rates; but even if it were possible, to attempt it would in many circumstances be both damaging and purposeless. For expectations play a large and unpredictable role in investors' decisions. Even when the Government is running a large revenue surplus, as at present, maturities of nearly £2,000 million a year require careful handling if adequate refinance is to be forthcoming. By the same token it would be mistaken to put much weight on short-term deviations in the path of the money supply or D.C.E., which can reflect not only these factors but also bunching in bank lending as well as purely random influences.

There has been much argument about our tactics in the gilt-edged market. There is no need, I think, to go over all the ground here. I suspect, however, that people do not always make a clear distinction between our tactics and our ends. Apart from the needs of government finance, our main end is to achieve the degree of monetary restraint judged to be appropriate to the economic situation and the overall direction of policy. Any particular degree of restraint in any particular circumstances will involve a certain level and pattern of interest rates which will have to be accepted. The burden of high interest rates on the Exchequer and balance of payments, though always a consideration, is not a foremost one. Rising nominal rates can often be illusory when seen in real terms; and to hold rates artificially low can only create a consistently weak market and lead to steady monetisation of the debt. It is this last consideration which has perhaps become more important in our minds recently as inflation has accelerated. Consequently unprecedentedly high nominal rates have seemed appropriate and our tactics in market management have become more flexible so that the market has been allowed to make sharper adjustments than in the past.

While we at the Bank naturally do not mind constructive and well-informed criticism of our market tactics – indeed we welcome it if it can help us towards improving the way we do our job – there is, I think, a real danger in much of the argument and criticism that is actually deployed. Many people apparently believe, or appear to believe, that a purely tactical change in the relatively arcane sphere of operations in the gilt-edged market can magically and painlessly do wonders for the real economy. It cannot be emphasised too strongly or too often that attacking a severe inflation simply by holding down the growth of the money supply means reducing real activity: or in more homely terms a lot of bankruptcies and unemployment. Thus the proper questions for discussion in a situation such as the present are first how much reduction in real activity is appropriate; and secondly how much weight should be placed on monetary policy in achieving it?

But in general it should be recognised that excessive reliance on monetary policy is bound to place severe strains on financial markets and the financial position of companies and may have serious effects on the nation's productive investment and housebuilding. At the same time it will have implications for external capital flows; and this raises doubt about how far monetary policy can in any case be pushed in an open economy without frustrating, at least in part, the authorities' objectives both domestically and externally.

External aspects
Sterling, like all currencies which are used internationally, is sensitive to capital flows, whether arising out of changes in yield differentials or from speculation on exchange rate adjustments. Exchange controls have limited the movement of resident funds; but leads and lags, transfers over intra-company accounts and switching by the banks in London are all important potential channels for capital movements. Meanwhile the growth of the euro-dollar market has seen a vast increase over recent years in the volume and mobility of international funds.

It is true that movements of interest sensitive funds will tend to slow down once investors have adjusted their portfolios and, in the case of covered transactions, as the forward rate reacts; but an attempt to offset them by further monetary action can renew the process. In Britain there has on the whole been little conflict of this kind since the war. During the sixties, for instance, when economic conditions generally pointed to the maintenance of high interest rates, arbitrage movements were often submerged by speculative flows which in themselves worked to tighten liquidity. But the dilemma has not been uncommon abroad; and it is one with which in future we may have to reckon ourselves now that the balance of payments is on a sounder basis.

Speculative flows present a special problem. There are a variety of techniques that can be used in an attempt to discourage arbitrage flows. These include attempting to change the relationship between short and long-term interest rates; intervention in the forward market; and the kind of specific measures applied by Germany and Switzerland in the face of speculative movements during the sixties. In practice, however, it is not simple to sustain an artificial relationship between short and long rates. Nor is it necessarily a straightforward matter to identify the nature of capital flows and to determine whether they would be susceptible to intervention in the forward market. Yet, once committed, it is impossible to withdraw from the market without intensifying speculation if the judgment should prove wrong.

As banks and corporations become more internationally-minded and sophisticated in their financial operations, the difficulties of conducting monetary policy in an open economy are not going to diminish. Recent years have underlined the pervasive influence, largely transmitted through the euro-dollar market, that credit conditions in the United States can have elsewhere in the world. For all these reasons we shall have to think hard over the next few years about the effects of our monetary policies on the rest of the world and the limitations imposed on us by the monetary policies of other important countries. It will be important to develop further the international co-operation and inter-dependence which has already been taken further than many would have thought possible a generation ago.

Forward view
I have tried to give a broad survey of the problems and possibilities of monetary management in Britain in the changing environment of the past twenty-five years. Before concluding, I should like to take a brief look forward.

The most pressing economic problem, not only for this country but in virtually all the major industrialised nations in the years ahead, is likely to be that of cost inflation. Much thought and discussion about this problem will be necessary, not merely among policy-makers, but among all the elements and individuals of our societies. Whatever role is assigned to monetary policy, there will doubtless be need to evolve our techniques and our thinking as we have done in the past. One obvious example of the necessity to adjust which has already made itself felt is the importance of distinguishing between nominal and real rates of interest.

Whatever our success in coping with inflation, the familiar problems of demand management will obviously continue with us. Here, to the extent that the financial position of the public sector remains under firm control and the balance of payments remains in surplus (and in my belief these two areas are very closely related), the strains on monetary policy and the institutional framework in which it operates could be significantly eased.

If this should prove to be the case, we may be able to make more progress with an aspect of monetary management to which I referred at the beginning of my talk, fostering the growth of an efficient and competitive financial system. As I have emphasised, our aims in this direction have in recent years been frequently in conflict with the need to maintain strict control over bank lending. It is true that, despite the heavy and unwelcome quantitative controls which we have imposed, the banking world has certainly not ceased to evolve. I have referred to the rapid growth of the subsidiaries of the clearing banks and of many other forms of British and foreign banks; and to the growth and development of new markets both in sterling and foreign currency. Individual banks have extended the range of their services in many ways and, by merging among themselves and forming international ties, have been able to match the financial needs of ever-growing industrial groupings and multi-national concerns.

I have no doubt that the banks will want to innovate further and in all sorts of ways. The clearers are experimenting rather more with term loans, for example, which afford them closer control over their advances. They recently increased the margin between their lending rates and Bank rate; and it may be that they will want to widen it further, or change their practices on interest rates completely. Developments of these kinds could lead to some breaking down of the line between the deposit banks and that other very heterogeneous group which, for want of a better term, we call simply the "other" banks. In these circumstances credit allocation could come to be determined more by price than by physical rationing throughout the banking sector.

The way in which the banking system evolves will be conditioned by credit control, and is bound to have implications for credit control. Some developments could make life easier, others could complicate it. In principle it is important that control should not be imposed and stifle innovation; but rather should allow innovation to take place and then adapt to it. We may hope that in the fullness of time a greater use of such mechanisms as Special and Cash Deposits, buttressed perhaps by the acceptance of greater variability of short-term interest rates, could lead to a more flexible framework for monetary management.

Key issues in monetary and credit policy

Text of an address by the Governor to the International Banking Conference in Munich on 28th May 1971

As many of you will be aware, we in the United Kingdom have recently embarked on a major change in our approach to monetary policy. Much of the detail of our new proposals, which are, of course, still being discussed with the banks and other institutions concerned, will be primarily of interest to banks operating in the United Kingdom. But I believe our proposals raise some fundamental questions which may be of general interest. Basically, they reflect a change in the official attitude towards two key questions: first, what monetary variable should the authorities attempt to influence; and, second, by what means should they attempt to influence it?

Let us first take the question of what monetary variable the authorities should attempt to influence. Of course, real life being more complicated than the textbooks, it is seldom possible or desirable for the authorities to put all their eggs in one monetary basket. One must in practice take account of movements in many financial indicators, varying the relative importance attached to them as circumstances change. With this qualification, however, it is fair to say that for the past six or seven years we in the United Kingdom have laid particular stress in our monetary policy on influencing the volume of bank lending in sterling to the private sector. There is some evidence that bank lending to particular elements in the economy – for example, to consumers – is an important direct influence on spending. Moreover, there may often be advantage in attempting to discriminate between different forms of economic expenditure – encouraging exports and restraining consumption, for example – and persuading the banks to be more generous to one activity and less to another may do something to help achieve this aim.

Against this, however, we must remember that financial systems are infinitely adaptable and the channels whereby money and credit end up as spending are many and various. We must beware of believing that if we do succeed in restraining bank lending we have necessarily and to the same extent been operating a restrictive credit policy. We may by our very actions stimulate the provision of credit through non-bank channels; we may introduce distortions into the financial system; and we may indeed be distorting in harmful ways the deployment of the real resources of the country. For these reasons we have increasingly shifted our emphasis towards the broader monetary aggregates – to use the inelegant but apparently unavoidable term: the money supply under one or more of its many definitions, for example, or domestic credit expansion.

My second basic question concerns the means whereby the authorities affect whatever it is they wish to affect. Obviously the more stress one lays on precisely controlling bank lending to the private sector, the more tempting it is to achieve that control in the most direct possible way by formal requests to the banks to lend no more than such and such an amount in total; to observe such and such priorities and so on. We in the United Kingdom have in fact been operating a system of bank lending ceilings with declared official priorities almost continuously since 1965. We have, however, been increasingly unhappy about the effects of operating monetary policy in this way over a prolonged period. In this audience I do not need to labour the ill effects. It is obvious that physical rationing of this kind can lead to serious misallocation of resources, both in the economy and in the financial system, and that inhibiting competition between banks can do much damage to the vigour and vitality of the entire banking system.

Here again we have over the last couple of years begun to move away from reliance on physical control, in that we have been prepared to see greater movements of interest rates throughout the system and consequently a greater reliance on the price mechanism in allocating credit. But as long as our major control continued to be ceilings on bank lending, we could not be said to have gone very far in this direction.

This month, however, we have taken a major new initiative. We have put proposals to all the banks for a new approach to credit control which, if agreement can be reached between the authorities and the banks, will enable us to abandon ceiling controls altogether.

Perhaps I could now outline the details of our new proposals. Basically what we have in mind is a system under which *the allocation of credit is primarily determined by its cost.* It accords with this general aim that the clearing and Scottish banks (the major deposit banks in the United Kingdom) should abandon their long-standing cartel arrangements, which have provided for uniform deposit rates linked to Bank rate, and also the convention which has governed the relationship of their lending rates to Bank rate. In future, the authorities would seek to influence the structure of interest rates through a general control over the liquidity of the whole banking system. In order to render such control more efficient and less imprecise, we are proposing a minimum reserve assets ratio applying uniformly to all the banks. At the same time our right to call for Special Deposits at the Bank of England would similarly be extended uniformly to cover all banks.

The minimum reserve assets ratio will be expressed as a fixed percentage of sterling deposit liabilities and will have to be held in certain specified reserve assets. These assets will comprise cash at the Bank of England and certain other assets which the Bank are normally prepared to convert into cash, either through open-market operations or by lending. These include Treasury bills, money at call in the discount market and gilt-edged stocks of up to one year's maturity. The ratio is designed to provide a known firm base on which the Bank of England can operate, both in market operations and by calls for Special Deposits, to neutralise excess liquidity which the banking system might acquire

As far as our interest rate operations are concerned, we shall of course continue to use the traditional instrument of Bank rate to affect short-term rates; indeed we envisage using Bank rate more flexibly than in the past. It was, moreover, important for the working of the new system that we should reduce the extent of our intervention in the long-term gilt-edged market. For this reason we announced on 14th May that the Bank of England no longer felt obliged to provide, as in the past, outright support for the gilt-edged market in stocks having a maturity of over one year. This does not mean that we have discontinued our normal operations of selling longer-dated gilt-edged against purchases of short-dated stocks, as a technically efficient way of refinancing maturities. But it does mean that we shall not generally be prepared to buy stock outright. Thus we shall not normally be prepared to facilitate movements out of gilt-edged by the banks, even if their sales should cause the market temporarily to weaken quite sharply.

These changes could, of course, mean that some gilt-edged holders may prefer to stay shorter than hitherto; but their policies will, no doubt, be influenced by the structure of rates as well as by the extent to which private institutions are stimulated to make a better market in gilt-edged than hitherto.

The second leg of our policy is represented by our ability to call for Special Deposits. Any calls would be made from all banks uniformly: and all the deposits called would bear interest at a rate equivalent to the Treasury bill rate. The call for Special Deposits might be related only to deposits obtained from overseas, or the call might be different for overseas and resident deposits; but in either case it would be applied uniformly to all banks.

It is not expected that the mechanism of the minimum asset ratio and Special Deposits can be used to achieve some precise multiple contraction or expansion of bank assets. Rather the intention is to use our control over liquidity, which these instruments will reinforce, to influence the structure of interest rates. The resulting changes in relative rates of return will then induce shifts in the asset portfolios of both the public and the banks. Of course, we do not envisage that there can be a nicely calculated relationship between the size of calls for Special Deposits and the achievement of a desired objective. We expect rather to achieve our objectives through market mechanisms. Special Deposits can be used not only to mop up any abnormal excess liquidity, but also to oblige the banking system to seek to dispose of assets not eligible for the liquidity ratio, for example gilt-edged stocks of over one year's maturity. By using Special Deposits in this way we shall be able to exert, when appropriate, upward pressure on interest rates — not only rates in the inter-bank market but also rates in the local authority market and yields on short-term gilt-edged stock.

Of course, the extent of the pressure we shall be able to bring to bear on interest rates by our open-market policies, backed up if necessary by calls for Special Deposits, will be affected by many factors: for example, the financial position of the central government or the current sensitivity of foreign exchange flows to short-term rates in London. However, no limitation is envisaged on the authorities' ability to neutralise excess liquidity or to bring about sufficiently strong upward pressure on bank lending rates.

What we are therefore adopting is a new approach to credit control designed to permit the price mechanism to function efficiently in the allocation of credit, and to free the banks from rigidities and restraints which have for far too long inhibited them from efficiently fulfilling their intermediary role in the financial system. At the same time, it is hoped that these changes will favour innovation and competition, and in their way make some contribution to faster and sounder economic growth. These changes are consistent with the broad policy aims of the present Government of the United Kingdom. We judge the present situation of low international interest rates, relatively slack demand for loans and a strong balance of payments to be a propitious moment in which to introduce these changes; and we also believe that they are not inconsistent with the United Kingdom's application to join the E.E.C. or out of line with the general movement towards the harmonisation of credit controls which seems likely to take place on the road to monetary union.

COMPETITION AND CREDIT CONTROL

The travails of Competition and Credit Control

From the outset, the removal of direct ceiling controls and the abolition of the cartel did, indeed, encourage much more aggressive competition within the banking and financial system. The Governor commented at the Lord Mayor's dinner in October 1972:

Last year we sought, by reforming the structure of the banking system and the official restraints under which it operated, to strike off the shackles that had been frustrating initiative and innovation in the provision of financial services. We believed that the forces of competition, working in an environment unencumbered by cartels and restrictions, would instil renewed energy to develop better and more efficient financial services.

A year's experience strongly suggests to me that we were right. Developments within the banking system during the past twelve months confirm not only the strength of competition but also the latent talent for new initiatives. It has been a period during which many changes have occurred and others have been foreshadowed. The banks have been re-arranging and improving the services they offer; they have provided a wider range of both lending and deposit facilities.

But, whereas the success in encouraging greater competition was manifest, the rate of growth of bank lending and the broad monetary aggregates accelerated sharply in 1972–73. There was a *prima facie* case that the credit control arrangements were proving seriously deficient. This was seen at the time, and thereafter, as an issue of major importance, requiring careful assessment and explanation. Accordingly, the Governor gave the subject detailed attention in his speech to the Mansion House in October 1972:

To all these efforts to improve the efficiency of the system, our critics tend to say: certainly we are getting the competition in the provision of financial services, but where is the credit control? And they point to the increase in the money supply over the past twelve months. This establishes a powerful *prima facie* criticism which we must take seriously.

It is, however, worth noting that the major structural changes introduced last year were bound to bring about considerable changes in the business of the banks, in the composition both of their assets and of their liabilities. If you encourage the banks to become more competitive, you must expect them to take a larger share of the available business, and this kind of expansion carries no connotation of excessive monetary ease.

Thus on the asset side, after so many years of controls and restrictions, it was hardly surprising that there was a large immediate surge in bank lending to those sectors against which the controls had been most severely directed, such as the personal sector. The extent of the shift was perhaps somewhat exaggerated both by the comparative stagnation in the demand from manufacturing industry for bank finance, though this now seems to be reviving, and also by the various measures taken, for example, in the field of taxation and in the abolition of terms control, which had the effect of encouraging personal borrowing still further.

Similarly on the liabilities side, the banks have sought to provide more varied attractions to potential depositors. In particular they have obtained a large volume of funds from large depositors by issuing sterling certificates of deposit at very competitive rates. There has, as a result, been some exaggeration in the pace of expansion of the broad definitions of the money stock, which include time deposits and sterling certificates of deposit. To put our own experience in perspective, M1, the narrower definition of the money stock, which I regard as less subject to bias, has been rising in the last six months at about the same rate as in France and Western Germany.

But even when all appropriate allowances have been made, I do not regard the record of monetary expansion of the past year with complacency. What lessons can we then draw about improving the operation of the new system? I have stressed on a number of occasions that in a system, free of direct intervention to ration the allocation of credit, the operation of credit control requires the flexible adjustment of interest rates both up and down and, as you will be aware, having with the new arrangements much reduced the importance of the old style Bank rate, we have recently taken an important step to restore flexibility and effectiveness to the rate at which the Bank lend to the money market.

In the last few months there have indeed been periods when prices in financial markets moved very sharply. Naturally this has proved an uncomfortable experience. But the rejection of reliance on direct controls implies the corollary of living with considerably more flexible interest rates. It follows that we must not temper our approach so as to protect whatever soft spots there may be at any particular time, and the emergency help which we extended to banks in the sterling crisis this summer is in no way inconsistent with that approach. This help arose rather from our proper concern to avoid an exceptional event having too disruptive an effect.

This leads me on to the question whether we did in practice last year operate with sufficient flexibility.

My opinion now is that late last year we should have resisted the downward movement in interest rates more strongly than we did; or that failing that, we should have moved earlier this year, perhaps even in February and March, to establish a higher level of interest rates. But when we did begin to shift to a more restrictive policy in June and July, we moved probably about as fast and as far as even hindsight would suggest was desirable.

We should probably have had a significantly higher level of interest rates last winter for several reasons. By then it was apparent that we had under-estimated the strength and persistence of the surge in lending to such groups as persons and financial institutions. Moreover the state of the property and housing market had become unruly with prices moving wildly ahead, unnecessarily far to provide an incentive for new building. Most significant of all, the outcome of the miners' strike dashed previous hopes for a steady deceleration of inflation.

Yet the objections at the time to higher interest rates were very powerful. Unemployment was still rising to new peaks: it did not turn down until April. Output was then barely rising, even after discounting the effect of industrial disruption. Until the settlement of the miners' strike there were some grounds for hoping that inflation would continue to decelerate. For all these reasons it was the Government's expressed policy to encourage by all means the expansion of activity. And perhaps I may be forgiven for recalling that over these months the whole tenor of press comment was that we should get interest rates lower still. If we had done so the necessary subsequent rise would have had to be even sharper than it was.

Certainly the appropriate direction for policy becomes easier to see at a time when real output is moving ahead at a fair speed, but inflationary concern mounts. And this was the state of affairs by the end of the second quarter, by which time the Budget measures were taking effect. The record shows that we did then shift sharply to a considerably more restrictive policy. The upwards movement in interest rates in the two months between the end of May and the end of July was remarkably abrupt by any historical standards. Base rates rose by $2\frac{1}{2}\%$ and representative money market rates by $3\frac{1}{2}\%$.

Monetary developments during the summer months were considerably distorted by the sterling crisis which led to the adoption and subsequent unwinding of abnormal monetary positions. Nevertheless it does seem possible to discern some slowing down in the rate of monetary expansion in recent months after the hectic pace of the second quarter, no doubt partly in response to the sharp upward increases in interest rates in June and July. However I am not confident that we have now done enough to ensure that monetary expansion will moderate to the desired extent in coming months. There are certain features ahead, the sharply rising deficit in the public sector, and the revival of borrowing by manufacturing companies, which could lead to a renewed acceleration in monetary expansion. We will need to be vigilant and active to prevent this.

I trust that this re-examination of past events will not have seemed out of place on an occasion so often devoted to invitations to ascend into a hopeful future. I have undertaken this re-examination because, particularly in an era of change, an appreciation of the lessons of the past must form the basis of our future plans. I accept, as most central bankers would, that control of the money supply is one of my principal, if not my most important, concerns and I have no wish to shirk it. But we cannot face two ways at once. There is no monetary policy which will simultaneously stimulate expansion and moderate inflation.

The new Governor, Mr G Richardson returned to the same issues as his predecessor in his first Mansion House speech in October 1973:

In September I issued guidance to the banks on the direction of their lending and asked them to limit it in the less essential areas. We saw a need to encourage an adjustment in the balance of demand as well as to support the higher interest rates in moderating the pace of monetary growth. For moderation in the rate of growth of the economy and in the pace of inflation requires moderation in the pace of monetary expansion.

It is not always easy to discern what these growth rates are. It is hard enough when dealing with the economy, but it is harder still in the monetary field. Many commentators appear to pass judgement on monetary policy almost exclusively by reference to the behaviour of the broader definition of money supply which we call M3. This is placing more weight on a single yardstick than it is capable either in principle or in practice of bearing. Thus there has been insufficient recognition both of the extent to which in the last two years business has flowed back into the banking system following the removal of earlier restrictions, and of the effects of investors' preference for liquidity at times when the future course of inflation and interest rates has tended to be uncertain. There are other indicators, and they do not all tell the same story. The narrow definition of the money supply, M1, which is the main focus of attention in the United States for example, has grown much less fast.

In so far as the faster growth of M3 has been due to business flowing back into the banking system, I regard it as healthy. I find it difficult to understand those who believe that the new structural system should be abandoned, because under it the banks are able to use their comparative efficiency so as to intermediate more between borrower and lender. That was the purpose of the exercise.

But, despite all the doubts and uncertainties that abound, one has to make a judgement about the pace of monetary expansion. And looking at all the monetary statistics, and perhaps in particular at the pace and direction of bank lending to the private sector, it appeared to have been overrapid. We acted this summer to raise interest rates sharply. The effects of this and of the guidance given to the banks take time to work through but I believe they will operate to stem the pace of monetary expansion. Hopes may be dupes but if they are—and there is a full-scale war in progress in the Middle East—we shall not hesitate to take such further action as may be necessary to secure our objectives.

I have dealt with the evolution of policy. I now turn to the framework within which it operates. But I should first state my firm belief that a framework which allows freedom for competition and innovation in the business of banking is good for the British industry and commerce and, by enabling banks to play a vigorous part in the world market for finance, is of further benefit to this country.

It is some two years since the Bank introduced the arrangements set out in *Competition and credit control*. At the time, these were widely acclaimed with a chorus of assent and very little qualification, no doubt partly because people then had vividly in their minds the difficulties, rigidities and inefficiencies to which the banking system had become a victim as a result of long years of restriction. Since that time the chorus has become muted, qualifications have been entered and there are sharply dissenting views.

Yet I do not suppose that anyone would deny that our banking system—and I speak especially of the big clearing banks—today shows an altogether new vigour and enterprise.

Many factors have been at work, but for myself I should want in their case to suggest disclosure, Competition and Credit Control, and the challenge of foreign banks, as three main agents of change. All this is good.

But the new competitive environment has posed some operational problems for both the banks and the central bank, including the so-called 'merry-go-round' which has added some further, very real, distortions to the monetary series. More generally banks have needed to learn new techniques in managing their resources and both they and others dealing in financial markets have needed to acquire new skills in assessing future developments generally and the course of interest rates in particular. In the same way, we in the Bank have needed to adapt and correct our approach and techniques in the light of experience.

What went wrong?

The Governors pointed in these speeches to a number of associated reasons to explain the rapid acceleration in bank lending and in the money stock, namely the reintermediation following the abolition of credit controls, the widespread desire for faster growth in 1971 and 1972 (which made it more difficult to raise interest rates), a general underestimation of the pressure of demand within the economy, and an accompanying expansionary fiscal policy. All these factors contributed, and were important, but they did not bear directly on the central problem. This was that the new system of credit control was intended to work through the influence of interest rates on banks' sterling business. There were expected to be two main transmission routes for this effect. First, an increase in bank lending rates was expected to reduce the demand for bank loans by making them more costly; second, an increase in interest rates on public sector debt, relative to the (presumed) stickier bank deposit rates, was expected to lead to a shift of funds by the non-bank private sector out of holding bank deposits into holdings of public sector debt.

Such transmission routes had apparently worked prior to 1971, since interest rates had a well-defined, significant effect on both broad and narrow monetary aggregates. The stability of this relationship between interest rates and the broader monetary aggregates broke down entirely after 1971, and has not reappeared since then. (This is described in the research paper on *The demand for money in the United Kingdom: experience since 1971*, included in the Econometric Appendix—page 172.)

Why did this happen? Answers are inevitably tentative. It is clear, however, that the structural changes in 1971 left the banks much freer to compete aggressively for (wholesale) deposits. Thus a rise in interest rates on public sector debt (Treasury bills and gilts), brought about by the Bank to restrict monetary expansion, would no longer necessarily lead to a shift in interest rate relativities, encouraging a shift out of deposits into public sector debt, since banks were now both willing and able to compete by raising interest rates on wholesale deposits and certificates of deposit, in line with increases in interest rates on other assets.

This put more of the weight of monetary control onto the first transmission route, through its effect on the demand for bank borrowing. But there were difficulties with this route also. First, although the relationships had been thoroughly obscured by the application of direct credit ceilings, over time research both in the Bank and elsewhere suggested that the demand for bank borrowing in the United Kingdom was, in the short run at least, rather unresponsive to movements in interest rates. Second, bank base rates remained administratively set, which tended to make them slower to adjust than market rates under most circumstances. Moreover, in the context of 1972–73, with high interest rates leading to banks obtaining large 'endowment' profits on their non-interest-bearing current accounts, and with the Government trying to restrict inflationary pressures at that time by the use of price and wage controls, there were broad political pressures limiting the upwards flexibility of bank lending rates. Indeed at times, bank wholesale deposit rates in those years rose above bank lending rates, causing an incentive to borrow simply in order to re-deposit the same funds with another bank, a distortion known as the 'merry-go-round'.

The result was that, by the latter half of 1973, the extent of the further rise in interest rates that might be needed to check the ballooning upsurge in bank lending and broad money appeared incalculable. Interest rates had already by then risen to unprecedented levels (MLR rose to 13% in November), though even this increase did not keep up with rapidly accelerating inflation. Against this background it was decided to revert to some more direct control over monetary expansion, and, after a short review of the alternatives, the supplementary special deposits scheme, commonly known as the 'corset' was devised, and introduced in December 1973. This scheme was described in a note 'Credit control: a supplementary scheme', included in the March 1974 *Bulletin*: its main features and an *ex post* survey of the working of the scheme are described in an article *The supplementary special deposits scheme* published in the March 1982 *Bulletin* and reprinted in Chapter 6 (page 117).

CHAPTER 3
Monetary targets

The choice of monetary aggregate

In their 1972 and 1973 Mansion House speeches the Governors repeated the theme that it was misguided to place too much weight on just one measure of monetary growth, ie the broad monetary aggregate (M3), and noted that narrow money, as measured by M1, was growing much more slowly. Moreover, the structural changes of 1971, which had altered the characteristics of interest-bearing wholesale deposits, left the characteristics of M1 deposits, which were primarily non-interest-bearing, unchanged. Thus, it might be expected that the relationships between M1, nominal incomes and interest rates, would remain stable and well-defined through this period. This, indeed, appeared to be the case as documented by the research article on *A transactions demand for money* included in the Econometric Appendix—page 188. Such findings might seem to provide a strong case for giving more weight to M1 as a second, or even perhaps the primary, target. Moreover, the initial adoption of sterling M3 as the main target had been originally due to somewhat fortuitous factors: the credit counterparts to changes in sterling M3 allowed the interaction between DCE and money to be more clearly articulated, and the statistical properties of sterling M3—it was less erratic and less dependent on arbitrary allocations of items in transit—were superior to those of M1. These considerations rather than a conscious preference for the one measure over the other determined the choice.

The case for giving greater weight to M1 relative to sterling M3 was reconsidered several times from 1973 onwards. Until 1982, however, these reviews, though sometimes finely balanced, left the Bank preferring to maintain the *status quo* for the following reasons.

First, the boom of 1972–73, and the oil price shock of 1973 were followed by an inflationary upsurge in 1974 and 1975. Many commentators blamed this directly on the expansion of broad money (M3) in 1972–73. With the general view being that monetary policy had been expansionary in 1972–73, the time path of broad money fitted in with that analysis; the time path of M1 did not. So, even though the relationship of past and current incomes and interest rates with M1 (as evidenced by its demand-for-money function) seemed much stronger and more stable than was the case with M3 (or sterling M3 which supplanted it in 1977), the influence of the latter broad aggregate on future movements of nominal incomes seemed then the stronger.

Second, as already noted, the movements in sterling M3 could be described and analysed in terms of the credit counterparts, which analysis could not also be done with M1. These credit counterparts included the public sector borrowing requirement (PSBR), government debt sales to the non-bank private sector, bank lending to the private sector and net external flows. Since these each reflected a major area of policy, respectively fiscal policy, debt management, credit policy and external policy, such analysis both allowed monetary forecasting and targetry to indicate coherent *ex ante* combinations of the separate arms of policy, and also to suggest *ex post*, which branch of policy needed adjustment when the broad monetary aggregate appeared to be going off course.

In the case of M1, no such counterpart analysis was available, so the only link between M1 and economic developments more generally was through its econometric relationship in the form of a demand-for-money function. In view of the manifold breakdowns of previously stable econometric relationships during the course of the 1970s, both in the monetary area and elsewhere, there was little enthusiasm for placing more weight on M1, purely on the grounds of a better econometric relationship with nominal incomes and interest rates. Moreover, towards the end of the 1970s and in the early 1980s, further structural changes seemed imminent, in the form of greater competition for retail deposits causing interest payments to be offered on transactions balances. These led to an expectation that the previously stable econometric relationships of M1 would be subsequently liable to considerable change.

Adoption of a monetary target

Despite the breakdown of the previously stable econometric demand for money relationship for broad money, the experience of the early 1970s, with the upsurge of inflation in 1974–75 following closely on the heels of the monetary explosion in 1972–73, led to even greater emphasis being placed on the need for a financial anchor in the form of a monetary target applied in order to constrain and control the rate of inflation.

In the immediate aftermath of the election of the new Government in March 1974, and with monetary growth being held down by the 'corset' and a fall-off in the demand for bank lending during the ensuing recession, attention swung back towards incomes and fiscal policies, and no particular mention was made of monetary policy in the 1974 Mansion House speech.

By October 1975, however, the Governor reverted to the theme of the importance of monetary control, and its desirable conjunction with complementary fiscal and incomes policies.

In commending an incomes policy I know that I disappoint those who believe that inflation should be tackled by monetary measures alone. But if we tackled it purely by controlling demand in general, or the money supply in particular, we would cause even deeper recession, even more unemployment, and even more damage to investment. The policy of pay restraint helps to minimise these losses: that seems to me pure gain.

That said, it is also true that an incomes policy should be complementary to fiscal and monetary policies—not a substitute for them.

There is much debate over the appropriate role of monetary policy in present circumstances. For my part I do not doubt that it has an important and powerful influence on the economy—though the force and timing of its impact may be difficult to predict. I also believe that, in view of the overriding importance of moderating inflation—a problem to be seen in the context not just of this winter, but of the next two or three years—we should strictly maintain a moderate pace of monetary expansion.

So far this year, as you will know, the rate of monetary expansion has in fact been moderate. Industrial and commercial demand for bank credit has proved unusually weak, because the developing recession has made it so. The financial appetite of Government, on the other hand, has been far from weak, and there has been room for it to be met in part by the banks. In the year to date, the rise in the money stock on the narrower definition has been a little less fast than the growth of money national income. On the wider definition, the money stock has risen much more slowly, by little over 10%: this I would regard as showing rather adequate restraint.

The most recent figures, coupled with the rise in interest rates, are indications that it is becoming more difficult to maintain so moderate a pace. The underlying reason is quite simple—the size of the public sector borrowing requirement. Until its growth can be halted and then reversed, we shall need to exercise special vigilance in our monetary management. The alternative of readily accommodating a further acceleration in monetary growth must, I believe, be rejected.

I should not conceal, my Lord Mayor, my anxieties about the public sector borrowing requirement. For some time the requirement has, on more than one occasion, proved much in excess of what was only recently forecast and assumed as an element of policy. I recognise that this has been due in part to the steeper decline in the economy and I accept that there are no absolute standards in this matter. But it is surely clear that such large unplanned increases will have to be brought under control, and that the deficit itself will need to be severely reduced over the next two or three years. I think it is now generally recognised that the reduction in the deficit will require not only the cautious planning of public expenditure for some years ahead, but also a mechanism of control over expenditure which is effective in the short run. We surely do not want a situation, in a few years' time, where the only way of controlling a bursting economy would be to impose a yet higher burden of tax.

Then in 1976, under the influence of severe and prolonged downwards pressure on the exchange rate, and in the light of experience abroad (for example in Germany and North America, which had adopted monetary targets), the Governor went further. He related the control of inflation primarily to monetary policy and advocated the adoption of a publicly-announced monetary target in order to buttress and to strengthen such policy. In June of that year, addressing the annual conference of the Chartered Institute of Public Finance and Accountancy, he noted some advantages and disadvantages of publicly-announced targets.

Looking ahead over the next few years, I am equally impressed by the difficulties to be overcome and by the opportunities to be taken advantage of. First among our problems will continue to be the problem of inflation, which I will therefore discuss first. Linked to the control of inflation is monetary policy, on which I will try to suggest some directions. Lying behind, in turn, there are major questions regarding general economic strategy— including questions about the size of the public sector borrowing requirement and the directions of budgetary policy. ...

We have to be single-minded in combating inflation; but not single-handed. Incomes policy has proved valuable, but it would be foolish if we placed all our reliance on it. No one should, and I certainly do not, underestimate the continuing and direct relevance of prudent management of demand in the economy, including a prudent monetary policy.

There have been other voices who, from various quarters, have urged the case for our expressing the monetary aims of policy in terms of a target figure, or alternatively a range, for the rate of expansion of one or more definitions of the money stock. The aims of policy thus formulated could be and would need to be, restated, at longer or shorter intervals in the light of the emerging situation. Some countries have found this a useful way of conducting monetary policy. The possible advantages are, I believe, that it may make clearer what the aims of monetary policy are, and may give the public a greater sense that the authorities are committed to the achievement of their stated aims. More generally, it may therefore have a useful effect on expectations, and may validate the belief of the public that inflation is being kept under proper control.

It is to be expected that the adoption of such a practice is not completely without attendant disadvantages, as would, I think, be generally recognised in the experience of countries which have adopted this approach. It is clear that close adherence to a target applying to one of the dimensions of monetary policy, namely the stock of money, may provoke greater instability in the other dimension of interest rates. The difficulties of adopting such an approach appear particularly great in a country like the United Kingdom, which is a much more open economy than is, for example, the United States, and where we have preferred to have much of the national debt in the form of long-term liabilities.

I believe that all these factors need to be carefully weighed. It is, in my view, important that we should not close our minds to any innovations in policy that would help in the task of controlling inflation. A quantification of the monetary aims of policy should not be adopted as an easy option. Such a procedure would seem to provide greater assurance that corrective action would be taken in time if this was required. From one point of view, this would be an advantage; from another, a potential obligation. Corrective action, if needed, could take either a monetary or a fiscal form: either further steps would have to be taken to finance the public sector deficit or, if these appeared disadvantageous, measures would be required to reduce the deficit.

Later that year, at the Lord Mayor's dinner, the Chancellor, with the Bank's encouragement, announced the adoption of a target for sterling M3.[1] The Governor, speaking on that occasion, said:

What is needed is again to live within our means. We must cease to be so dangerously beholden to others. Unhappily, there are no easy remedies available, and no course that is not, at least for a time, painful and destructive to some hopes. But nothing can now absolve us from the need to put our national finances on to a more stable basis.

All arms of policy will have to contribute. But I begin with monetary policy, because I regard it as having a pre-eminent place among the responsibilities of the Bank.

Monetary policy, and the money supply, remain the subject of expert, and inexpert, controversy. Myself, I take a simple view. We live at a time of all-pervasive inflationary danger. That being so, I think it must be right to aim publicly for a growth in money supply which will accommodate a realistic rate of economic growth but not accommodate, more than in part, the rate of inflation. Operating against that background, monetary policy becomes a powerful weapon in the fight against inflation.

So I believe it is right to have a publicly-announced monetary target, set in conjunction with fiscal policy, so that the relative weights placed on fiscal and monetary measures in the attainment of the target can be clearly seen.

The target for the growth of M3 is currently 12%. Next financial year it ought to be lower than that. Over the past few weeks, by raising interest rates and calling for special deposits, we have demonstrated our determination to keep within the limit set. The purpose of these measures was twofold: to restrain the growth of bank lending to the private sector within the bounds set by the 12% target; and to secure adequate official sales of public sector debt to the general public, so as to neutralise the creation of liquidity arising from the public sector deficit and thereby also moderate the rate of monetary expansion.

In this latter context, the Bank have been criticised for their orthodoxy in relation to the marketing of gilt-edged stocks and for being slow to experiment with new methods. I confess to being sceptical over how far technical ingenuity could have overcome the basic arithmetic, but we have naturally been taking a hard look at the various possibilities. It has always to be remembered, however, that we have in this country the most efficient market for government debt that exists in the world; and for my part, I should want to be sure before agreeing to any proposed innovation, that this efficiency would be fully preserved. Perhaps I may add that, during the last month, we have sold gilt-edged stocks on a massive scale.

The fixing of monetary targets is a new development in this country; so when formulating our monetary aims for the financial year to come, it will, I think, be desirable to look in detail at the methods used in some other countries. In particular, it would be useful to consider the practice of the United States, under which targets are redefined periodically, more especially if this can be done at times when we are able to review the whole mix of policy.

Monetary and fiscal policy—and I would add incomes policy— each have their part to play, and should form a coherent whole. At present there is, undeniably, a growing question over the balance between our monetary and fiscal stances. The record level of interest rates reflects in large part the difficulty of financing, without excessive monetary expansion, the present public borrowing requirement. The current stance of monetary policy will have to continue for the time being. But it is far from costless, and if interest rates remain so high for long, they will begin to be a powerful deterrent to investment, only now showing signs of recovery. In that case, as the Chancellor has pointed out, one would have to ask whether this impact on industrial revival was acceptable or whether public sector borrowing should not be reduced more rapidly, so as to provide more scope for the borrowing of industry.

The operation of monetary targets

The adoption of a target for sterling M3 was widely seen as representing a major change of stance in monetary policy. In the course of the next year, therefore, the Governor described the circumstances, rationale and

---

[1] Some ambiguity, however, attaches to the precise date of the first announcement of a monetary target in the United Kingdom. The Chancellor, in an earlier pronouncement in July 1976, stated that monetary growth in the United Kingdom over the following period 'should' proceed at a particular quantitative rate. There remained, however, a degree of ambiguity about the extent of normative force to be attached to the phrase 'should'.

advantages of such a target in two speeches. The first, at the biennial dinner of the Institute of Bankers in Scotland in January 1977, is reprinted on page 49. The second was at the Mansion House in October 1977.

Monetary restraint and the containment of inflation have been my constant preoccupation over these last years, and I see nothing to suggest that they will not continue to have a crucial importance in the period ahead. I want therefore to say something about our experience.

Financial stability requires monetary stability; and I regard the adoption of published monetary targets, first formally enunciated at this dinner last year, as an essential foundation. Allow me, my Lord Mayor, to indicate again the reasoning that leads me to this view.

Probably the most immediate benefit from publicly announced monetary targets derives from the assurance that money will not itself be a source of instability. Beyond this, monetary targets give a clear indication to those responsible for economic decisions—including those affecting the course of future costs and prices—of the limit to which the authorities are, in effect, prepared to see inflation financed in the months ahead: the implication being that inflation at a faster rate will inevitably put output and employment increasingly at risk. I would not myself look for any short-term relationship between changes in the money supply and changes in prices: but, over time and as they are persevered with, I would expect monetary targets to be an increasingly pervasive influence in moderating inflation.

Such perseverance with monetary targets in the longer run would require a changed perception of monetary policy. Monetary instruments have hitherto tended to be seen as providing essentially flexible support for other tools of economic management. But if monetary targets are to provide, as I believe they should, a continuing and long-term constraint on the inflationary bias which our economy, along with others, has been shown to possess, it would follow that the availability of monetary instruments for other purposes would, over time, be significantly reduced. This seems to me to be a logical and desirable extension of the course we are now on.

Having lived with published monetary targets for only a year, I am sure that we still have much to learn about them, but I think we can look on our experience in the first year with cautious satisfaction. If one goes back to July last year, we had a succession of months when the money supply grew unduly rapidly, so that for a time it seemed we were going to fail to live within the limit we had set for the financial year. Yet over the whole fifteen-month period since July last year M3 has grown by 9½% at an annual rate, comfortably within our target range. And so we have done what we said we would do, and I am greatly encouraged by the general recognition, by people of widely differing political views, that our monetary policy has been a key factor in turning the financial situation.

This achievement has not been without its problems. But we have, I think, shown some ingenuity in meeting them. Our use of debt management techniques such as the partly-paid issue and the variable rate stock has helped us to match the Government's funding programme more closely to the needs of monetary control. I should, however, remind you how difficult it is to forecast month by month what these needs may be, for the behaviour of the money stock reflects a wide array of financial flows which may vary considerably in the short run. Not only do external capital flows defy prediction. The central government borrowing requirement itself fluctuates widely, as also does the scale of bank lending to the private sector. Fluctuations on the domestic side frequently tend to offset variations in external factors. Nonetheless, it is inescapable that there will be erratic variations in the figures, as the statistics for the latest two banking months illustrate.

Then, in February 1978, the Governor took the opportunity of an invitation to give the inaugural Mais Lecture at the City University in London, to deliver a major address on the role of monetary policy. This is reprinted on page 51.

Extract from a speech by the Governor of the Bank of England

given at the biennial dinner of the Institute of Bankers in Scotland on 17 January 1977.

Last year also saw us announcing quantitative targets for the rate of monetary expansion. This brings me to my main subject tonight, namely monetary policy, which has of course to be seen as part of the Government's overall economic policy. In particular, it seems appropriate that I should discuss not so much our recent monetary actions but more generally what monetary targets are likely to involve, and give some account of the Bank's thinking on this matter.

In the past we have naturally had aims as to the rate of monetary expansion we wished to see, though before last year we did not announce them in terms of a quantified target for the money supply. At the end of 1973, for instance, we raised interest rates and introduced the supplementary special deposits scheme, with the object of achieving a reduced rate of growth of M_3. Our aim since then has been to keep the growth of money supply moderate. In the event, the growth of M_3 in the three succeeding years was in a region lying either side of 10%; and this was achieved in the early stages, largely no doubt because of the slowdown in the economy, without great difficulty. Last summer, however, there was a marked acceleration of monetary expansion, due to the concurrence of continuing high public sector borrowing, a resurgence of inflationary expectations, and increased bank borrowing associated with foreign exchange pressure. These developments forced us to a series of corrective measures. We are now back on course, and in line with the monetary aims stated by the Chancellor in July and explicitly formulated in October. Recently, we have agreed targets with the International Monetary Fund, which as you know have been framed in terms not of the growth of the total money supply, but of the growth of its domestic component — that is, of what we have come, for short, to call domestic credit expansion. I will come later to the reasons for this change of emphasis. Though domestic credit expansion is now given greater prominence, it is not of course a newcomer to the scene. We published over a year ago the figure which we provided to the IMF of the domestic credit expansion we foresaw in this financial year, and we expect the outturn to be within the figure of £9 billion then forecast.

What advantages do we see in having quantitative monetary targets? We start from the presumption, as I hardly need say, that monetary developments and monetary policy have important effects. Monetary developments affect the decisions both of firms and individuals. Too expansive a policy will unduly stimulate demand, exacerbate domestic inflation, worsen the balance of payments both on current and capital account — and thus tend to worsen the exchange rate, which, as we have seen, will also add to the rate of inflation. In the same way, too restrictive a policy, while helping with inflation and the balance of payments for a time, would unduly depress demand, swell unemployment and discourage industrial development and investment.

Second, a principal line of our thought is that it is useful to seek to be more precise about our monetary aims. This is helpful to us in formulating the aims of policy. It also appears advantageous to us to try to give the public a clearer idea of those aims. This in turn is helpful to the Bank in carrying out monetary policy.

Third, we have come to the view that, in present conditions especially, the best way of giving a clear indication of the thrust of monetary policy is to state quantitative aims for the rate of expansion of one or more of the monetary aggregates. It is sometimes argued that this is too simple an approach, given the complexity of the financial system, and that we should therefore pay regard to a wider collection of financial and real indicators. I think the answer to that is, 'By all means look at all relevant factors when setting the target; but let us try to define clearly what we are aiming at.' The growth of the monetary aggregates, properly related to the circumstances of the time, is perhaps the best indication of monetary conditions; and targets set in terms of monetary aggregates are useful in providing checkpoints against which current developments can be compared and monitored.

I have sought to make the general case for having monetary targets. I must now say something about the factors which should, in our opinion, determine what numbers we choose as our targets.

Major considerations affecting our judgment about the appropriate rate of monetary expansion have been the pace of inflation and the balance of payments. In recent years, both have in our view called for a relatively restrictive stance of monetary policy. One purpose of announcing monetary targets is to serve notice that excessive increases in domestic costs will come up against resistance. If people believe that the money supply will be expanded to accommodate any rise in costs and prices, however fast, inflationary fears are likely to be increased. If, on the other hand, people are convinced that the rate of growth of the money supply will be held within well-defined limits, this should help to reduce inflationary expectations. Monetary policy should therefore aim to act in concert with other branches of policy, including incomes policy, in slowing down inflation. For these reasons, there has appeared to be a good case in recent years for aiming at a rate of monetary expansion below the increase in money national income. Over the last three years, as I have indicated, the money stock has risen, broadly speaking, by about 10% a year, while the money national income has risen nearly twice as fast.

Though we have agreed our monetary targets with the IMF for the period ahead, this does not mean that the targets are entirely inflexible. While we do not expect it to be necessary, it is open to us to review the targets with the IMF if they appeared to be leaving insufficient room to meet the financial needs of industry.

In general, I do not take the view that monetary targets can sensibly be fixed for all time in accordance with a predetermined formula. There are perhaps two main reasons for insisting on the need for some degree of flexibility. The first is of a somewhat technical character. In the United Kingdom we have not recently been able to observe a continuing stable relationship between money and incomes. Moreover, there can be structural changes in the financial, and more particularly within the banking, system which can change the amount of money that the economy needs. Second, and more fundamental, we need to look, as I have already said, at what is happening to the economy at large. For the true objective of policy is not to keep monetary expansion at a particular level; but to bring about a reduction in inflation and a recovery in employment, growth and the balance of payments.

I appreciate that many monetarist thinkers would, in principle, prefer an unvarying figure or — if we start off course — a pre-set approach to such an ideal figure. While maintaining a need for discretion, I do not have in mind sharp variations in the rate of monetary growth and would emphasise that the flexibility required is likely to be limited. Other central banks which have adopted monetary targets have retained a degree of flexibility, for instance in choosing bands for the rate of growth of their chosen monetary targets or in providing for the updating of the targets, as appropriate. For those who require reassurance I would suggest, too, that if we continue to have publicly announced monetary targets in the years ahead, as I think we should, changes in the targets will need to be justified; this in itself is likely to provide a protection against excessive variation.

We have stated our monetary aims for the years immediately ahead in the form of targets for the domestic component of credit expansion — not for the total growth in the stock of money as measured, for instance, by the M_3 statistics. I must now say a word as to why we thought it best — and why the IMF thought it best — to couch our aims in this form.

The difference between domestic credit expansion and M_3 mainly comprises what might be called the foreign component of credit expansion — very roughly, the balance of payments position on current account plus net private sector capital flows. There are two reasons for choosing a DCE target rather than a money supply target in present circumstances.

First, an excessive growth of domestic credit is likely to be associated with a worsening balance of payments, both directly, if surplus liquidity leaks abroad, and indirectly, if the excessive growth undermines external confidence.

The second consideration is that it is the domestic element of credit expansion that is most directly under our control. To focus attention on DCE as a control variable appears the best means of ensuring that the domestic financial situation is kept under the proper degree of constraint, especially when the need remains to rectify our external payments position.

Reflections on the conduct of monetary policy

The first Mais lecture, given by the Governor at the City University, London on 9 February 1978.

I must begin by saying what a privilege and pleasure it is for me to have been invited to inaugurate this new series of lectures in the field of banking and finance which are to take place annually at the City University. It is a fitting tribute to the energy and broad interests of Lord Mais, who in 1973 as Chancellor of this University and Lord Mayor launched the appeal for funds to set up this University's Centre for Banking and International Finance, that these lectures should bear his name.

This academic occasion provides me with a welcome opportunity to speak at greater length than is usually possible—or indeed acceptable—at a public function, and I propose to use it by sharing with you some reflections on the conduct of monetary policy, as they have formed in my mind over the past five eventful years. By so doing I shall hope to contribute to the public debate on monetary policy—a debate which I wholeheartedly welcome.

The City University is an especially appropriate place for me to do so. A personal reason is that it gives me the occasion, before the departure of Dr Parkes for the University Grants Committee where his expertise in the elasticity or dynamic plasticity of academic structures will be fully tested, to discharge some part of my debt of gratitude for the Honorary Doctorate of Science conferred on me some two years ago by this University during his Vice-Chancellorship—although the moral of my lecture, that the conduct of monetary policy is an art rather than a science, might be taken to suggest that he gave me the wrong degree.

Another reason is that this University, through its relationship with the City and its institutions, established with them in the ten years of its existence, has been able to combine intellectual rigour and practical relevance in its academic approach to banking and international finance: this is one of the objectives of the Centre and finds its personification in its Director, Professor Brian Griffiths.

We are now at an historical juncture when the conventional methods of economic policy are being tested. The principles on which we have conducted economic policy since the war are having to be reassessed, because, with changing conditions, we are no longer so certain of being able to achieve what once seemed possible. At the same time, the greater emphasis on monetary policy has occasioned new initiatives in ways of conducting it. The present is therefore a suitable time to try to take stock.

What I have to say today falls conveniently under three main headings. First, I shall review the change in our ideas about monetary policy since the Radcliffe Committee reported, and will discuss the shift of emphasis towards concern with the monetary aggregates. Secondly, I shall attempt to consider more systematically the place of monetary policy in the management of the economy. And thirdly, I shall review some of the problems of implementing monetary policy—of management of the growth of the aggregates; of the choice of aggregate for the control variable; and the case for what are sometimes known as 'rolling targets'.

The recent development of monetary thought

It may be helpful to start with an historical perspective. We tend to forget how much our ideas change in only a few years. It makes our present ideas clearer if we see them standing in contrast to what we thought earlier; and it is salutary to have to work out why we think that we now know better than we did five or ten or twenty years ago. A convenient landmark is the Radcliffe Report published in 1959.

The change in ideas since the Radcliffe Report
The doctrine of the Radcliffe Report was always complex and is perhaps difficult to summarise fairly in today's changed climate of ideas. The Radcliffe Committee saw the monetary system more as a set of institutions supporting numerous flows of funds, than as a set of institutions providing a stock of means of payment. Monetary policy was seen as acting on total demand mainly by affecting the ease of access to finance, or what was more vaguely called the 'liquidity of the economy'. Changes in monetary policy took their effect through changes in interest rates: the latter (it was argued) altered the liquidity position of financial institutions, and this in turn affected the availability of funds to borrowers. The difference from present-day thought is illustrated by a quotation from the Report. 'The authorities thus have to regard the structure of interest rates rather than the supply of money as the centre-piece of the monetary mechanism. This does not mean that the supply of money is unimportant, but that its control is incidental to interest rate policy.'

The Committee were mainly looking, as we do not today, for quick tangible effects from monetary measures on the level of demand. The Report left a clear impression that its authors believed that monetary policy had little such effect, and that what effect it did have was not all to the good. They found it difficult to believe that 'any of the changes in interest rates' had much influence—though some effect on demand probably resulted from the 'diffused difficulty of borrowing'. But 'the really quick substantial effects', they concluded, 'were secured by the hire purchase controls' —though these had disruptive effects on particular industries. That, as they said, was 'far removed from the smooth and widespread adjustment sometimes claimed as the virtue of monetary action; this is no gentle hand on the steering wheel that keeps a well-driven car in its right place on the road'.

The Bank did not entirely share this scepticism, as their evidence to the Committee demonstrated. The Radcliffe Report failed to establish a consensus. It did, however, provide a focus for monetary debate, and one strand of the Bank's thinking—and indeed practice—which found an echo in the Report was the importance attached to operations in the gilt-edged market having a wider objective than merely financing the Government—though the objective suggested was couched in terms of the long-term rate of interest rather than, as today, in terms of the monetary aggregates.

Since those days ideas about monetary policy have undergone further evolution. On the theoretical plane, arguments advanced by Keynes and later by Friedman suggesting that there might well be a stable relationship between the demand for money and the level of income and interest rates found apparent statistical verification in the late 1960s. The identification of this function appeared to provide a sound intellectual basis for monetary policy; but it left a practical choice whether the money supply or the level of interest rates should be taken as the proximate objective of policy.

What swung the argument in favour of choosing a quantity rather than a price as the best indicator of the thrust of monetary policy was the acceleration of inflation. Since 1970 not only have prices risen much faster than in the 1950s and 1960s but the rate of inflation has varied considerably from year to year. With increased inflationary expectations, interest rates also have risen greatly. We can, if we like, think of the nominal interest rate as having an 'expected inflation' component and a 'real' interest element. But we can never observe expectations, which are in any case likely both to differ from person to person, and to be volatile. The real rate of interest is an abstract construct. This has made it very difficult to frame the objectives of policy in terms of nominal interest rates.

For these reasons we were led to pay increasing attention to the monetary aggregates as a better guide—though not of course a perfect guide—to the thrust of monetary policy. In this we were not alone; a move in this direction occurred quite widely in the Western world towards the end of the 1960s. This emphasis was reflected in the new approach to monetary policy put into effect in September 1971, on which I must now say a few words.

Competition and credit control
The aims of competition and credit control were twofold. First, it was a move away from reliance on direct restrictive controls in the monetary sphere. They had remained in being far longer than appropriate for the health of the banking system, and such restraining effects as they had were being increasingly eroded. More positively, it was a move towards a system in which market forces could play a predominant rôle. As I have already indicated, importance was now attached to the monetary aggregates; their rate of growth was to be controlled by the market instrument of interest rates.

A change on these lines was clearly desirable and indeed overdue. Nonetheless the results over the ensuing two years have provoked serious criticism. There was rapid expansion of the monetary aggregates, and the economy did in fact expand rapidly—though in some large part no doubt because the stance of fiscal policy was strongly expansionary. And prices later started to rise rapidly —though here again other factors, including a world-wide commodity boom, have also to be taken into account. I shall not attempt to disentangle the complex strands of causation, but some points may be remarked.

The removal of earlier restrictions over the growth of bank lending allowed the banks to recapture a share of the business which controls had caused to be undertaken through non-banking channels. Such reintermediation was indeed natural, as the banks benefited from their comparative efficiency in the provision of services. In addition we had hoped that this process would go further: that some of the business undertaken by the fringe institutions which had grown up during the 1960s would be taken over by the longer-established banks. In the event, however, this transfer was to some considerable degree frustrated by the more general expansion in lending which took place.

In the two years to September 1973, M_3 grew at an average annual rate of about 26%, compared with about a 10% rise in M_1. Part of the increase in broad money was possibly associated with a general preference for increased liquidity at a time of uncertainty surrounding the future course of inflation and interest rates; part undoubtedly reflected the sort of reintermediation I have touched on above; and part reflected the arbitrage which developed when companies found it profitable to borrow on their lines from the banks and on-lend in the wholesale money markets. To the extent that these factors represented shifts in the demand-for-money function rather than an excess creation of money, their effects on the real economy were likely to have been much less significant.

The process of reintermediation was accompanied by a number of other developments. In the financial sphere the banks—here and in many industrialised countries —were shifting towards 'liability management'. In expanding their loan books they began to pay less attention than before to the resources already available to them, since they could if necessary make up any deficiency by recourse to the wholesale money markets. This was facilitated by the encouragement of competition in the banking system in 1971. With banks increasingly prepared to compete for wholesale deposits in this way, the development of the broader monetary aggregates came increasingly to depend on interest-rate relativities—between wholesale money rates, Treasury bill and local authority rates on the one hand and bank lending rates on the other—rather than on the average level of rates. In 1972 and 1973 for example the major banks competed extremely vigorously to expand the size of their books and their individual share of the market; this helped to bring about a pattern of interest rates conducive to very rapid expansion. The supplementary special deposits scheme was precisely tailored to arrest this development: after its introduction at the end of 1973 the differential between rates of interest offered on wholesale deposits and charged on loans widened and the rate of growth of wholesale deposits fell back. However, it is hard to know how much this was due directly to the impact of the scheme and how much due to other factors.

The Government over this period were deliberately promoting a faster rate of economic growth. To revive slack domestic activity against a background of mounting concern for unemployment, an expansionary Budget in the spring of 1971 was followed by further tax reductions and increases in expenditure in July, and another reflationary Budget in the following spring. The PSBR began to move upwards.

The monetary expansion which occurred largely resulted from the conjunction of these separate factors—reintermediation, the banks' aggressive search for new business and with it their move to liability management, and fiscal expansion. Monetary expansion must have contributed to the rapid rise in asset prices that occurred, notably in real property. It is more difficult to decide how far it caused the boom in the real economy, and the acceleration in the rate of inflation that began to set in. Some would regard the monetary development as the sole, or at least the dominant, cause; others would see it as a minor contributing factor accompanying, and in part reflecting, other more powerful forces. Despite such uncertainties about the nature and the effects of the monetary expansion, it cannot be judged other than excessive.

It had proved difficult to raise interest rates sufficiently to match the worsening inflationary environment, and braking the monetary expansion by this means was in any case proving unacceptably slow to show its results. In these circumstances, after raising minimum lending rate from $7\frac{1}{2}\%$ to 13% during the second half of 1973, the Bank introduced the new mechanism of supplementary special deposits.

Since then emphasis has continued to be placed on controlling the growth of the monetary aggregates as a specific proximate target for policy. Only since 1976 has this taken the form of publicly declared quantitative targets. Before that it constituted an internal aim: I think it is not therefore entirely accidental that during each of the three years 1974–76 the growth of sterling M_3 was about 10%, well below the rate of expansion of national income in current prices. This was achieved during a period in which inflation, though latterly declining, was at an explosive rate and in which the financing requirement of the public sector increased notably.

The place of monetary policy in the scheme of things

I now turn to discussing the place of monetary policy in the context of economic policy generally, and what we hope to accomplish by monetary policy.

I am conscious that this aim is ambitious. This is a subject much written about and much disputed by economists and non-economists alike. Moreover a statement of view by an institution is something very different from that of an individual expert. An institution like the Bank differs in being first a collectivity, a team; in having primarily operational responsibilities; and, as such, in operating in a political environment. We hope to be sensitive to new currents of thought; yet at the same time we must exercise our judgment and not be too ready to accept every change of intellectual fashion. Formulating a line of practical policy and trying to stick to it, while yet remaining appropriately flexible amid the uncertainties of day-to-day affairs, feels very different from devising ideal solutions in the seclusion of a study.

It is, however, reasonable to expect us to seek to abstract ourselves from day-to-day pressures, and to try to systematise the philosophy that underlies our actions, though of course I have no illusions that I am stating the last word. Indeed, I hope that our critics will say why they disagree, and that thus we will together participate in a dialectic which will contribute to the evolution of a new climate of public opinion.

Monetary targets and their part in general economic policy
I will start by trying to say something about the nature of monetary targets; and go on to touch on some current issues about the proper way to conduct economic policy.

The achievement of a monetary target is not an end of policy in itself. The real objectives of policy include economic growth—in the short term, and also in the long term: and stemming from this the provision of sufficient investment for the future, and of adequate employment opportunities. They include also price stability, both as a major end in itself, and as a means to much else; and as a means if not an end, they include maintaining an appropriate relation to the rest of the world and a prudent balance of payments stance. It could be argued that monetary policy is but one instrument of policy, along with fiscal policy, exchange rate policy and, to the degree that it is possible, incomes policy; and that all such policies should be jointly set so as to achieve the desired feasible combination of final objectives, and should be adjusted from time to time as circumstances change.

In such a context, is there a place for having a target for the single instrument of monetary policy? Might this not introduce an element of undesirable rigidity—particularly inappropriate, it might be thought, for monetary policy, whose advantage has often been claimed to be that it was flexible?

To this, however, it can be replied that we should beware of over-reacting to changing circumstances, and of being over-active in economic management. Policy changes are unsettling and disturbing in themselves. It is right that people should know what the broad lines of policy are, and that such policy should be kept on its stated course until circumstances clearly call for a reappraisal. There has in any case been a reaction against frequent policy adjustments, or attempts at what has popularly been dubbed 'fine tuning'—a reaction which is part of a wider disillusion with the possibilities of economic policy and the post-war enterprise of trying to manage the economy.

This spirit of disillusion with demand management is justified up to a point, but is capable of being carried too far. To eschew demand management entirely would involve tenacious faith in the self-correcting properties of the private sector of the economy, for which the evidence is not strikingly clear. Moreover, the economic functions of government have become so extensive that it is difficult to define what a neutral policy is.

What, however, does seem clear to me is that the conventional methods of demand management can only work well against a background of financial stability. In recent years the economic system has received so many shocks that the stability of the post-war world has been fractured.

Our first order of business must, therefore, be to restore confidence in the framework of the system. The crucial economic decisions, for example to undertake investment, involve an act of faith in the future. That faith has been undermined by uncertainty—uncertainty in particular about the future value of money, externally and internally. In times past other features of the economic system, such as fixed exchange rates or Gladstonian budgetary principles, were thought to provide some guarantee of stability. These restraints have now gone. The main rôle therefore that I see for monetary targets is to provide the framework of stability within which other policy objectives can be more easily achieved.

It is essential for this purpose that monetary targets should be publicly announced, and that the authorities' resolve be sufficient to make that announcement credible. Our acts have, I believe, given observers cause to regard our resolve as strong. This in itself has dampened fears of worsening inflation, and provided an appropriate backdrop against which we can continue the struggle to bring inflation steadily down. I would not claim that monetary policy can or should be left to fight inflation singlehanded —I shall turn to this subject again later. But monetary targets have an important place in the relevant armoury.

Monetary targets represent a self-imposed constraint or discipline on the authorities. This can at times seem irksome, the more so perhaps because the permissible thresholds cannot be precisely and scientifically set, involving a considerable element of judgment. Yet the layman's apparently intuitive perception of the broad relationship between monetary growth and inflation —clearer perhaps to him than to the professional who knows all the necessary qualifications—may well make it easier to explain and justify measures necessary to achieve the goal of stability but with immediately unpopular effects. We need a basis of public support and understanding of the limits to prudent action. Furthermore, quantitative monetary targets can provide a useful trigger for more expeditious policy decisions.

The main purpose of having publicly announced monetary targets is, therefore, to provide a basis for stability. Stability does not, however, imply rigidity. There can be occasions when policy needs to be adjusted because circumstances have changed. There is a case for adjusting monetary policy, as well as fiscal policy, to offset cyclical swings in the economy. In recent years, however, severe cyclical disturbances have been overlaid and accompanied by an even more menacing inflationary trend. We will not, in my judgment, be able to deal satisfactorily with the present recession until we can conquer our inflation problem, whose implications for monetary policy I now turn to discuss.

Monetary policy and inflation
There is, I think, a two-way connection between inflation and economic expansion. The common wisdom used to be that there was a trade-off: high levels of activity led to high rates of inflation, and lower levels of activity similarly to lower rates of inflation. Nowadays, with the elusiveness of what economists call the 'Phillips curve', this route to controlling inflation has seemed to become less sure. And yet some important part of that connection must surely remain. The governments of almost all industrial countries have acquiesced in low rates of economic expansion in the last three years. Their motives have been manifold, but a main one has been fear of inflation; and inflation rates have fallen. And in this country, I think it is generally accepted that the practicable rate of economic expansion will depend in large part on how successful we are in moderating the pace of inflation. The connection is in part a matter of market forces—strong demand pressure would generate larger wage increases, in part semi-political —unrestrained expansion would erode the braking power of the present policy of pay restraint.

The reverse connection is that—quite apart from this connection via economic policies—inflation impedes economic expansion by inducing caution among consumers, and by making business, and in particular investment, so much less predictable. If we could reduce inflation, this would itself generate a faster expansion in the private economy. The expansion we sacrifice in order to deal with inflation is less than might appear.

One should recognise that the blame for inflation rests not on any simple cause, but rather on a multitude of political and economic pressures. Is it not clear enough that our system has a strong inflationary bias? In recent years annual wage increases have become the accepted norm, though there is no logic in this. The size of wage increases moreover depends on an unco-ordinated and to some degree competitive process in which, to say the least, the collective effect on price stability does not naturally act as a dominant consideration. Governmentally-inspired efforts at pay restraint take their rationale from these circumstances. In our post-war history there has been a succession of attempts at such policies, some more successful than others; and I would guess that we are destined to continue the effort. Such policies have their obvious shortcomings and considerable attendant disadvantages. Nevertheless from the point of view of monetary policy we should welcome whatever success they can achieve, while giving them in turn all the support from monetary policy that we can devise.

I would not want to suggest that there is always a direct, simple chain of causation running from the money supply to the price-level. Indeed, it is generally recognised that inflation can, at least for a time, follow a life of its own quite independent of current or past monetary developments. The peak of recent inflation in the United Kingdom three years ago owed much both to the rise of world commodity prices in 1973 and to the repercussions this had—through the unfortunate accident of the threshold agreements then in force—on domestic wages. Equally, exchange rate movements had important effects—though I know this raises more complicated issues on which I shall comment later.

But though the causation may not be simple, there is an observable statistical relation between monetary growth and the pace of inflation. I am not here thinking of the short-term relationships which underlie the demand-for-money equations to which I have already referred. There has been a fair measure of success in establishing such relationships, even though the success is far from complete. I think however that what is far more important is the relationship between monetary growth and inflation over the longer term. A great deal of work has been devoted to the study of this relationship over long time periods and in many countries; and that there is such a relationship cannot, I think, be doubted. To many this provides adequate intellectual justification for establishing medium-term aims for the rate of growth of the money supply.

Some I know may still feel doubts as to how the statistical relationship between money and prices should be interpreted. Governments and central banks are often in effect under pressure to validate price increases stemming from non-monetary sources because the alternatives have seemed to be pressures on interest rates or on employment. It might then be questioned whether under such circumstances the causality could not run as much from prices to money as from money to prices.

To those who doubt on some such grounds how far monetary policy can be of help in dealing with inflation, I would venture to address a more general defence of our present line of policy. The latest issue of the *National Institute Economic Review* suggests for instance that the Institute are of this school. The Institute base their contention on the grounds that labour market pressures in general and unemployment in particular do not serve greatly to moderate the wage spiral, unless extremely severe. With wages in their view thus determined by non-market pressures, they argue that financial targets will either fail to bite, and thus be ineffective, or alternatively that they will have their major impact on real output. But in the same issue I note that the Institute declare that the early re-establishment of reasonably full employment would be foolhardy until a solution is found to the problem of inflation—which, from the viewpoint of the Institute, depends on the adoption of incomes policies on a permanent basis. Until then, it is implied, the pace of expansion will have to be kept down to a strictly moderate pace.

I concur with this last judgment—as I have already indicated, I take the view that we cannot allow the economy to expand very vigorously until inflation has been brought down to a lower level and we have some assurance that this achievement will not be threatened by faster expansion.

A monetary target both provides an overt public expression of this need for caution, and embodies some assurance that action will be triggered if the need for it arises. In the short term, if things go wrong adherence to an unchanged monetary target will be the equivalent of early restraining discretionary action. In the longer term, the commitment to monetary targets will also ensure a general degree of caution. One may therefore say that in a figurative sense to announce such a commitment is to serve notice on all those concerned, including those concerned with wage bargaining, how far the authorities are prepared to finance inflation. It will be said that those involved in wage bargaining pay no heed to the size of the monetary targets. This may be so—though I would think it better if it were not. Yet, over time, perseverance with a policy of the sort I have outlined will, I believe, have an increasingly pervasive effect. As it becomes clear to all that faster growth can only be had with less inflation, will there not be more pressure to see how this can be done?

I think one thing will be evident from what I have said. Monetary policy is often classed as an instrument of demand management: in practice, until we have made more progress with inflation, its services are likely to be pre-empted by the need to use it as an instrument against inflation. Nevertheless, it is clear also that we need a reasonable rate of expansion; and the prospect I see is not of no expansion, but of a reasonably controlled expansion.

I should now refer to the relation between monetary policy and the exchange rate. Many monetarists would I know see the chief influence of monetary policy on prices as coming via this route, and would regard a floating exchange rate as an essential concomitant of a sound monetary policy.

It will be plain that the Bank have not adopted the whole of this intellectual position. The advantages of an appreciating rate for domestic prices are evident enough. But as a recent issue of the Bank's *Quarterly Bulletin*[1] made plain, we are also concerned with the effect on export prices and on the profitability of exports. Nor did we wholly accept the argument that capital inflows, arising at a time when we were intervening on the exchanges to keep the rate lower than it would be on a free float, must necessarily undermine the effectiveness of our monetary control. Indeed for ten months of last year—when massive inflows occurred—this was not the case. A time came however when we felt unable any longer to maintain full control over the growth of the money stock without setting the exchange rate free to float—concern about exports notwithstanding. The decision made in those circumstances emphasises our commitment, in conditions of conflict, to controlling the monetary aggregates.

The implementation of monetary policy

I should now like to turn from the broad general principles

[1] See the September 1977 issue, page 299.

of policy to the more technical problems of implementing monetary policy in practice.

Management of the monetary aggregates
The difficulties of achieving the desired path for the monetary aggregates can be described in various ways. Let us start by considering what influences the demand for money. Given the level of national income, and neglecting temporary influences, we work on the theory that interest rates are the main determinants of the demand for money. That is the logic of our method of operating, as I have sought to describe it earlier in this lecture—we seek to manage the course of the monetary aggregates by bringing about changes in interest rates. But it is, of course, difficult to predict the level and structure of interest rates at which the stock of money the public wants to hold will be brought into equality with the stock the authorities would like to see being held. I need not apologise for this: the converse of this ignorance is that how interest rates will be influenced by various factors is highly uncertain, a fact of life known to all market operators.

In practice we often try to get round this difficulty by building up a forecast from, as it were, the 'supply' side. Thus, we look separately at the main items which statistically speaking are the components of the money supply on a broad definition—such as the PSBR, sales to the public of government debt, the volume of bank lending to the private sector and external flows to the private sector. What we are in effect doing in such an exercise is to attempt to predict what the rate of monetary expansion will be if we refrain from trying to change interest rates— as a preliminary to considering the need for intervention. This may disguise, but does not really evade, the central difficulty of prediction which I have just mentioned.

We are, of course, kept constantly awake to this difficulty by the sheer erratic variability of the counterparts of the money stock with which we are dealing. For example, since 1974 the mean error of forecasts of the PSBR made at the beginning of each financial year has been of the order of £3 billion. Again, the monthly growth of bank lending frequently fluctuates from its trend by over £100 million; extreme fluctuations in recent years have been as much as three times as large as this. Moreover, in the last two decades bank lending has been greatly affected by numerous types of official intervention and control; and, partly no doubt in consequence, we do not now know at all exactly how it is likely to respond to changes in economic or financial conditions.

The essence of monetary management, as I see it, is to act to offset divergences from forecast in these sources of monetary expansion—difficult to predict and control—as soon as it becomes reasonably clear that inaction is likely to undermine achievement of the monetary target. Such divergences from forecast are difficult to identify quickly, partly because of inevitable delays in statistical information about the recent past.

A corollary is, I believe, that so long as we can see our way to bring it back within a few months to the charted path, we should not be unduly concerned when monetary growth goes temporarily off course. I do not for example see much case for supposing that the temporary slow-down in monetary growth last winter, or the temporary acceleration last autumn—largely influenced by massive inflows of funds from abroad—had or will have a significant effect on the development of the economy. Nevertheless, the long run is a summation of short periods; and what is above all important is that we do not allow monetary developments to diverge too long from trend.

I know that there are critics and commentators who believe that the problem of maintaining control over these short-term developments could be more satisfactorily achieved by a change in our form of operations. They argue that control over some form of high-powered or base money would be more effective in controlling monetary growth than are our present methods. This same debate is occurring in several countries between central banks and their academic critics. It is the case that most central banks, including most of those with publicly quantified monetary targets, seek to affect monetary growth by varying the general level of interest rates. The monetary authorities in the United States, in Canada and in Germany, for example operate by this method. I would not seek to suggest however that the methods adopted by the major central banks are, *ipso facto*, right.

This is too large a subject to enter at this stage in my address, and I would hope to return to it on some future occasion. What I want to say now is that I doubt whether a move to base money control would enable control to be achieved with less variation in interest rates than at present. Indeed, the extent of interest-rate variation that the system would have to tolerate might be considerably greater, in the short run at least, if base money control was to be rigorously imposed.

Choice of monetary aggregate
I turn now to the question of which of the monetary aggregates is the most appropriate series on which to set the target. If you plot the rate of growth of the alternative monetary series in the United Kingdom since 1970, particularly the series of M_1 and M_3, you will see that they have followed markedly differing paths. For the technically minded, the correlation of the quarterly changes in these aggregates over this period has been only $+0.1$. Which series one chooses to look at can clearly affect one's interpretation of monetary developments.

The broad monetary aggregate, sterling M_3, in terms of which our present target is expressed, has a number of advantages over its rivals. As I have already said, it can be linked to changes in certain key credit counterparts, such as the PSBR, bank lending, government debt sales, DCE and external financial flows, in a way that helps our understanding of the course of monetary developments. It has also some comparative statistical advantages; for example, it is proportionately less disturbed by transit items—somewhat arbitrarily treated as they are—than M_1.

Nevertheless, there are certain shortcomings in this series which call for caution in its interpretation. The velocity of M_3, the ratio of incomes to broad money, has exhibited very sharp fluctuations, with a major fall during the period of adjustment to competition and credit control, and subsequently a return to—or above—its previous average level. The econometric equations, estimated earlier, neither forecast nor have since adequately explained this development. It probably arose because (as I have already noted) the rate of growth of one of the major constituents of M_3, wholesale deposits, depends on relative interest rates, rather than their general level.

Increases in minimum lending rate and in the general level of interest rates do not of themselves bring about a shift in the relative pattern of interest rates that would serve to moderate the growth of wholesale deposits within M_3. Indeed, if the increase in rates is closely connected, as it often is, with pressure on banks' liquidity, the relative pattern of rates is liable to adjust adversely, leading to even faster growth in wholesale deposits, at least temporarily. On occasions the path of M_3 can be significantly influenced by changing competitive conditions within the banking industry—conditions which can change for reasons quite separate from the course of nominal incomes in the economy, or the actions of the monetary authorities.

There is also, I believe, worthwhile information to be obtained from looking at series other than M_3. Over the period for which we have complete data since 1963 the relationship between movements of narrow money (M_1) on the one hand and of incomes and interest rates on the other has been closer and more stable than has been the case with M_3. Though for some economists that alone would be reason for putting chief emphasis on M_1, I would not go that far. First, the relatively stable relationship involving M_1 has been observed for a comparatively short period, during which the authorities have not given emphasis to controlling M_1: this does not guarantee that the relationship would remain as stable under differing conditions, particularly if the authorities were to seek to control it more closely. Secondly, I value the broader descriptive analysis that reference to M_3 allows, which one cannot obtain with M_1.

Reasons could also be advanced for paying attention to wider liquidity series than M_3. There is a high degree of substitution between some assets included in M_3 and some excluded, Treasury bills and certificates of deposit for example. Moreover, the growth and evolution of the building societies has blurred the distinction between deposits with banks and shares and deposits with building societies. This development raises a number of issues, among them the scope and coverage of any series intended to measure private sector transaction balances.

One specific proposal put to us is that we should once again provide a refurbished M_2 series, which would aim to exclude wholesale deposits (whose course is so hard to predict or control) and to include retail-type time deposits. We welcome and seriously consider suggestions of this kind. However, we have certain doubts about this particular suggestion. We doubt whether the addition to the existing M_1 series of seven-day deposits with the clearing banks would provide much additional information. A theoretically better split between retail and wholesale-type deposits might be obtained by grading deposits by size, over and under £50,000 for example. However, not only would any such dividing line be arbitrary, but it would impose a new, onerous burden on the banks' statistical systems. Moreover, for the reasons I have already indicated, I am not sure that it would be sensible to restrict a statistic measuring private sector retail-type deposits to the banks alone, excluding similar-type deposits with building societies.

More generally, there will be some information to be had from observation of virtually any financial and economic indicator. But we cannot and should not translate all such indicators into targets for policy. That would be a recipe for confusion. We need to have clear and simple targets, and I am satisfied that in the present state of the art we have chosen best in selecting sterling M_3.

Rolling targets
Finally, I might comment on the question of how often targets should be reviewed and revised. The present monetary target was set in last March's Budget to last without review for the whole financial year. But it is open to question whether this is the optimum strategy. New information on the economy is continually becoming available and it is my view that we should reassess developments as often as sufficient information makes this worthwhile.

A drawback of the present annual targets has been the implied requirement to hit a particular number on a particular date. The various time-lags in the system make it difficult, and certainly highly undesirable, to try to offset undesired monetary movements very rapidly. Firm deadlines can force one either to try to adjust too fast to an unforeseen trend developing late in the period; or to appear to accept a failure to reach one's target. For such reasons it is for consideration whether it would not be advantageous to rebase the target before the previous target period has been fully completed.

The Federal Reserve undertakes a reassessment each quarter. I believe that for us that would be too frequent. Such a reassessment might however be undertaken along with a review of fiscal policy, for instance at the Budget and again in the autumn.

Targets operated in this way have come to be called 'rolling targets'—yet another addition to our growing dictionary of economic jargon, though perhaps a useful and expressive one. I am aware that some people fear that a move to rolling targets would permit much greater elasticity, so that over a period monetary growth could drift further and further away from a desirable medium-term trend. The ability to reassess policy at six-month intervals, however, would not necessarily entail altering course. Indeed I would hope that, more often than not, it would validate staying on the same course for an extended period. I need hardly stress again the value that I place on the importance of maintaining monetary stability.

I would not of course support the adoption of rolling targets if this implied a change of direction in our present strategy. But I could see it as a minor, but useful, technical change to our continuing policy of having publicly announced monetary targets—a policy which I have sought to defend and explain this afternoon.

In doing so, I have covered a lot of ground and will therefore spare you—and myself—the added burden of summarising what I have had to say. We have not, it is plain, adopted a wholehearted monetarist philosophy. But what we do is likely to give a monetarist a good deal of the prescription he would recommend, which may be what Mr Volcker, President of the Federal Reserve Bank of New York, implied in his phrase 'practical monetarism'. But the essence of what I have been saying is indeed very old-fashioned—the predictable caution of a Central Banker.

CHAPTER 4
Reflections on the role of monetary targets

The adoption of a publicly-announced monetary target for sterling M3 gave yet more emphasis, a higher profile, to monetary developments, without making the problems of (short-run) monetary control any easier. There were some difficulties from the outset. The attempt, during the course of 1977, to pursue independent objectives separately both for the exchange rate and for the broad money stock led to an attempt to deter massive capital inflows by sharp reductions in short-term interest rates (which were brought down during the year from 15% to 5%), while trying to mop up the monetary consequences of the capital inflows by equally large gilt sales (themselves encouraged by the prospect of capital gains). This attempt to maintain two inconsistent objectives simultaneously was eventually abandoned in October 1977, but not before interest rates had been dramatically lowered. This sharp fall in interest rates led immediately to a surge in M1, and was also a factor in the sharp increase during the next year in bank lending. With financial markets later becoming suspicious about the continuing counterinflationary strength of the Government's fiscal and incomes policies, debt sales also faltered in the spring of 1978. Faced then with an acceleration of monetary growth, the Government reimposed the 'corset' for the final time in June 1978.

Inflation worsened through the winter of 1978 and into the autumn of 1979; and against that background the Governor urged the need to bring down the rate of inflation, and to use monetary policy for that end, in the Mansion House speech in October 1979.

It is inflation, not the policies needed to counter it, that threatens the ideals of the welfare state and of full employment, by undermining the basis of the sound economy on which they depend. It is sometimes said that we have been forced to abandon these ideals and the post-war consensus on which they rested. But let me read you the following words:

> Action taken by the Government to maintain expenditure will be fruitless unless wages and prices are kept reasonably stable.

and then these additional words:

> ... the stability of these two elements is a condition vital to the success of employment policy ...

These words were not written in the 1970s. They are taken from the classic statement of that consensus—the 1944 White Paper on Employment Policy. It was recognised then, as our actual experience teaches us to recognise more emphatically now, that there is no real trade-off between inflation on the one hand and employment and growth on the other—that action to maintain employment will be fruitless without reasonable price and wage stability.

The truth is that if we do not defeat inflation now, because the treatment is unpalatable, it will be worse tomorrow. Some feel that living with inflation of, say, just within single figures would be good enough. Inflation, however, is unlikely to be so obliging. At such a rate it is much more likely, left to itself, to increase further than to slow down; and there would be little restraint or limit to how fast it might go.

In the course of this last year, our rate of inflation has increased substantially. A year ago, a combination of monetary, fiscal and incomes policies had succeeded in reducing inflation from the peak levels of 1974 and 1975 to around 8%. But one leg of that tripod, incomes policy—inherently liable to erosion—collapsed last winter. By February it was clear that the turn in industrial relations and the size of pay claims threatened faster inflation. The threat only too quickly became reality.

Price levels have since been further boosted by the rise in energy prices, and by the shift—desirable for the longer-term health of the economy—in the structure of taxation from direct to indirect. That effect is once for all, not a continuing source of inflation.

In all these circumstances, it is essential to hold firm to our monetary policy. It is precisely at a time like this that monetary discipline is most needed—though inevitably it is at such times that discipline becomes most painful. To hold monetary growth substantially below the rate at which nominal incomes are rising must involve pressures—pressures associated with fiscal restraint, a strong exchange rate and high nominal interest rates.

Some people blame the monetary authorities for these pressures. But a central banker is surely entitled to ask precisely where lies the cause of any sense of monetary tightness in an economy whose output is not growing in volume terms, but where money supply is rising above 10%. If the escalation of costs could be held within saner bounds, such monetary growth would provide ample room for real growth and improvements in real living standards.

As you know, the rate of monetary expansion has in recent months been running at a rate around the upper limit of our monetary target, or higher if one allows for the distortions that have resulted from the enforcement of the 'corset'. We have been facing strong pressure resulting from a high government borrowing requirement so far this year, combined with unusually strong borrowing from the banks by the private sector; and the need for the action we took on minimum lending rate at the time of the Budget has been fully demonstrated by subsequent events. The September money figures published today suggest some slowing down in the pace of monetary expansion. But no-one can judge from one month's figures, and the future is far too uncertain to come to a view that there has yet been a change in the trend.

Sustained reductions in interest rates depend on success in reducing inflation. That in turn will be influenced by the rate of monetary expansion; the way to get lower interest rates is to persevere with monetary control.

The new government was putting major emphasis on monetary control, in the form of controlling the rate of growth of sterling M3, as a main instrument for controlling inflation. At the same time, the abolition of exchange controls in October 1979 necessitated the subsequent removal of the 'corset', since otherwise the direct control of domestic financial intermediation would increasingly have been avoided by financial intermediation abroad.

Squeezed between the worsened and intrenched domestic inflationary trends in costs on the one hand and the Government's determined counterinflationary monetary and fiscal policies on the other, the company sector, particularly manufacturing companies engaged in selling tradable goods, found its profit margins coming under increasing downwards pressures. Moreover, the combination of tight monetary policies, tight at least in relation to the underlying demand for financial intermediation, and the second oil shock, occurring at a time when North Sea oil was coming on stream, raised the real effective exchange rate very sharply. Thus, simultaneously, further pressure was put on the company sector, the rate of inflation was lowered, and the real earnings, savings and financial surplus of wage earners were raised. These factors had a marked effect on the pattern of sector financial balances, and thence on the demand for financial intermediation through the banking system.

The consequence of this combination of forces was to bring about a faster decline in nominal incomes, with both output and the rate of inflation declining faster than had been earlier expected or forecast. At the same time the rate of monetary growth, as represented by the broader monetary aggregates, increased; during both the 1980–81 and 1981–82 target periods monetary growth rose well above its stated target. The Governor reflected upon this experience in his Mansion House speech in October 1980.

One of my important tasks tonight, My Lord Mayor, to which I must now come, is to discuss the behaviour of the monetary aggregates. As we all know, our target aggregate, sterling M3, showed a rapid increase in the summer. It is therefore important to determine the nature of that acceleration.

It is, first, clear that the 'corset' seriously distorted the monetary statistics, both in the two years while it was in effect, and after its removal in June. The effect was not unexpected: the uncertainty related to its extent.

One general lesson from this experience with the corset and from our earlier experience with quantitative lending ceilings is that we need to be deeply sceptical of the value of direct controls of this kind.

It also seems clear that, making all due allowance for the effects of the corset, the true underlying rate of growth of sterling M3 accelerated sharply in the late spring and summer to well outside the target range. This followed a period of some months in which monetary growth had moderated.

These swings in the rate of monetary growth reflected quite largely the fluctuations in the scale of public borrowing. At the turn of the year the public sector borrowing requirement was relatively low, while heavy funding continued. In the spring and summer there was a resurgence in public borrowing—which perhaps approached a rate of about £7½ billion in the first six months of the financial year. This resurgence was no doubt in considerable degree temporary, but it was much larger than expected. It was in consequence more than could then be financed outside the banking system from the capital market, even though sales of gilt-edged stock were made to domestic non-bank investors in that period of over £4½ billion.

In face of such swings in the borrowing requirement, the difficulties for short-term control of sterling M3 are, I submit, bound to be increased.

At the same time, net external outflows from the private sector, which exercise a contractionary effect on monetary growth, diminished as the current account went into surplus.

There was, in addition, one other powerful force, arising from the condition of the economy—persistently strong demand for bank credit from the private sector. The bulk of this borrowing has been by industrial and commercial companies and, increasingly since the recession really began to bite in April, a proportion of it has been undertaken to maintain the substance of businesses intact.

The large financial deficit of companies has gone along with a large surplus of the personal sector. Given that companies effectively lacked an alternative channel of finance, via the capital market, the marrying of these large negative and positive imbalances has fallen to a very considerable extent on intermediation through the banking system. The aggregate that is the target of policy, sterling M3, was correspondingly inflated in a way that may well misrepresent the degree of stringency with which monetary policy is affecting the economy.

Assessment of what has happened must also take into account the likelihood that these pressures on sterling M3 may now begin to ease. Inflation is past its peak. There are some tentative signs that private sector demand on the banks may be beginning to slow down. Public borrowing should also fall off: its enormous scale in the first half of the financial year must be judged to have been of a pseudo-seasonal character, which in some degree will correct itself. Taken together, such changes would at least hold out the prospect that the recent inflation of the sterling M3 statistic may not persist. This suggests that over the whole of the target period to next April the rise in sterling M3 after proper allowance for the distortions of the 'corset' may turn out to be much less than has been generally supposed.

The recent experience illustrates the strength of the forces of monetary creation with which we are contending in our monetary aims, forces which derive their current power from the pressures and distortions prevalent in the economy. It is of course possible to imagine a tighter or more rigid control of the creation of money achieved on a more continuous and shorter-term basis. Temporary pressures and distortions would then be turned back more abruptly on the real economy instead of being reflected in temporary variations in monetary growth.

In reflecting on this whole experience my final observation is to emphasise the sheer erratic variability—words again from the Mais lecture—of the counterparts contained in sterling M3. The lesson, perhaps, is the need to avoid attaching undue importance to short-term developments in any single monetary aggregate; it is sounder to take into account, as we in fact do, the underlying developments both in the aggregates as a whole and in the real economy. Taken overall, this evidence suggests that policy has been restrictive rather than otherwise.

The tenor of these remarks is to suggest that monetary control, as any central bank practitioner will confirm, is not a simple matter.

That said, it is of course right that we should at all times be active in the search for improved methods of monetary control. This subject has been under intensive official consideration, and we have recently had the benefit of advice both from experts in the City and our own universities, and from central banks and universities in other countries. It will be a little time yet before the conclusions to be distilled from these extensive consultations can be put forward.

Meanwhile, some important changes are already in train. The abolition of the corset means that we shall soon have a system in which the distortions it caused will be a thing of the past. Furthermore, it has already been agreed that there will be an important extension to the availability of index-linked national savings. This move, which could doubtless be extended, and the projected sale of British National Oil Corporation bonds, should materially ease a situation that has complicated monetary control. The Bank welcomes these developments: they should enable an increasing proportion of the public sector's needs for finance to be met directly from personal savings and should constitute a helpful step on the road to opening the capital markets again to corporate borrowers.

These are adjustments and modifications to our present system of control. Proposals have been made that we should move to a rather different system, a monetary base method of control. It is an attraction of such a system that the monetary base—held by the banking system as the basis for its operations—is more directly controllable by the monetary authorities than are the monetary aggregates, particularly the wider aggregates such as sterling M3. I will not embark on a discussion of the exact way in which changes in monetary base might be related to the behaviour of the wider aggregates, for the hour is late and the subject complex. But two things are, I think, clear. It would create a rather different environment for many of our financial institutions, and it would require a perhaps not inconsiderable period for experience to be gained as to the response of the system under the new conditions.

It would be premature to attempt to come to a definitive view on these questions. For some time to come we shall, in any event, continue to face the sort of tensions besetting monetary policy which I have set before you, and which are the background to monetary management.

During the 1981–82 target period the course of monetary growth, and assessment of it, were further affected by the Civil Service strike and by the incursion of the banks, for the first time in a large way, into the mortgage market. The Governor again reflected on the experience of the preceding year, and of five years of monetary targets, in his Mansion House speech in October 1981.

What I then have to do tonight is to give you the reasons why our monetary policy had to be what it has been. I shall do this, not in theoretical terms, but in terms of the obvious considerations which the Bank cannot neglect if it is to discharge its central and time-honoured responsibility—the responsibility, not least in today's unsettled climate, to seek to protect the integrity of the nation's currency, both domestically and internationally. That objective is constant. ...

It is clear that our resolve to pursue the path of financial discipline has manifestly not weakened. But it may be asked, My Lord Mayor, how we now view monetary targets, of which we have had five years' experience since their first adoption. A monetary target, for all its difficulties of interpretation, here and elsewhere, provides a necessary discipline. But in the short term our actions need to be guided by a range of considerations. Last year, with the economy moving sharply into recession, money supply on the broad definition grew very rapidly, yet policy was evidently severe—as was clearly shown by the other aggregates and the exchange rate, then very strong. This year, we have had the prolonged statistical fog created by the Civil Service dispute; we have had to consider the growth of bank lending at a time when demand in the markets to which the credit has gone has been weak: and we have had the decline in the exchange rate.

Despite these complexities, it remains imperative to keep the rate of monetary growth under control. To give weight to exchange rate considerations would on some occasions have meant loosening our monetary control. But in present circumstances pursuit of the two objectives has been complementary and mutually reinforcing. The fundamental objective remains that of providing a financial climate in which inflation can be progressively brought down, and preserving a stable base from which expansion of the economy can be progressively resumed.

In the light of this experience with monetary targets during the course of the later 1970s and early 1980s, certain lessons may have emerged. On the one hand changing structural and conjunctural conditions may so change the nature and form of existing relationships between any monetary aggregate and economic developments more widely that one cannot reliably predict velocity in any single case. On the other hand, the experience of those years suggests that the adoption and maintenance of monetary targets played a major and important role in the successful reduction of what had earlier appeared a sharply worsening inflationary situation.

These and other lessons about the nature of monetary policy and the role of monetary targets were discussed on two occasions. The first was an address by the Governor to the Italian Senate in Rome in April 1983 in which monetary developments formed part of a wide ranging review of *British economic policy over the last decade*; an extract from this speech is printed on page 63. The second occasion was a paper by J S Fforde on *Setting monetary objectives* (page 65), presented to a conference on monetary targeting organised by the Federal Reserve Bank of New York in May 1982.

British economic policy over the last decade

This extract is taken from an address by the Governor to the Italian Senate in Rome on 12 April 1983.

Earlier, before our decade of discontent, an element of discipline had been provided, under the Bretton Woods arrangements, through a fixed exchange rate and the need to adjust fiscal and monetary policy—and hence the growth of nominal income—in order to maintain the rate. Formally, the external discipline was removed for the United Kingdom when sterling was floated in 1972, though I believe it is one of the enduring lessons of the period since then that the fundamental external constraint cannot be escaped, whatever the exchange rate regime.

Twice in the subsequent period we had resort to an incomes policy—a formal policy of restraint over the growth of wages that placed considerable reliance on the co-operation of the trade unions. This policy appeared at the time to offer promise; but each attempt turned out to be short-lived. Following its breakdown in the winter of 1978–79, this approach to policy has not been an option. It nevertheless remains the case that governments cannot avoid responsibility for wages in the public sector; and it is widely—I would hope increasingly widely—recognised that wage moderation more generally, within a policy framework directed at influencing nominal income, is an essential element in achieving lower inflation in combination with lower unemployment. But we have not yet found an effective means through which these considerations can be translated into a structured complement to other policies.

Alongside this experience the role given to monetary policy has grown. In its ultimate objective the aim of monetary policy has been to constrain the growth of nominal income to a rate that is consistent with the productive capacity of the economy. By exerting downward pressure on inflation in this way the goal has been to establish a framework of stability as a necessary precondition for sustainable long-run growth of output and employment. With fast inflation, and changing expectations about inflation, nominal interest rates had become an unreliable guide to monetary conditions. Throughout the past decade, therefore, we have had control of the money supply as the intermediate objective of our policy.

One can have a policy of this kind without formally announcing it, but it is likely to be both clearer and more effective in reinforcing political resolve and in affecting expectations, if it is publicly stated. We started to announce quantitative targets for the growth of the money supply in 1976, under the previous, Labour, administration. In 1980 the present Government made the innovation of projecting the money supply targets for several years ahead, as the central element of a medium-term financial strategy. The increase of the money supply was projected at declining rates of growth to emphasise the permanence and consistency of its counter-inflationary purpose.

Unlike some other countries we have always thought primarily in terms of a broad definition of money. While this choice of definition may not be critical—and indeed has had disadvantages of its own—it has the particular merit of being capable of analysis in terms of the counterpart sources of monetary growth, which include the public sector borrowing requirement. This has helped considerably to focus attention on the vital need for consistency between fiscal and monetary policy. The same link between fiscal and monetary policy is made in the Government's medium-term financial strategy. This sets out, alongside the monetary targets, an illustrative path for public sector borrowing in future years— also on a declining scale. Thus we have attached particular importance to the need for budgetary restraint which is essential if monetary control is to be effective without undue reliance on interest rates. For big changes in interest rates have serious economic effects of their own, for instance on exchange rates or on the viability of businesses, that are too important to ignore.

Our experience, like that of others operating this form of monetary policy, has not been without difficulty. Whatever can be said about the stability of relationships between monetary growth and nominal income over the medium term, it is plain that there can be substantial variations in that relationship over shorter periods. These problems have been made worse in recent years—in North America as well as in my own country—by the speed of innovation, which is changing the characteristics of the various financial assets and the boundaries between them. While, therefore, particular measures of the money supply may be the best available individual indicators of monetary conditions, it would be naive to think that, on their own, they can be relied upon to capture at any moment the full measure of the pressure which policy is exerting on the economy.

This presents the operator of policy with a dilemma. Too rigid or mechanical adherence to the monetary targets can impose a traumatic pressure working through financial markets on the real economy, and in particular on the private industrial sector. On the other hand, allowing the targets to be overshot—particularly in the early years—can damage the credibility of the policy and harmfully weaken its effect upon inflationary expectations.

This situation, I am convinced, can only be met through the exercise of judgement and discretion in operating monetary policy. The monetary targets have to be continually interpreted in the light of the range of available supplementary evidence bearing on the prospect for inflation, including the behaviour of the exchange rate. And the outward form of monetary targets may itself have to be adapted from time to time to meet changing circumstances as we ourselves have found most recently a year or so ago. More than its form, what matters—indeed is of vital importance—is that the substance of policy should be resolutely adhered to, and its aims pursued continuously and consistently. And it is this that we have endeavoured to achieve.

The process of squeezing out entrenched inflation is painful and slow—more painful and slower than it would have been had our economy been less rigid, and had expectations been readier to adapt than they have been. But the only sure way to change attitudes built up over a long period of years is to demonstrate consistency of purpose—equally over a sustained period. This approach is now beginning to show the first signs of success. These signs are to be seen in our continued progress against inflation, to which I referred earlier. But they are to be seen too in improved productivity, in turn reflecting the beginnings of more flexible working practices in the labour force and greater determination on the part of management. If persisted in, this will reduce the rigidities of the supply side of the economy.

Setting monetary objectives

This paper by J S Fforde, an adviser to the Governor, was presented at a conference on monetary targeting organised by the Federal Reserve Bank of New York in May 1982. [1] *In it Mr Fforde reviews the political economy and history of monetary targeting in the United Kingdom since the early 1970s.*

Temporal references have not been altered so that, for example, 'last year' refers to 1981.

Our monetary objectives were reset early last month, when the Chancellor of the Exchequer presented his annual Budget to the House of Commons and reformulated the medium-term financial strategy of Her Majesty's Government. The stated monetary objectives comprised a single target range for 1982/83 encompassing three different monetary aggregates, one narrow and two broad. The range was appreciably higher than the one set a year ago for M_3, as the target for 1981/82. This was accompanied by an important qualifying text. It explained how the development of these aggregates, whether individually inside or outside the target range, needed to be interpreted when forming judgements about the monetary situation that relate to policy decisions about short-term interest rates.

In addition to a variety of qualifying factors pertaining to the behaviour of the monetary aggregates themselves, the text mentioned above referred to such other matters as the course of the exchange rate, the apparent real interest rate, the state of certain asset markets, and the concurrent course of nominal GDP. In brief, the UK monetary authorities again confirmed that while the counter-inflationary strategy remained unaltered in substance, their presentation of the money supply as an intermediate target in pursuit of that strategy had been modified in the light of experience since 1979. It remains to be seen how this relatively pragmatic approach will evolve, both in its practical application and in its intellectual and political presentation. But it clearly represents a rather greater emphasis on empiricism in the monetary policy field; though an empiricism purged, it is intended, of earlier permissiveness which was its downfall.

The occasion of this return most conveniently sets the framework of this paper. It does so because it permits an examination of the evolution of strict monetary targeting in the United Kingdom, a demonstration of why we chose to concentrate on broad rather than narrow aggregates, an analysis of the difficulties which we have found to be present in the use of monetary intermediate targets, and an assessment of what of value remains of the experiment that has been conducted.

The political economy of M_3

When discussing our monetary problems among ourselves, we have come to distinguish rather sharply between the 'political economy' of a money supply *strategy* and the 'practical macroeconomics' of a money supply *policy*. The former expression has to do with political presentation to the wide variety of audiences that constitute the public, and whose perception of the strategy presented is very diverse. Our own political economy is also much affected by the constitutional and governmental structure of the United Kingdom which, though by no means unique, differs considerably from that in, for example, the United States and West Germany. The latter expression, 'practical macroeconomics', is concerned with macroeconomic relationships and their stability or instability. It is concerned, for instance, with relationships between the money supply as an intermediate target and the ultimate objectives of policy regarding prices, output and employment. These distinctions seem both simple and useful, and will continue to be made in what follows.

The United Kingdom is a unitary state and a parliamentary democracy. Subject to parliamentary and ultimately electoral approval, macroeconomic policy is decided and carried out by a unified executive branch. This includes, for purposes of this paper, both the Treasury and the Bank of England. The latter is institutionally and operationally separate from the Treasury but is best regarded as the central banking arm of a centralised macroeconomic executive. For the past decade or more, this structure has worked in an economic environment characterised by sluggish or zero growth, a very large public sector, persistent and volatile inflation, pronounced external constraints, and often frustrated expectations of real-income growth.

Such conditions, which have on two occasions compelled us to borrow from the IMF, are clearly those in which there is a relentless need to restrain the size of fiscal deficits, to minimise the monetary financing of such deficits, to avoid conditions of financial laxity in the private sector of the economy, and more often than not to pay particular and close regard to the external repercussions of all aspects of domestic policy. The macroeconomic executive can only ignore those restraints at the risk of losing all control of financial stability and of the economic situation generally. This being so, it follows that there will be found great advantage in a method of formulating and presenting

---

(1) Copies of the conference proceedings, *Central Bank Views on Monetary Targeting* are available from the Public Information Department, Federal Reserve Bank of New York, New York 10045, USA.

Chart 1
Economic growth and inflation

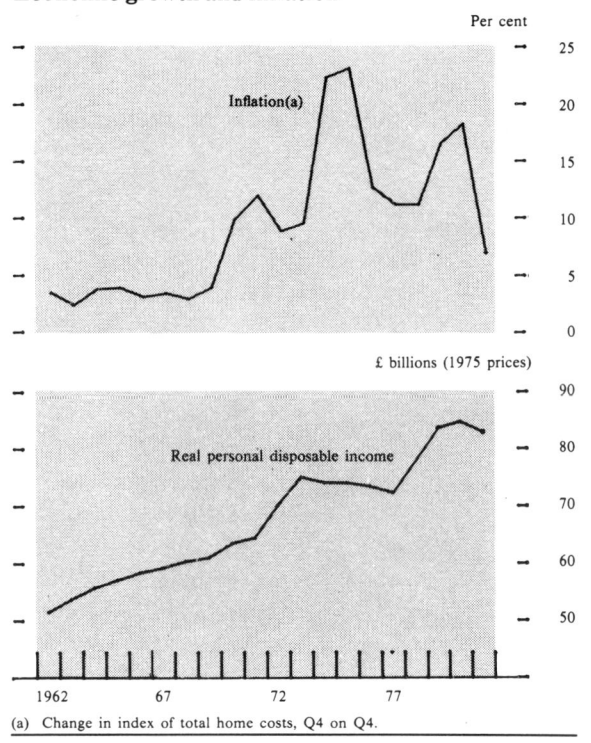

[Chart showing Inflation(a) in per cent, ranging roughly 0-25%, and Real personal disposable income in £ billions (1975 prices), ranging roughly 50-90, from 1962 to 1977.]

(a) Change in index of total home costs, Q4 on Q4.

policy that can bring together in one single analytic and statistical framework the interrelated complex of well-known fiscal and monetary magnitudes.

The use of such a framework helps to achieve a proper consistency and coherence of fiscal and monetary decision-making within the wider governmental apparatus, and to provide a convincing and persuasive public presentation of such decisions, at least to Parliament, to the 'informed' media and to financial markets. Indeed the practice of intermediate targetry in the United Kingdom is due only in part to its associated and often 'monetarist' economics. It is as much due to the evolving political and administrative needs of a macroeconomic executive that has to maintain control in the environment mentioned above, and to do so in a democratic society with a relatively free and open economy.

Specific intermediate targetry was, however, first introduced in the United Kingdom by the IMF when standby facilities were negotiated with the Fund following the devaluation of sterling in 1967. The IMF had presumably become accustomed to lending money to countries beset with problems similar to those experienced in the United Kingdom, and to imposing conditions that would so far as possible ensure that the loan was repaid on time. The conditions obliged the borrowing country to carry out an internally consistent macroeconomic policy along the lines mentioned above, so as to restrict the fiscal deficit, restrain the provision of finance to the private sector and by these and a variety of other means[1] bring about control of a specially devised broad credit aggregate (DCE). The containment of this aggregate within an agreed numerical limit was intended to ensure that the medium-term external loan from the IMF would be repaid on time. But although DCE is a credit aggregate, the strength of this assurance did in practice depend upon some workable degree of stability in the relationship between money and income rather than 'credit' and income.

The requirements of the IMF fitted readily into the established flow-of-funds accounting matrix and could thereby be made analytically consistent and visibly interrelated. It did not matter too much, for the purposes of political economy, that a set of accounting identities yielded of themselves relatively little information about causality; or that financial forecasts of the way such identities would turn out *ex post* were extremely imperfect. It sufficed that the various 'intermediate' fiscal and monetary magnitudes could be presented in directly interrelated form, through the financial accounts, and directly related to externally imposed conditions (DCE) which had perforce to be met.

These combinations of external compulsion, governmental structure, financial accounting and the persistence through time of the range of economic problems mentioned earlier, together propelled us towards the use of intermediate targets. But they also predisposed us to a concern with broad rather than narrow money. Narrow money relates to short-term interest rates and to income—in the economic sense of 'relates'. So, at least in principle, does broad money. But, unlike the latter, the former cannot be closely related in the accounting sense of the word to such other important magnitudes as, for instance, the fiscal deficit, non-bank absorption of government debt, or external monetary flows. This is not to suggest that narrow money, as an intermediate target, had no attractions. But for us these would have had to rely on a rather straightforward version of the quantity theory and on behavioural characteristics that were in practice very useful, reliable, superior to those of broad money, and known by markets to be so, rather than on demonstrative interrelationship with other monetary magnitudes.

If the targeting of narrow money seemed to rely rather exclusively on the quantity theory, the use of a broad money target could be justified by reference to rather different theories, about the importance of 'liquidity' and 'credit', as well as by regard for the quantity theory itself. Since the climate of thinking on these matters in the United Kingdom in the early 1970s was more eclectic than monetarist, this property of broad money was an additional reason for its adoption as an intermediate target.

The practical macroeconomics of M_3 in the early 1970s

At the outset, some twelve years ago, the behavioural characteristics of broad money seemed quite promising and in some respects superior to those of narrow money both in terms of controllability and in terms of reliable and useful relationships with ultimate goals. Experience of the 1960s suggested an adequately reliable demand-for-money

---

(1) Such as setting an appropriate rate of exchange, conducting enforceable incomes policies, or strict use of exchange controls.

function, or reliable relationship between M_3 and nominal incomes. Experience also suggested an adequately reliable relationship between M_3 and nominal interest rates of a form implying that sufficient control of the former could be obtained without movements in interest rates so large as to set up intolerable economic side effects. These inferences could be made because by the end of the 1960s econometric analysis could, for the first time, fully use the comprehensive monetary statistics that had only become available in the United Kingdom earlier in that decade, following the Radcliffe Report.[1] The initial results being promising, they served to reinforce a natural enthusiasm. For it now looked as if the combination of econometric method and adequate statistics would enable monetary policy to acquire a positivist or 'scientific' flavour in place of the qualitative and 'artistic' nature with which it was thought to have been tainted.

This econometric research into the properties of M_3 strongly encouraged the monetary authorities to attach greater importance than hitherto to the money supply itself, for two separate reasons. First, because it could be cogently argued that nominal interest rates, in conditions of persistent and volatile inflationary expectations, were a poor guide to real interest rates and hence to the 'thrust' of monetary policy. Money supply growth, relative to GDP, was a better guide; so 'money mattered' after all. Second, because the supposed responsiveness of this better guide to acceptable movements in nominal interest rates suggested that the needs of monetary policy could be met without persistent recourse to direct controls over bank lending to the private sector. This was a very attractive suggestion. By 1970, because of their diminishing effectiveness, and in the interests of competitive efficiency in banking, there was a lively disposition to move sharply away from the direct controls which had become a feature of monetary policy.

Neither of the two reasons just mentioned had much to do with 'monetarist' economics. In the early 1970s UK monetary policy, though more interested in the money supply and in the analytical and accounting framework described earlier, remained along with fiscal policy essentially 'Keynesian' in outlook, the more so after the IMF had been repaid and the associated DCE constraint had lapsed. Nevertheless the behaviour of the UK money supply, both broad and narrow, attracted increasing attention from monetarist writers both in the academic world and in the financial community.

An expansionist fiscal policy was adopted early in 1972, followed within months by abandonment of the fixed parity of exchange. Severe inflationary stresses ensued, notwithstanding the reintroduction late in 1972 of formal controls over prices and wages. In addition to familiar symptoms of a high pressure of demand on real resources, the signs of stress included booming markets in commercial and residential property, fuelled by a ready supply of

Chart 2
Monetary conditions 1970–74

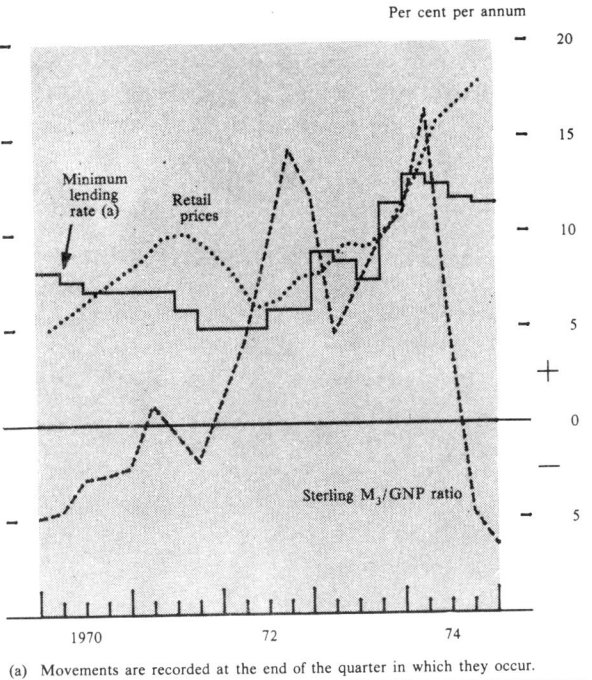

(a) Movements are recorded at the end of the quarter in which they occur.

finance from banks and savings institutions. Responding to domestic and external pressures, interest rates were raised sharply in June 1972 and again in the summer of 1973. Despite this, there persisted an extremely rapid growth in M_3 relative to nominal incomes, although by 1973 the growth of M_1 gave much less cause for monetarist alarm. Towards the end of 1973 'overheating' became acute and inflationary pressures were intensified by the rise in energy prices. Corrective action had to be taken. Fiscal policy was tightened, short-term interest rates were raised to levels not hitherto experienced, and a form of direct control was reimposed on the banking system. But at the same time, the statutory incomes policy became subject to severe strain which culminated in industrial action in the coalmining industry. A general election was held in March 1974 and the Conservative Government lost office. The incoming Labour Government abandoned its predecessor's incomes policy; though one feature of that policy, a form of partial wage-indexation, continued to affect wage levels for some time thereafter.

The intensity of the inflationary pressures that developed in 1973 was evident enough from a very wide range of economic and financial information. But it was not clear whether the rapid growth of M_3 was either accurately corroborating all the other available evidence or reliably predicting the level of inflation which would ensue in 1974–75.[2] The problem with M_3 was one that has since become familiar to executants of monetary targetry in many countries. It had undergone structural change following the simultaneous abandonment late in 1971 of the direct credit controls and the collective agreements between principal banks regarding the setting of deposit

---
(1) *Committee on the Working of the Monetary System — Report*, HM Stationery Office, Cmnd 827, 1959.
(2) A much higher level did in fact ensue. But the massive rise in energy prices, whose effect was aggravated by the partial indexation of wages, was a very important contributory factor that had nothing to do with the British money supply in the preceding period.

and lending rates. Monetary econometrics that relied upon the statistics of the 1960s proved useless once the banking reforms of 1971 had taken effect. But precisely because this could so readily be attributed to structural change, and because that change itself so obscured underlying monetary trends, there remained some justifiable optimism among monetary economists that normality would soon return and the econometric reliability of M_3 be restored. Regrettably, this optimism was to prove unfounded. But for the time being it underpinned professional economic support for the political economy of 'monetarism' which became increasingly influential in the United Kingdom during the later 1970s.

Furthermore, the breakdown of the previously established relationships between M_3 on the one hand and interest rates and nominal income on the other did not of itself mean that the usefulness of M_3 to the macroeconomic executive had been fatally undermined. For one thing, political and market opinion subsequent to 1973 remained very sensitive to the development of the money supply. This accordingly influenced the exchange rate as well as the state of domestic financial markets. For another, it now seemed that the growth of M_3 within reasonable limits could be directly influenced, occasionally to a high degree, by a combination of direct controls (now more acceptable again) and an active policy of debt management. So although there was at first no formal or published money supply target, the course of M_3 was a fairly strong policy constraint after 1973, and one that could be brought to bear on decisions about the level of government borrowing, about the pattern of its financing, and about short-term interest rates.

M_3 as an overriding constraint: 1976–79

From an unpublished M_3 objective as a moderate constraint on other aspects of macroeconomic policy, it was but a short step to a published M_3 target as an overriding constraint upon policies which might otherwise fail to stop inflation reaccelerating to 20 per cent per annum and more. This was the speed that had been reached by the middle of 1975, just before the reimposition of direct control (this time non-statutory) over wages and salaries. The short step to published annual targets for M_3 was taken in the autumn of 1976 when it became clear that financial confidence was unlikely to be obtained without it. For at that time the UK authorities had become caught in a spiral of declining confidence. Concern about official intentions regarding the rate of exchange heightened a persisting concern about the level of government borrowing and the stance of fiscal policy. Concern about the effects of these matters upon the viability of incomes policy then further increased concern about prospective inflation. All these things made the required policy of debt management more difficult to carry through. This in turn caused difficulty with M_3. In the end, a published M_3 target was announced and short-term interest rates were raised to 15 per cent, even higher than the level reached at the end of 1973. Recourse was again then made to borrowing from the IMF, with its accompaniment of a tightened fiscal policy and agreed limits on DCE.

The use of a published M_3 target as an 'overriding constraint' upon other aspects of policy, which then continued to be conducted broadly along Keynesian lines, lasted until the change of government in May 1979. It was notably reinforced in the autumn of 1977. During the spring and summer of that year, following restoration of external confidence during the winter of 1976–77, there was strong upward pressure upon the exchange rate. After a time, this caused concern for the external competitiveness of British industry. Attempts were therefore made to contain the appreciation by heavy intervention in the exchange market and by a progressive reduction in short-term interest rates.

These measures, though technically effective, were carried to the point where they were clearly undermining restraint on the domestic money supply. In short, they collided with the overriding monetary constraint; and they were abandoned. That constraint was further reinforced in the early summer of 1978 when the fiscal policy of the government again failed to command adequate market confidence for the containment of M_3 to be secured without additional measures. So fiscal policy had to be corrected and in addition a degree of direct credit control was once again reimposed. But despite these reinforcements of a published monetary constraint, the containment of inflation still depended importantly upon persistence with the direct, though largely voluntary, restraint on prices and incomes. This latter became relatively ineffective during the winter of 1978–79. It had no place in the electoral programme of the Conservative opposition which won the general election of May 1979 and embarked upon a radical change in

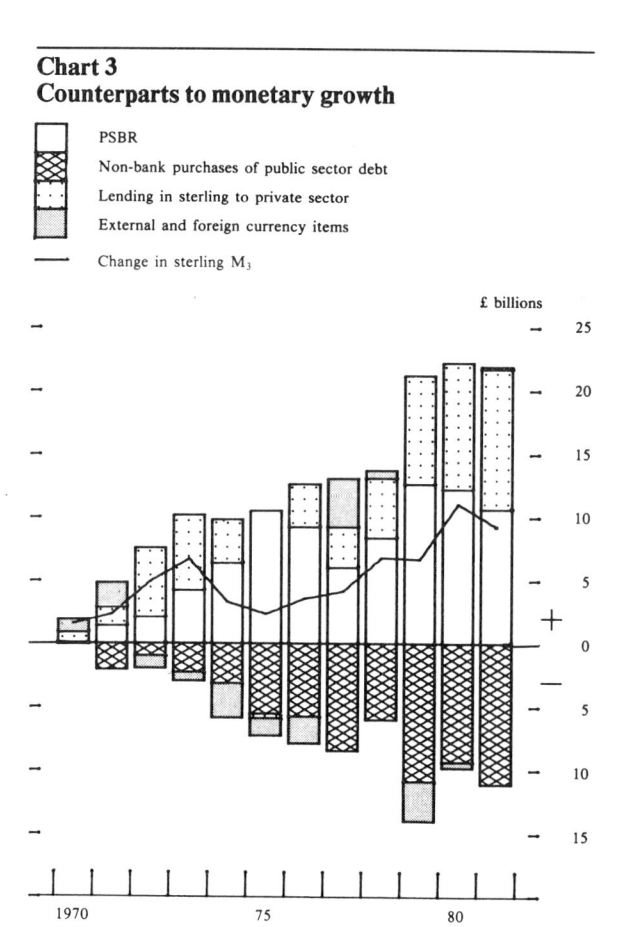

Chart 3
Counterparts to monetary growth

PSBR
Non-bank purchases of public sector debt
Lending in sterling to private sector
External and foreign currency items
— Change in sterling M_3

macroeconomic strategy. Colloquially, monetarily constrained 'Keynesianism' was replaced by 'monetarism'.

The medium-term financial strategy and the problems of M_3: 1979–82

The incoming Government retained the use of M_3[1] as the single target aggregate. It was recognised that experience hitherto in achieving fairly close control of this aggregate was not entirely reassuring. But it was felt that the answer to this might lie in changing the methods of control rather than the target aggregate itself. Retention of M_3 may also have been encouraged by further econometric research which made allowance for the troubles that followed the reforms of 1971. This was thought to support a view that success in controlling M_3 within a narrow and restricted range over the *medium* term would reliably be followed by a predictable success in steadily reducing inflation. But retention of M_3 was also due to those same advantages of targeting a broad money aggregate in the United Kingdom that had first appeared ten years earlier: namely, the direct accounting linkage with the level of government borrowing and financing, with the level of bank lending to the private sector, and with external monetary flows. In this context it will be recalled that the 'monetarist' counter-inflationary strategy of the present Government has always included great emphasis on the need to control and reduce the public sector borrowing requirement so as to obtain a fiscal/monetary mix more favourable to enterprise in the private sector.

The change of strategy altered and intensified the 'political economy' of M_3. In place of the overriding constraint against run-away inflation there now emerged a published programme for reducing the growth of the money supply over a period of years and, it was stated, bringing about thereby a steady reduction of inflation down to a minimal pace. In pursuit of this programme, considerable importance was attached to the favourable effect that official monetary declarations and performance could have upon expectations about prices and employment, and therefore on behaviour with respect to wages and salaries. Success, first in keeping M_3 within the published target range, and second in doing so without producing unacceptably damaging side-effects, was clearly most important. Yet the change of strategy did nothing of itself to alter the shorter-term behavioural characteristics of M_3. Opinions about these differed but experience since 1974 was not entirely encouraging. For whatever that experience might suggest about relationships applying over a *medium* term measured in years, the 'political economy' of the strategy seemed to require a demonstration of quite close control, and an absence of intolerable side-effects, in a *short* term measured in months. Herein turned out to lie much of our problem with single-aggregate broad-money targetry.

The structural context of UK monetary policy was changed in the autumn of 1979 by the abolition of exchange control. This rendered direct credit controls virtually useless. For the first time in their history, and on this occasion they had been in force since May 1978, such controls could now be avoided wholesale by offshore disintermediation. Moreover, avoidance through domestic disintermediation was already growing and confidence in the ability of direct controls to deliver a worthwhile amount of additional monetary restraint, as opposed to 'cosmetic' manipulation of the target aggregate, was declining. Accordingly, direct controls were abolished in the summer of 1980. The growth of M_3 was markedly inflated for some months afterwards by reintermediation. This episode came at a time when the money supply policy was encountering other and more fundamental difficulties and therefore cast important additional doubt on the credibility of our single-aggregate targetry.

Without direct controls, there remained short-term interest rate policy and debt management. But pursuit of the former was unlikely, on the available evidence, to begin to have a worthwhile effect on M_3 until a time lag of at least six months had elapsed. The effect, when it came, was seen to be through a fall in demand for bank loans; though it was unclear whether this itself would be a consequence of the income effects of interest-rate changes, or whether it would be a precursor of those income effects. Indeed, discovery of reliable relationships between the demand for bank loans to the private sector and a whole variety of other variables, including short-term interest rates, had proved very elusive. Yet in the absence of effective direct constraint on their supply, and given a banking system fully adapted to 'liability management', it was the *demand* for bank loans that had to be influenced in the cause of M_3 control. So with these uncertainties and time lags surrounding the course of bank lending, monetary control in the shorter term came to depend critically upon debt management; and despite the progressive introduction of a variety of technical improvements, there were rather close limits to what could be achieved by this means. For one thing, the short-run predictability of the government's own borrowing needs was at that time very poor.

These problems of short-run control, though serious, need not of themselves have led to a de-emphasis of M_3 as the single target aggregate. For, provided the existing techniques had been able over a rather longer period, say between six months and a year, to contain the money supply within the kind of target range required, but without the emergence of severe conflict with ultimate objectives of policy, all might have been well. But this latter condition proved not to apply. The apparent relationship between M_3 and nominal incomes, in the shorter term, began to display alarming properties. Pressing policy to the point where the monetary target might have been achieved would seemingly have risked unacceptably severe and immediate consequences for the real economy, consequences that were unintended and strategically damaging. In short, progress with the *ultimate* objectives of policy had, by the summer of 1980, to be taken into account as well as progress with the

---

[1] Or sterling M_3 as it had become since the removal of a foreign currency element from the definition in 1977.

intermediate targets. At the time this seemed to call into question the political economy that had been expressed in the government's medium-term financial strategy, which had only been fully presented to the public, in quite strict numerical terms, as recently as March of that year. But as time went by it came to be realised that the strategy was more likely to be judged by its actual effect on the economy, and on the actual behaviour and expectations of the principal agents in it, than by the puzzling short-run behaviour of a particular monetary aggregate.

What was actually happening? Beginning in the second quarter of 1980 the British economy moved steeply into a recession marked in particular by a cutback in inventories. Industrial production fell fast, profits (already low) were sharply reduced, unemployment rose very rapidly, and in the autumn there began a marked slowing down in the growth of prices and wages which had at first failed to respond to the change of strategy. Short-term interest rates at first remained at the 17 per cent to which they had been raised in the previous November in response to excess growth of M_3 and, most importantly, the rate of exchange rapidly appreciated after external competitiveness had already been reduced by the relative growth in unit labour costs in the United Kingdom over the preceding two years. Yet the course of M_3 relative to its target did not properly justify a cut in interest rates. Rather did it at times suggest a further rise. It was affected upwards by a rise in the fiscal deficit, associated with the recession, and by a continuing high corporate demand for bank loans despite the run-down of stocks. At the same time, the personal saving ratio rose to a very high level; and this increased saving flow helped finance the corporate and public sector deficits through the intermediation of the banks.

Throughout the summer and autumn of 1980 M_3 continued to grow outside the top of its target range. But short-term interest rates were reduced to 16 per cent in July 1980, to 14 per cent in November, and to 12 per cent in March 1981. On each occasion it had to be judged that the performance of M_3 required interpretation in the light of other indicators, including the exchange rate, and that the thrust of policy was in practice as restrictive as had been intended. In particular it seemed that the increase in personal savings, and their flow to the business sector through the banks, had inflated M_3 without adverse implications for the future. This factor may have diminished in force during at least part of 1981. But in that year the performance of M_3 was additionally affected, first by a structural change following entry of the principal banks into the market for residential mortgages, and second (but in the opposite direction) by the growth of foreign currency balances held by UK residents in preference to sterling. These structural changes were a lagged consequence of the abolition of exchange control in 1979 and of direct credit controls in 1980. M_3 was also affected in 1981 by a prolonged alteration in the timing of tax receipts resulting from industrial action in the civil service.

Within this catalogue of special factors influencing M_3, the effect of prolonged inflationary uncertainty and high nominal interest rates on the pattern of corporate financing should also be mentioned. By the mid-seventies, these pressures had for practical purposes forced corporate borrowers to abandon the market in long-term fixed-interest debt. Although recourse to the equity market remained an option that continued to be used on a significant scale, medium-term variable rate borrowing from banks became an attractive and readily available substitute for long-term bond financing.[1]

Chart 4
Industrial and commercial companies' finance

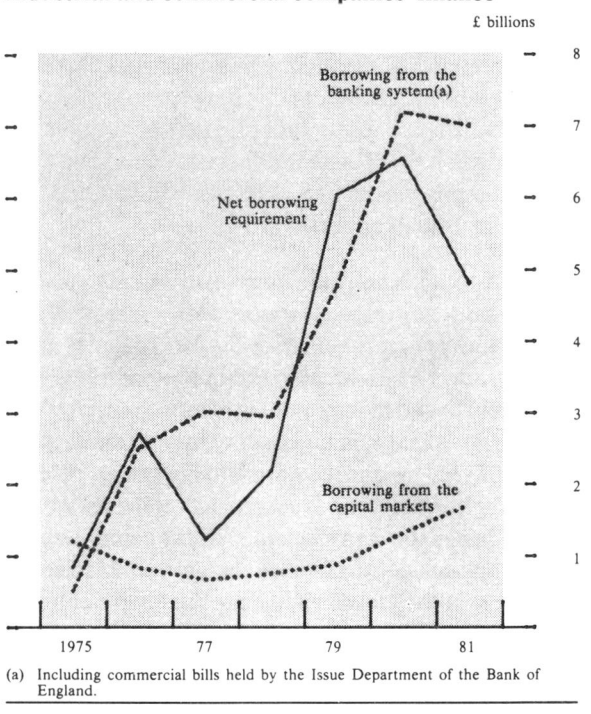

£ billions

(a) Including commercial bills held by the Issue Department of the Bank of England.

With the 'borrowing requirement' of the corporate sector being persistently large, this tended substantially to increase the degree of banking intermediation, and the growth of M_3. Recently, however, it has been counteracted by a debt management policy of 'overfunding'. By this process, the government borrows funds outside the banking system, that the corporate sector would formerly have borrowed directly, and in effect uses them to finance variable-rate lending by the banks. This was in the first instance done by repaying government debt in the hands of the banks and thereafter by repaying government debt in the hands of the Bank of England which in turn acquired short-term corporate debt from the banks.

This prolonged distortion of the financing patterns, resulting mainly from persistent and volatile inflation, has added to the uncertainties surrounding both the ability of policy to influence bank lending and the actual desirability of seeking the severe restriction of bank lending, as such, which M_3 targets of around 10 per cent per annum would

---

(1) Latterly there has also been a rapid growth in the leasing of fixed assets by banks to industrial and commercial companies. This development has owed a lot to the 'tax-efficiency' of the (profitable) banks leasing plant and equipment to those industrial and commercial companies who themselves had at the time no liability to corporation tax.

at first sight seem to imply. The success of the banking system in filling the gap left in corporate financing by the abandonment of long-term fixed-rate debt can be considered satisfactory and laudable. Yet counteracting its effect on M_3, by overfunding, must in the end raise questions about the politico-economic 'interface' between the central government and the corporate sector that are unlikely to remain unanswered indefinitely.

Alternative solutions

It is not surprising that all these difficulties with M_3 should have provoked close interest both in alternative target aggregates and in different techniques of control. If, for instance, another aggregate could have been found which had greatly superior behavioural characteristics, then it might have been worth sacrificing the advantages derived from the accounting linkage of M_3 with government borrowing, bank lending, etc. Indeed, many of us in the Bank of England have at one time or other undergone road-to-Damascus conversions to M_1; only to find that the new faith soon loses its apparent attractions.

To control M_1 there is only one single instrument to use, namely the short-term rate of interest. Other aspects of macroeconomic policy, for instance the fiscal balance and its financing, affect M_1 indirectly. But in this context they would scarcely be called instruments of money supply control. It follows that a change cannot in practice be made from M_3 to M_1, having started out with the former, at least unless the single instrument of control can convincingly be shown to be reliable and efficient. This we cannot do. Neither the amount of interest rate change needed to secure a given change in the growth of M_1, nor the length of time before the change is secured, can be estimated within limits sufficiently narrow. To reply that the actual amount of interest rate change needed does not matter, so long as M_1 is held within its target range, is to brush aside the risk of unacceptable side-effects on, for instance, the rate of exchange. Whatever the advantages of a visibly controlled money supply, no monetary executive in a democratic society can be blind to the risks and consequences of policy becoming so unintendedly severe as to forfeit the degree of public support needed to command authority.

As to ultimate objectives, M_1 has not recently shown superiority to M_3 in its relationship to income. Indeed there is some evidence that while M_3 tells us something about the future, M_1 merely confirms the present, most of which is already apparent from other sources. Nor, moreover, is M_1 at all immune from structural change caused by financial innovation. Finally, in order to steer by M_1 the policymaker is almost totally dependent on the findings of econometric research. The judgemental consideration of flow-of-funds forecasts, useful when brooding over M_3, is not much help with M_1. This is not a mark in favour of the latter. For whatever reason, but perhaps because the turbulent economic and financial climate of the past decade has led to frequent alterations of economic habit, or financial behaviour, policy makers in the United Kingdom have come to regard econometric optimism with some caution.

It is almost as if relationships are in practice more likely to change than remain stable. In addition, there is no such thing as *the* econometrics of M_1. There are several, as with other aggregates. They carry differing messages, and all are vulnerable to upset by fresh research on the same data.

If we had started with M_1 we would no doubt have seen formidable disadvantages in a change to M_3. But we did not so start and for the wide variety of reasons sketched above the monetary authorities in the United Kingdom have not seen any net advantage in changing to M_1 as the target aggregate, although it was later included in the multi-aggregate target range that we now have. What then of a radical change in the technique of control? The modifications to the existing system which came into operation last August did not constitute such a change. In some respects they opened up the possibility of further and more radical change at a later date. But their main purpose was to improve the operation of the existing system, by better adapting it to current circumstances.

Radical change was considered in enormous depth by the monetary authorities and by outside commentators (not exclusively British), over a period of several years prior to 1981. The change debated was known as 'monetary base control'; though towards the end this seemed much more a generic term, with a whole range of sub-species, than a single specific technical construction. At one end of the range it amounted to medium-term targeting of the 'wide monetary base', defined as bankers' reserve balances at the Bank plus notes and coin in circulation, without close concern for month-to-month changes. Technically this would not have been very different from a rather loose targeting of M_1. At the other end of the range, monetary base control amounted to close control, perhaps almost week-to-week, either over a mandatory reserve base of the banks, regarded as a close proxy for money supply, or over non-mandatory operational balances of the banks at the Bank, regarded as a loose proxy for money supply loosely defined.

All these proposals presented difficulties that seemed just as formidable as those actually encountered by the existing control system when we endeavoured to carry out the task initially set us in 1979 and 1980. Targeting the note issue seemed to mean allowing whatever flexibility in short-term rates was needed to control an aggregate whose interest-elasticity was extremely low but whose income-elasticity was quite high. This looked like trying to use short-term interest rates to manipulate nominal GDP in order to control the note issue. This did not seem a particularly sensible way of pursuing a strategy in which nominal GDP was supposed to be affected by control of money rather than vice versa. The proposal to target a mandatory reserve base, to go to the other end of the scale, set out to impose on the authorities an almost total abandonment of discretion over the setting of short-term interest rates, with the aim of thereby achieving 'automatically' a close control of the money supply itself. The proposal to target a non-mandatory reserve base seemed designed to achieve the same ends but with less rigidity.

It is not easy to do justice to the controversy about reserve-base targetry in the United Kingdom in a single paragraph. But it might perhaps be summarised as follows. On the one side were those who were much influenced by the manifest behavioural characteristics of the monetary aggregates themselves and who judged that reserve base targetry would lead to an extreme instability in short-term interest rates, directly and indirectly damaging to industry and commerce, and damaging to government financing. This they judged would in turn probably lead to a serious renewal of cosmetic disintermediation, as the community sought to repair the damage by operating in ways which did not provoke the instability. In effect, on this view, monetary base targetry might conceivably achieve close control of a monetary aggregate or aggregates but at the cost of unacceptable side-effects and the setting in motion of structural changes that would undermine the meaning of what had been controlled. On the other side were those who argued that the discretionary setting of short-term interest rates would always in practice result in their being set too low to achieve proper control and that the inflationary expectations of financial institutions, industrial and commercial companies, and trades unions, would remain insufficiently reduced. Against the charge of extreme instability, advocates of base control tended to stress that while short-term rates might for an initial period move much higher than hitherto experienced, the effect on expectations and on economic and financial behaviour would be so dramatically favourable that proper control of money could thereafter be achieved without the damaging instability that some people feared. Moreover the rigidity of the base target, rather like martial law, could be eased once this favourable revolution had occurred. As one advocate put it, monetary base control would be a modern version of the discipline forced on monetary authorities by the gold standard, with its statutory obligations regarding maintenance of the gold convertibility of banknotes.

The arguments in favour of monetary base control did not in the end prevail. Perhaps this was because by the autumn of 1980 the attractions of a monetary revolution, never very great, had become less apparent to a macroeconomic executive which was having to deal with circumstances rather different from those with which the revolution was supposed to deal. For by then the need to have regard to a range of indicators, including the exchange rate, when judging the appropriateness of policy in respect of ultimate objectives, was becoming very evident. The behaviour of the target aggregate itself did not seem to be giving a reliable signal. Monetary base control did not seem relevant to this problem.

Conclusions

Among the many conclusions that could be drawn from the British experience with monetary targeting, this paper draws attention to four. The first of these is that it would scarcely have been possible to mount and carry through, over several years and without resort to direct controls of all kinds, so determined a counter-inflationary strategy if it had not been for the initial 'political economy' of the firm monetary target. Though not considered at the time, it would have been possible to initiate such a strategy with a familiar 'Keynesian' exposition about managing demand downwards, and with greater concentration on ultimate objectives than on intermediate targets. But this would have meant disclosing objectives for, *inter alia,* output and employment. This would have been a very hazardous exercise, and the objectives would either have been unacceptable to public opinion or else inadequate to secure a substantial reduction in the rate of inflation, or both. Use of strong intermediate targets, for money supply and government borrowing, enabled the authorities to stand back from output and employment as such and to stress the vital part to be played in respect of these by the trend of industrial costs. In short, whatever the subsequent difficulties of working with intermediate targets, they were vitally important at the outset in order to signal a decisive break with the past and enable the authorities to set out with presentational confidence upon a relatively uncharted sea.

The second conclusion is that the difficulties that have come to seem inherent in short-term monetary targetry are by no means fatal to the associated counter-inflationary strategy once its practical credibility can be established by the perceived behaviour of policy in response to the developing and disinflationary economic situation. For what matters is the refusal of the authorities to stimulate demand in 'Keynesian' fashion, or to 'reflate', as conditions develop that would in the past have justified and provoked such a response. The fact that the monetary targets have not concurrently been met, or that the meaning of particular developments in this or that aggregate has become very ambiguous, is of much less importance. At one time it was indeed feared that the difficulties encountered with M_3 would leave the strategy bereft of a vital ingredient. Experience now suggests that this fear was exaggerated. But it is recognised that maintaining the 'coherence' and credibility of strategy in such circumstances may be easier in a country where the conduct of macroeconomic policy is highly centralised, and where broad money is accorded greater importance than narrow.

The third conclusion concerns the continuing reinforcement of the strategy that has to be provided by annual statements of quantified macroeconomic intent. It is about the question: does it suffice just to continue with modified and qualified monetary targets, guidelines, or 'expected ranges' for a year ahead, accompanied by an ongoing policy of fiscal restraint, or has it become desirable to indicate an acceptable *medium-term* path for nominal GDP as well? On balance it is beginning to look as if the answer to this latter question may be 'Yes'. Without it the desired strategy can seem negative and stale, instead of offering a prospect of revival and recovery. Indicating an acceptable medium-term path for nominal GDP enables a greater emphasis to be placed on the favourable development of demand and output that could be accommodated within it if, for example, unit labour costs grew sufficiently slowly for the stance of policy to be made much less restrictive. This emphasis becomes more necessary once the level of unemployment, and other aspects of recession, are as much in the public mind as the falling level of inflation.

The fourth conclusion endeavours to answer the question of whether modifying and qualifying the monetary target leaves us so prone to a weakening of counter-inflationary resolve that there is need to reconstitute a published 'overriding constraint' or 'long-stop'. The obvious and indeed only remaining candidate for this vacancy, certainly in the United Kingdom, is the rate of exchange; and it looks as if the answer to the question is both 'not quite' and 'not yet'. It is clear that we pay close attention to the exchange rate when taking policy decisions, in particular it was clear last autumn, when short-term interest rates rose 4 per cent in the trough of a deep recession, that a further depreciation of sterling would have been most unwelcome to the UK authorities. It is equally clear that although the behavioural characteristics of the exchange rate, as an intermediate target, can be as tiresome as those of a monetary aggregate, its political economy is much superior. Everyone knows what it is. But in present international monetary conditions a pegged exchange rate regime for sterling, in isolation, would be sufficiently vulnerable to volatile short-term flows that such an open commitment would seem on operational grounds better avoided; there is in any case economic as well as operational advantage in preserving room for manoeuvre. As with the money supply so with the exchange rate, the attempt to honour too rigid a commitment may create unintended and intolerable side effects. So for the present, an exchange rate 'long-stop' may be better provided through the practical evidence of official behaviour than by publicised alteration of the present regime.

Reference was made at the beginning of this paper to British empiricism. As may now be visible, this means that setting objectives for the money supply, and endeavouring to carry them out, has become a more humble pursuit. It does not lack resolve, or a clear sense of direction, but it recognises once more that the successful execution of monetary policy requires the exercise of judgement, and of a constantly interpretative approach to the evolving pattern of evidence. Except in some grave emergency, or in the initial phase of a novel strategy, the abandonment of judgement in favour of some simple, rigid, quantitative rule about money supply does not reliably deliver acceptable results. This has been disappointing for those who distrust discretion and admire rules. But the humble pursuit is also disappointing for those who admire discretion and have no use for rules at all. The right balance has to be found empirically, as we go along.

CHAPTER 5
Operations in the gilt-edged market

The Bank's operational objectives in the gilt-edged market have changed considerably over the last two decades as the objectives and techniques of monetary policy more generally have evolved. These objectives and accompanying operating techniques are described in four articles which form the substance of this chapter.

In the mid-1960s the volume of outstanding gilt-edged securities was much higher in relation to GDP than it has been since the mid-1970s; moreover, persistent concern about the balance of payments and the exchange rate created repeated anxieties in the gilt-edged market. The monetary aggregates did not, however, at this time play a central role in monetary policy, so that the Bank was not under such strong pressure as it is now to achieve quantitative sales targets. Against this background, the authorities operated both as buyer and seller in the gilt-edged market (as 'jobber of last resort') with the purpose of avoiding large short-term fluctuations in prices and thereby seeking to maximise the longer-run demand for gilt-edged stocks. At the same time they endeavoured through market operations to lengthen the maturity of the government stocks in the public's hands so as to ease the refinancing burden.

This mode of operation was described in the first article entitled *Official transactions in the gilt-edged market* (page 75) published in the June 1966 *Bulletin*.

At times of market weakness, the Bank could find itself buying large amounts of stock in the process of smoothing price fluctuations. By late 1968 these purchases had come to conflict with the wider objectives of monetary policy, which was by then restrictive. Accordingly, the Bank began to make less attractive bids for stock offered to it by the jobbers.

This move towards less intervention by the authorities in the gilt-edged market was taken further in the consultative document on *Competition and credit control* issued in May 1971 (see paragraph 13 of this document on page 116). In November 1971, shortly after these changes, the Chief Cashier explained some of the background to them in the *Sykes Memorial Lecture* to the Institute of Bankers (page 83).

In the event, yields rose steadily between 1971 and 1974, and in the environment thus created it was difficult for the Bank to sell large amounts of stock, though there were heavy sales after yields had fallen back sharply early in 1975. The adoption of a target for M3 in 1976 (later, the targets were set for sterling M3) put further pressure on the Bank to sell gilt-edged stocks, particularly because, as noted in the article *Setting monetary objectives* in Chapter 4, government debt sales appeared to be the main means at the authorities' disposal of achieving short-term influence over this aggregate. The role of gilt-edged funding in monetary policy was described in an article *The gilt-edged market* (page 86), published in the June 1979 *Bulletin*. This article comments on a number of alterations in technique which had been made, and on some other changes which had been suggested at that time.

After 1979, the pressure on the Bank to sell stock for reasons of monetary control persisted. The dominance of the gilt-edged market within the UK capital market in this period was described in a paper on *The Bank's operational procedures for meeting monetary objectives* (page 98); this paper was presented by A L Coleby, an Assistant Director of the Bank, as a companion paper to that on page 65, to the conference on monetary targeting organised by the Federal Reserve Bank of New York in May 1982, and was subsequently reprinted in the June 1983 *Bulletin*. Further evolutionary developments in the techniques of selling stocks are described in this article as well as the more radical introduction of index-linked gilt-edged stocks—initially on a restricted basis in March 1981 but a year later restrictions were dropped.

In 1980/81 and 1981/82 the need to restrain the broad monetary aggregates led to central government funding (including sales of national savings instruments) being conducted on a scale substantially greater than the total central government borrowing requirement, so that the government was able to repay much of its short-term debt represented by Treasury bills: the size of the weekly Treasury bill tender was reduced to the minimum practicable level (£100 million). Having exhausted the possibilities for repaying Treasury bills, the authorities then began to acquire short-term claims from the banking system in the form of commercial bills. These changes in the financing of the central government had important implications for the Bank's operations in the money market, which are discussed in the next chapter.

Official transactions in the gilt-edged market

The management of the national debt is a central part of monetary management and at the same time a branch of Exchequer financing; as the Radcliffe Committee observed, it now consists of much more than a search for the cheapest way of dealing with a nuisance. The reconciliation of the diverse and often conflicting aims involved, and the methods and tactics adopted in pursuing them, are as much issues of monetary policy as of good housekeeping for the Government, though clearly they are not the whole of either.

This article is not a comprehensive review of the management of public sector debt in all its forms. It deals only with the nature of the market for gilt-edged stocks (government stocks and stocks of the nationalised industries carrying government guarantees), and with the purposes, tactics, and limitations of stock issues and official transactions in this market.

Debt management as an instrument of policy First, management of the gilt-edged market and Bank rate are together the principal means of executing interest rate policy. Almost all fixed rates for government borrowing and lending, such as the rates for national savings certificates, national development bonds, tax reserve certificates, and Exchequer loans to the nationalised industries, are fixed from time to time by reference to the current yields on gilt-edged stocks. The structure of these yields therefore has a strong influence on the structure of prime rates generally; and the authorities can pursue their aims for interest rates throughout the economy by seeking to influence the behaviour of prices and yields in the gilt-edged market. Secondly, management of the gilt-edged market, and the outcome in terms both of prices and of the net amounts of stock sold or bought in official dealings, have a considerable bearing on credit policy and the liquidity of the banks and others, creating conditions that may help or hinder policy in this field. Neither interest rate policy nor credit policy, however, is the dominant long-term consideration in debt management; this is rather to ensure so far as possible that suitable finance for the Exchequer is available, and will continue to be available in the future, so that there need be no excessive recourse to short-term borrowing from the banks on Treasury bills and accompanying increase in the money supply.

The Government's need for long-term finance The total of British government and government guaranteed marketable stocks outstanding is about £19,500 million (nominal); of this total £16,000 million is in stocks which have to be redeemed by fixed dates, and some £3,500 million in stocks, such as $3\frac{1}{2}$% War Loan, with no final redemption dates. The fact that the dated stocks, of which about £11,500 million is currently in the hands of the general public, will have to be repaid by the final date given in the prospectus is one certain element in the Government's future need for finance. Moreover, about a third of the total amount of dated stocks falls due for repayment over the next five years, with an average amount of more than £1,000 million reaching its final date each year; these magnitudes are likely to be at least maintained while the patterns of demand in the gilt-edged market continue as they are.

The certain need to provide for debt redemption year after year on such a scale is a suitable point from which to begin a statement of purposes in debt management. This, however, is not the only need for finance to be borne in mind; it is almost as certain that the Government will also need to raise new funds each year for capital requirements, and will thereby also add to the redemption problem in the future. It is not that the central government's own capital expenditure requires financing in this way; on the contrary, their revenue has been more than enough, over recent years, to provide for all their expenditure, both on capital and on current account. But the central government also provide substantial sums for the capital programmes of the nationalised industries and, through the Public Works Loan Board, for those of the local authorities. In the five years from March 1960 to March 1965 the central government have financed capital investment other than their own to the extent of nearly £3,000 million.

The need to refinance maturing debt together with the need to borrow to finance new capital investment, and the certain prospect for many years to come that these pressing needs will both persist, enable the chief purpose of debt management to be stated simply; it is to maintain market conditions that will maximise, both now and in the future, the desire of investors at home and abroad to hold British government debt.

Demand for gilt-edged stocks The turnover of stocks in the gilt-edged market is large and varies quite considerably from time to time; the figures published by the London stock exchange for 1965, a year in which activity was somewhat below the recent average, show that, including official dealings, the amount of stock passing from one investor to another during the year was about half the total of £19,500 million outstanding. Much the greater part (in money terms) represents the business of the large financial institutions, sometimes investing new funds, more often switching between stocks. These institutions— the banks, discount houses, insurance companies and pension funds—and the large industrial and commercial companies with substantial sums which they need to invest in highly marketable securities hold between them something like half of the gilt-edged stocks in the hands of the general public. The banks and discount houses hold mainly the shorter-dated stocks; the insurance companies and pension funds mainly the medium and longer-dated. Most of them have large individual holdings and expect to be able to buy or sell, or to switch between stocks, in amounts of several million pounds at a time. This ability to deal freely at all times is highly important for them; although an institution may not often wish to deal in such amounts, yet if it thought that there was a risk of its not being able to do so at any time that it wished, it would feel that its liquidity and its freedom of manœuvre were becoming impaired and would become increasingly reluctant to maintain its investment in gilt-edged stocks.

Alternative investments for the financial institutions are the stocks of local authorities and industrial debentures, many of which offer unquestionable security with a somewhat higher yield than is to be had on gilt-edged stocks. But these alternatives are not so readily marketable in large amounts that the institutions can feel sure of being able to sell at once whenever they choose; it is the assured and, for practical purposes, limitless marketability of gilt-edged stocks that gives them their chief advantage over the best alternatives, and their greatest appeal for the institutions.

The institutions have for many years taken the unrestricted marketability of gilt-edged stocks for granted. Their investment decisions in the gilt-edged market have in consequence come to be governed principally by their expectations of future movements in prices; not surprisingly there is often a substantial consensus of view among such investors, and there is therefore likely to be, at any one time, a preponderance either of buyers, or of sellers, in the market.

The aggregate of the resources that the jobbers in gilt-edged stocks are able to commit, however, is small in relation to the volume of trading; unsupported, they might not be able, even with the help of wide swings in prices, to absorb the kind of pressures that build up when sentiment in the market veers sharply one way or the other. It has therefore become a prime consideration in official dealings to keep the pressures on the jobbers within supportable limits, and so contain the risk that a holder of government debt might find it impossible to deal either way in the market for whatever amount of stock he wished—subject only, if he is a buyer, to the particular stock he wants being available.

Official dealings
Official dealings in the gilt-edged market comprise those of the National Debt Commissioners and those of the Issue Department of the Bank of England. The National Debt Commissioners are responsible for the management of the National Insurance Funds, the funds of the Post Office Savings Bank and the trustee savings banks, and many smaller funds of an official nature. The timing and extent of their operations are matters in the first instance for the National Debt Office to decide in the light of the needs of those funds; and, except when the National Debt Office are buying or selling large amounts of stock, the Government Broker will usually be able to deal for them in the market on normal terms. If, however, any of their operations is likely to have a significant effect on prices inimical to debt management policy at the time, it may be preferable to keep the transaction wholly within the official group; the deal will then be done between the National Debt Office and the Bank, at current market prices but without effect in the market. In this way the National Debt Office are at all normal times able to manage the funds for which they are responsible without subordinating their decisions to tactical considerations of debt management. But they also stand ready to vary holdings in the interests of debt management policy, where to do so is not prejudicial to their other interests.

The Issue Department has resources of nearly £3,000 million invested in government securities, a large part of which is invested in marketable gilt-edged stocks; this provides the means for dealing in the market in whatever way seems most likely to help achieve the current aims of debt management. With such a *masse de manœuvre* in their hands, it would be possible for the Bank to intervene vigorously in the market, taking the initiative in dealing and instructing the Government Broker to sell or buy specific amounts of stocks at the best prices he could get. In normal official dealings, however, the Bank leave it to the jobbers in the market to take the initiative; the Bank offer stock—when they have it to offer—in response to bids made by the jobbers to the Government Broker, and bid for stock, if conditions justify doing so, when it is offered by the jobbers through the Government Broker. In this way they stand behind the jobbers in the gilt-edged market—acting as the jobbers' jobber, or a jobber of last resort. Though the Bank give no formal commitment to buy or sell when asked, they are in fact normally willing to do so at prices of their own choosing. They thereby give the market a very much greater capacity to meet the needs of investors than the jobbers' own books would provide. The choice of this method of dealing rests on a judgment that it broadens the market, increases its activity, enhances its appeal to institutions with large sums to invest, and in the long run increases their desire to hold government stocks, and that the alternative method would strike investors as being more arbitrary and capricious and would therefore make them reluctant to commit themselves to the same extent in the gilt-edged market.

The Bank's role in these dealings is nevertheless not a passive one. Although they deal in the market only in response to offers originating there, they pursue an active policy in the great majority of cases through their choice of the prices at which they are prepared to respond. Moreover, the Bank's continuous presence in the market, not seeking business but normally willing to deal at prices reflecting official policy, and in practice dealing almost every day and often in substantial quantities, provides ample opportunity for seeking to influence prices, even on the minority of days when supply of stock is roughly in balance with demand. This close involvement in the daily turnover of an active market both enables the Bank to pursue their aims continuously and without undue attention being drawn to individual transactions and gives the Bank a useful degree of flexibility when they are seeking occasions for implementing a shift of policy on prices. It is worth mentioning that not only is the identity of the Government Broker well known throughout the market, but all official bargains are done by him and there is seldom any doubt as to whether or not he is dealing for one or other of the official funds. The prices he bids in response to an offer are therefore seen as the expression of the Bank's current policy, and are closely watched by the jobbers for any sign of a change of emphasis in the policy, such as might lead the market to expect new movements in prices.

New issues   Because the gilt-edged market is so largely made by the financial institutions, and because these institutions fall into fairly homogeneous groups with broadly similar investment preferences, new issues do not need to be made in great variety. There are at present just under fifty gilt-edged stocks for investors to choose from; new interest in the market and increased demand from the institutions can usually be encouraged, and can then be satisfied, by making a small number of relatively large new issues, which in each case will probably be sufficient to meet the demand from investors for some months to come. These are the 'tap' stocks which the Issue Department, having taken up the unsubscribed balance at the time of issue, gradually sells as public demand develops. When a new stock is issued, and becomes available on tap, many investors who have had their funds invested in other stocks will decide, because the price is attractive or for some other reason, that the new stock is more suitable for their portfolios, and they will therefore wish to switch out of other stocks into the new one. The jobbers will probably be able to facilitate many of the switches, by taking the stocks offered on to their own books until they are able to resell them. Where these are shorter-dated than the tap stock for which they are being exchanged, the Bank will generally be willing to facilitate the switch by themselves taking the shorter-dated stocks from the jobbers, if the jobbers so wish, in exchange for the tap stock; in this way the Bank may ease the pressure on the jobbers' stock holdings that is caused when large-scale switching is taking place into a stock available through the tap.

Redemptions   The redemption of maturing stocks, if they were always firmly held by investors to the last, would be likely to cause considerable disturbance, both in the money market—as most of the cash paid out sought employment—and in particular in the gilt-edged market as the investors receiving the money took steps to reinvest it. Fortunately, not all investors are equally attracted by the prospect of being repaid in cash on the redemption date. The Bank therefore stand ready, as a stock approaches maturity, to buy it in when it is offered, usually at a price that gives, over the remaining life of the stock, the current rate on Treasury bills. This is a widely known practice; and many large investors find it convenient to sell their holdings on these terms, so that they can reinvest at times of their own choosing, rather than wait for the redemption proceeds at a time when many others may be moving in the same direction. It is quite usual for the Bank to acquire in this way three-quarters or more of the maturing stock; and most of these purchases will be matched one way or another by sales of other stocks by the Bank. The investor who sells the maturing stock may reinvest his money in a stock which the Bank do not at that time hold; but his purchase will bring a seller into the market and may initiate a sequence of switches, perhaps involving a number of investors and jobbers, and leading eventually to a purchase of a stock that can be met by a sale by the Bank. This is a very common form of switching which both appeals to the investors and suits the Bank.

Switching   Between these two special kinds of switching—into the new tap stocks or out of the next maturing stock—which together may amount to several hundred million pounds of stock over a period of a few months, there will be a variety of individually matched purchases and sales attractive to particular investors. An institutional holder of gilt-edged stocks, except where the lives of his assets are already closely matched to his liabilities, is likely to pursue a regular policy of exchanging shorter-dated for longer-dated stocks in order to push on the average life of his portfolio and offset the continual shortening that occurs with time. This alone gives rise to many substantial switches; and the Bank can often help this process along, with advantage to their own position, by being prepared to sell the longer-dated stocks, when the Issue Department has them to sell, against purchases of shorter-dated.

There are occasions, of course, when some investors are switching, not into longer-dated stocks, but into shorter-dated. This may be because a new stock with a shorter life than the one already held is seen by the investor to have greater attractions for him, such as, perhaps, a higher coupon, giving a higher running yield, or because he expects prices to move in a way that would make it advantageous to be invested for a time in shorter-dated stocks. Such switches are seldom much help to the Bank in managing the debt; on the contrary, if the counterpart is provided by the Bank, they would—unless later reversed—increase the weight of maturities for which refinance would have to be provided sooner rather than later. The Bank therefore normally do little or nothing to facilitate them; but if the pressure from investors is more than the jobbers between them can well support, so that there is a real risk of dealings becoming difficult, or if it appears likely that intervention will rapidly restore conditions more favourable to the execution of current policy, then the Bank may step in, but normally only at prices fully reflecting the disadvantage for the authorities of switches of this type.

Other switches are made attractive to particular investors by the differences in their liability to tax and the different effects of the tax laws as between one stock and another. A recent and particularly striking example of this has been the extensive switching provoked by the provision in the Finance Act 1965 that, as regards gilt-edged stocks issued before the Budget in 1965, capital gains taxes would not apply to gains or losses caused by price movements within the range between the lowest issue price and the redemption price.[1] Some gilt-edged stocks now outstanding were issued at or near par, and others were issued well below par; under the new provision this difference brings a new and quite significant factor into the calculation of yields.

Normally the Bank will provide a counterpart to switches of any of the kinds described where the investor is moving into longer-dated stocks than he already holds. These transactions will ordinarily be done at current market prices and will leave those prices unaffected. As already mentioned, the price at which the Bank will buy the next maturity is usually kept in line, in terms of yield, with the average price of Treasury bills at the tender. A new stock is issued at a price that is closely in line with market prices of other stocks; when it is put on sale by the Bank on the first day of dealings it is generally offered at a price fractionally above the issue price, so as not to undermine the position of those who applied for the stock at the time of issue. As demand for the stock grows and sales through the tap increase, and provided that other prices in the market are firm, the price of the tap stock can be moved upwards in steps; the steps are typically $\frac{1}{32}\%$ in a short-dated stock and $\frac{1}{8}\%$ in a medium or long-dated stock. But, if the market suffers a general weakening and prices of other stocks fall so far that the Bank's price for the tap stock becomes out of line with other prices, the tap price will not ordinarily be lowered immediately lest to do so should depress the market further. It is allowed to remain out of line until it seems that demand is capable of being restimulated, and is then reduced in a single step to bring it back into line with other prices.

The aims of debt management   The chief purpose of management of the gilt-edged market was stated above to be to strengthen the demand for government stocks. It is not immediately concerned with the day to day finance of the Exchequer's payments: as an earlier article has explained,[2] the machinery of the money market ensures that enough government debt is always taken up to provide for residual needs, and the Bank's techniques for managing that market smooth out the day to day irregularities. In the gilt-edged market the principal concern is to encourage the widest possible variety of investors, other than the banks, to increase their holdings, and to hold longer rather than shorter-dated stocks. These are essentially long-term aims; in the long run success will depend on investors' confidence in the market and this in turn will rest decisively on their experience of dealing in it.

The tactics used to attract and hold the interest of investors have already been described: to issue new stocks that are tailored to the current demands of large investors; to ensure that dealings do not become seriously inhibited by the absence of buyers to match sellers, or that the market does not become too volatile due to a preponderance of buyers unable to satisfy their demands for stock; to

---

[1] September 1965 *Bulletin*, page 221.
[2] "The management of money day by day"; March 1963 *Bulletin*, page 15. (Reprinted on page 107.)

spread the impact of the issue and redemption of large blocks of securities, and in particular to minimise the fortuitous disturbances, always less than welcome, that these give rise to in the market and in the banking system; and generally to slow down and moderate violent movements in the market unless there is likely to be a particular advantage in a rapid adjustment, as in the case of a change in Bank rate.

Other aims of debt management become important from time to time; and to keep down the cost of the Government's borrowing is important at all times. Of these additional aims the principal ones are, in normal times:

(i) to assist economic policy by promoting or sustaining the most appropriate pattern of interest rates; and

(ii) to assist credit policy, usually by increasing sales of government debt, so that the Government's needs can be met with less recourse to the banks, less addition to their liquid assets, and less scope, in consequence, for them to increase their lending.

These short-term aims are not, of course, alternatives but usually present themselves in combination. The actions on prices that they suggest can at times conflict, either between themselves or with actions that seem necessary to preserve the attractions of government stocks in the long run; and they cannot be pursued without regard to the danger of causing damage in the long run to the health and capacity of the market—a limitation that may sometimes preclude all but a fairly narrow choice of policies in the short term.

This can well be illustrated by the problems which arise when policy is judged to require interest rates to move upwards. Circumstances may sometimes allow an adjustment to be easily and smoothly achieved. A number of investors may read the economic scene as pointing towards higher interest rates. They may therefore enter the market as sellers and an insufficiency of buyers then leads to offerings of stock to the Bank which allow the Bank, by bidding at successively lower levels, to secure a drop in market prices of broadly the dimensions thought desirable. This drop may then prove sufficient to discourage other investors from selling, so that the market stabilises itself naturally at the new level.

At other times the process may be more difficult to achieve smoothly. The economic scene may not be read in such a way that a preponderance of sellers appears. Or, while there may be sellers, a first small downward movement in prices may be enough to cause them to hold off and the selling movement to come to an early end. In different circumstances a downward movement, once started, may feed upon itself and threaten to go much further than the authorities would desire, perhaps even to the extent of risking serious demoralisation of the market. Another possibility is that, perhaps because of outside circumstances or because investors take alarm at the pace of the adjustment, signs of demoralisation may appear at an early stage. In all these circumstances the Bank may, because of their overriding concern for the long-term health of the market, have to modify their tactics.

It is sometimes argued that in such circumstances the desired results could more often or more nearly be attained if the Bank regularly adopted a more positive line in their market dealings. For instance, they could take steps to initiate a downward movement in prices by themselves entering the market as determined sellers; or, if there were sellers already in the market, an adjustment to a desired new level of prices could be made more quickly, and so with the prospect of quicker recovery and an earlier reappearance of buyers in the market, if the Bank were to decline to buy stock until the level of prices was reached at which they hoped to see it settle.

One of the problems of applying such techniques is that of judging where this new level should be established. This can seldom, if ever, be clearly discerned at the outset, not least because it depends in substantial part on the reactions of investors as the market movement gets under way and on other changing circumstances and expectations. By remaining in the market the Bank can better judge, from market reactions to their offers, when a stabilising move should be developed. Another important consideration is that the pace of a decline in prices can build up very rapidly once expectations that it will continue have taken hold; if such expectations are further strengthened by the visible withdrawal of the Bank from the market, to arrest or retard the fall may in the end require a disproportionate amount of official support. Not only will additional liquidity then accrue to the banks, despite the probable desire at the time to restrain credit, but the authorities may also be led, in order to get the movement under control, to adopt so definite a stand as will seriously restrict their freedom of manœuvre in the period ahead. Finally, a market in which downward movements of prices is too abruptly initiated by selling by the Bank or, if originating elsewhere, is generally left unmoderated and then as abruptly halted by official intervention at some predetermined level, may come to be viewed by investors as arbitrary and unpredictable in its behaviour; there is then a danger that they would be seriously discouraged from investing their funds in it. The likely consequence would be that the capacity of the market would be permanently reduced and with it the ability of the Government to borrow at long term.

A change in Bank rate might at first sight appear to be in contradiction to this approach. But even here the change to a new basis of gilt-edged yields is substantially influenced both by the guidance given by the Bank in announcing the new Bank rate and by the new prices that the Bank subsequently quote for the tap stocks, or bid for any stock that may be offered to them.

The opposite case, in which policy aims to encourage a rise in prices and a fall in interest rates, can present almost as many problems. It is more obviously true in this case that an attempt by the Bank to induce a movement is unlikely to succeed, without inordinate expenditure on the purchase of stock, unless investors generally hold the view that the movement is justified by the state of the economy, or by some development such as a substantial reduction in the amount of borrowing in prospect for the Exchequer. But it is also true that the Bank can, when conditions are right, stimulate the market's appetite for stock by selling at gently rising prices; and once the market has come to expect an upward movement, it may absorb very considerable quantities of stock and yet bid prices further upward in the market. In this case, too, it is important that the movement should not gather too much momentum or go too far, because once a rise is judged to have become excessive the reaction of the market is likely to be abrupt and damaging to investors' portfolios, and in the end is probably harmful to their confidence in the gilt-edged market. But if the Bank are to moderate a rise in prices which the market is convinced, at least for the moment, will go further, they must sell stock to meet the demand, whatever level it may reach; and these heavy sales could be as little in tune with credit policy at the time as the purchase of stock is at times of credit restriction.

Conclusion The examples given above by no means exhaust the possible variations, in policy and in market behaviour, with which debt management may be faced. The market is dominated for most of the time by its own expectations of future movements in prices, or occasionally by its uncertainty and nervousness about the future. The market's expectations about the prices that the Bank will quote in future official dealings are an important factor in its assessment, but not one that in the end carries greater weight than the balance of supply and demand among the holders of the £14,500 million of stock in the hands of the general public. This is a market in which, however, total supply is highly elastic and responsive even in the short run, both because there are normally tap stocks available for purchase by the market, and because the Bank are normally willing bidders, even if only at prices that discourage the sellers, when stock is offered. Variations in demand in the market are therefore likely to lead to variations in supply at unchanged or only slowly changing prices, rather than to immediate variations in prices big enough to bring demand back into balance at nearly the same level of supply. Policy on interest rates can, and in all the circumstances must, concentrate largely on fostering demand, in the future as well as in the present.

With the demand for gilt-edged stocks so fully satisfied, a shift in the holders' expectations can quickly give rise to a strong tide in dealings that may owe nothing to any stimulus from the Bank, for there are many other factors contributing to the market's views and expectations, or causing it to be uncertain. It is hardly surprising therefore that the business of debt management is less often a matter of stimulating a movement than of retarding one that is gathering momentum, or moderating the more exaggerated day to day fluctuations that occur when markets are thin or nervous. And even in this limited field of action, the fundamental forces of the market are usually too strong to be contained or diverted for long. Thus the daily concern of debt management is usually to steady the market without opposing it too rigidly, but always within the context of its aims for interest rate and credit policy and for the maximisation of demand for British government debt.

Competition and credit control: extract from a lecture by the Chief Cashier of the Bank of England

The text of part of a Sykes Memorial Lecture given by the Chief Cashier to the Institute of Bankers, 10, Lombard Street, London EC3 on 10 November 1971.

... First, the gilt-edged market; as you will know, last May at the time of the publication of *Competition and credit control*, the Bank announced and put into effect a modification of the extent of their operations in the gilt-edged market. This was no simple decision, representing as it did a substantial change in the basis upon which dealings in the gilt-edged market had taken place for some years.

To put this decision into perspective, it is necessary to review briefly the origin and development of the Bank's place in the gilt-edged market. In origin, the Bank deal in the gilt-edged market in discharge of their function of banker and issuing house to government. In this capacity, the Bank are concerned with the issue of securities, both short and long-term, to finance the needs of government whether these arise from its current financial position or from the maturity of existing debt. Thus, the Bank first entered the gilt-edged market in order to improve the efficiency and smoothness with which they discharge this function, selling one or two new securities and buying in those approaching maturity. Gradually the Bank became willing to deal in a wider range of securities because by so doing it appeared possible to improve the effectiveness of their operations. At the same time, in the late 1950s and early 1960s, smoothing out the fluctuations in interest rates which market forces tended to bring about had come to seem an appropriate objective. Both these considerations worked together to lead the Bank to a position in which they were prepared, at prices of their own choosing, to deal in the whole range of British government securities in the market.

The changes to these arrangements introduced last May were based on three considerations: the effectiveness of monetary policy, the health of the market and the need to preserve the Bank's ability to finance and refinance the needs of government.

The first change, as stated in the document *Competition and credit control*, was that the Bank were no longer prepared to respond to requests to buy stock outright except in the case of stocks with one year or less to run to maturity. This change was intended—I quote—to 'help to limit, further than can be achieved solely by alterations in the Bank's dealing prices, fluctuations in the resources of the banking system arising from official operations in the gilt-edged market.' Some time before the reappraisal of monetary policy which led up to *Competition and credit control* had been completed, the conclusion had been reached that the Bank's operations in the gilt-edged market should pay more regard to their quantitative effects on the monetary aggregates and less regard to the behaviour of interest rates. In application of this conclusion, the Bank's tactics in the gilt-edged market became much more flexible in respect of both the techniques they employed and the prices at which they were prepared to deal. But, for the effectiveness of the new arrangements this did not go far enough. So long as monetary policy was closely concerned with the total of bank lending, the banking system's operations in the gilt-edged market were not of critical importance for monetary policy. Under the new arrangements the ability of banks—and others—to deal in large quantities of stock at moments of their own choosing at prices not far removed from those ruling in the market at the time would clearly be unacceptable.

By implication this part of the change made last May was designed to help the effectiveness of a restrictive monetary policy. But any modification to existing arrangements to be complete had also to provide for the implementation of an easy monetary policy under which it might come to be appropriate for expansionary open-market operations to be engaged in. For this reason the Bank reserve the right to make outright purchases of stock with more than a year to run at their discretion and initiative.

The limitation on the extent of the Bank's operations was also addressed to the health of the market. The extension of the Bank's operations to which I have already referred was in part inspired by a developing inadequacy in the resources of the market in relation to the volume of business; that is to say, the Bank extended their operations because they thought that otherwise the marketability of gilt-edged securities, which is one of their principal attractions, would be unduly impaired to the disadvantage of government financing and refinancing. In retrospect, this decision itself probably contributed to the attrition of the market's resources. So long as the Bank were prepared in effect to put substantial resources into ensuring the marketability of gilt-edged, there was no particular reason why others should do so. Furthermore, and especially with the advent of greater flexibility in pricing on the part of the Bank, a market dominated by a dealer with resources far and away beyond those which any other single dealer could possibly command was not one likely to be attractive to newcomers. Also, it is the essence of a market that there should be a variety of views among operators of similar size. The Bank's close presence in the market often meant that in practice there were only two views—those of the Bank and those of everybody else. This situation gave rise to very large speculative transactions and made the speculative management of portfolios altogether too easy. We thus sought to make room in the market for others to operate in more realistic conditions. It is as yet too soon to judge whether or not this objective has been achieved but I have reason to think that we have already made some progress towards it.

Finally, the changes of last May leave intact the system of continuous financing and refinancing of the central government. Alternatives to this system can be conceived but none seems likely to be so effective. The Bank thus continue to be buyers of near-maturing stock, sellers of tap stocks and to engage in switching transactions which help this process and help investors to maintain the length of their portfolios as time elapses.

The second domestic market with which the Bank are concerned is the money market and, most directly, that part of the money market which deals in short-term debt of the central government, for here too we are concerned both as an issuing house and as an executant of monetary policy. In framing the proposals in *Competition and credit control* it seemed to us that our objectives could be met without structural change because, despite what the critics may say, that structure serves the interested parties very satisfactorily. Thus, although the discount market's agreements among themselves and with the banks on Treasury bill prices and money rates would go, along with the banks' agreements on interest rates, it seemed desirable and possible to maintain the discount market's rôle in underwriting the Treasury bill tender and as the channel through which our influence on short-term rates of interest was exerted. Thus we concluded the agreements with the London Discount Market Association described in the paper *Reserve ratios and special deposits*.[1]

The structure thus remains basically unchanged, but modifications to our techniques have already taken place and further change will be considered as and when necessary. The first change is that the Bank are now free to determine day by day the prices at which they are prepared to deal in Treasury bills. Up to the middle of September, the discount market agreed prices among themselves not only for the tender each week but also for subsequent dealings in long bills in the market. Consistently with this agreement, the Bank themselves dealt in line with the market's prices for Treasury bills and influenced changes in those prices by acting so as to bring about a change in the price at each tender, notably by requiring the market to borrow at a penal rate. It has yet to be decided how far the Bank would be prepared to make use of this new-found flexibility and what therefore might be the implications for the rôle of Bank rate. The second change of technique, which arises only in part from the new arrangements, is the extension to the discount market of limited borrowing facilities which each house may use at its own discretion for the management of its portfolio—a change which in part restores a position that used to prevail. These facilities are intended to give houses time—but strictly limited time—for adjustment if fluctuations in short-term interest rates become more frequent and larger than recently; and to make a clear distinction between the use of last resort facilities for this purpose and borrowing forced on the market by the Bank, whether in the interests of smoothing out large fluctuations in money flows or as an act of monetary policy.

I now turn to the arrangements made with banks and finance houses. I shall confine myself to certain important matters: the next issue of the Bank's *Quarterly Bulletin* will include an article explaining these arrangements in some detail.[2] First, in any arrangement intended to give the central bank influence over monetary conditions, there is a problem where to draw the line across the field of financial intermediaries so as to separate those who can appropriately and effectively be influenced by the actions of the central bank and those who cannot. So long as the technique of credit control was the requests made by the Bank of England for the observance of quantitative limits on lending, the drawing of such a dividing line gave rise to considerable difficulties for there were always some institutions who did not appropriately come within the purview of the central bank but whose lending activities were only marginally different from those which did. The essential difficulty was that of maintaining equity between those to whom requests were addressed and those to whom they were not.

In the new approach, as I have already said, the essence is a generalised influence on credit conditions through variations of interest rates. In the context of such a system, a clear distinction can be drawn between on the one hand those institutions who finance their activities to a significant extent by taking deposits from the public and those who do not. The former group have a capacity to compete for funds which is not available to the latter. Furthermore, the influence of the Bank is capable of being backed up by the provisions of the Bank of England Act 1946. As you will be aware, the terms of that Act which could be used for the purpose of monetary policy relate only to banking undertakings. Now there is, of course, and has been, room for argument about what constitutes a banking undertaking. But it is eminently clear that an institution not taking deposits is not a banking undertaking. Thus, although there may be room for doubt as to whether or not certain deposit-takers are banking undertakings, confining the provisions for reserve assets and special deposits to deposit-taking institutions is not only appropriate but also justified on grounds of efficacy, although I by no means intend to suggest that the use of the provisions of the Bank Act is contemplated.

The arrangements made with banks and deposit-taking finance houses are intended to ensure the responsiveness of those institutions to modifications of policy. For this purpose it appeared not possible for the authorities to rely on the voluntary observance of ratios which banks and finance houses habitually maintain for reasons of commercial prudence for two reasons. First, the dictates of commercial prudence are by no means immutable. A ratio that seemed appropriate at one

[1] Issued as a supplement to the September 1971 *Bulletin*.
[2] See page 482 of the December 1971 *Bulletin*.

point in time could well change with circumstances and change appreciably. The impact of monetary policy whether conducted through market operations or through the use of special deposits would therefore be uncertain and the degree of uncertainty appeared to be capable of being too great to be acceptable. Secondly, the composition of the liquid assets held for reasons of commercial prudence might also change. In particular, individual deposit-takers might substitute claims on the private sector for claims on the public sector thus once again introducing an uncertainty as to the impact of acts of monetary policy.

Having decided that for the sake of the effectiveness of monetary policy deposit-takers must be required to observe a minimum holding of liquid assets, it does not necessarily follow that the ratio should be the same for all. The diversity of the deposit-taking institutions in this country is well known and as well known to the Bank as to anyone else. It can fairly be argued that the volume of liquid assets needed by one institution or one set of institutions is significantly different from that needed by others. The cash deposits scheme negotiated in early 1968 but never implemented sought to recognise this diversity in full. It did so by relying for its effectiveness on the possibility of cash deposits bearing a low or nil rate of interest rather than on the pressure which a call for cash deposits could have exerted on holdings of liquid assets. But the application of such a penalty requires that those who may be liable to it should be told of the action they need to take in order to avoid it. Such guidance would most likely be indistinguishable from the system of quantitative rationing which the new approach was designed to replace. In the new arrangements recognition of diversity without slipping back towards ceilings would have meant for the Bank a type of handicapping exercise involving putting weights on each of the horses at the start of the race and being prepared to change those weights as circumstances and fortunes altered. This would have been inappropriate, indeed absurd, and, I would think, unwelcome to the horses. Also, examination of recent practice suggested that the adjustments which uniformity would require of banks were not very large. For these reasons it was decided that the ratio should be the same for all deposit-taking institutions except the deposit-taking finance houses which do not achieve full recognition as banks . . .

The gilt-edged market

The principles on which the marketing and management of marketable government debt other than Treasury bills (gilt-edged stocks) are at present based have been long established and may be summarised as follows.

- Investors and traders are free to determine the size and composition of their gilt-edged portfolios in the light of their own assessment of current and prospective economic and financial conditions, and of the prices and yields determined by a market made in the stock exchange by jobbers.
- The Bank deals or is prepared to deal continuously in this market within a well-defined and well-known framework, an essential element of which is that the Bank operates at prices close to those determined by the general body of transactions in the market.
- The Bank issues periodically on behalf of the Government new stocks which normally are intended to replenish the portfolio which is available for market operations, although recently some issues have been fully or nearly fully subscribed on application. The terms of new issues too are pitched so as to offer yields very close to those prevailing in the market at the time of the announcement of the issue.

An article in the June 1966 *Bulletin*[1] described the objectives and techniques of the Bank's management of the gilt-edged market within the above framework. The present article describes subsequent changes in those objectives and the consequent adaptation of techniques and instruments, and considers, against that background, a number of proposals for further change that have been the subject of recent public discussion.

The evolution of objectives and techniques

In the 1966 article, the main objective of gilt-edged management was stated to be to maximise the long-run desire of investors at home and abroad to hold British government debt. This main objective followed from the Government's continuing need for large amounts of long-term finance both to meet its current borrowing requirement (at that time for new capital investment by the public sector) and to replace maturing debt. Other aims of gilt-edged management which were seen as important from time to time were to assist economic policy by promoting or sustaining the most appropriate pattern of interest rates, and to assist credit policy by limiting government borrowing from the banking system. These two aims were regarded as shorter-term and were clearly subsidiary to the longer-run aim of preserving the attraction of government stocks and sustaining the health and capacity of the market.

This concern to maintain the longer-run, structural health of the market has remained an important objective of gilt-edged management. Since 1966, however, as the main emphasis of monetary policy has shifted to controlling the trend in the growth of the money supply (and in particular, in recent years, the growth of sterling M_3), the raising of government finance from domestic investors outside the banking system has become an increasingly important shorter-term objective of gilt-edged market management. This change of emphasis came about by stages and was accompanied by adaptations of the Bank's operating techniques.

In 1966, the principal quantitative objective of monetary policy was limitation of the growth of bank lending in sterling to the domestic private sector, and the principal method of achieving that objective was quantitative rationing. The short-term development of bank lending to the public sector was not a principal consideration. Finance for the Government could be obtained as necessary from the banking system—through the tender for Treasury bills and the Bank's financing operations in the money market—and this left

Net official sales of gilt-edged stock

£ millions

	Total net official sales(+)	Purchased by:							
		Other public sector	Banking sector	Non-bank private sector					Overseas sector
				Savings banks	Insurance companies and pension funds	Other financial institutions	Industrial and commercial companies	Persons (residual)	
1972	− 519	− 1	−1,114	193	305	− 68	16	− 23	173
1973	1,543	− 13	− 35	113	509	79	39	735	116
1974	664	− 29	− 146	− 4	201	97	− 39	603	− 19
1975	5,208	− 5	812	31	2,503	776	92	1,005	− 6
1976	5,399	4	68	270	2,976	84	123	1,744	130
1977	7,293	2	708	579	3,346	764	88	822	984
1978	5,052	108	− 60	519	3,958	310	− 2	319	−100
Total	**24,640**	**66**	**233**	**1,701**	**13,798**	**2,042**	**317**	**5,205**	**1,278**

[1] Reprinted on page 107.

a degree of flexibility over the timing of government funding in the gilt-edged market, which allowed the Bank, consistently with, and indeed in pursuit of, its main aim of strengthening demand for government stocks in the longer term, to seek to moderate changes in yields arising from changes in market sentiment.

The essence of the technique of gilt-edged management employed at that time was summarised by the phrase 'jobber of last resort'. Thus the Bank was prepared to deal in gilt-edged stocks of all maturities at prices close to the market level, prime considerations being to preserve the almost unlimited marketability of gilt-edged stocks and, to that end, to limit the pressures experienced from time to time by the gilt-edged jobbers. This technique did not and could not preclude, as a part of interest-rate policy, changes in prices and yields in response to market developments, but it was considered that sharp changes, other than any that might be consequent on a change in Bank rate, would be likely to be disruptive to the market and liable to impair the demand for gilt-edged stocks over the longer term.

Starting in 1968, more importance came to be attached to a wider quantitative aggregate than bank lending as a target for the conduct of monetary policy. In 1968 and 1969, in agreement with the International Monetary Fund, quantitative limits were set for domestic credit expansion (DCE). This step was of limited importance for the management of the gilt-edged market, however, partly because the Government's requirement for finance was quite small at that time and partly because it was not then regarded as a lasting change in the objectives of monetary policy. The basic technique described above remained unchanged but the Bank, while still concerned to avoid disruptive volatility in the market, tended to move more quickly the prices at which it was prepared to deal.

A more significant step was taken in 1971 when direct quantitative control of bank lending was abandoned, and the arrangements for credit control were modified, with the broader aim of regulating the growth of the money supply, principally by variations in interest rates. This new emphasis on the money supply, rather than on interest rates *per se*, as the immediate goal of monetary policy has been carried further since, leading to the public announcement, from 1976, of quantitative targets for the growth of a particular monetary aggregate—sterling M_3 in the last two years—for periods of twelve months ahead.

In May 1971, preparatory to the change in credit control arrangements which took place the following September, the extent of the Bank's operations in the gilt-edged market was modified; and the Bank's position in relation to the market was codified as follows.

- The Bank is not prepared, as a general rule, to buy stock outright except in the case of stocks with one year or less to run to maturity.
- It reserves the right to make outright purchases of stock with more than a year to run solely at its discretion and initiative.
- It is prepared to undertake, at prices of its own choosing, exchanges of stock with the market except those which unduly shorten the life of the debt.
- It is prepared to respond to bids for the sale to the market of tap stocks and of such other stocks held by the Bank as it may wish to sell.

This remains the framework of the Bank's operations.

These adaptations of technique were primarily intended to improve the effectiveness of monetary control. It was clear that the ability of banks and other investors to sell to the Bank large quantities of stock at moments of their own choosing, at prices not far removed from those ruling in the market at the time, was incompatible with monetary policy in its modified form. The principal change was therefore that the Bank ceased to be prepared to respond to requests to buy stock outright, except in the case of stocks with one year or less to run to maturity.

Inevitably this change implied greater short-term fluctuations in gilt-edged prices and some reduction in marketability. It was not felt, however, that the longer-term health of the market need suffer in consequence. It had become clear by 1971 that the Bank's willingness to deal at prices close to the market level allowed speculation too large and too easy a rôle in the management of portfolios; it often meant that in practice the Bank provided the counterpart to dealings by the rest of the market. The curtailment of the Bank's operations therefore made room in the market for others to operate in more realistic conditions.

Nevertheless, tension for gilt-edged market management can arise between the objectives of shorter-term monetary control and of sustaining the longer-term health of the market. And this tension became more marked during the 1970s as the emphasis on control of the broader money supply increased.

The choice of the broader monetary aggregates, DCE and sterling M_3, as the immediate target for monetary policy has tended to concentrate attention on the rôle of gilt-edged market management in implementing monetary policy, in a way that has become increasingly evident. An important characteristic of such broader aggregates—which does not apply to narrower measures of the money supply such as M_1—is that they can be closely analysed, in an accounting sense, in terms of their credit counterparts. Properly interpreted, and allowing for the inter-relationship between the counterparts, this has the considerable advantage that it can help in understanding the factors contributing to monetary growth. It highlights the extent to which the public sector borrowing requirement (PSBR)—and, indeed, other sources of monetary growth such as bank lending to the private sector or inflows from abroad—are offset by sales of government debt, and more particularly of gilt-edged stocks, to domestic investors outside the banking system. This direct accounting link between the gilt-edged market and the behaviour of the broader money supply, month by month, means that the extent to which the momentum of official sales of stock is being maintained has assumed much more significance—both for the authorities and for the general public—as an indicator of how far monetary policy is succeeding in its quantitative objective than was the case when the link was seen to be with the liquidity of the banking system.

This development has occurred against the background of a sharply higher government borrowing requirement and of a higher and more variable rate of inflation. In the eight years to 1970, the PSBR averaged a little over £¾ billion (2% of GDP at current market prices). Since then, it has averaged £6 billion (6% of GDP), with a peak of over £10½ billion (10¼% of GDP) in 1975. This huge expansion of government borrowing took place during a period in which not only the rate of inflation but also its variability from year to year increased sharply. In the eight years to 1970, inflation—measured by the increase in the monthly retail price index over the previous twelve months—averaged 4%, ranging from under 1% to 8%; in the eight years since then inflation has averaged just over 13%, ranging from 7½% to 27%. Nominal interest rates have naturally been not only higher but also more volatile as a result, and this volatility, and the associated volatility of expectations about the future rate of inflation, have greatly added to the problems of gilt-edged market management.

Public sector borrowing requirement and purchases of gilt-edged stock by non-bank private sector

[Chart showing Public sector borrowing requirement and Non-bank purchases of gilt-edged stock, £ millions, from 1963/64 to 1976/77, scale 0 to 12,000]

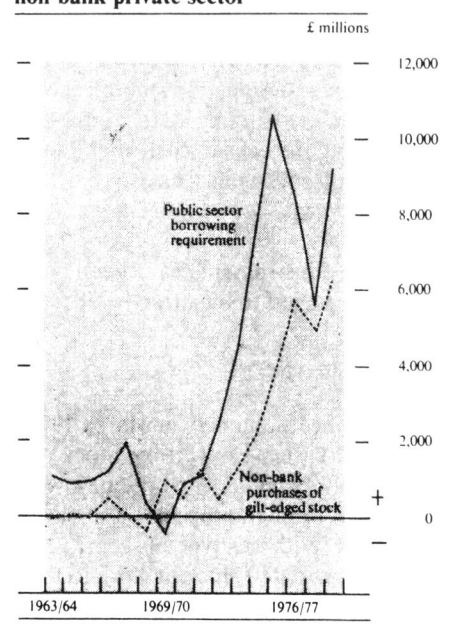

Despite the unfavourable background, management of the gilt-edged market on the basis described above has proved capable of raising finance for the Government on a very large scale indeed over a prolonged period, as is shown in the accompanying chart. And this has helped to contain the trend in the growth of the money supply in the last five years to a rate that has been generally consistent with official policy objectives. Thus, sterling M_3 increased at a rate of around 10% in most calendar years since 1974, which has been well below the rate of growth of nominal national income. This has not been without a cost in terms of high nominal interest rates. Inflation, and the scale of government borrowing, have necessitated high nominal yields, which—given the uncertainties regarding the future rate of inflation—have largely excluded potential private borrowers on fixed-interest terms from the capital market.

Adaptations to deal with the effect of uncertainty

Government finance on this scale involves continuous borrowing. From time to time, however, investors may lack confidence in the outlook, for example in respect of wage demands and industrial disturbance and their implications for future inflation, and in the economic and financial policies being pursued. Some uncertainty and risk are of course always present, and it is for investors and their advisers to assess them. At times, the uncertainties are such that investors cannot be confident that the level of interest rates will not rise, and hence do not feel justified in committing the funds they manage—generally in the interest of others—to investment in fixed-interest securities at that time. Sometimes the extent of uncertainty may be such that some investors are disposed to sell their existing holdings of gilt-edged stocks, keeping the proceeds liquid, and this, within the framework of the Bank's operations described earlier, is allowed to bring about whatever rise in yields may arise from market transactions. Once such an adjustment is completed—and how long that takes will depend upon the degree of uncertainty and the range of investors affected by it—the Bank is then able to resume the Government's funding programme on the higher yield basis. But at other times, perhaps when it is less clear which way a situation will develop, investors generally may lack the conviction to sell their existing holdings but still decide to keep their accruing funds in liquid form. In such situations, while prices in the gilt-edged market may remain relatively stable for some time, turnover contracts, and the market effectively becomes immobilised until the way ahead becomes clearer.

The principal effect of such periods of uncertainty, given the present emphasis of monetary policy on controlling the behaviour of sterling M_3, is to interrupt the contribution which sales of gilt-edged stocks outside the banking system make to that control. It should be noted, however, that the other factors affecting the growth of sterling M_3 are also subject to similarly large and erratic short-term fluctuations: the PSBR, the growth of bank lending, and the impact of external transactions can all vary from month to month by amounts which are very large in relation to the average monthly increase in the money supply that is consistent with the monetary target. And such variations are predictable—even for just a short period ahead—only with large margins of error. The short-term interruption

Variability of the main credit counterparts of the money stock (sterling M$_3$)[a]

£ millions: *seasonally adjusted*

	Financial years[b]			
	1975/76	1976/77	1977/78	1978/79
Central government borrowing requirement	490	260	440	700
Other public sector	70	200	220	350
Purchases of gilt-edged stock by non-bank private sector	520	650	530	480
Sterling lending to the private sector	120	260	250	310
External finance	240	370	450	360
Money stock (sterling M$_3$)	420	490	280	580

[a] The table shows root mean squares of first differences which indicate the general magnitude of month-to-month changes for each year.
[b] Banking May to banking April, except for 1975/76 where the figures are for banking July 1975 to banking April 1976.

of the flow of official gilt-edged sales is therefore not the only reason why there may from time to time be random month-to-month fluctuations in the growth of the money supply; and even if a more regular flow of sales could be achieved, this would not in itself be enough to remove such fluctuations arising from other factors.

The purely temporary divergence of the growth of the particular target aggregate, sterling M$_3$, from the intended trend—whatever the origin of the divergence—is not in itself a cause for concern, in the sense that such erratic fluctuations are unlikely to have any significant effect either on the real economy or on inflation. This is more especially true when the origin of the divergence is a temporary interruption of the gilt-edged funding programme, since in this case the additional monetary balances which result are, in some large part, held by long-term investment institutions awaiting commitment in the capital market, and so are not in any direct sense available to finance transactions in goods and services. If, therefore, one could be confident in any particular case that a funding pause would indeed prove to be short-lived, the proper course would be simply to ride it out.

In practice, however, a central difficulty—for financial analysts generally, including investors in the gilt-edged market, no less than for the authorities—is to determine at the time whether an incipient divergence of sterling M$_3$ from the intended trend is merely erratic or whether it marks the beginning of an important acceleration of monetary growth in some more fundamental sense. Although, as noted above, interruption of official gilt-edged sales is not the only possible cause of short-term fluctuations in the growth of the money supply, any uncertainty on the part of investors in the gilt-edged market is likely in present circumstances to pose this question quite quickly. The size of the PSBR, and the continuous, heavy funding programme it involves, mean that if investors delay their purchases of gilt-edged stocks for only a month or two there is likely to be a noticeable upturn in the growth of sterling M$_3$. The authorities then have to assess—in the light of the causes of uncertainty and of other developments (including, for example, the behaviour of other aggregates, such as M$_1$, and particularly the non-interest-bearing element of M$_1$, which are much less directly affected from month to month by the timing of gilt-edged investment decisions)—the significance of this upturn and whether it is likely to continue. They may decide that the hesitation on the part of investors generally is well-founded and make policy changes; or they may decide that policy changes are not necessary. If, in either case, a sufficient body of investors remains unpersuaded, sterling M$_3$ will continue to grow above the required trend, and this can lead to more active selling in the gilt-edged market, until yields eventually rise to a point where investors come back into the market and the funding programme can be resumed.

In many cases, such a yield adjustment (or the policy action taken to forestall it) may be accepted in retrospect as having been necessary in the light of outside circumstances to maintain monetary control. But in other cases it may appear to have been part of a self-generating spiral, with the initial uncertainty causing an acceleration in sterling M$_3$ which in turn affects expectations about interest (and possibly exchange) rates, leading eventually to upward adjustments of yields which are in excess of those justified by the underlying situation and which may subsequently therefore be reversed. The danger of such unnecessary disturbance and interest-rate fluctuations would be reduced if a somewhat smoother pattern of sales of gilt-edged stocks to the non-bank private sector could be achieved in the first place.

Partly-paid stocks
Faced with this problem, the Treasury and Bank introduced an adaptation in their issue technique in March 1977 by providing for only part of the subscription money for a new issue to be paid at the time of application with the balance being payable in instalments timed by reference to the Government's expected funding need. This adaptation, which has been used with varying degrees of success on a number of subsequent occasions, was designed to smooth the flow of funds from outside the banking system into gilt-edged stocks by staging the calls to correspond with the expected funding requirements in successive banking months.

In addition, new gilt-edged instruments have been introduced which were designed to be attractive in conditions of uncertainty.

Convertible stocks
Even before the recent concern, namely in March 1973, a convertible stock, 9% Treasury Convertible Stock 1980, was issued, which offers holders an option, in 1980, to convert at predetermined terms into a stock maturing in the year 2000. With this type of security, investors are offered a short-dated stock at close to the current market yield for that maturity at the time of issue, with an option to convert at a later date into longer-dated stock at a yield close to that prevailing for the longer maturity at the time when the convertible short-dated stock was issued. Such a security gives the investor the option of holding a short-dated stock to maturity, or, by exercising the conversion right, of moving into the long end of the market at a specified

later date (or dates) on terms which are known in advance and which may then no longer be available in the market. The attractiveness of a stock of this kind depends in part upon the relationship between short-term and long-term yields at the time of issue. The attractiveness of the conversion option in particular depends on investors' assessment of the likely course, beyond the immediate future, of long-term interest rates. If they judge that there is a good chance that long-term interest rates will be lower by the time the conversion option may be exercised, they will find the option attractive. To the extent that it does, in the event, produce an advantage to the investor, it will of course prove correspondingly expensive to the Government, although this risk may be worthwhile if it enables the momentum of the funding programme to be maintained without a rise in interest rates. There are a number of possible variations on this general theme.

Variable rate stocks

The second instrument designed to cater for conditions of uncertainty is the Treasury Variable Rate Stock, of which three issues have been made, maturing in 1981, 1982 and 1983. These stocks offer investors a degree of insurance against rising short-term interest rates, always provided that their market price is relatively stable. The insurance takes the form of six-monthly interest payments based on the average discount rate for Treasury bills over the preceding six months. At par, the interest rate payable is a half per cent over the Treasury bill discount rate, and for every one point discount on par the prospective capital gain to maturity effectively widens the margin over the Treasury bill rate, if the stock were held to redemption, by about a quarter per cent. In practice none of these stocks has traded at par, so that the effective margin over the Treasury bill discount rate has always been larger than a half per cent. The variable rate stocks have not yet, however, proved to be more than modestly attractive to investors outside the banking system as stocks to be held; they have not been very actively traded in the market, and, partly as a result, they have not perhaps so far enjoyed sufficient price stability. They have none

Prices of variable rate and other selected gilt-edged stocks

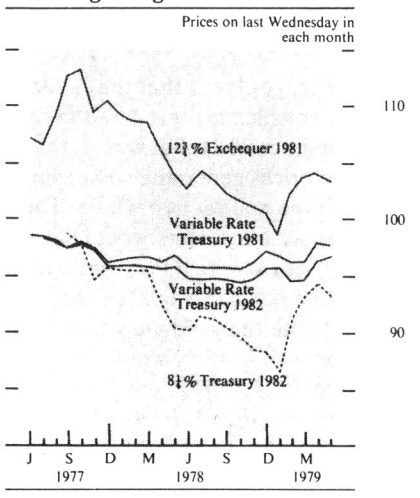

the less played some small part in smoothing the flow of funds to the Government, coming into demand when the outlook for interest rates seemed particularly uncertain and when official sales of conventional stocks were depressed, and being bought back by the Bank, against sales of conventional stocks, at other times. This rôle could grow with increasing market experience of the stocks. In the case of variable rate stocks, too, a number of variants are possible. One such variant that has already been adopted by a number of local authorities has the interest rate set half-yearly at a fixed margin above the six-month inter-bank deposit rate ruling at the beginning of each interest period, though these stocks too have yet to establish any significant market outside the banking system.

Some suggested possible further changes in technique and instruments

The adaptations so far described have not involved any departure from the established principles on which official management of the gilt-edged market has been based. It remains the case, however, that uncertainty among investors continues to cause occasional interruptions to the Government's funding programme. The rest of this article, therefore, considers a number of possible further changes—some more radical than others—which, it has been suggested, might be introduced to achieve a smoother path of official sales despite recurrent periods of uncertainty attributable to factors external to the gilt-edged market itself. These would involve changes, either of operating technique, or in the range of gilt-edged instruments.

A number of these changes could have significant implications for the structure of the gilt-edged market, and in particular for the market-making mechanism. Despite the developments since 1971 described above, a gilt-edged investor is still normally able to deal almost instantly at his own initiative in large amounts of stock of any maturity at—or at something very close to—a known market price; and this liquidity, provided by the gilt-edged jobbing system, remains an important element in the attraction of gilt-edged investment. It is difficult to avoid the conclusion that the present market-making mechanism would be seriously affected by some of the changes that have been advocated, but it is not easy to predict what alternative mechanism might emerge and how effective such an alternative might be. These questions are touched upon in the discussion that follows, but they would need to be very fully considered in a complete analysis of the proposals.

Changes in technique

In the area of technique, the changes that have been suggested fall into two main groups. The first group of suggestions would involve sharper changes in the prices and yields at which gilt-edged stocks are made available. The second group would involve some form of more direct relationship between the authorities and major investors through which the amounts, the timing and the terms of gilt-edged stocks to be taken up would be determined in advance.

Suggestions for greater flexibility in the price at which government stock is marketed are based on the proposition that a sufficient fall in the price at which the stock is obtainable will, in any surrounding circumstances and without any associated policy action, produce the required demand. In the Bank's judgment this proposition needs qualification, as is explained below.

These suggestions for greater price flexibility are of two kinds. The first relates to the prices at which the Bank markets stock out of its own portfolio through transactions on the stock exchange, where the initiative for varying the price would fall upon the Bank. The second relates to the method of public issue of government stocks, where proposals have been made for issues by tender (or auction) which, in this variant, would not be underwritten, and under which the variation in price would be determined entirely by the investors.

The pricing of tap stocks
At present, a new stock is normally issued at a price closely in line with the prices of other comparable stocks already in the market, and the amount of the stock not taken up by the public—usually a large proportion—is taken into the Bank's own portfolio, with the Bank acting in effect as an underwriter. If the market remains firm, this tap stock is subsequently sold by the Bank through the market at prices raised in fractional steps above the issue price. If, on the other hand, as a result of a change in conditions giving rise to uncertainty among investors, demand for the stock does not develop, the Bank does not immediately reduce the price at which it is known to be prepared to sell. Instead, the Bank waits until the market recovers or, if the market generally weakens, until the yield adjustment is completed and the market has stabilised, when the tap price will be lowered in a single step in response to bids from the market. This established practice provides assurance to investors who subscribe for stock on issue, or purchase it through the market soon afterwards, that, short of a general weakening in the market, their position will not be undermined by the Bank's supplies being subsequently made available at lower prices.

The main suggestion that has been made in relation to more flexible pricing of stocks from the Bank's own portfolio is that, in order to maintain the momentum of sales through periods of uncertainty caused by changes in outside circumstances, the Bank should be more willing to lower the tap price in one step, going beyond the fall in market prices generally, or in smaller steps, in line with the decline in the market, without necessarily waiting until the market yield adjustment is completed. A difficulty with this approach is that such behaviour, in the conditions of weakening confidence where it would be relevant, could tend to add to, rather than diminish, the uncertainties in the minds of investors.

If the Bank—as by far the largest seller in the market, and with earlier knowledge of some important developments likely to affect the market, such as imminent policy steps, statistics, etc.—had had to reduce its price once, why should it not do so again shortly thereafter? Given this evidence of official urgency to sell stock, investors might well conclude that, by waiting, they might obtain still higher yields. There could be a danger that prices in the market would move away from the Bank, simply falling further in response to each successive reduction of the official price of the tap stock. At some point one must presume that this process would stop, and that yields would reach a level at which investors were prepared to commit the required funds; but the increase in yields might need to be unnecessarily large in these conditions, and, in the case of the proposal for a single step change, it would be difficult to arrive at a reasoned judgment in advance as to the tap price which would ultimately need to be set. In these circumstances, it could, as a practical matter, become necessary to find other means of establishing an appropriate price, perhaps through tenders or through a process of negotiation with major investors, with the further implications discussed below.

The argument has been put that the authorities already act on prices in the gilt-edged market by changing minimum lending rate (MLR), and that shifts in the tap price would only differ in degree. But the difference in degree would be very considerable. Changes in MLR are made as a result of varying considerations, not necessarily immediately related to developments in the gilt-edged market, and their effect on gilt-edged prices is indirect and may be greater or smaller depending on the surrounding market circumstances. Furthermore, a change in the yield on a three-month bill from, for example, $9\frac{1}{2}\%$ to 10% changes its price by only one tenth of one percentage point, while to secure a similar change in the yield on a 20-year stock would require a change in price of about 5%. Such changes in price imposed unilaterally by the authorities would involve heavy capital losses which operators would be likely to regard as beyond the normal hazards of business; and the only defence for the market-makers against such behaviour on the part of the authorities would be to narrow the market drastically whenever such conduct appeared to be in prospect.

A modified version of this suggestion is that the Bank should lower the tap price at which it is prepared to sell during periods of a weakening market, but by less than the full extent of the fall in prices generally, so keeping the price a little way above the market as a whole. The intention would be that, because investors would have greater certainty as to the price at which they could re-enter the market, they would be encouraged to sell their holdings and so accelerate the yield adjustment. It would seem, however, that such a policy would in practice be almost indistinguishable from the previous suggestion, and that the Bank's price adjustments would have much the same effects upon market expectations.

More generally it has been suggested that the Bank's technique in pricing tap stocks is too easily predictable: investors, it is argued, can, if they are uncertain, postpone their purchases of stock in the knowledge that if prices should improve, they will not, while a tap stock is active, move ahead too rapidly so that the cost of delay is likely to be small. This argument sometimes prompts the suggestion that the Treasury and the Bank could price a new issue some way ahead of the market, or that the Bank could adjust its selling price of the tap stock upwards by larger amounts, so encouraging investors to accelerate their purchases in the immediate situation and weakening their complacency over the longer term. There are circumstances where, within generally rather narrow limits, this tactic can be—and indeed has been—used. But it can only be used where the Bank is reasonably confident that the surrounding conditions in fact justify an unusually sharp decline in yields and where this prospect is likely to carry conviction with investors. If used where the overall circumstances did not in fact justify a fall in yields to the extent implied by the pricing decision, the tactic would be likely to induce an otherwise unnecessary interruption of the funding programme as yields subsequently adjusted back to more appropriate levels. In a similar way, it has been suggested that the authorities should vary their tactics in introducing new stock issues, by periodically standing aside from the market, but this possibility has been largely precluded by the recent size of the funding programme, which has involved more or less continuous borrowing.

In considering these various proposals for a more active pricing policy, the Bank is conscious that a securities market cannot function satisfactorily if there is an operator in a position to exercise overwhelming influence who is liable to enter the market unpredictably both as to timing and behaviour. All of the proposals would—if carried very far—introduce an important new element of uncertainty into the determination of gilt-edged prices. This in turn would seriously impede the making of a market, in any size, in gilt-edged stocks—whether by jobbers, as at present, or under some different institutional arrangement. The restriction on marketability which could then result would tend to reduce one of the principal attractions of the gilt-edged market for investors, damaging its long-term capacity.

Tenders
A different kind of suggestion for achieving a smoother pattern of gilt-edged sales through greater price flexibility is for the adoption of a tender system for new issues. Again there are a number of possible variants, but a common element would involve the Government announcing from time to time the volume of securities it wanted to sell on particular dates, or in a given period, and then leaving it to investors to determine the price and yield at which they were prepared to buy it. As with the suggestion for a more active policy of lowering of the tap price, the object would be to enable the authorities to sell the amounts of stock expected to be required in any given period to achieve shorter-term control over the growth of sterling M_3, unhampered by interruptions in government funding arising from changes in outside circumstances. (This would of course still leave sterling M_3 subject to erratic short-run fluctuation arising from unpredicted variations in the other credit counterparts, as mentioned earlier.) The proposal may derive in part from the regular use of the tender technique for new issues of US government securities by the US Treasury. In considering it, however, one needs to bear in mind that there are substantial differences in the size and structure, and in the rôle, of the government bond market in the two countries.

In the United States, the $330 billion of government bonds outstanding are equivalent to only some 16% of GNP, whereas the £57 billion of gilt-edged stocks outstanding is equivalent to some 42% of GNP in this country. Although government borrowing has increased in the United States—as in the United Kingdom—in recent years, government bonds have not dominated the capital markets to the same extent: in 1977 government bonds absorbed only some 30% of the total funds raised in the US domestic capital market, whereas the comparable figure for the United Kingdom was nearly 90%. In the United States, too, government bonds are typically of much shorter maturity. They include a large proportion of two-year issues, and only about 16% have a life beyond eight years; whereas in this country gilt-edged stocks are rarely issued for less than four to five years, and some 60% are of more than eight years' maturity. This results in an average maturity of US government bond issues of about five years, compared with about twelve years for gilt-edged stocks in this country. Finally, the institutional arrangements in the two government bond markets differ: prices are made in the US market, for example, by dealers in government securities rather than through the stock exchange as in this country. Such differences suggest the need for considerable caution before one can conclude that arrangements found helpful in the United States would be similarly effective in the United Kingdom.

A major difference in the present context is that the US Treasury's debt management objectives are not the same as the present objectives of debt management in this country as described above. In particular, the US Treasury is not directly involved in the implementation of monetary policy and its use of the tender technique for new stock issues is not primarily directed to the achievement of short-term monetary control. In the United States, the main emphasis of monetary policy in recent years has been on controlling the narrower monetary aggregates, which the Federal Reserve authorities influence essentially through management of the level of short-term interest rates. There is consequently not the same direct link between government debt management and the chosen monetary target in the United States as there is here, and debt management policy can therefore be directed to a far greater degree to the narrower objective of providing finance for the Government at the lowest cost consistent with maintaining an appropriate maturity structure. In this context, the use of the tender technique would seem to be designed to deal with the difficulty that can at times arise with a fixed-price offering if market sentiment should change (in either direction) between the announcement of terms and subscription, rather than as a means of keeping up the volume of sales in circumstances of uncertainty without regard to the effect on market yields. On the contrary, in framing its programme of debt sales, the US Treasury pays considerable regard to the advice given by the Federal Reserve authorities, and by the main government securities dealers (who effectively underwrite the tenders and act as intermediaries in on-selling a large part of new issues to final investors) on the capacity of the market to absorb new issues—particularly of longer maturities—without an undue effect on market prices.

A form of tender technique, with a minimum tender price set in line with market yields at the time of announcement of the issue and designed to secure for the Government—through a lower borrowing cost—a part of the benefit from any sharp improvement in market sentiment between the announcement of terms and the date for subscription, was in fact adopted by the Treasury and the Bank for a new issue (12¼% Exchequer Stock 1999) in March 1979. This followed the uniquely heavy oversubscription, resulting from an abrupt reversal in market expectations about the future course of interest rates, of two stocks issued a month earlier. The use of the tender technique for this purpose, however, is basically different from its use to achieve greater short-term control over the growth of the money supply by ensuring the necessary volume of gilt-edged sales in any given period. If that were the objective, it would at times involve pressing ahead with an issue even in a market which was unsettled by outside conditions, and accepting the resulting yield; the objective would in such conditions be likely to be frustrated if there were a minimum tender price, unless it were set on a yield basis substantially higher than the prevailing market level. A change to this method of issue would not of itself help to diminish investors' uncertainties about the future, nor make it easier for them to make a judgment about the future course of yields, and hence about the yield at which they should commit any large volume of funds to long-term fixed-interest investment. Given that they would still have open to them the possibility of buying stock in the secondary market or—because of the continuous nature of the Government's borrowing need—of entering a subsequent tender, by which time the particular uncertainty might have lessened, they could, in uncertain conditions, continue to find it more prudent to stay short and wait. Investors would, therefore, not necessarily enter a tender even of this sort, in the required volume, at the times when it mattered. And to the extent that they did so, it would probably be at prices and yields that discounted an unfavourable outcome in those areas that were the source of uncertainty.

The effect of tenders of this second kind, in terms at least of short-term price volatility, might be somewhat similar to that of a more active policy of moving the official tap price, with similar longer-run implications for the capacity of the market. Used with the object of selling a predetermined volume of stock, the tender technique would have a further corollary. It would run counter to this objective for the Bank itself to enter the tender on any substantial scale; the Bank's own dealings in the market would, therefore, be curtailed and would no longer provide a reservoir for adjusting the level of sales to the level of investor demand as under the present tap arrangements. At the same time, as things stand at present, the gilt-edged jobbers do not have the resources to bid regularly at tenders in amounts that would enable them to assume this function. If the tenders were to be successful, therefore, given the present institutional arrangements in the United Kingdom, virtually all the stock offered would have to be taken up directly by investors—whatever the state of market confidence happened to be—with no large intermediary to cushion the impact on prices. In part, the gap left by the implied change in the Bank's rôle might be filled if the capacity of the present jobbers were to increase or if new intermediaries emerged, perhaps of the kind of short-term dealer in government securities that exists in the United States. Such a development would be unlikely to come about overnight, and the market in gilt-edged stocks could be severely affected in the meantime. But even in the longer term, the change in market structure and the greater short-term price volatility that could result from the tender technique—if used to achieve closer short-term monetary control—might well lead to both reduced marketability and a significant shortening of the maturity structure of government debt. In the conditions envisaged, market-makers might be prepared to run a sizable book in short-dated stocks, but they are less likely to be prepared to take in the longer maturities on the same scale because of the higher risks. Any development in this direction would involve a considerable change in the management of the government debt, in view of the already heavy burden of annual maturities that have to be refinanced.

Because of structural changes in the gilt-edged market that could result from a general shift to tenders, some commentators have alternatively suggested that tender issues might be made on occasion, at times of particular uncertainty rather than as the normal method of issue. This more modest step might still, however, have the disadvantage that it would tend to increase rather than diminish uncertainty. There would be the danger that once the tender technique had been used in the manner suggested, the possibility that it would be used again could damage confidence in a hesitant market on subsequent occasions: prospective buyers might be deterred from investing when they would otherwise have done so, by the fear that a subsequent tender would impose capital losses on them. Experimentation in this area is not, therefore, wholly straightforward.

A more direct relationship with the major investors
The suggestions for possible changes in technique discussed so far would maintain the traditional arms-

length nature of the relationship between the authorities and investors in gilt-edged stocks. An entirely different approach would involve a more direct relationship between the Government, as borrower, and major investors, for example, the larger pension funds and life assurance companies. Suggestions under this heading include:

- the negotiation of underwriting of government stock issues by the long-term investment institutions, rather than by the Bank as at present (whether such issues were on a fixed-price or tender basis); and
- the negotiation of direct placings of government stock with the institutions.

Purchases of gilt-edged stock by insurance companies and pension funds

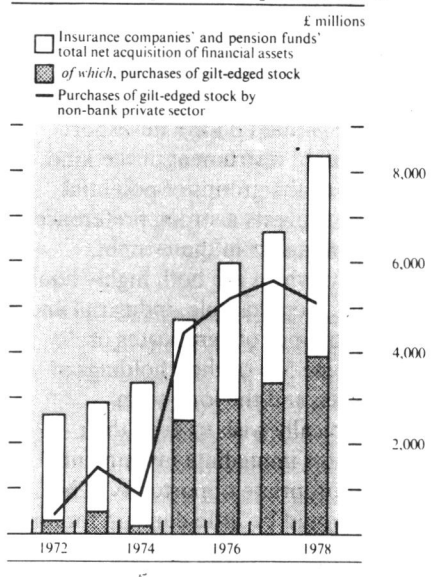

The rôle of the long-term investment institutions in the gilt-edged market has grown rapidly in recent years. Even so, these institutions do not generally account for more than about half of all net purchases of gilt-edged stocks by investors outside the banking system, and their combined holdings of gilt-edged stocks still amounted to only a third of the total nominal amount outstanding at the end of 1977. The institutions do not represent the small, tightly-knit grouping that is sometimes supposed: at the end of 1977 there were some 300 life assurance companies and over 2,000 pension funds in the United Kingdom, with over 100 institutions with assets of over £100 million accounting for two thirds to three quarters of the total long-term institutional investment. Thus, while suggestions of this kind might in principle be applied to a significant part of the Government's gilt-edged market borrowing, they would not of themselves provide a total solution to the funding problem.

A key question—as in the case of the proposal for tenders—is whether the suggested change in new issue technique would in itself make it easier for the long-term investment institutions to maintain their purchases of gilt-edged stocks through periods of uncertainty, without wide fluctuations in interest rates. Other things being equal, there is little reason to suppose that institutional investors would be willing to commit their funds—at times of uncertainty—to fixed-interest stocks offered by way of a placement where they were not prepared to buy the same stock offered by way of a public issue, unless they were given the inducement of a significantly higher yield. Nor is it clear that the institutions could prudently, in the interest of their pension fund members or insurance policyholders, take on the very considerable risks of loss that would be involved in the regular underwriting of government stock issues (which are at present underwritten by the Issue Department of the Bank) on anything like the recent scale, unless they were free to move the underwriting price quite widely to protect themselves in adverse conditions. While, therefore, it is possible to see how this approach could function in market conditions that were reasonably favourable—when the present technique is satisfactory—it is hard to see that arrangements of this sort could be freely negotiated in those conditions where they would be most helpful, without producing much the same effect of greater short-term price fluctuations that would result from the earlier suggestions.

Some suggestions for a more direct relationship between the authorities and major investors would go some way towards displacing a free market and would involve varying degrees of government influence over the decisions taken by the major investors. In the extreme this could extend to statutory direction. It is beyond the scope of this article to discuss the general arguments for and against such an extension of government influence. It is reasonable to assume, however, that the use of such influence would tend, in the first instance, to hold yields on gilt-edged stocks below the level that would otherwise be established in the market; and that this in turn would tend to reduce the attraction of investment in gilt-edged stocks to other investors not subject to similar influence or control. Though it might be possible to achieve in this way a smoother flow of investment in gilt-edged stocks by the major institutions, it would not necessarily follow that gilt-edged sales to the non-bank private sector as a whole would be more regular; nor perhaps that a higher overall volume of sales would be achieved.

The last three suggestions considered—for tenders; for negotiated underwriting of government issues by the institutions; and for some element of direction by the Government of the institutions' investment—have been discussed separately, as logically distinct proposals. In practice, however, this distinction could prove difficult to maintain. The pressures on the Government could tend to lead to a progressive development: in order to avoid the disturbance to interest rates that might be expected to result from the adoption of tenders, there would be a temptation to look for some underpinning of the tenders by institutional investors, and, in negotiating the terms of such underpinning, the Government would need to exercise considerable restraint if a free market was to be preserved. To this extent, therefore, the implications of the various proposals in these areas need to be looked at together.

New forms of gilt-edged instrument
Suggestions advanced for possible new types of gilt-edged stocks fall into two main groups. First, there have been various proposals for new short-term marketable government debt instruments, with maturities ranging from perhaps three months up to about two years. Secondly, some commentators have advocated the introduction of a marketable government stock indexed in some way against inflation.

Short-term instruments
The short-term instruments suggested are principally designed to attract into government debt institutional funds awaiting investment (including longer-term investment in the gilt-edged market) and some part of the liquid resources of industrial and commercial companies currently held with the banking system and so forming a part of the money supply. They could also appeal to personal investors, though in this area particularly they would compete with the range of (non-marketable) national savings instruments already offered by the Government.

At present, there are two marketable short-term central government debt instruments generally available to investors: Treasury bills and gilt-edged stocks approaching maturity. Both Treasury bills and gilt-edged stocks with less than one year to run to maturity are eligible reserve assets for the banking system. They consequently have a particular value to banks as compared with most other short-term assets with which they compete, and their yield, therefore, tends, on occasion, to be bid down to a level unattractive to investors outside the banking system. The suggestion has, therefore, been made that a new instrument could be issued which would not be an eligible reserve asset, and in relation to which—because of the short maturity—a more active pricing policy could be adopted without the implications such a policy would have if adopted in relation to the gilt-edged market generally.

Although there is no central government instrument of this kind available to the market, it is an area which is already quite heavily drawn upon by local authorities, through deposits, mortgages and negotiable bonds, none of which is eligible as a reserve asset. The total of such temporary local authority debt outstanding is around £4 billion, of which some £1½ billion is held by non-bank financial institutions and about £½ billion by industrial and commercial companies and persons taken together. If the central government raised additional funds from outside the banking system by marketing a new short-term instrument, it would be in competition with local authority short-term borrowing; this would tend to limit the net additional inflow of funds to the public sector as a whole.

It is difficult to establish how large a market, outside the banking system, there would be for a new short-term central government debt instrument of the kind proposed. The behaviour of the groups of potential investors identified above suggests a strong preference for holding their short-term assets in the form of conventional bank deposits which are both highly liquid and wholly capital-certain. For example, industrial and commercial companies' holdings of certificates of deposit amount to only some 5% of their holdings of conventional bank deposits; and the long-term investment institutions typically wish to keep their liquid resources available for immediate investment when they perceive an appropriate opportunity. This might suggest that there would be little demand for any short-term central government instrument that was not a close substitute for bank deposits. If the Government offered such a close substitute, this would not produce a meaningful reduction in the liquidity of the economy. If

Local authority short-term debt by type of holder[a]

£ millions: *amounts outstanding at end-year*

	Total	Banking sector	Building societies	Insurance companies	Other financial institutions	Industrial and commercial companies	Personal sector	Other
		of which:[b]						
1972	2,408	475	298	83	329	359	294	330
1973	3,274	660	346	236	460	483	266	541
1974	3,976	376	741	582	465	484	242	704
1975	3,758	371	649	362	524	459	211	746
1976	4,349	497	452	407	768	579	243	974
1977	3,013	332	842	269	110	229	203	585
1978	3,872	632	1,405			387	233	716

[a] Includes all loans repayable within one year of their inception.
[b] Excluding revenue bills.

Distribution of main sterling liquid asset holdings at end-1978

£ millions

	Bank deposits	Building societies	Other financial institutions	National savings	Local authority debt	Tax instruments	Treasury bills and gilt-edged stocks
Holders							
Persons	24,174	36,616	4,578	11,238	233	146	..
Industrial and commercial companies	11,904[a]	337	230	—	665	763	509
Insurance companies[b]	1,537	139		—	269	..	10[c]

.. not available.

[a] *of which*, certificates of deposit £440 million.
[b] 1977 book value (net).
[c] Treasury bills only.

holdings of the new instrument were excluded from the definition of sterling M_3 (which does include certificates of deposit issued by banks), the growth in sterling M_3 might statistically be reduced; but this effect would be seen by the financial markets as largely optical.

To attract such liquid funds into a less liquid asset, the Government would need to offer a higher yield. Indeed, action has already been taken to make both national savings instruments and certificates of tax deposit more attractive. The contribution that a new general-purpose, short-term, marketable security could make would depend in part on how far this higher cost was regarded as acceptable.

Indexation

The final suggestion to be considered is some form of index-linked marketable government security. There is little doubt that an appropriately priced, inflation-proofed marketable security could be attractive to a wide range of investors. This is not because it would necessarily yield a higher return to maturity than a conventional fixed-rate security—that would be difficult to judge in advance and would depend upon whether, in the event, the future rate of inflation proved to be greater or less than the rate presently discounted in nominal market yields. (By the same token, the real cost to the borrower would also be difficult to predict in advance and might prove to be greater or less than on a conventional stock.) The attraction would be that the 'real' rate of return to maturity would be fairly clear; this would provide a measure of protection to investors, and would be particularly attractive to institutional investors such as pension funds whose liabilities also rise with inflation. It would also mean that investors would be substantially protected against capital loss as a result of a fall in the market price arising from an upward shift in inflationary expectations (though not from price fluctuations associated with changes in real interest rates). This characteristic particularly means that indexed gilt-edged stocks would remain attractive to investors when they feared accelerating inflation, which is the predominant cause of interruption to the government funding programme at present. The introduction of indexed stocks almost certainly could in principle, therefore, make an important contribution to smoothing the pattern of official gilt-edged sales.

The question of an indexed stock cannot, however, be looked at solely in this narrow context. Frequent recourse to an instrument of this type—and once a start had been made down this road it would be difficult to draw back in future conditions of uncertainty—would create considerable pressure for indexation in the capital markets more generally. There is room for differences of view about how far the introduction of indexed gilt-edged stocks would lead to the spread of indexation through the economy as a whole. But if this were a significant possibility, the authorities would need to be assured that the implications of indexation (e.g. for the tax structure, for the financing of industry, etc.) were fully understood and that the economic and social consequences were acceptable. Whether or not the generalisation of indexation through the economy would be advantageous is a question that probably cannot be answered in an absolute sense: it would depend to a considerable extent upon the prospect for the development of the economy, in the light of the other available policy options, at the time. But it is not the purpose of this article to discuss that much wider question: the immediate point is that the argument for indexed gilt-edged stocks needs to be made in that wider context, and not considered solely as an expedient to facilitate gilt-edged market management.

Conclusion

The purpose of this article has been to explain the evolution of the rôle of gilt-edged market management, and of the techniques and instruments employed, during the past decade or so; and to contribute to the public discussion of certain possible further developments.

Present policies have enabled the funding in the gilt-edged market of the Government's borrowing requirement—which has itself been very large—to make an important contribution to the objective of controlling the trend in the growth of the money supply over the past years. Closer month-by-month control over the growth of sterling M_3 is not, however, achievable. One reason for this—but one reason only among others—is because the contribution of gilt-edged funding can be interrupted from time to time as a result of a weakening of confidence among investors, particularly relating to the outlook for inflation and the adequacy of economic and financial policies to contain it, which makes yields seem unattractive. Steps have, however, been taken to secure a smoother flow of government funding and to moderate the effect of such interruptions.

The latter part of the article has discussed various suggestions for further change put forward with the aim of improving the authorities' capacity for short-term monetary control, and of reducing the risk of the authorities having to accept interest-rate fluctuations, or to take preventive policy action, not justified by the underlying economic circumstances. Some at least of these suggestions would seem likely to add to, rather than diminish, the short-term volatility of interest rates without necessarily leading to greater stability, or to lower interest rates, over the somewhat longer term. Most of the suggestions that have been put forward would be likely to have far-reaching implications—for the structure and capacity of the gilt-edged market in the longer term, for the nature of the relationship between the Government and the major institutional investors, or for economic management in general—and the question arises whether the objectives aimed at justify such possible consequences.

As noted earlier, erratic, short-run, month-to-month fluctuations in the rate of growth of sterling M_3, or indeed of any other monetary aggregate, may derive from a number of causes, and are not likely in themselves to be important. Monetary control is therefore properly directed to the trend of monetary growth over a longer period. As this emphasis becomes more widely understood, and provided that investors are convinced that the authorities are prepared to take the steps necessary to maintain this control, unjustified reaction in the gilt-edged market to erratic short-term fluctuations in monetary growth may diminish. While there may, nevertheless, be scope for further technical changes in gilt-edged market management, which are designed to improve the authorities' capacity for shorter-term monetary control, one cannot properly expect that such changes will serve in place of substantive policy changes that become necessary from time to time in other areas.

The Bank's operational procedures for meeting monetary objectives

This paper by A L Coleby, Assistant Director responsible for the Bank's Money Markets Division, was presented at a conference on monetary targeting organised by the Federal Reserve Bank of New York in May 1982.[1] *Mr. Coleby explains how debt management and interest rate policy have been used to pursue economic objectives in the shape of intermediate monetary targets. The structure of the UK gilt-edged market and recent technical developments in it are described, along with changes in the Bank's means of operation in the money market and of influencing short-term interest rates.*

Temporal references have not been altered so that, for example, 'last year' refers to 1981.

Introduction

John Fforde's paper on 'Setting monetary objectives' in the United Kingdom provides the starting point for discussion of the Bank of England's operational procedures for meeting monetary objectives. His paper brings out the central role played over the past dozen years by the accounting framework designed to give coherence and consistency to the various 'intermediate' fiscal and monetary magnitudes in relation to ultimate economic objectives. It comments on the operational implications of the choice of a single target for a broad money aggregate, especially when close control within the short term came to be desired. And it records the historical experience of direct credit controls.

Enough is said in that paper about direct credit controls for them to be dealt with fairly summarily here. Experience in the 1960s and earlier led the UK authorities to conclude that prolonged or heavy reliance on them was extremely damaging to the competitiveness and efficiency of the financial system. The arrangements introduced in 1971 assigned to direct credit controls, at most, a part to play in emergency restraint in a rapidly deteriorating monetary situation. They were so adopted on three occasions in the 1970s. Experience showed that, unless the controls quickly became redundant because money pressures subsided of their own accord, they were extremely difficult to remove, partly because it was rarely timely to give such a clear signal that restraint could be eased, and partly because it could never confidently be predicted how much activity they had suppressed or how quickly it might resume. This discouraging evidence of their value as an occasional instrument of monetary control was compounded by growing signs that the increasingly sophisticated banking and financial system could find ways round them with no great difficulty; and with no difficulty at all once exchange control was abolished in October 1979. Their real, as opposed to their cosmetic, monetary effect was therefore questionable.

This paper will therefore make no further reference to direct credit controls, but will concentrate on the Bank of England's two main operational areas in domestic markets—debt management in the government bond market and interest rate management through money-market operations. The context for both is set in the manner described in John Fforde's paper. The setting of a monetary target, which typically accompanies periodic decisions on fiscal policy, is related to a companion set of forecasts for the real economy and for a wide range of financial flows. The coherence and consistency of the whole projection rests on the building-in of some econometrically-derived relationships, and the testing for plausibility of a variety of others. The problems that have arisen with the variability of these relationships have been described; but the forecasts nevertheless provide *ex ante* a consistent projection for the period ahead.

Among the ingredients are the fiscal policy that is to be followed, projected paths for short-term interest rates, for bond yields and for the exchange rate, and projections for the amount of non-monetary finance of the public sector, all intended to be consistent with successful achievement of the declared monetary target. Inevitably, the process may call for some adjustment of starting assumptions before a consistent outcome can be identified, and it is at this stage that decisions about fiscal policy, and notably about the size of the fiscal deficit, can be illuminated by examining, for example, the interest rate implications of various choices. Once those decisions have been taken, and the monetary targets set, then the accompanying projections of interest rates, bond yields and debt sales become 'best guesses' of what monetary operations will be seeking to deliver over the coming period.

The description 'best guess' is to be preferred to that of 'target', or even 'indicative target'. The relationships involved in the forecasting process are imperfectly understood, and seem perpetually variable. Once fiscal decisions have been taken, it then is for monetary

---
[1] See also paper by J S Fforde on page 65. Copies of the conference proceedings, *Central Bank Views on Monetary Targeting* are available from the Public Information Department, Federal Reserve Bank of New York, New York 10045, USA.

management to respond to any variations so as to achieve the monetary target, because fiscal changes can take place only infrequently, and even when made will usually require considerable time before becoming fully effective.

It is equally true that changes in short-term interest rates take a long time to achieve their effect on a broad money aggregate such as M_3. As emphasis has grown on the desirability of keeping close control in the short run over the monetary target, so has attention concentrated on the operational area that has the most immediate and direct quantitative linkage with it, namely, debt management. So the first main section of this paper will look at that subject, to be followed later by a discussion of interest rate and money-market management.

Debt management

The sale of any form of public sector debt to the non-bank public will, in principle, help to restrain M_3, because the public sector will have a correspondingly reduced need to borrow from the banking system. It seems reasonable to presume that the deposits that the public sector can bid away from the banks are those most sensitive to alternative rates of return, and unlikely to be drawn at all heavily from M_1 balances, so that debt management would probably have attracted less prominence had we been on an M_1 target. Some of the sums subscribed to government debt might not in fact be attracted from bank deposits but from other assets such as corporate shares and bonds; if, as a result, corporations are in their turn obliged to borrow more from banks, the effect on M_3 of selling public sector debt is reduced.

Central government is by a long way the biggest public sector borrower in the United Kingdom, partly because it channels to local authorities and to public corporations most of the finance they need, and restricts their direct access to the longer-term markets.[1] Central government borrows partly through non-marketable instruments, but mainly through marketable debt, principally in the form of bonds (known as 'gilt-edged'), with much smaller amounts obtained by way of Treasury bills, largely held by the banking system.

The non-marketable borrowing is mainly from the personal sector through various national savings instruments, including since 1975 an index-linked certificate. It is not possible to vary the terms offered on these instruments at all quickly or precisely in response to market rates and yields, because of the elaborate retail network involving post offices up and down the country. Partly for this reason, when interest rates began, in the mid-1970s, to be high and variable, national savings were for a period not used aggressively as part of the funding programme. More recently they have received renewed emphasis, so as to ease the load on other forms of borrowing, and their share in total net purchases of central government debt by UK non-banks has risen as high as 31 per cent in 1981. They have an important part to play in government financing, but do not provide instruments for adjusting monetary control from month to month. Moreover, some national savings instruments are relatively short term, eg, deposit accounts, and are included in the wider liquidity aggregate PSL_2 for which a target range has now been adopted.

The gilt-edged market

Sales of gilt-edged stocks, managed by the Bank on behalf of the Treasury, have consistently provided the bulk of total debt sales. They have also frequently exceeded, usually by a large margin, the amount projected in the forecasts when the fiscal and money target decisions were taken at the beginning of the year. This is illustrated in the table. The table is cast in terms of the total purchases by the domestic non-bank public. That is because it is those which count for monetary control purposes, rather than total official sales, although it is the latter that the authorities can most closely influence. Purchases by banks, or by overseas residents,[2] do not contribute directly to the restraint of sterling M_3.

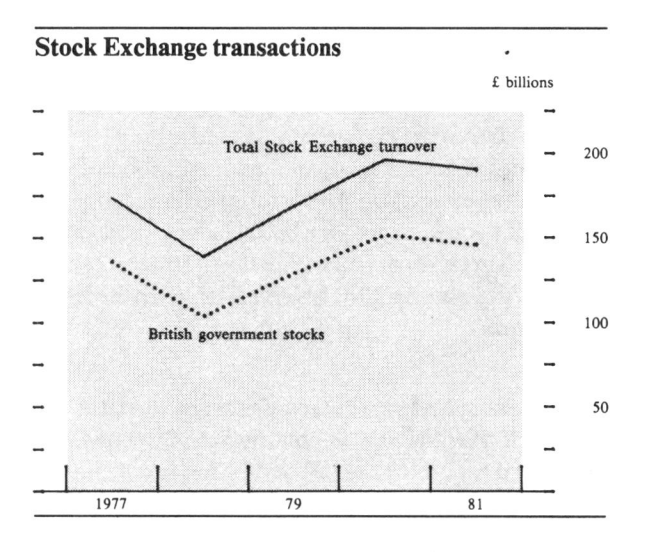

Stock Exchange transactions

£ billions

[Chart showing Total Stock Exchange turnover and British government stocks, 1977–81, with values up to 200 £ billions]

The gilt-edged market dominates the UK capital market. Net new issues of gilt-edged over the years 1977–81 inclusive amounted to nine times all new private sector issues of equity and debt combined, and turnover in gilts accounted for 75 per cent by value of the total on the UK stock exchanges. The techniques of issue and operation reflect the organisation and structure of the UK securities market, based on The Stock Exchange. This embodies a single capacity system, which makes a sharp distinction between jobber and broker. Jobbers are market makers, dealing for their own account and are not permitted to deal directly with the public, only through broker members of the market. Brokers may execute their client's orders only by dealing with jobbers, and may not take positions on their own account. These arrangements serve to concentrate secondary market transactions with the jobbers,[3] enabling them to conduct very heavy turnover on fine margins and to

---

(1) Local authorities undertake some longer-term borrowing through the capital market and directly from the public but it is fairly limited in extent.
(2) Overseas resident's holdings of sterling deposits are excluded from the UK definitions of money.
(3) Principal may deal direct with principal outside the market, but there is no active dealer network for doing so.

make a continuous market, preserving a high degree of liquidity for holdings of gilts.

The ample capacity of the secondary market in gilts compares with a virtual absence of a large primary market of the sort provided in New York by the specialist dealers. These structural features have led the Bank of England to rely on the 'tap' system for selling gilts. Under that system, new issues are brought by public offer at a fixed price—or, more recently, offered for tender with a fixed minimum price. Any stock unsold on those terms is taken up by the Bank for sale in the secondary market, through its own brokers, when there is demand to be met. As by far the largest participant in the market, the Bank established certain conventions in its behaviour in the market, in the interests of developing that market to the fullest extent and of minimising the long-term cost of selling the desired amount of debt. Thus, for example, the Bank does not, by convention, move the price of a tap stock down aggressively when prices generally are falling, on the view that this would disrupt the market and that any additional sales gained in the short run would be at the cost of conceding higher risk premia in the long run. Instead, the Bank waits until the market has found a new level at which demand has resumed, and then responds to it after a period of consolidation.

The table shows that, using the tap system, offering various types of stock to meet the particular investment horizons and tax positions of different classes of investor, the Bank was able persistently to exceed the volume of sales which the financial forecasts had suggested would be needed. Overperformance was necessary because other elements of the projections, eg the fiscal deficit, departed from their projected path. In the period before 1976, when money targets were not published, there was no publicly visible measure of the additional debt sales needed to satisfy monetary objectives. From 1976 onwards, there was. It became increasingly necessary not only to attempt over target periods as a whole to compensate by debt management for variations in other elements of the monetary forecast, but to keep closely to target throughout the period so as to avoid disturbances to markets. For once the actual figure departed from the target path, the expectation formed that there would be a compensating change in the level of debt sales pressed on the market, with a resulting change in yields. Demand was either dampened, if the target was being overshot, or stimulated, if the target was being undershot, threatening an explosive departure from the target path, and corresponding volatility in yields and interest rates.

Despite the experience of periods of feast and famine in official gilt sales, analysis has shown that gilt operations were on balance a stabilising factor in the management of M_3, which suffered even greater variability from other sources. But it was an entirely natural reaction, both within the Bank and on the part of outside commentators, to ask whether changes in technique could be found to improve performance. The persistent tendency during much of the late 1970s and early 1980s for M_3 to grow above target—especially if adjustment is made for growth concealed by the reaction to direct credit controls—compelled a search for any technique that might promise, simply through increased efficiency, to sell more. Beyond that, difficulty came in deciding which of various potentially conflicting objectives to pursue. One suggested objective was a smoother path, over a period, for gilt sales themselves. A more ambitious form was to achieve whatever level of gilt sales was necessary to deliver a smooth path, within its target, for M_3.

The last objective throws up many problems beyond those of being able to sell a specified quantity of gilts at will. It requires knowledge of the behaviour of the other components and counterparts of money which have to be compensated; and it requires knowledge of how much of the gilts being sold is being taken up by the non-bank public. None of that knowledge is available until some time after the event. But it has in common with the lesser objective of smoothing gilt sales the need for a technique that avoids 'feast and famine'.

Technical developments

Since 1977, there have been four evolutionary developments of technique each designed to contribute to that end:

- The issue of a number of variable rate stocks, where the coupon was linked to the yield on three-month Treasury bills and varied weekly. This was intended to enable the stocks to maintain their capital value which was thought likely to be an attractive feature when the market was uncertain about the future course of interest rates; but in practice they have been bought primarily by the banking system and therefore have been little help in restraining sterling M_3.

- The reintroduction after a long absence of partly-paid issues of gilt-edged, where only a part of the total price is due at the tender, with the balance coming in one or two 'calls' over the next couple of months. Thus at times when immediate funding needs have been met, a new issue can be announced, with perhaps as little as £15 to pay at tender per £100 of stock. If this is sold to the public in partly-paid form, a significant contribution to the funding needs of the next couple of months is assured.

The importance of gilt-edged stocks
£ millions

Fiscal years	Net purchases by UK non-banks of: Gilt-edged Forecast(a)	Actual	All central government debt Actual	Purchases of gilt-edged as a percentage of all debt
1975/76	1,350	3,850	5,150	75
1976/77	3,000	5,800	6,400	91
1977/78	3,900	4,900	6,750	73
1978/79	5,800	6,200	8,300	75
1979/80	6,400	8,350	8,200	102
1980/81	5,350	8,900	11,500	77
1981/82	7,200	7,100	11,650	64

(a) Forecast at the time of the relevant Budget: ie roughly at the beginning of the year.

- The development of two ways by which the Bank can acquire modest amounts of additional stock to sell, without launching a full new issue. These are by creating additional tranches of existing stocks, and by taking existing stocks from other official holders in return for new non-marketable stock of a similar maturity. This increases the Bank's flexibility of operations, for example by allowing it to supply small amounts of a variety of stocks to a market it judges to be too weak to welcome a single large new stock.
- The offering of a short-dated stock with conversion rights into a longer stock. This refined an experiment made in 1973 and was launched at a time (ahead of a Budget) when a conventional stock might have been less attractive. Although the conversion rights of this particular stock currently have no value, because of changes in yields since it was issued, and the stock is accordingly not one of the market's favourites, there would seem to be a permanent—if limited—place for other such stocks in future.

Consideration has also been given to two changes, one of instrument and one of issuing technique, which have to be regarded as revolutionary rather than evolutionary. As regards issuing technique, one modest change was made in 1979, when the fixed price offer was replaced by minimum price tender. This safeguards against an unseemly scramble for allotments should there be a sharp rise in gilt-edged prices in the three or four working days between the announcement and the completion of the issue. All allotments are made at the lowest accepted price—in contrast with US practice—and, unless there is heavy application at above the minimum price, the practical effect is no different from that of a fixed price offer, and the outcome normally expected is undersubscription and subsequent operation as a tap stock.

A proposal widely discussed was to adopt instead the practice of making issues by free auction, with no underwriting, relying on the whole amount being taken up and, therefore, abandoning the tap system. The Bank and Treasury have not accepted that proposal, for two reasons. First, they are not persuaded that, in just those conditions of uncertainty when the tap system encounters difficulty, a free auction system could be relied on to take up the quantities of gross sales that are typically needed—currently about £1 billion per month. In other conditions, when the tap system works well, so might an auction system. But, even then, it would almost certainly require substantial change both in the structure of the gilt-edged market, described earlier, and in the UK securities market generally. It would be necessary to develop much greater capacity in the primary market, involving the creation of retailing networks, that would inevitably put great strains both on the ability of jobbers to maintain the present active secondary market, and on the separation of function between jobbers and brokers. Such changes would not be reversible, and would be disruptive while they were taking place, so that there is little attraction in experimenting for experiment's sake.

Index-linked debt

The second radical change under discussion has been the introduction of index-linked gilts. This proposal raised both technical market questions, and wider ones about taxation policy and other implications for the economy generally. In the first category, it was argued that indexed debt would be a useful addition to the menu of public sector borrowing instruments and that, in particular, it would be valuable whenever a pause occurred in the demand for conventional debt because of developments threatening higher inflation and so higher nominal interest rates. It was also argued that indexed debt would prove to be a much better bargain for the government as borrower than would fixed coupon debt at current nominal yields, on the assumption that counter-inflation strategy succeeded. Somewhat in contradiction, the argument was advanced that gilt-edged investors had for too long been defrauded by having the real value of their assets eroded by inflation, and that simple honesty required the government to provide an asset which was protected from that risk. In a wider context, there was disagreement whether indexation would be regarded as implicit acceptance of inflation, with the risk of widespread adverse effects on expectations both in financial markets and in the economy at large, or whether it would be accepted as evidence of the strength of the Government's determination and confidence that inflation would come down. Finally, there was concern over the difficulty that might follow, if developments such as sharp increases in the price of oil required the acceptance of reductions in real wages, from giving protection to the real income of rentiers.

As early as 1975, there had been a limited acceptance of the 'honesty in borrowing' argument when the index-linked national savings certificate was introduced. This avoided most of the problems just mentioned by being confined to investors past the age of retirement, and being limited in amount even to them, so that the loss of revenue through exempting the inflation mark-up from both income tax and capital gains tax was contained. Subsequently the range of eligible holders was enlarged, and in 1981 the certificates were made available to all, but still with a limit on individual holdings. Meanwhile, in March 1981 the indexation of government debt was carried a stage further through the offering of an index-linked gilt-edged stock. This too was related to the protection of the real income of the retired, by restricting eligibility to hold it to pension funds and, in respect of their UK pension business only, to life insurance companies and friendly societies. As all those funds are permitted to accrue their income without deduction of tax, there was no risk of fiscal loss.

There was no existing yardstick by which to judge the real yield at which such a stock would be subscribed, and the issue was therefore made by auction with no published minimum price. In the event, the stock, which carried a coupon of 2%, was fully subscribed at par—all successful applicants being allotted at the same price whatever their actual bid—so establishing a real yield of 2%. Subsequently, however, the price fell in the market. Two further stocks issued on a similar basis failed to attract sufficient bids from the public to absorb the full amount offered at any price, and the Bank was obliged itself to take up a large proportion of the offer, which was then available to be operated as a tap stock. By early March of this year, real yields on these stocks had risen to 3%–3¼%.

In his Budget of 9 March, the Chancellor of the Exchequer announced the ending of all restrictions on the holding of index-linked stock. Real yields on existing indexed gilts fell back to below 2½%. But the first new unrestricted stock to be offered, in mid-March, attracted an even lower level of applications than any of the previous ones, and the Bank again acquired a substantial holding.

It is too early to draw any confident conclusion about the contribution that indexed stocks will make in the long run to the funding of the Government. Obviously investors will need some time to get used to the new instrument and to decide the appropriate real yield at which to buy. The timing of the first opportunity given to the general body of investors must have made that decision a difficult one, because the yields currently available on conventional gilts are high in relation to the recent level of inflation, which in turn seems to be heading downwards. It would be reasonable to assume that an indexed issue would have greater appeal when inflation was thought likely to increase—the circumstances in which the sale of conventional stocks becomes difficult. Indexed stocks will certainly add to the range of options in debt management. The auction technique of issue, on the other hand, must on experience to date have a question mark against its suitability in the UK market structure.

Interest rates and money-market operations

The description in the introductory section of this paper of the preparation of periodic real and financial projections did not claim that they led to firm targets for short-term interest rates. The projected path provides no more than a starting point for decisions in the ensuing period on interest rate objectives. The more immediate and powerful influences, then, are the actual behaviour of the target variable, hitherto quantified only for M_3 (both in terms of its target path and in its relationship with the real economy), and the state of financial markets including the foreign exchange market. A departure from target that cannot be regarded as transient leads to a reappraisal of interest rate levels; it does not necessarily lead to change in the desired level, if the ultimate objectives of monetary policy seem to be being achieved despite the behaviour of M_3. Such reappraisals could be hastened by market anticipation of an impending change in official interest rate policy, or prompted by markets responding to other influences such as the course of interest rates in other countries.

Until recently, and despite variations and appearances to the contrary, the operational technique for giving effect to official interest rate objectives has stayed close to the classical model. That involved the setting, and periodic variation, of an official discount or lending rate, which, when necessary, is 'made effective' by open market operations in the money market. 'Making Bank rate effective' means restraining a decline in market rates from an unchanged Bank rate, or bringing them up to a newly established and higher Bank rate; it is accomplished by limiting the availability of cash to the banking system so as to 'force the market into the Bank' to borrow at the somewhat penal level of Bank rate. There have been some actual or apparent departures of practice in the past dozen years from this simple model, which need to be mentioned, as do some features of the institutional structure within which it has operated.

The first departure proved to be more apparent than real. It came with the introduction in 1971 of the reserve asset scheme, which required banks to maintain holdings of certain short-term assets in a certain ratio—12½ per cent was the general level—to a measure of their deposit liabilities. The effective level of the ratio could be raised by requiring the banks to place special deposits with the Bank of England. These arrangements were in no way intended to provide the means of operating a reserve base/money multiplier form of control. But they did provide a supplementary or alternative means of managing interest rates, by containing the supply of reserve assets. Experience soon showed that, in a world in which banks were increasingly relying on liability management to square their books, this technique for managing interest rates was markedly inferior to the classical one, especially with a monetary target expressed in terms of a broad aggregate. The banks reacted to a shortage of reserve assets simply by bidding for more deposits, driving up interbank rates to levels that made it profitable for customers having overdraft facilities linked to the rather sticky base lending rates of the banks to draw on them and earn arbitrage by redepositing elsewhere. The immediate effect on M_3 of seeking to manage interest rates in that way was accordingly perverse, and the technique was effectively abandoned very soon, though the reserve asset scheme did not finally lapse till last August.

The second departure came in 1972. There was upward pressure on market interest rates at a time when the Government's economic strategy was expansionary and it was unwilling to indicate a change of approach by endorsing an increase in Bank rate. Changes in Bank rate, though initiated and put into effect by the Bank of England, took place only with the agreement of the Chancellor of the Exchequer. In order to give such changes a less high political profile, while still enabling the official lending rate to stand at a modestly penal level in relation to market rates, Bank rate was replaced by minimum lending rate (MLR), itself derived from a formula linking it to the result of the most recent weekly tender for three-month Treasury bills, though with provision for the formula to be overriden. This was at first a more satisfactory system than its immediate predecessor, but was itself found to have shortcomings especially when high and variable inflation was accompanied by sharp changes in interest rate expectations and in the term-structure of short-term rates. Lending was never undertaken for longer than seven days or so, and a three-month market rate was frequently a rather poor guide. The formula-related MLR was replaced by an explicitly administered MLR—virtually back to Bank rate—in 1978.

There are three features of the institutional structure to be mentioned. The first is that facilities to discount and to borrow at the Bank of England have not been made available to banks in general, but only to the money-market specialists known as discount houses. It is also, in the main, with the discount houses that the Bank conducts its money-market operations, using bills—Treasury bills, local authority bills and bankers' acceptances. The second feature is that there is a need for a substantial volume of activity in the money market for purely housekeeping reasons. The accounts of the central government are centralised at the Bank of England, with no spare cash balances either there or with commercial banks. Any net balance of cash flows to or from the government therefore has to be absorbed by, or financed from operations in the money market. In order to accommodate such transactions without disturbance to interest rates, the Bank for many years made known each week the rates at which it would conduct its operations—buying or selling—for bills of any maturity up to three months. The third feature is that the only banks required to maintain balances at the Bank of England were, until last year, the London clearing banks. They had an operational need for balances, so as to be able to meet settlements against them in the cheque clearing at the end of the day. A conventional level had been established, in relation to their deposits, which they had to maintain on average over a period. It provided an ample margin above actual operational needs, enabling them to draw down the balances somewhat when overnight interest rates moved up, and vice versa.

The wide-ranging debate in the United Kingdom on monetary control, punctuated by the publication in 1980 of a Green Paper (or official discussion document), left the Bank unpersuaded that there would be an advantage in replacing its approach to setting interest rate objectives by the more direct control of quantity—some form of monetary base; and wholly convinced that no practical basis existed for the early adoption of such a system. But there were aspects of interest rate management which looked good candidates for change. First, it seemed sensible to try to remove any bias to delay in changing official objectives for interest rates that might be attributable to the high political profile associated with formal government approval. Second, it seemed likely that more effective and prompt official responses to market pressures could be facilitated by imparting greater technical flexibility to the way in which our day-to-day operations were conducted, and by adjusting the pattern of those operations so as to allow more scope for market influences to determine the term structure of money rates. Institutional features tending to produce rigidities in rates needed to be questioned.

New arrangements

By November 1980, the way ahead was sufficiently clear for the authorities to outline a programme of limited but useful change, the impact of which was concentrated on the money markets and upon the Bank's exercise of its influence over short-term interest rates. These proposals were developed further publicly in March and June 1981 and detailed arrangements discussed with the banking system in time for the changes to become fully effective in August 1981. The parallel changes in the Bank's operations in the money market began in the autumn of 1980 and were complete by last August.

The starting point for description of the new arrangements is the reformulation of official interest rate objectives. MLR has been suspended and the Bank's operational aim is now set primarily in terms of an 'unpublished band for very short-term interest rates'. The aim of this change was to make shifts in the official interest rate objectives less obtrusive, thereby reducing both the political sensitivity of a shift and the extent of official influence over longer money rates. To this end, market operators were denied guidance not only to the position of the band at any point in time, but even to the instrument or term to which it applied.

A complementary set of changes introduced in the year to August 1981 sought to place an increasing weight on market factors in determining the structure of short rates, by a radical alteration in the Bank's daily dealing methods. Progressively, over a short period of time, the Bank disengaged from setting official dealing rates, putting the onus upon market participants (notably the discount houses) to bid for cash. Thus, now on a day when cash is short, the houses may offer bills to the Bank twice in the day, quoting a rate (or rates) at which they will sell. The Bank has complete discretion to take which offers it chooses. The houses know that if their offers of bills are not sufficiently aggressive and they are obliged to borrow from the Bank, they are likely to be charged somewhat above prevailing market rates. Lending at market rates is now done only rarely and in response to exceptional (largely technical) factors.

The purpose in seeking, through making borrowing terms unattractive, to concentrate the demand for cash on the offering of bills is to provide a competitive basis for determining rates. An alternative means of putting cash into the system, advocated by some as simpler and technically more efficient, would have been for the Bank to lend directly in the interbank market. That method did not seem, on examination, to offer a satisfactory means of determining interest rates, because the highly concentrated structure of sterling deposit banking would have confronted the Bank with only a handful of large takers of funds—the clearing banks. Rate determination in those circumstances would have come close to a bilateral haggle. So the decision was taken to continue to provide cash through bill operations, dealing largely with the discount houses.

An essential ingredient in this process—given that it is not intended as a vehicle for management of a quantity of base money—is that there should be broad equivalence between the quantity of cash supplied and the actual demand for it. The Bank's stated objective is 'broadly to offset the cash flows between the Bank and the money markets' and to leave the clearing banks within reach of their desired operational balances. As part of the new arrangements, the clearing banks were relieved of their former obligation to hold balances well in excess of their operational needs, and they now aim for whatever level they judge necessary to avoid overdrawing their account at the Bank, which is not permitted. At the same time, to maintain the income of the Bank (all the profits of the note circulation passing by statute to the Government), all banks and licensed deposit-takers above a certain minimum size have agreed to maintain a non-interest bearing and non-operational balance at the Bank.

The first six months of the new arrangements have passed in an often difficult and volatile external and domestic environment. Within the first six weeks, the combination of downward pressure on sterling, and domestic concern about monetary conditions, pushed short rates up by between 3%–4%. A period of uncertainty in October was followed by one of quite marked downward market pressures in November; and, after renewed uncertainty around Christmas, there has been further downward pressure on rates since. One problem of market management which has arisen is that this period has seen the unwinding of much of the effect of the civil servants' dispute last spring and summer which, at its peak, had delayed perhaps £7 billion of net government revenue. The process of catching up on these arrears has made the task of forecasting the daily cash position of the banks unusually hazardous. More recently, the combination of this catching up, heavy funding of the government's borrowing requirement and a seasonally heavy period for normal tax revenue have combined to draw massive amounts of cash from the banking system, which the Bank has recycled through its open-market operations.

In general, the new operating techniques have worked well so far and the discount market has normally made offers at a sufficiently wide range of rates over the day for the authorities to avoid overtly setting an interest rate by lending through the discount window. However, on the first occasion when a major rise in very short rates was desired by the authorities (in mid-September) lending was necessary at a specified rate. In November and again early in March the Bank lent through the discount window to discourage too rapid a decline in rates.

Market forces have, as intended, played a more important role than before the new arrangements were established. On occasion, the signals given by longer rates in the money markets have been an important element in determining the authorities' objectives for very short rates; thus, after longer rates had risen persistently in the second half of September, the authorities did not seek to resist the market when, at the end of that month, it offered shorter-dated bills to the Bank at significantly higher rates than hitherto. But at other times, for example in the first week of October when longer rates continued to rise, the authorities have considered it appropriate to assert their view by leaning against the market movement.

It is, of course, too early to judge the technical merits of the arrangements as a whole but it does appear that the authorities' own operations do indeed have considerably greater flexibility. A similarly cautionary note is appropriate in considering whether the changes have lowered the political temperature of interest rate policy. Market pressures, however, clearly played a significant part in the sharp rises in rates in September and probably did help the authorities to establish both the fact and, fairly quickly, the extent of the needed increases. In general, it does indeed seem that the authorities have been able to keep a lower profile.

Conclusions

Monetary policy has had to operate in an often difficult environment over the last five years. Its main objective—to counter inflation—has remained unchanged, although there has been a wide-ranging debate over almost every aspect of its aims and operations and there have been changes (particularly in the last eighteen months) in the weights given to particular factors considered in formulating policy.

Along with these changes have gone developments in the Bank's operations in the money and gilt-edged markets, the nature and roots of which have been explored in this paper. In many cases, the changes have not been in effect long enough for us to judge their contribution. Moreover, it cannot be claimed that the period of change is necessarily over. We now move to a period in which less primacy is to be given to M_3 as the sole quantified target; targeting is now more explicitly a matter of interpretation in the light of a number of factors, such as the behaviour of exchange rates, and is moreover expressed in terms of three aggregates including a narrower one, M_1. This will add further considerations to the already difficult task of setting the path for interest rates. But the changes of the last five years in the flexibility of the Bank's operations in the gilt-edged market and those of the last two years in the money market, will leave us the better equipped to tackle the problems to come.

CHAPTER 6
Operations in the money market

The Bank's operations in the money market have changed substantially in some respects over the last two decades, but its main objectives have remained the same throughout—namely to give effect to official interest-rate objectives and to manage the day-to-day financing of the Exchequer and the liquidity of the banking system.

The Bank's operations have been conducted against the background of agreements between the Bank of England and the commercial banks about the way in which the latter would manage their liquidity. The voluntary nature of these agreements was explained in a booklet *Monetary policy in EEC countries: UK institutions and instruments* published by the Bank in February 1974:

There has never been any legal requirement in the United Kingdom for the observance by banks of cash or liquidity ratios, or calls for special deposits. Where such arrangements have been in force, they have been based on voluntary agreements made either among the banks themselves or between them and the Bank of England, with the powers under the Bank of England Act 1946 remaining untested in the background ...

These agreements, and the Bank's operational methods, have undergone two major revisions—in 1971 and 1981—and they now constrain the banks' liquidity management much less than they did. It is therefore convenient to divide this chapter into four sub-sections, dealing with, respectively, the situation up to 1971; Competition and Credit Control and its effect on the Bank's money market operations; the 1979–80 debate on monetary base control; and the consequent changes in the arrangements relating to the Bank's operations.

Money market operations up to 1971

The terms of the agreements between the Bank of England and the commercial banks that were operative during this period were summarised as follows (*ibid* page 26):

Before the changes introduced in September 1971, the London clearing banks (originally by agreement among themselves, but later at the request of the Bank of England) had since 1946 held a minimum of 8% of their total deposit liabilities in cash (coin, bank notes and balances with the Bank of England). At the request of the Bank of England, they also held from 1951 a minimum proportion of their total deposit liabilities in liquid assets (cash, money at call and short notice, UK Treasury bills and other bills and refinanceable credits), set at 28% from 1963 to 1971. Until 1971 there was a similar, but less formal, agreement between the Bank of England and the Scottish clearing banks concerning a minimum liquidity ratio. Between 1960 and 1971, the clearing banks' liquidity ratios were the fulcrum on which from time to time they were required to place special deposits, expressed as a percentage of total deposit liabilities, with the Bank of England. Other banks had no arrangements with the Bank of England up to September 1971 for observing any minimum cash or liquidity ratios; but in 1968 all banks other than the London and Scottish clearing banks and the Northern Ireland banks agreed, when called upon to do so, to place cash deposits, expressed as a percentage of certain of their deposit liabilities, with the Bank of England. This scheme, however, was never used.

Special deposits bore interest at a rate closely related to the Treasury bill rate; in combination with the 28% liquid assets ratio they were used to bring about changes in the banks' liquidity position, generally for the purpose of influencing bank lending to the private sector. Increasingly during the 1960s, though, the main techniques for restraining bank lending became the imposition of official lending ceilings. These were difficult to maintain, both for the authorities (because of the large number of claims for exemptions) and for the commercial banks themselves (because they normally had undrawn loan commitments to their customers); moreover they stifled competition among banks, penalising the efficient and sustaining the inefficient.

The Bank's operations in the money market during this period were described in some detail in an article *The management of money day by day* (page 107), first published in the March 1963 *Bulletin*. At that time the Bank made a weekly announcement about Bank rate, which was the rate at which the Bank would normally lend to the discount houses against approved security and to which clearing bank deposit and lending rates were conventionally linked. The article describes how Bank rate was 'made effective'—ie how the Bank was able to prevent market interest rates from falling far below Bank rate. It also describes the arrangements for the day-to-day financing of the Exchequer and the management of the commercial banks' liquidity and the accounting thereof; in essentials this description remains valid today.

THE MANAGEMENT OF MONEY DAY BY DAY

The responsibilities of the Bank of England include the management of the money market and, as the Bank are the Government's bankers, of the Exchequer accounts also. This article describes the way in which the two tasks impinge upon each other—being in many ways indeed opposite sides of the same coin —and how they are discharged from day to day.

It is first necessary to define some terms. The title "Exchequer" is used in this article to cover a group of accounts in the books of the Banking Department of the Bank of England. These are the Exchequer in the formal sense, the revenue Departments, the Paymaster General (including the Exchange Equalisation Account) and the National Debt Commissioners. Paradoxically, it is convenient to include also in this group the Issue Department—although it is constituted as a part of the Bank of England—because of the nature of its transactions in government debt, as will appear below. The Exchequer Group is not synonymous with the total of "Public Deposits" shown in the weekly Bank of England Return which includes numerous other balances at the Head Office and branches, as well as the working balances maintained by Government Departments.

The term "Bankers" corresponds to "Other Deposits: Bankers" in the weekly Return, except in so far as these Deposits are held with the Bank's branches. It will be used to describe what is in effect the London money market, in a broad sense. Transactions by the Exchequer or by the Banking Department (including the issue and payment of bank notes) will generally result in a credit or debit to the account of a bank or a discount house at the Head Office of the Bank of England : and these are the main transactions that cause a change in the total of Bankers' balances. There remains the group of the Bank's customers other than the Exchequer Group and the Bankers, referred to as "Customers", the most important of which are other central banks.

The working balances of Government Departments are kept to a minimum each day, any surpluses being transferred or lent overnight to the account of the Exchequer proper. This account, with the complementary account of the Paymaster General, is also operated as far as possible so that, after taking account of such transfers and the rest of the day's payments and receipts, no large idle balance is left overnight; the objective is a balance of £2 million between the two accounts, a small figure in relation to the huge total of daily government payments and receipts which may amount to some hundreds of millions of pounds. The flow of these payments and receipts is, of course, distinctly uneven from day to day and from one time of the year to another. It is the Bank's task, working closely with H.M. Treasury, to ensure that finance is available to meet each day's spending; at the same time it is necessary to see that large surpluses do not remain unemployed but are used each day to buy back Treasury Bills from holders outside the Exchequer Group, so minimising the net cost of the service of the National Debt.

The other main objective, the management of the London money market, is linked to the management of the Exchequer accounts since the net flow day by day of government payments to and receipts from the Bankers is the main cause of ease or stringency in that market. On a day on which the banks need, for example, to pay over large sums of tax monies to the Exchequer, they are likely to be drawing upon the most liquid reserves among their assets, notably their money lent at call to the London discount houses and similar institutions. The discount houses find themselves short of funds in consequence, and unless the Bank take steps to relieve the shortage— usually by buying Treasury Bills either from them (the so-called 'direct' method of giving help) or from the banks (the 'indirect' method)—they may be forced to borrow from the Bank at Bank Rate or over. The enforcement of such borrowing increases the average cost of the houses' total borrowings and is one of the main ways (short of a change in Bank Rate) in which the Bank of England exert an influence on short-term interest rates and particularly on the rate at which the discount houses may be expected to bid for Treasury Bills at the following Friday's tender.

If the Bank are to operate effectively, therefore, it suits them if there is an initial shortage of funds in the market which they may then at their discretion relieve with or without the penalty of forcing houses to borrow at the Bank. If the market has a surplus, the Bank do not have this choice. They may sell Treasury Bills to the market to provide employment for surplus funds, and this may also be helpful for smoothing purposes in putting Bills into the market's hands which will mature on days when its funds are expected to be particularly short; but the market cannot be expected to straiten itself by buying Bills in such quantities as to bring the risk of having to borrow at the Bank later in the day. In these circumstances the Bank's influence lies largely in their discretion as to the rate at which they offer to sell the Bills.

In practice the normal operation of the weekly Treasury Bill tender will usually create such an initial shortage of funds. This is because the number of Bills which is put on offer at the tender each Friday, to be paid for day by day in the following week, is calculated so as to cover the Exchequer's estimated needs with, if anything, a small margin to spare; and the authorities can be sure that this total will be taken up because of the understanding that exists that the members of the London Discount Market Association will, between them, always bid for something close to the full amount of Bills offered. They thus accept an informal responsibility to underwrite the total issue although, in practice, there are normally many other tenders for Bills besides their own. Over the week as a whole, therefore, there will be a potential net movement of funds from Bankers to the Exchequer.

To go into a little more detail, the appropriate size for the tender is decided broadly as follows. Towards the end of each week H.M. Treasury forecast Exchequer receipts and disbursements for some weeks ahead. These figures are combined with the amount, which is known, of Treasury Bills maturing each week in the hands of the market and the Banking Department of the Bank of England, *i.e.*, all Bills other than those held by the Exchequer Group. And the two, taken together, give the main indication of the amount of new Bills which will need to be issued each week. In its simplest form, the sum for a particular week might be as follows:

£ millions

1. Expected net Exchequer deficit on receipts and disbursements ... ... — 40
2. Maturing Bills held outside the Exchequer Group:
   Banking Department 10
   Other 175   —185   —225
3. *Add* Bills for which tenders are to be invited, say ... ...   +230
   _____
   + 5
   ===

The figure of +£5 million is the measure of the Exchequer's estimated net cash receipt during the week in question. As virtually all Exchequer receipts and payments must represent transactions either with Bankers or with the Banking Department of the Bank of England, the Bankers' position in that week in relation to the Exchequer can be estimated by taking out of the calculation those maturing Bills (£10 million) the proceeds of which will accrue to the Banking Department and not to Bankers (and the amount, if any, of the new Bills that may be allotted to, and paid for by, the Banking Department) and reversing the sign of the remainder. The Bankers' position for the week is then seen to be a deficit of £15 million, assuming that the Banking Department does not tender for any new Bills. The spread of this deficit over the days of the week will usually be uneven and particular days may well show a surplus. This is partly because of the uneven flow of Exchequer receipts and payments and partly because the market's tender for Treasury Bills can be divided between the days of the week at its discretion.

In practice, the calculation is a little more elaborate. Allowance is also made, for example, for the likely course of official transactions in government stocks and in foreign exchange; and for Treasury Bill business or other transactions by overseas central banks and other private customers of the Bank of England. Transactions by Customers—like transactions by the Banking Department itself—will affect either Bankers or the Exchequer individually without producing an opposite impact upon the other. Other items may also need to be brought into the calculation, as will become clear later when the daily work is described.

The number of Bills to be offered each Friday is always announced a week ahead, on the preceding Friday afternoon, when the results are published of that day's tender. But it is still possible on the day of the tender to 'take the top off the tender', *i.e.*, allot less than the full amount of Bills on offer. Alternatively, the authorities may lessen the effect of the tender on Bankers—but this time without reducing the amount accruing to the Exchequer—by putting in an application on behalf of the Banking Department. It is not possible to increase the number of Bills on offer beyond that already announced.

Attention may now be drawn to the two-page table at the end of this article, which is a simplified version of a working sheet used in the Bank. The figures are illustrative only and shown in round £ millions.

Bankers and Exchequer each have half of the sheet, several of the entries in the two halves representing transactions between the two and thus giving rise to the same entries but with the sign reversed; and each half of the sheet primarily serves one of the two main objects, namely, the management of the money market (Bankers) and the Exchequer accounts. The Banking Department intervenes as necessary in either half, as explained below.

Taking the Bankers' section first, the "Actual Balance" in the last column relates to the total balances held at the close of business on the drawing accounts at the Head Office of the Bank of England of the banks and discount houses which make up the greater part of the London money market. The "Bankers' target", which appears above the table, is the total of these same balances which it is estimated they would wish to hold at the close of business on the current day. This target is estimated each morning (and altered, if need be, as the day proceeds) partly by projection and partly—for the banks whose balances are most likely to change—by direct enquiry. Balances at the Bank of England are regarded by the commercial banks as part of their cash base (along with their notes and coin), and each bank sets as its target the figure which, after taking into account the business expected during the day, will ensure that at the close of business the desired ratio of total cash to deposits, usually about 8% for the clearing banks, is broadly maintained.

The remaining entries in this section represent transactions which it is known or estimated will occur during the day and which will affect the "Actual Balance". For example, the take-up or maturity of Treasury Bills day by day will be known in advance, and the Exchequer's receipts and disbursements can be estimated. In the other columns, too, known figures or estimates will be entered in advance whenever it is at all reasonable to do so (as, for instance, in foreign exchange or stock transactions which are customarily settled a day or two after the deal is done); and throughout each day additions or amendments are being made to the table as information becomes available from the Treasury or from the different offices of the Bank. More detailed explanations of the items included are given in the footnotes to the table.

At any time in the course of the day the net total of the day's entries—entered in column 11—can be applied to the previous night's "Actual Balance" to give an estimate of the new day's closing balance; and this in turn can be compared with the "Bankers' target" at the top of the sheet to give a measure of the shortage or surplus of funds in the market. On this understanding, the table shows a prospective market shortage on Tuesday of £29 million, that is £206 million (237−31) compared with the target of £235 million.

At the same time as they are collecting this information the Bank are keeping in touch with the money market both by direct contacts and through consultation with their Bill brokers. Market reports may or may not tell quite the same story as the figures: information on one side or the other may not be quite complete; some transactions may have been a little delayed, leading the market to believe itself perhaps shorter of funds than it will prove to be later; or, within the market, surplus funds seeking employment may not yet have found the points of shortage. In such circumstances some judgment is needed in assessing the true situation.

If we assume, however, that the indicated shortage of £29 million in the illustration is unchanged in the early afternoon shortly before the day's business must be completed, and assuming again that market reports are broadly in line with this estimate, various courses are open to the Bank. The first is to do nothing, in which case one or more of the discount houses will almost certainly be forced to borrow from the Bank at Bank Rate or above in order to balance their books. In the table, the appropriate 'plus' entry would be made in column 10. If, on the other hand, it is not desired to force the market into the Bank—or to do so only to a limited extent—the authorities will give help, usually by instructing their brokers (the 'special buyer') to buy Treasury Bills in the market. These purchases, which are made at market rates, put cash into the market's hands; at the same time, by choosing to buy Bills of particular maturities, the Bank can do something to shorten the market's cash either later in the same week or in some future week in which the Exchequer forecasts suggest that this is appropriate.

Because a shortage of funds in the market will often be accompanied by a surplus in the Exchequer Group, such purchases will usually be made by the Issue Department, acting for the Exchequer Group. On the working sheet, they will give rise to a 'plus' entry in column 4 and, if the Bills purchased are due to mature later in the same week, a 'minus' entry of the same amount on the appropriate day. Similar entries, but with signs reversed, must be made in the Exchequer half of the sheet in column 16.

Cash is always available for the Issue Department to make such purchases. This is because the Department's assets are so disposed as to ensure that a number of Treasury Bills or other loans to the Exchequer mature each day. Should the proceeds of these maturities not be required, they are re-lent to the Exchequer at the end of the day.

If the Exchequer Group has not a sufficient surplus of funds, some or all of the Treasury Bills in question may be bought by the Banking Department, giving rise to similar entries in the Bankers' section of the sheet, but in column 3; since the Exchequer is not affected, no entry is required in that section. If the Bank are buying Bills for Customers (notably, in this context, overseas central banks), limited help can also be given to the market by placing these 'special orders' in the market (a 'plus' in column 8).

A note on the day's timetable may help to make these operations clearer. The large banks do not usually seek to withdraw call money from the discount market after 12 noon; but their 'calling' by this time will be on a large enough scale to provide for their estimated cash needs at the end of the day. If, therefore, there is a general shortage of funds in the market on a particular day, this will be the time when it appears most acute. From then until the close of business at 3 p.m. funds will continue to become available and there will be a progressively narrowing gap between the market's needs as reported by itself and as indicated in the Bank's figures, which relate to the position as it will be at the end of the day. In the 'early afternoon' of the illustration, shortly after 2 p.m., when the Bank's operations in the Treasury Bill market are being concluded, it can generally be assumed that the discount houses will be able, if in need, to find before the close of business between £10 million and £30 million more money from the market than has so far become available: the amount can only be estimated, and is one of the matters referred to earlier as calling for judgment according to the circumstances of the day. Thus, if the figures at this time of day indicated, as in the illustration, a shortage of £29 million, it would not necessarily be inconsistent with this if market reports suggested that the discount houses were still looking for anything up to twice that amount.

If a discount house borrows from the Bank, it must do so by 2.30 p.m., at which time it must make its own estimate, based on experience, of what other funds may yet become available to it in the next half hour. Allowing for these funds, it will then borrow from the Bank the minimum which will be required to balance its books. Occasionally, of course, money expected will not materialise, and in such circumstances the house in question must make what arrangements it can with the commercial banks to balance its books.

With these operations concluded, there is still time for some of the entries in the table to alter before the final balances are struck, although substantial changes are unlikely. In particular, the estimates of receipts and disbursements in column 2, despite revision earlier in the day, may prove to have been a little off the mark, and there may be late transactions of one kind or another to be put through the Bank's books after the formal close of business. The true day's movement in the note circulation entered in column 9 may also differ somewhat from the earlier estimate. Amendments are made as new information becomes available, and in due course the actual total of "Bankers' Balances" as at the close of business can be entered in column 12. There will usually be a small discrepancy (shown in brackets in column 11) between the recorded changes totalled in column 11 and the true change now revealed in column 12. This arises mainly from the rounding of the figures (in practice a number of entries are made to the nearest £¼ million), and from incomplete recording of the transactions by Customers shown in column 8. There are some Customers' accounts which rarely throw up any sizeable net movement on the day and, to save unnecessary complication, transactions on these accounts are not all recorded on the working sheet; large transactions by such customers can be, and are, allowed for.

The Exchequer section of the sheet is used in much the same way as the Bankers'. It may be recalled that the objective here is to leave the accounts of the Exchequer and Paymaster General with a combined balance of approximately £2 million at the end of each day. As with the Bankers', the final right-hand column records the previous day's finishing position, whether as being on target or as a surplus or shortfall on the £2 million. And this is the starting point for the day's work. The earlier columns show the various transactions, whether with Bankers or the Banking Department, which will affect the Exchequer Group in the course of the day, the total change being shown in column 20. Transfers within the Group such as, for example, sales of stock between the Issue Department and the National Debt Commissioners, can be ignored.

Looking at the illustrative figures for Tuesday, the Exchequer has in prospect a surplus of £35 million (36 less 1 needed to repay outstanding Ways and Means Advances). At the same time, as we have already seen, Bankers face a shortage, compared with their target, of £29 million on the day and need help if it is not intended to force the discount market to borrow from the Bank.

If the Issue Department gives this help by purchasing exactly £29 million of Treasury Bills from the market, with entries in columns 4 and 16 such as have already been described, the Exchequer still has a prospective surplus of £6 million to dispose of. This it does by purchasing Treasury Bills from the Banking Department (a 'minus' entry in column 15). Again, so far as possible, Bills will be chosen of maturities which will smooth operations either later in that week or in the weeks ahead. Conversely, if on any day the Exchequer should appear short of funds after allowing for all other known transactions, this can be remedied by selling Treasury Bills to the Banking Department.

These purchases or sales of Treasury Bills are made by the Issue Department, which is thus used either to spend a net surplus of the Exchequer Group as a whole, or to cover a net deficit by selling its Bills and lending the proceeds to the Exchequer.

For practical reasons the final 'switch' of Bills between the Banking and Issue Departments has to be made before information about the transactions of the Exchequer Group is complete and, as with Bankers, some small late amendments to the figures must usually be expected. To the extent that these could not be foreseen and allowed for in the 'switch', the Exchequer will end the day with a surplus which it will be the object to employ the next day, or with a debt to the Banking Department in the form of overnight Ways and Means Advances which are made, in multiples of £250,000, to restore the Exchequer balance to the desired minimum.

£ millions

BANKERS

	1	2	3	4	5
	Treasury Bills	Exchequer receipts/ disbursements	Treasury Bills — Banking Department	Treasury Bills — Issue Department	Stocks
Monday	−19	−10	+6	+21	−2
Tuesday	−17	−24			+8
Wednesday	+ 5	+ 3			

EXCHEQUER

	13	14	15	16	17
	Treasury Bills (inc. Banking Department)	Exchequer receipts/ disbursements	Issue Department (Treasury Bills) with — Banking Department	Issue Department (Treasury Bills) with — Market	Stocks
Monday	+16	+10		−21	+2
Tuesday	+17	+24			−8
Wednesday	−10	− 3			

Column 1. The net cash figure resulting from the market's subscriptions for new Bills (arising out of the weekly tender) less its receipts from maturing Bills.

2. All government receipts and disbursements, other than those specified elsewhere in the table [receipts are (−)].

3 and 4. Transactions in Treasury Bills with the market by the Banking and Issue Departments, purchases from the market (which put cash into the market's hands) being (+) to Bankers.

5. Transactions in gilt-edged stocks between the market on the one hand and the Issue Department or the National Debt Commissioners on the other. Purchases from the market are (+) to Bankers. As deals are usually done for settlement the next day, the day's total is usually known the previous evening.

6. Subscriptions by Bankers for Tax Reserve Certificates [always (−)]. The forecasts of government receipts included in column 2 take account of estimated surrenders of these Certificates in payment of tax.

7. The change in the sterling assets of the Exchange Equalisation Account resulting from the sale of foreign currencies to Bankers or purchases from them. A purchase of foreign currency by the Exchange Equalisation Account will be paid for in sterling, appearing here as a receipt (+) by Bankers. Most deals are done for value one or two days ahead, allowing reasonably accurate forecasting.

8. The net total of transactions between Bankers and the Bank of England's principal other private customers, notably overseas central banks.

9. The movement of notes between the Banking Department and the commercial banks. If notes in circulation outside the Bank are increasing, the accounts of the commercial banks at the Bank of England will be debited [a (−) entry in this column] to pay for the notes passing from the Banking Department's reserve. The week's movements are estimated in advance.

Bankers' target 235

6	7	8	9	10	11	12
Tax Reserve Certificates	Foreign exchange	Customers	Note circulation	Market advances	Bankers' Balances Estimated + or −	Actual
						Saturday 241
−1	+9	−2	−5		− 3 (−1)	237
	+3	+1	−2		−31 ( )	
	+1	+2	−1	−5	+ 5 ( )	

18	19	20	21
Tax Reserve Certificates	Foreign exchange	Total + or −	Surplus + or Ways and Means Advances −
			Saturday +1
+1	−10	− 2	−1
	+ 3	+36	
	− 2	−15	

Column 10. Advances at Bank Rate or over made by the Banking Department to the London discount market. Advances are usually made for seven or eight days, and repayments are known beforehand (as on Wednesday in the illustration).

11. The total change in Bankers' Balances as estimated in columns 1 to 10. The difference between this total and the actual change is shown in brackets: the causes of this difference are explained in the text.

12. The total balances at the Head Office of the Bank of England at the close of business of the London clearing banks and other financial institutions which, broadly, comprise the London money market (see text).

13. Column 1 with sign reversed, adjusted to include Treasury Bills taken up by, or maturing to, the Banking Department or Customers. The subscription accrues to, and the Bills are a liability of, the Exchequer, although Bankers are not affected.

14. Column 2 with sign reversed.

15. Transfers of Treasury Bills between the Issue and Banking Departments. These are made either to put the Exchequer in funds or to employ a surplus (see text).

16 and 17. Columns 4 and 5 with sign reversed.

18. Usually column 6 with sign reversed; but an addition is necessary if the Banking Department buys Tax Reserve Certificates on its own account.

19. Column 7 with sign reversed, adjusted to include foreign exchange transactions by the Bank's customers.

20. The total of columns 13 to 19.

21. The total surplus on the Exchequer and Paymaster General accounts at the close of business, as compared with the desired balance of £2 million (see text), or the Banking Department's Ways and Means Advances to the Exchequer.

Competition and Credit Control and after

The objective of the Competition and Credit Control reforms was described in Chapter 2. It was a system in which credit was rationed by price rather than by credit ceilings set by the authorities, and in which banks were affected more equally by official credit control measures. The Bank's proposals for the new system were published in a consultative document on 14 May 1971 entitled *Competition and credit control* (page 115).

The new arrangements for reserve asset ratios and liability to place special deposits with the Bank, which applied equally to all banks, were set out in paragraph 7 of this document. In addition, the London clearing banks agreed to hold as part of their reserve assets an average of $1\frac{1}{2}$% of their eligible liabilities in the form of non-interest-bearing balances with the Bank of England; these balances were used for clearing purposes.

The Chief Cashier described how the new system was expected to impact on the money market, and in particular on the discount houses, in his *Sykes Memorial Lecture* to the Institute of Bankers in November 1971 (page 83); he went on to explain parallel arrangements which were introduced for certain deposit-taking finance houses outside the banking system.

Under the new system the role of quantitative controls on lending was to be reduced and greater weight given to market-determined interest rates in the allocation of credit. Initially, the weekly announcement of Bank rate continued, but in October 1972 this arrangement was changed, as described in the Commentary of the December 1972 *Bulletin*:

> With the introduction in September 1971 of the new arrangements for the control of credit, the significance of Bank rate as a conventional reference point for other rates was reduced. In particular the clearing banks ceased to tie their lending and deposit rates to it. But the function of Bank rate as a market instrument remained, being the minimum at which the Bank would normally lend to the discount market. The increased flexibility of interest rates envisaged by the changes of September 1971, however, requires a last resort lending rate which can respond flexibly to changing conditions in the money market, without movements in it being interpreted as signalling major shifts in monetary policy.
>
> With the approval of the Chancellor of the Exchequer, the Bank accordingly published on 9th October new arrangements for determining and announcing their minimum rate for lending to the market. From 13th October, the lending rate was to be $\frac{1}{2}$% above the average rate of discount for Treasury bills at the most recent tender, rounded to the nearest $\frac{1}{4}$% above. The rate would be automatically determined by this formula and announced each Friday afternoon with the results of the Treasury bill tender, the weekly Bank rate announcement on Thursday being discontinued. A change in the lending rate independent of these arrangements, however, was not to be excluded if, for example, it was required to signify a shift in monetary policy. When the Bank decided, with the approval of the Chancellor, to make a special change of this kind, the announcement would normally be made on a Thursday at mid-day and the operation of the minimum lending rate formula would be suspended until market rates had moved into line.

This formula remained in operation for over five years, though it was overriden on occasions. But in May 1978 the authorities reverted to setting their minimum lending rate administratively. This was principally to enable short-term interest rates to be set at a level thought to be consistent with the achievement of monetary targets:

> On 25th May, the Bank announced that minimum lending rate would, in future, be set by administrative action rather than by the formula normally used since October 1972. Although the formula had in general worked well, it had been found that a close automatic link with the Treasury bill rate could on occasion lead to undesirable erratic movements in interest rates; MLR will continue to be adjusted flexibly, taking account of market developments.
>
> (June 1978 *Bulletin* page 166)

Mr A L Coleby, an Assistant Director of the Bank, commented briefly on these changes in a speech reprinted in Chapter 5 (page 98). They are reviewed more thoroughly in Annex A of the Green Paper on *Monetary Control*[1] prepared jointly by the Treasury and the Bank and published in March 1980 (page 143).

As the Green Paper noted (see also page 44), in the economic circumstances of 1973 the authorities were forced into a partial retreat from the principles of Competition and Credit Control and introduced the supplementary special deposits scheme, known as the 'corset', in December of that year. It was, in effect, a form of direct control on the size of the banks' balance sheets. The background to this scheme and its operation are reviewed in an article *The supplementary special deposits scheme* (page 117) published in the March 1982 *Bulletin*.

---

1 *Monetary Control*; HMSO, Cmnd 7858 1980.

Competition and credit control

Text of a consultative document issued on 14 May 1971 as a basis for discussion with banks and finance houses.

1   The Chancellor of the Exchequer announced in his Budget speech that the authorities wished to explore with the banks and finance houses the possible development of new techniques of monetary policy, with the objective of combining an effective measure of control over credit conditions with greater scope for competition and innovation. He said: 'I believe it should be possible to achieve more flexible but still effective arrangements basically by operating on the banks' resources rather than by directly guiding their lending.'

2   This paper sets out some proposals to this end as a basis for discussion.

3   In recent years the authorities have paid particular attention to certain categories of lending in sterling by banks and finance houses who have been asked and have agreed to observe quantitative limits on that lending. In practice these limits have been applied individually to most of the banks and finance houses affected and consequently have impeded competition and innovation so that the efficient have been prevented from growing and the less efficient have been helped to maintain the level of their business. Competition in the banking system is at present also limited by the agreements between the Bank of England and the London and Scottish clearing banks which require these groups, but not other banks, to hold certain specified classes of assets to an amount not less than a fixed percentage of their deposit liabilities (the cash and liquidity ratios). In addition, the London and Scottish clearing banks adhere to collective agreements fixing the rates which they pay on deposits and setting minimum rates charged on advances.

4   The authorities, for their part, propose that the impediments to competition arising from the existing liquidity and quantitative lending controls should be replaced by other means of influencing bank and finance house lending in sterling, including the application of a reserve ratio across the whole banking system. It would be part of these proposals that when the changes are introduced, the London and Scottish clearing banks should abandon their collective agreements on interest rates (subject to the proviso in paragraph 15 below about the terms offered on savings deposits).

5   The techniques of monetary policy now proposed would involve less reliance on particular methods of influencing bank and finance house lending and more reliance on changes in interest rates, supported by calls for special deposits on the basis of a reserve ratio across the whole of the banking system. There would be similar arrangements for deposit-taking finance houses.

6   For the banking system it is proposed to modify the special and cash deposits schemes so as to put banks on a common basis so far as the operation of these schemes is concerned. The special deposits scheme provides for calls for deposits by the Bank of England to whatever extent the authorities deem necessary for the purposes of credit control and for payment of interest on such deposits close to the Treasury bill rate. Its effectiveness rests in part on the agreement by the London and Scottish clearing banks, mentioned above, to hold certain specified assets to an amount not less than a fixed percentage of their deposit liabilities. The cash deposits scheme places a narrow limit on the extent to which the Bank of England may call for deposits but allows the Bank in certain circumstances to pay a low or even nil rate of interest on outstanding deposits. No agreement exists with the banks participating in the cash deposits scheme regarding any minimum ratio of specified assets. The effectiveness of the cash deposits scheme rests predominantly on guidance being given by the authorities, which in practice may differ little from requests for quantitative restriction.

7   It is now proposed that all banks should:

(i)   hold not less than a fixed percentage of their sterling deposit liabilities in certain specified reserve assets; and

(ii) place such amount of special deposits with the Bank of England as the Bank may call for from time to time.

The proposal that all banks should observe a minimum reserve assets ratio is intended to provide the authorities with a known firm base for the operation of monetary policy.

8   It is proposed that the reserve assets should comprise cash at the Bank of England and certain assets which the Bank will normally be prepared to convert into cash. The principal assets which would qualify for inclusion are balances with the Bank of England (other than special deposits), British government and Northern Ireland government Treasury bills, money at call with the London money market,[1] British government securities with a year or less to run to maturity, local authority bills eligible for rediscount at the Bank of England and, up to a proportion of deposits to be specified, commercial bills eligible for rediscount at the Bank of England. The Bank will wish to discuss with the London clearing banks the understanding which for the future should govern the level of their balances with the Bank within the reserve ratio. It is not proposed that notes in tills should be included in the ratio because they are held mainly as a stock-in-trade to meet the needs of the banks' customers.

9   The amount of reserve assets to be held by banks would be calculated by reference to their sterling deposits obtained outside the banking system, including sterling resources acquired by switching foreign currencies into sterling.

---

[1] The exact definition of this item is to be agreed in the light of discussions. It is not proposed to include money placed in the inter-bank or local authority temporary money markets.

10 The objective of putting banks on a common basis leads to a strong presumption that the reserve ratio in **7**(i) above should be uniform for all banks. It is recognised that there is a wide diversity of business between banks in the United Kingdom but in that part of their business which involves the taking of sterling deposits and their employment in sterling assets—which is all that the present proposals seek to control—the similarities of function are more important than the dissimilarities. Moreover, according different treatment to different parts of the banking system would be difficult to reconcile with the objectives of the proposals in this paper, and would impede the authorities in making uniform calls for special deposits.

11 A preliminary examination suggests that a uniform reserve ratio as defined above could be set close to the average practice of the banking system in recent years without causing inequity or undue disturbance arising from banks needing to rearrange their portfolios. Such an average would suggest a ratio of $12\frac{1}{2}\%$ of relevant deposit liabilities. In addition, it would be for consideration from time to time what level of special deposits was required. The need for a call for special deposits would be determined by the authorities, in the light of monetary conditions generally, including the behaviour of total sterling lending by all banks, and of the intention of the authorities to maintain adequate control. The amount of special deposits to be placed with the Bank of England might be calculated by reference to all or only some of the banks' liabilities to which the reserve ratio would be applied. In particular, a call could be related to domestic or to overseas deposits, or the rate of call might be different for domestic and overseas deposits. The rate or rates of call would be the same for all banks; and all deposits called would bear interest at a rate equivalent to the Treasury bill rate.

12 Problems would be likely to arise in moving from the existing methods of control to the arrangements just described. Where reserve assets were appreciably below the prescribed ratio, there would be problems of adjustment for the banks concerned. Where reserve assets were appreciably above the prescribed ratio, there would be problems for the authorities in ensuring maintenance of adequate control over monetary conditions. Special provisions to meet each set of problems would need to be devised and agreed.

13 In the context of the above proposals it has been decided to restrict the extent of the Bank of England's operations in the gilt-edged market. With immediate effect, these will be conducted on the following general basis:

(i) the Bank will no longer be prepared to respond to requests to buy stock outright, except in the case of stocks with one year or less to run to maturity;

(ii) they reserve the right to make outright purchases of stock with more than a year to run solely at their discretion and initiative;

(iii) they will be prepared to undertake, at prices of their own choosing, exchanges of stock with the market except those which unduly shorten the life of the debt; and

(iv) they will be prepared to respond to bids for the sale by them of tap stocks and of such other stocks held by them as they may wish to sell.

This modification by the Bank of their mode of operation in the gilt-edged market represents a return towards the position in the market which they occupied up to some ten years ago. In the present context, it will help to limit, further than can be achieved solely by alterations in the Bank's dealing prices, fluctuations in the resources of the banking system arising from official operations in the gilt-edged market. It is being put into effect now so that it can be taken into account in discussions of the proposals on credit control outlined in this paper. More generally, it is considered appropriate to accompany changes in credit control intended to allow greater freedom of competition in the banking system with lesser intervention by the authorities in the gilt-edged market so as to leave more freedom for prices to be affected by market conditions and for others to operate if they so wish.

14 Notwithstanding the abandonment of quantitative ceilings, and the adoption of the above proposals, the authorities would continue to provide the banks with such qualitative guidance as may be appropriate. For example, so long as hire-purchase terms control remains in force, banks will be asked that personal loans related to the purchase of goods subject to terms control should be made on terms no easier that those permitted by the Department of Trade and Industry for hire-purchase contracts.

15 The greater freedom afforded to banks by the above proposals might lead them to compete for individuals' savings at present invested in public sector debt or in the finance of housing. The impact of such competition on savings banks and building societies would need careful consideration and the Bank of England would wish to discuss this matter with the banks. It might be that a need would be recognised, for example, to observe some limits on the terms offered for savings deposits. The need for such limits would be open to reconsideration in the light of changed circumstances.

16 The members of the London Discount Market Association are not parties to either the special deposits or the cash deposits schemes; separate proposals are therefore being made to the Association to ensure that their operations do not undermine the authorities' arrangements with the banks.

17 The Bank of England would wish to discuss with the Finance Houses Association arrangements for their members parallel with those for banks proposed above. The Bank would wish to discuss this question also with those finance houses not members of the Association who have been receiving the Bank's requests for credit restriction.

18 Some amendments to and amplification of existing statistical information provided by banks and finance houses would be required to put the arrangements proposed above into practice. It would be essential for the authorities to receive this modified information, accurately compiled, promptly each month.

The supplementary special deposits scheme

This article reviews the supplementary special deposits scheme, known as the 'corset', as an instrument of monetary control.

The scheme was introduced in response to the growth of 'liability management', which made it difficult for the authorities to restrict the growth of the broad monetary aggregates in the face of strong demand for credit. It was designed to have the minimum impact on the structure of financial markets.

The scheme was largely effective in containing the growth of wholesale deposits. But it tended to encourage the diversion of banking business into other channels.

The scheme exemplifies the difficulties of relying excessively on direct controls on the banking system as a means of influencing monetary developments.

I Introduction

The supplementary special deposits (SSD) scheme was a system of direct controls on the sterling operations of banks (and deposit-taking finance houses) in the United Kingdom. It imposed penalties on individual institutions whose interest-bearing eligible liabilities (IBELs — essentially their interest-bearing sterling deposits) grew faster than a prescribed rate. The penalties became increasingly severe, the greater the excess over the prescribed growth in IBELs. The scheme was activated three times—from December 1973 to February 1975, from November 1976 to August 1977, and from June 1978 to June 1980.[1]

Part II of this article outlines the developments which led to the adoption of the scheme as a supplement to the then existing arrangements, known as *Competition and credit control* (which had been implemented in September 1971). The reasons for modifying *Competition and credit control* in this way, rather than adopting one of a number of other possibilities, are also considered. For example, the authorities could have reverted to a system of ceilings on bank lending; other options would have been to introduce incremental controls on bank lending, or interest rate ceilings.

Part III describes the way in which the scheme operated in practice. The scheme was intended as a simple adjunct to existing arrangements. It was hoped that it would directly tackle the unhelpful response (for monetary control purposes) of the banking system to reserve asset shortages, without requiring any radical, and unintended, changes to the structure of financial markets. In many respects the scheme achieved these objectives, but the practical operation of the scheme—in particular, its interaction with the reserve asset ratio—became quite complicated.

After the adoption of published monetary targets in 1976, difficulties were also encountered in relating the aggregate on which the SSD scheme was based, interest-bearing eligible liabilities, to the target monetary aggregate, sterling M_3.

Part IV assesses the impact of the scheme on monetary developments. Such an assessment is difficult, not only because the scheme may have had a direct effect by discouraging the banks from competing for business, but also because the announcement of the scheme may itself have created an environment conducive to sales of gilt-edged stocks, thereby influencing the money supply indirectly. On the other hand, the direct effect of the scheme on the recorded monetary aggregates may, at least in an economic sense, have been partially offset by the tendency for borrowers and lenders to circumvent the controls by redirecting funds through uncontrolled, parallel markets (a device known as disintermediation).

The relaxation of exchange controls in June 1979 and their abolition in October 1979 enabled UK residents to place deposits with, and borrow from, banks overseas. The possibility of large-scale offshore disintermediation further undermined the effectiveness of the scheme, and in June 1980 it was abolished.

In Part V the contribution of the scheme to the maintenance of monetary control is assessed in the light of the circumstances which prevailed at the time, in particular the prior existence of *Competition and credit control* and exchange controls.

The glossary on page 119 explains some of the key terms used in this article.

---

[1] Because a period of grace was allowed before the banks became liable to pay penalties, the scheme could have been a direct constraint on the banks only from April 1974 to February 1975, February 1977 to August 1977, and August 1978 to June 1980.

II Historical background and the design of the scheme

In 1973, the UK economy appeared to be nearing the limits of its capacity. In the fourth quarter, unemployment fell to 2.2% and unfilled vacancies rose to 1.6%, both of which subsequently proved to be turning points. The current account of the balance of payments deteriorated throughout 1973, with a deficit of £400 million in the fourth quarter.

The pressures on the economy were also apparent in financial developments. The banks were faced with a strong demand for credit and, unconstrained by quantitative ceilings (which had been abandoned in 1971), bank lending to the private sector grew by 33% during 1973. The banks funded this increased lending by bidding aggressively for deposits in the wholesale money markets. As a result, the broad monetary aggregates, which include (UK residents') large denomination deposits and certificates of deposit, grew rapidly: M_3, for example, grew by 28% during 1973. In contrast, the narrow monetary aggregate, M_1, grew by only $5\frac{1}{4}$%, probably reflecting a switch from non-interest-bearing to interest-bearing accounts prompted by the rise in short-term interest rates. (During 1973 bank base rates rose from $8\frac{1}{2}$% to 13%.)

Liability management

The importance of the demand for credit in the determination of the overall size of the banks' balance sheets, at least in the short run, arises in part because of an asymmetry in the flexibility of interest rates on each side of the banks' balance sheets. The overdraft system has the general effect of enabling customers to increase their borrowing, effectively at their own discretion, at rates which have tended to be relatively inflexible in the short run. This inflexibility was enhanced because the banks used to tie their base rates—to which ordinary overdraft rates were related—to Bank rate (later minimum lending rate—MLR).[1] Changes in MLR involved an administrative decision, with the delays that that entailed, and for a time an increase in the demand for credit did not provoke a rise in lending rates.[2] In contrast, wholesale deposit rates have been highly flexible in the short run, and the banks have tended to accommodate the demand for credit by bidding whatever rate is necessary in the wholesale markets to attract sufficient funds to meet their lending commitments. This behaviour is known as liability management.

Some have argued that control of the broad monetary aggregates is virtually unattainable if liability management is allowed. Further, it has been suggested that in order to control the broad aggregates the authorities should induce the banks to react to unexpected shortages or surpluses of funds by adjusting their assets rather than their liabilities. It would appear, however, that private sector demand for bank credit has been insensitive—at least in the short run—to changes in the absolute level of interest rates. Indeed, the immediate effect of a rise in interest rates may, on occasion, have been to raise the demand for bank credit, in order to pay the increased interest charges. Attempts by the banks to stem sudden changes in the demand for credit by varying their lending rates might therefore have involved sizable fluctuations in short-term rates, if not an unstable interest rate spiral. If the banks had been induced to manage their assets by rationing the supply of credit, parallel markets would doubtless have developed to provide the services which the banks would no longer be offering.

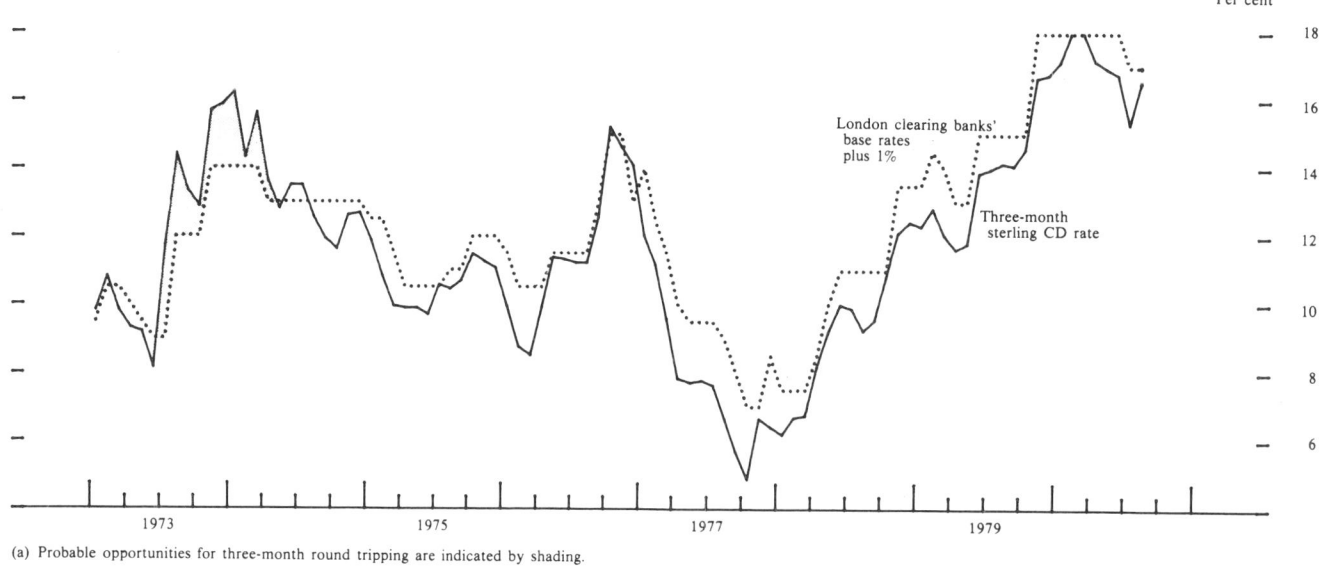

Chart 1
Bank base rates and wholesale money market rates[a]

London clearing banks' base rates plus 1%

Three-month sterling CD rate

(a) Probable opportunities for three-month round tripping are indicated by shading.

(1) Throughout the 1970s, an increasing proportion of bank lending was undertaken by means of three-month roll-over credits, rather than by overdraft lending. Whereas the interest rate charged on overdrafts was set at a margin over the banks' administratively determined base rates, roll-over credits tended to be charged at a margin over the London inter-bank offered rate (LIBOR)—a market-determined rate. However, the actual rate charged on roll-over credits was still inflexible in the short run because the rate was adjusted only every three months.

(2) In October 1972 Bank rate was replaced by MLR. MLR was to be determined in an automatic manner at $\frac{1}{2}$% above the average rate of discount for Treasury bills at the weekly tender, rounded to the nearest $\frac{1}{4}$% above. However, the Bank retained the right to override the normal formula. In May 1978 it was announced that MLR would in future be determined by administrative decision. Since mid-August 1981, MLR has been suspended.

Glossary of terms

Bank bill
A commercial bill on which a reputable bank has placed its name, thus accepting the obligation to honour the bill on the due date.

Bill leak
Bank bills held outside the banking sector.

Commercial bill
A bill of exchange drawn by a commercial firm to finance a short-term self-liquidating transaction such as the export of goods.

Competition and credit control
A package of measures implemented in September 1971, following the abolition of direct controls on bank lending. It involved, among other things, the introduction of a common reserve asset ratio requirement, which applied to all banks.

Disintermediation
The process whereby business that is essentially banking business is conducted in such a way that it does not appear in the banks' balance sheets. Cosmetic disintermediation is encouraged by the imposition of controls on the banking system.

Eligible liabilities
Essentially the sterling resources available to a bank for on-lending to other sectors of the economy. Between 1971 and 1980, these mainly comprised:

- All sterling deposits, of an original maturity of two years or under, from UK residents (other than banks) and from overseas residents (other than overseas offices).
- All sterling deposits, of whatever term, from the UK banking sector *net* of sterling claims (including non-reserve asset lending to listed discount market institutions).
- All sterling certificates of deposit issued, of whatever term, *less* any holdings of such certificates.
- The bank's net deposit liability, if any, in sterling to its overseas offices.
- The bank's net liability, if any, in currencies other than sterling.

Suspense accounts were also included, as were 60% of net debit items in transit.

Interest-bearing eligible liabilities
The interest-bearing element of eligible liabilities.

Liability management
Process whereby the banks adjust the volume of their deposits by operations in the wholesale money markets so that the liability side of their balance sheet accommodates changes in the demand for loans. (Asset management is the process whereby loans granted or marketable instruments held are adjusted to equal the supply of deposits.)

Money at call
Typically, a deposit with a discount market institution which is placed on a day-to-day basis and which can be withdrawn any day before noon. When placed with a discount market institution, and both at call and secured, such a deposit counted as a reserve asset.

Reserve asset ratio
Between September 1971 and January 1981, each bank was required to hold at least $12\frac{1}{2}\%$ of its eligible liabilities in the form of reserve assets. (The reserve asset ratio was reduced to 10% in January 1981, temporarily reduced to 8% for most of March and April 1981, and abolished in August 1981.) Reserve assets comprised:

- Balances at the Bank of England (other than special or supplementary deposits).
- British government and Northern Ireland Treasury bills.
- Secured money at call with London discount market institutions.
- British government stocks with a residual maturity of less than one year.
- Local authority bills eligible for rediscount at the Bank.
- Commercial bills eligible for rediscount at the Bank (ie eligible bank bills), up to a maximum of 2% of eligible liabilities.

Round tripping
Process whereby bank customers borrow in one market (eg on overdraft at a base rate-related rate) and redeposit the funds in the wholesale markets at a higher rate.

Special deposits
The authorities can require the banks to place a certain percentage of their eligible liabilities in a special deposit at the Bank. This deposit did not constitute a reserve asset. Special deposits bear an interest rate broadly equivalent to the Treasury bill rate.

Trade bills
A commercial bill which has not been accepted by a bank.

Wholesale deposits
Large deposits, bearing an interest rate in line with market rates (rather than base rates). Includes certificates of deposit.

Chart 2
Three-month interest-rate differentials

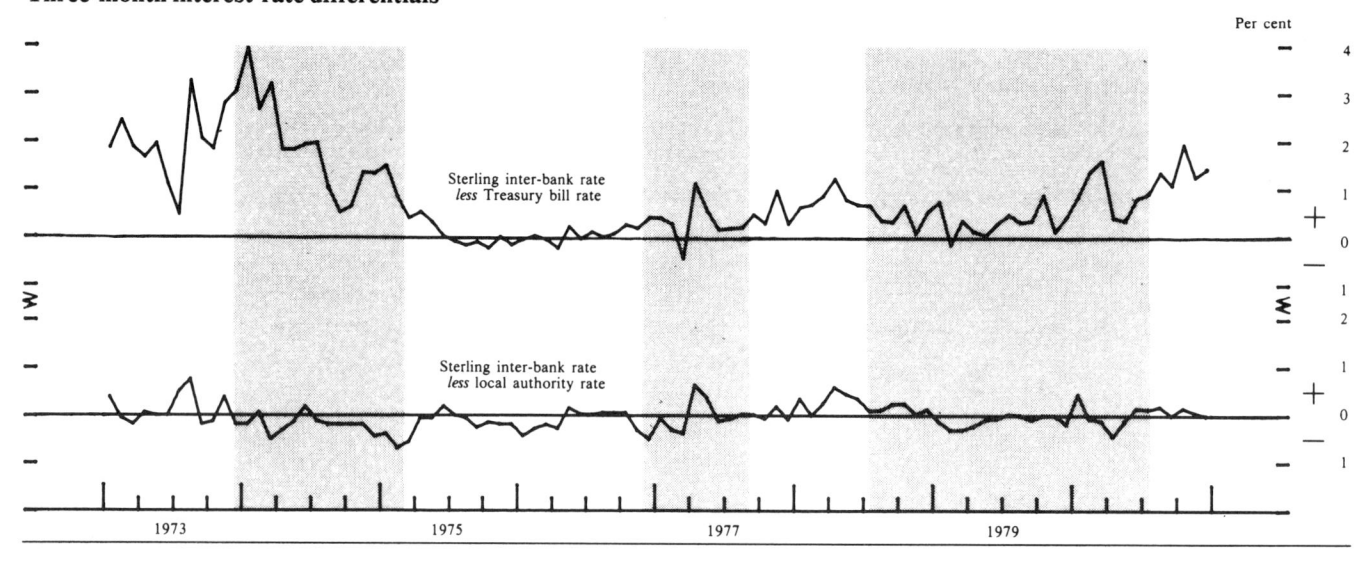

As a result of these limitations, the authorities have found it difficult to restrict the growth of the broad monetary aggregates in the face of strong demand for credit, as in 1973. Moreover, increases in wholesale deposit rates have tended to have perverse effects on the broad aggregates because of changes in relative interest rates. Since base rates have been less flexible than wholesale deposit rates, rises in short-term rates have generally led to base rates falling temporarily behind wholesale deposit rates. On occasion, prime borrowers have been able to make a profit by borrowing on overdraft at a base rate-related rate, and relending these funds at a wholesale deposit rate (see Chart 1). This 'round tripping' has artificially inflated the banks' balance sheets and thereby the broad monetary aggregates.

In 1973 liability management and round tripping may have become more widespread because of the authorities' attempts to curb monetary growth by applying increasing reserve asset pressure to the banks. In December 1972 a $\frac{1}{2}$% special deposit call was made, and by December 1973 special deposit calls had risen to 5%. This had the effect of reducing the banks' reserve asset ratios towards their $12\frac{1}{2}$% minimum.[1] Rather than curb their lending (ie asset manage), the banks tended to bid more aggressively for deposits (ie liability manage) in order to finance their increased holdings of reserve assets. Thus, yields on reserve assets such as Treasury bills and money at call tended to fall relative to inter-bank and other non-reserve asset yields (see Chart 2). In the short run, the banks seemed prepared to absorb the increased cost of funding; later they began to include explicitly in their margins the cost of acquiring reserve assets, perhaps with little short-run impact on the demand for credit. Moreover, while the 'formula' for setting MLR was in operation, the relative decline in Treasury bill yields tended to reduce the pressure to raise MLR.

The authorities responded to these difficulties by announcing the SSD scheme for the first time on 17 December 1973. Under the scheme, banks (and finance houses[2]) agreed individually to place non-interest-bearing supplementary special deposits with the Bank if their interest-bearing eligible liabilities grew faster than a specified rate. Since the banks did not, and presumably could not, vary their non-interest-bearing deposits to accommodate changes in the demand for credit, non-interest-bearing liabilities were excluded from the system of controls.[3] The size of the deposits required to be placed with the Bank varied progressively according to the excess growth of IBELs. The details of how the penalties were calculated are outlined in the box (on next page).

The scheme therefore forced the banks either to accept lower profits (or even large losses) on additional lending, or else to widen the margins they quoted to customers. The cost of placing non-interest-bearing SSDs with the Bank was considerably greater than the (opportunity) cost of acquiring reserve assets, particularly in the second and third penalty zone (see box on next page), so the financial incentive to widen margins was greatly increased. To the extent that they widened their margins, a 'wedge' was driven between their deposit and loan rates. Even if higher lending rates had only a small short-run impact on the demand for credit, lower wholesale deposit rates relative to base rates were expected to reduce the opportunities for profitable round tripping. There was also some hope that the reduced profitability of marginal business might deter the banks from expanding their balance sheets either by

---

[1] Between September 1971 and January 1981, each bank was required to hold an amount equivalent to at least $12\frac{1}{2}$% of its eligible liabilities as reserve assets. The reserve asset ratio was reduced to 10% in January 1981, temporarily lowered to 8% for most of March and April 1981, and abolished in August 1981. In broad terms, reserve assets comprised certain types of deposit with the discount market and some short-term public sector debt. A more detailed definition can be found in the glossary.

[2] Certain of the larger deposit-taking finance houses were subject to the provisions of *Competition and credit control*. But the aggregate size of their business was small in relation to that of the banks, and they are not discussed further in this article.

[3] The relative inflexibility of the implicit yield on non-interest-bearing deposits (including the value of transmission services *less* bank charges) suggests that these deposits are largely determined by non-bank demand for them, rather than by the demand for credit. The residual between non-bank demand for credit and demand for non-interest-bearing deposits has to be met by the banks bidding for wholesale deposits.

How the scheme worked

- The scheme applied in principle to all 'listed' banks and deposit-taking finance houses; but small institutions and (because of the special circumstances there) institutions in Northern Ireland were exempt.
- Institutions were required to lodge non-interest-bearing deposits with the Bank of England if their interest-bearing eligible liabilities (see next box) grew faster than a specified rate. The rate of deposit was progressive from 5% to 50% as the amount of excess growth increased.
- The liability to pay SSDs was calculated monthly, on a moving three-month average of IBELs.
- The precise details which applied to each activation of the scheme are shown below.

Scheme announced	Base period[a]	Allowable growth	Rate of deposit	Exemption[b]	Scheme terminated
17 Dec. 1973	Oct.–Dec. 1973	8% over first six months; 1½% per month thereafter	*Until Nov. 1974* 5% in respect of excess of up to 1% 25% ,, ,, ,, ,, of 1%–3% 50% ,, ,, ,, ,, of over 3%	£3 million	28 Feb. 1975
			From Nov. 1974 5% in respect of excess of up to 3% 25% ,, ,, ,, ,, of 3%–5% 50% ,, ,, ,, ,, of over 5%	£5 million	
18 Nov. 1976	Aug.–Oct. 1976	3% over first six months; ½% per month thereafter	As above	£5 million	11 Aug. 1977
8 June 1978	Nov. 1977–Apr. 1978	4% over period to Aug.–Oct. 1978; 1% per month thereafter	As above	£10 million	18 June 1980[c]

(a) The base level was the average level of IBELs over the period shown.
(b) The scheme did not apply to institutions with IBELs below the amount shown.
(c) The announcement of the termination of the scheme was made on 26 March; final deposits were repaid in August.

pursuing innovative lending policies, or by making loans with a higher default risk. The ability of the SSD scheme to encourage such non-price rationing by the banks might have been important because of the interest insensitivity, at least in the short run, of the demand for credit.

Alternatives to the scheme

In constructing a direct control in 1973, designed for intermittent use, the authorities had to have regard to the structural changes that had occurred since 1971, and to the longer-run objectives of *Competition and credit control*. Although the SSD scheme limited the extent to which the market share of the individual banks could change, the scheme was intended to operate for short periods only. During periods when the scheme was in abeyance, the competitive pressures introduced under *Competition and credit control* could reassert themselves. A system of financial penalties rather than absolute ceilings (which had been used in the pre-1971 controls) was also preferred because of the greater flexibility it afforded the banks.

A temporary system of controls with financial penalties could have been applied to changes on either side of the banks' balance sheets. A system of controls on bank lending, like the French *Encadrement du credit*, could have been tried, but it was thought that there were a number of advantages in favour of applying the controls to the liability side of the banks' balance sheets. In fact, an individual bank's eligible liabilities (ELs), of which IBELs are the major component over which the bank has some control, consist essentially of the sterling funds available to the bank for on-lending to non-bank customers. As well as including all sterling deposits (including net sterling deposits from other banks) with an original maturity of less than two years, ELs also include net sterling funds acquired by switching foreign currencies into sterling.[1] In consequence, and in contrast to the pre-1971 controls, the SSD scheme did not discriminate between bank lending to the public and private sectors.

It might have been possible to inhibit liability management by imposing an interest rate ceiling on deposits. Indeed, between September 1973 and February 1975 the banks were asked not to pay more than 9½% on deposits of up to £10,000. In the United States, *Regulation Q* has been applied more widely, but not (since 1973) to certificates of deposit; partly as a result, most wholesale business has been conducted in marketable instruments. In practice, it would be difficult to impose an interest rate ceiling on marketable instruments, and, because of the ease of substitution between non-marketable large denomination deposits and certificates of deposit, the use of a ceiling similar to *Regulation Q* would have been unlikely to contain liability management. Moreover, interest rate ceilings tend either to be binding, causing dramatic flows out of the controlled institutions (as with the 'credit crunch' in the United States in 1966), or to have no effect. The switch from not being binding to being a major restriction can be abrupt and far from smooth.

---

(1) Switching out of sterling into foreign currencies was not allowed as an offset. See glossary.

III The SSD scheme in practice

The scheme was designed to have as little impact as possible on the structure of financial markets. This objective was pursued not because of any particular commitment to the *status quo* by the authorities, but because it was felt that changes in financial markets should not be initiated as a, possibly unexpected, by-product of an intermittently used system of monetary control. As a result, the SSD scheme was designed to operate in tandem with, rather than independently of, the $12\frac{1}{2}\%$ reserve asset ratio adhered to by the banks.

IBELs were chosen as the variable to be controlled, in some large part because ELs were already used as the base for calculating the reserve asset ratio and calls for special deposits. Banks were allowed to offset not only funds placed with other banks (since these funds would be included in the recipient bank's IBELs), but also funds placed with the discount market, if these funds did not have reserve asset status.[1]

Since the discount houses were not subject to the SSD scheme, money at call held by the banks with the houses (a reserve asset) could be redesignated as money not at call (not a reserve asset) thereby reducing the total IBELs of the banks. These transactions for reducing IBELs could continue until the banks' excess reserve assets were exhausted. The banks could increase their non-reserve asset lending to discount houses, and the funds could then be used by the houses to purchase commercial bills or other assets from the banks. In this way, a fall in IBELs could be arranged without falls in reserve assets, in non-bank deposits with the banking sector, or in lending to the non-banks by the banking sector. In effect, lending to non-banks could be shifted from the banks to the discount houses. Ultimately, these transactions were constrained by the undefined assets multiple. (Undefined assets,[2] which included lending to the non-bank private sector, could not exceed twenty times the capital and reserves of each discount house.) But, if the houses were below their limit, the imposition of the SSD scheme might have made it profitable for them to increase the size of their balance sheets up to that point.

It was therefore not surprising that significant SSD penalties were paid only when the banking system as a whole was under reserve asset pressure and the discount houses were close to their undefined assets limit (see Chart 3). In the first SSD period, some penalties were paid, mainly because of operational errors by a few banks, but on the whole the banks were able to run down their excess reserve assets, and through this, and other means, avoid penalties. In particular, the undefined assets multiple rose sharply after the announcement of the scheme. Had the demand for credit continued to grow at a rapid rate in the first half of 1974 the banks might have incurred significant penalties; but in the event the economy began to turn down and the demand for credit slackened.

Chart 3
Pressure on the banks and the discount market

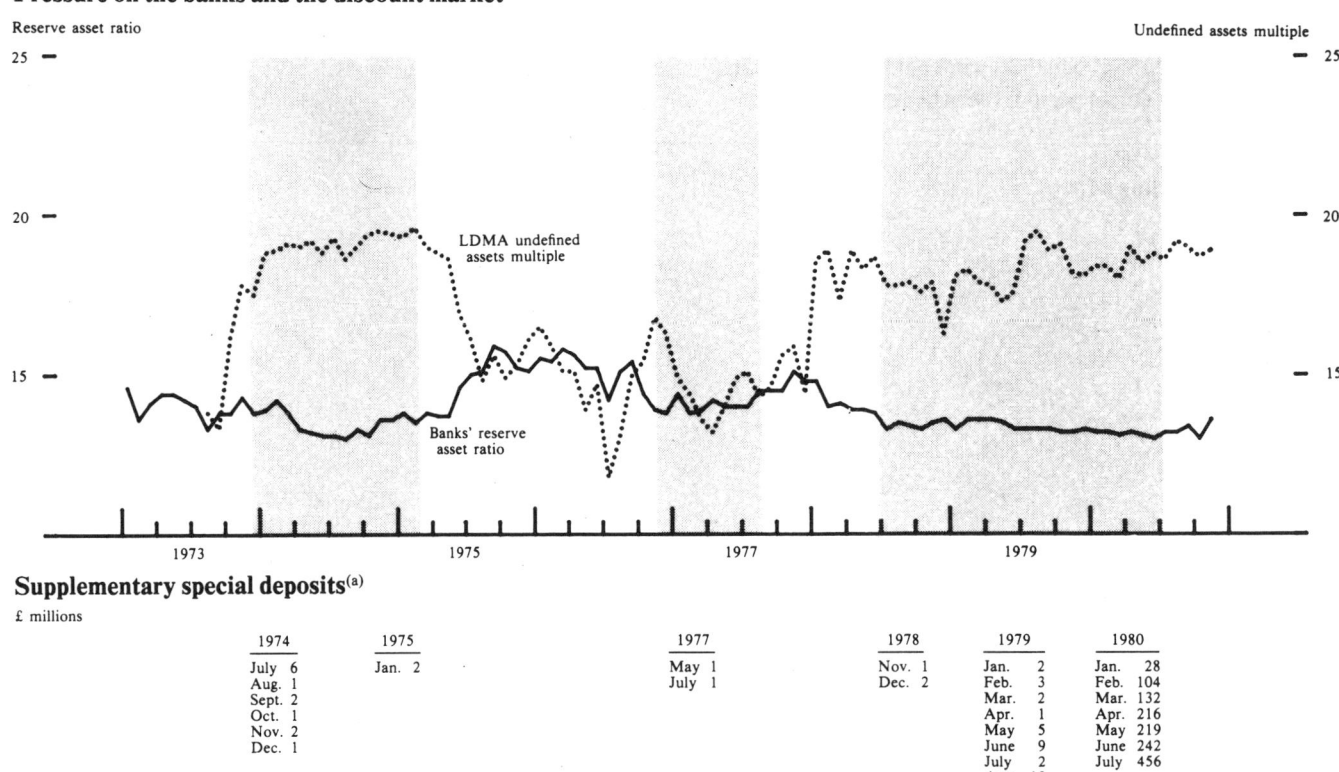

Supplementary special deposits[a]
£ millions

1974	1975	1977	1978	1979	1980
July 6	Jan. 2	May 1	Nov. 1	Jan. 2	Jan. 28
Aug. 1		July 1	Dec. 2	Feb. 3	Feb. 104
Sept. 2				Mar. 2	Mar. 132
Oct. 1				Apr. 1	Apr. 216
Nov. 2				May 5	May 219
Dec. 1				June 9	June 242
				July 2	July 456
				Aug. 10	
				Sept. 4	
				Oct. 1	
				Nov. 3	
				Dec. 19	

(a) A more detailed analysis of deposits can be found in the appendix: this shows the number of banks incurring penalities and the size of deposits in each tranche

---
(1) To qualify as a reserve asset, money placed with the discount market institutions had to be secured and immediately callable.
(2) All assets other than certain public sector assets, such as balances at the Bank, Treasury bills, and government stock with a residual maturity of less than five years.

The SSD scheme was activated for the second time in November 1976, when there was concern to constrain the growth of domestic credit in order to try to protect a weak exchange rate. As it turned out, the exchange rate soon recovered dramatically, mostly for reasons unconnected with the scheme, and this was followed by very heavy sales of public sector debt and reduced demand for credit. Throughout this period the banks continued to hold excess reserve assets, and there was also considerable scope for increasing the size of the discount houses' balance sheets. Since no attempt was made to make full use of these 'loopholes', it is perhaps not surprising that very few SSD penalties were paid, even though the penalty-free rate of growth of IBELs appeared to be tighter than under the first scheme.

In the third SSD period, only minimal penalties were paid between November 1978 and late 1979, but the banks' combined reserve asset ratio fell from around 13.5% towards its minimum operational level of between 13.1% and 13.2% by the summer of 1979. The undefined assets multiple remained above 18 once both the reserve asset ratio and the SSD ceilings became effectively restrictive. By February 1980, twenty-two banks had placed £104 million as SSDs, and the demand for credit continued to grow rapidly. Indeed, after February 1980 the number of banks in the second and third penalty tranches increased dramatically.[1] In these higher tranches the cost of undertaking additional lending became onerous, in contrast to the first penalty tranche which imposed only a modest marginal cost.

Although sizable SSD penalties were paid only in the latter part of the third corset period, the scheme did appear to reduce the aggressiveness with which the banks bid for wholesale deposits. In all three episodes, wholesale deposit rates tended to fall relative to both base rates and yields on other liquid assets (see Chart 2). At its inception this was the main purpose of the scheme—to curb the growth of wholesale bank deposits. Since December 1976, however, formal target ranges had been announced for sterling M_3,[2] and although any restraint on the growth of wholesale deposits was likely to have contributed towards the attainment of these targets, the scheme had not been designed for that purpose.

The relationship with monetary targets

In translating a sterling M_3 target into prescribed IBELs growth, adjustments had to be made for items included in IBELs, but not in sterling M_3, and *vice versa*. In particular, IBELs included overseas sterling deposits, which are not in sterling M_3, while sterling M_3 includes notes and coin held by the public and non-interest-bearing deposits, all of which were excluded from IBELs.[3] As a result, even if the prescribed IBELs path was achieved, errors in forecasting the other components could lead to the overshooting or undershooting of the sterling M_3 target.

In general, sterling M_3 tended to grow faster than IBELs when the corset was in operation, and this divergence tended to unwind when the scheme was in abeyance (see Chart 4). This discrepancy arose mainly as a result of the transactions with the discount houses described above, but other factors might have been the increased use of non-interest-bearing deposits or over-two-year deposits. Customers might, in theory, have been induced to increase their non-interest-bearing balances as a result of 'compensating balance' arrangements for corporate

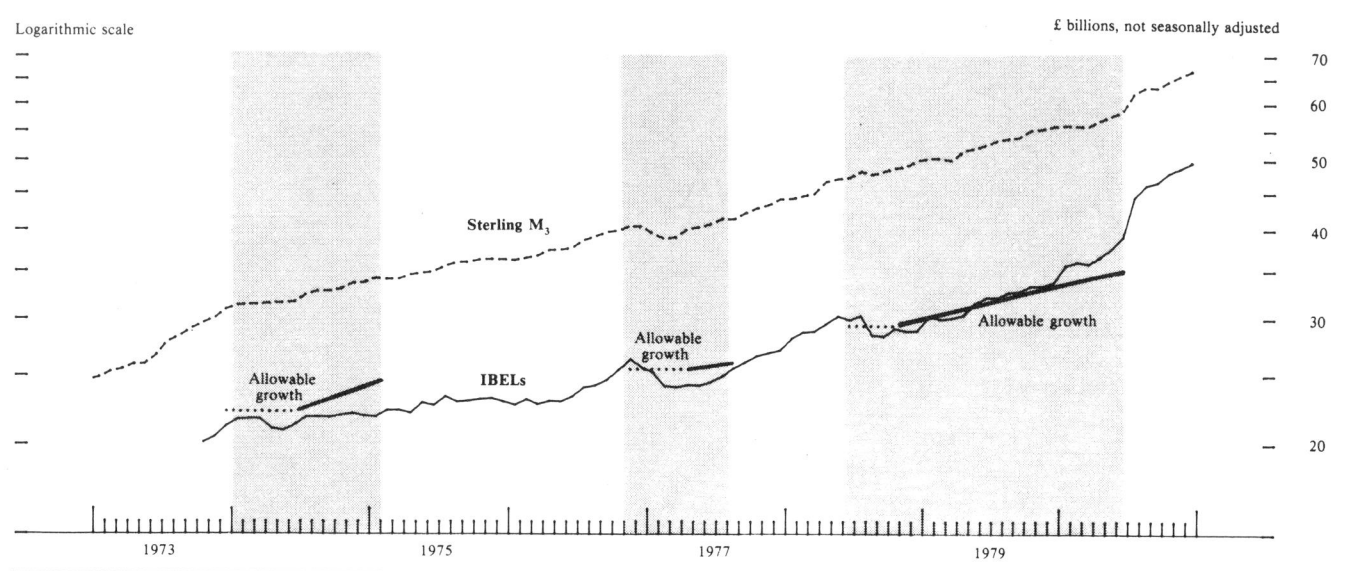

Chart 4
IBELs and sterling M_3

(1) In the March 1980 Budget it was announced that the scheme would lapse with effect from June 1980. Some banks may have been prepared to incur penalties in the higher tranches for this limited period in order to maintain or even increase their market share.
(2) The April 1976 Budget set guidelines for M_3 in line with money gross domestic product. In July 1976 it was announced that M_3 should grow by 12% in the financial year 1976/77. M_3 comprises UK residents' sterling and foreign currency deposits with UK banks (including discount houses), and notes and coin held by the public. In December 1976, the Letter of Intent to the IMF included a commitment to ceilings for domestic credit expansion: £9 billion for 1976/77, £7.7 billion for 1977/78, and £6 billion for 1978/79. In the same month, the Chancellor announced a 9%–13% target range for sterling M_3 (which comprises UK residents' sterling deposits with UK banks—including discount houses—and notes and coin held by the public).
(3) UK residents' sterling deposits with an original maturity of over two years and UK residents' sterling deposits with the discount houses are also included in sterling M_3, but excluded from IBELs.

customers or 'free banking' for personal customers, but there is no evidence of this having occurred on any large scale.[1] The banks apparently did not attempt to attract longer-term deposits, possibly because the higher rates required on such business rendered it unprofitable.

In principle, the SSD scheme could have been redesigned so that the controlled aggregate bore a closer relationship to sterling M_3. However, if the scheme had discriminated between resident and non-resident deposits it might have induced artificial switching of resident deposits into balances which nominally belonged to non-residents, but which would have been at the disposal of residents. Also, because of the secondary market in certificates of deposit, it would have been impossible to distinguish between certificates of deposit of individual banks held within the banking sector and those held outside. (It is, however, possible to estimate the total of certificates of deposit held by UK residents outside the banking sector and these are included in sterling M_3.)

Finally, even if the scheme could have been specified in terms of sterling M_3, a discrepancy would still have arisen because the monetary targets have been specified in seasonally adjusted terms. In practice, it would have been difficult to require individual banks to keep within an SSD ceiling in seasonally adjusted terms, in part because seasonal adjustments tend to be revised as more information becomes available.[2]

Impact on different types of bank

Although the SSD scheme applied to nearly all banks above a certain size (see below) it may, nevertheless, have had a differential impact on the various types of bank within the banking sector. Banks with a potential for rapid growth were constrained to the same penalty-free rate of growth from an arbitrarily set base level of IBELs. Also, the corset penalties were calculated for each bank individually and not on a consolidated basis for each banking group. As a result it was argued that the scheme discriminated against the smaller and more specialised non-clearing banks, which started from a low base and could not switch business within a group of banks in order to avoid or reduce penalties.

Partly for this reason, small banks were excluded from the scheme. Initially, banks with IBELs of less than £3 million were exempt, but the *de minimis* limit was later raised to £5 million and then to £10 million. As a result of the *de minimis* limit and various other adjustments, 'operational' IBELs, ie IBELs on which SSD penalties were calculated, tended to be lower than 'statistical' IBELs, ie IBELs as published in the *Bulletin* and elsewhere. In the first two corset periods, this discrepancy was not large, but in the third period the *de minimis* banks grew at a disproportionate rate, creating another leakage. Indeed, there appears to have been some scope for intra-group switching between banks included in the scheme and the *de minimis* banks.

On the other hand, some of the non-clearing banks may have been able to maintain a high level of lending within each banking month, while persuading some of their customers to switch to overdraft borrowing from the clearing banks over the monthly make-up day. This sort of 'window dressing' may have redistributed the liability to pay penalties, and allowed effectively higher lending by the non-clearers at the expense of the clearers.

IV Impact on monetary developments

Any assessment of the impact of the SSD scheme on monetary developments is complicated by three factors. First, the activation of the scheme was in each case announced as part of a package of economic measures, so it is difficult to disentangle the effect of the scheme from the impact of other instruments of government policy.

On 13 November 1973, MLR was raised from $11\frac{1}{4}\%$ to 13% and a further 2% call was made for special deposits, primarily in response to adverse domestic monetary developments and the general overheating of the economy. As well as introducing the SSD scheme on 17 December, the Chancellor announced a £1,200 million cut in previously planned government expenditure for 1974/75 (amounting to 2% of GNP).

The fall in the effective exchange rate index from 73 in January 1976 to 57 in October 1976 resulted in a similar package. In September 1976, MLR was raised from $11\frac{1}{2}\%$ to 13%, and the rate of call for special deposits was increased by 1%. In October, MLR was raised to a then record 15%, and a further 2% call for special deposits was made. In November 1976 exchange controls were tightened on the sterling finance of third-country trade and the SSD scheme was re-imposed. In January 1977 agreement with the IMF was reached on a borrowing facility, the markets having confidently expected such an agreement for some time.

Fears about the Government's resolve to control the public sector borrowing requirement, and worries about the buoyancy of loan demand and the possibility of overshooting the monetary target, led to a gilt-edged funding pause in the early summer of 1978. The authorities' inability to sell debt aggravated the problems caused for monetary control by the strength of loan demand, and precipitated the re-imposition of the corset and a number of other measures in June 1978. MLR was raised from 9% to 10% and a package of fiscal measures was announced, including a $1\frac{1}{2}\%$ surcharge on employers' national insurance contributions, to offset the forecast loss of revenue arising from opposition amendments to the Budget proposals.

In all three cases it is impossible to know what would have happened to monetary developments if the corset had not been imposed.

---

[1] 'Compensating balances' and 'free banking' are arrangements whereby customers pay for their financial services by holding an agreed level of non-interest-bearing balances.
[2] An element of seasonal adjustment was allowed in calculating IBELs for operational purposes: banks were allowed to 'smooth' the interest credited to seven-day deposit accounts.

The second problem associated with assessing the scheme's usefulness relates to its indirect impact on the monetary aggregates. Sizable SSD penalties were paid only in the latter part of the third corset period, but on all three occasions the announcement of the scheme may have indicated to the markets that the banks were likely to moderate the aggressiveness with which they would bid for wholesale deposits. Although the imposition of the scheme did not guarantee that the authorities would not have to raise interest rates further, it may have reduced the chance of this happening. Certainly, if the markets believed that interest rates had reached their peak, gilt-edged stocks became easier to sell and this tended to reduce the money supply.

The third problem in assessing the impact of the scheme is to evaluate the extent to which the improved control of the recorded aggregates, in particular sterling M_3, was undermined by offsetting developments elsewhere. While it would appear that the impositon of the scheme retarded the rate of growth of IBELs, they may have grown faster than otherwise would have been the case during 'corset-off' periods. The re-imposition of the corset was widely anticipated prior to November 1976 and June 1978, and the banks may have been encouraged to raise their IBELs so that they started from a higher base level.

The re-imposition of the corset was expected in the spring of 1976, and the banks' ineligible (non-reserve asset) lending to the discount houses, an offset to IBELs, fell quite markedly during that period. Prior to the second and third corset periods, the banks also appear to have raised their IBELs by issuing more sterling certificates of deposit and using these funds, at least in part, to purchase bills from the discount houses; during the 'corset-off' period between July 1977 and June 1978, IBELs grew by 21%, whereas sterling M_3 grew by 14%. Thus, there may have been a tendency for the corset merely to redistribute the rate of growth of IBELs over time. The authorities responded to this by backdating the base level: the base for the third corset period, announced in June 1978, was the average of IBELs between November 1977 and April 1978. Nevertheless, the redistribution of wholesale deposit growth over time may be an inherent feature of any temporary system of control.

Disintermediation

The efficacy of the SSD scheme was also undermined by disintermediation of a purely cosmetic nature. Even though the scheme restrained wholesale deposit taking, and therefore lending by the banks, frustrated lenders and borrowers could often be brought together in parallel markets. For example, some corporate customers could be induced, at minimal cost, to borrow by means of an acceptance, rather than an advances facility. Under this arrangement, a bank would agree to accept (ie guarantee) bills issued by a customer up to a specified limit. Accepted bills, known as bank bills, would be almost identical in terms of marketability and default risk to certificates of deposit, and as such could be sold at a similar price to holders other than banks. Thus, although bank bills held outside the banking sector are regarded as close substitutes for, and as liquid as, certificates of deposit, they are only a contingent liability of the accepting bank, and therefore an off-balance sheet item excluded from IBELs and sterling M_3.

The growth of bank bills held outside the banking system (known as the 'bill leak') when the corset was in operation was widely known and measurable. Before the first activation of the corset in the fourth quarter of 1973, bills held outside the banking system stood at an estimated £350 million, but by the end of that corset period they had grown to £500 million. During the second corset period, the bill leak grew from £320 million in the fourth quarter of 1976 to a peak of £430 million in the second quarter of 1977. Thereafter bills outstanding fell to £150 million in the first quarter of 1978. After the third corset was announced the bill leak grew to £710 million in the third quarter of 1978, and reached a peak of nearly £2,700 million in the second quarter of 1980. After the corset had been abolished bills held outside the banking system fell back to less than £500 million.

The authorities could have included this leakage in the corset controls, and even in the official definition of money. In the event, market participants were able to make reasonably accurate estimates of changes in the bill leak from published figures and thereby calculate changes in 'adjusted sterling M_3'. These adjustments were widely quoted and understood. From September 1979, figures for the bill leak were published as a component of the private sector liquidity series (Table 12 in the statistical annex). Including the bill leak in the system of controls would not, however, have curbed the problem of disintermediation. Indeed, without such a safety valve, less measurable forms of disintermediation might have grown more rapidly. The inter-company market might have expanded, by-passing the banking sector altogether, and large, creditworthy companies might have issued trade bills of similar marketability and default risk as bank bills. The funds acquired by issuing trade bills could have been used to extend trade and other forms of credit to less well-placed suppliers and customers. Some large industrial and commercial companies might therefore have become quasi-banks.

Once exchange controls were abolished in October 1979, UK residents could place deposits with, and borrow from banks located outside the United Kingdom. Since the corset could be applied only to banks in the United Kingdom, there was a possibility that all wholesale deposits in excess of the penalty-free amount would be booked offshore. Whereas it might have been possible to maintain precise control over the recorded aggregates, such control would have been largely cosmetic. Some restrictions could perhaps have been placed on offshore subsidiaries of branches of UK banks, but little or no control could have been exercised over the sterling business of offshore banks whose parent bank was not located in the United Kingdom. In the event, the Governor of the Bank of England asked UK banks not to evade the corset by booking business offshore, but it was recognised that this request, which did not and could not cover foreign banks, could not provide a lasting solution to the problem.

It is doubtful whether there is any definition of money for which close substitutes could not be developed in the event of direct restrictions being placed on the growth of such money balances; this is perhaps particularly so in the case of wholesale deposits. Disintermediation is likely to undermine most permanent or semi-permanent systems of direct control. A temporary scheme, however, may have a (non-cosmetic) effect because it takes time for parallel markets to emerge; set up costs have to be incurred and there is a learning process. In fact, it is possible to argue that systems of direct control have to be changed every few years in order to be effective. On the other hand, if schemes have to be suspended from time to time, the problems of reintermediation and anticipatory behaviour by the banks have to be faced.

Post-corset reintermediation
The rapid growth of IBELs and sterling M_3 after the abolition of the SSD scheme in June 1980 illustrates the problems of an on/off system of direct controls. In banking July 1980,[1] the bill leak fell by £1,000 million, while private sector deposits rose by £3,000 million, sterling lending to the private sector by £2,200 million, and sterling lending to overseas by £700 million, suggesting some reintermediation of sterling business driven offshore by the corset. Banks tended to rebuild their holdings of public sector debt, which had been run down during the corset period; in particular, non-reserve asset lending by banks to the local authorities rose by 11% in banking July alone. IBELs rose by some 14% in the month and total ELs by around 9%.

Although the size of the bill leak was known, the extent and speed with which it would unwind were unpredictable. Also, after a long period in which the corset had operated there was considerable uncertainty over how many acceptances would continue to be held outside the banking system when the corset was abolished. The split between UK residents' and overseas holdings of acceptances could not be ascertained, and the implications of the unwinding of the bill leak for sterling M_3 were therefore to some extent a matter of conjecture. On top of this, the size and speed of the unwinding of other forms of disintermediation, both offshore and domestic, were largely unknown.

In the event, sterling M_3 grew by $7\frac{3}{4}\%$ in the three banking months (July to September) following the abolition of the corset and by $5\frac{1}{4}\%$ in banking July alone. This was more than had been expected, and the authorities had considerable difficulty in distinguishing between the effects of reintermediation and an increase in the underlying rate of growth of the broad monetary aggregates. The narrower definition of private sector liquidity (PSL_1) grew at the somewhat slower rate of $4\frac{1}{4}\%$ in the three months. This may have been because PSL_1 includes bills held outside the banking sector as well as other liquid assets, some of which tended to contract as funds were reintermediated back into the banking system. But all the broad monetary aggregates may have been inflated during this period as a result of reintermediation from the eurosterling market and other largely unmeasurable domestic markets.

The question arose as to whether an allowance ought to be made for reintermediation in interpreting the monetary target. If sizable reintermediation had indeed occurred, keeping to the existing target would have represented an unintended tightening of policy. On the other hand, estimating the size of the reintermediation involved a considerable element of judgment, and, if an *ex post* adjustment was to be made for the removal of the corset, consistency would presumably require adjustments for its imposition and also for the relaxation of exchange controls. When the quarterly eurosterling figures became available, the evidence for adjusting the targets upwards to allow for reintermediation from offshore sources appeared to be slight. In the event, no explicit adjustment was made, but implicit judgments about reintermediation and other factors still had to be made when the target was rebased in the spring of 1981.

As might have been expected, borrowing from, and lending to, the eurosterling market by UK non-banks rose—by around £0.6 billion—in the period after the relaxation of exchange controls. It might have been reasonable to suppose that this rise was largely at the expense of domestic deposits and lending because of the ease of substitutability between the two markets. In the quarter following the abolition of the corset, eurosterling deposits from, and lending to, UK non-bank residents fell by £0.2 billion, but in subsequent quarters this fall was reversed. Since the abolition of exchange controls, the ratio of UK residents' eurosterling deposits to domestic deposits has risen from around 1% to 2%. This shift may have occurred largely at the expense of sterling deposits with UK banks.[2]

Longer-term effects
As well as encouraging the temporary redirection of conventional bank business through parallel markets, the SSD scheme itself, or the threat of its reimposition, may have had a longer-term influence on the structure of UK financial markets. The periodic imposition of restrictions on the growth of sterling deposits may have encouraged some UK banks to promote other types of business. Exchange controls severely limited the extent to which UK banks could take deposits from, and lend to, UK residents in foreign currencies. The UK authorities did not, however, attempt to restrict UK banks from taking deposits, or from lending to overseas residents, in foreign currencies. Between 1973 and 1980, overseas residents' foreign currency deposits at UK banks grew, on average, by 25% per annum, whereas UK residents' sterling deposits grew by 13% per annum.

Other factors may have affected the UK banks' overseas business. The growth of international trade may have increased the need for overseas residents to hold balances in London. Not only were foreign currency deposits exempt

---
(1) That is, the month to mid-July.
(2) Until August 1981, when the reserve asset ratio was abolished, there were periods in which the banking sector was short of reserve assets, and the yields on reserve assets fell relative to the yields on non-reserve assets (see Chart 2). This interest rate differential effectively constituted an implicit tax on the UK banks, and an incentive arose for funds to be redirected offshore. On occasion there was an incentive for eurosterling round tripping to occur, which had complicated effects on the broad monetary aggregates.

from the SSD scheme (provided that the banks did not use them to acquire sterling resources), but they were also excluded from the reserve asset ratio. In contrast, the United States and West Germany have imposed relatively onerous reserve requirements on their domestic banks, without there being exchange controls on their residents. This has given rise to disintermediation from these countries, and some of these funds may have been channelled through UK banks.

During the 1973–80 period, the banks' share of UK personal sector savings declined in relation to that of the building societies. In 1973, the building societies and the banks each had deposits of around £17 billion from the personal sector. By 1980, the banks' deposits had risen to £30 billion, whereas those of the building societies had reached £42 billion. During the 'corset-off' period in 1977–78, some banks sought to promote lending to the personal sector for house purchase, but total bank lending for house purchase remained small. Excess demand for mortgage finance tended to be met by 'topping-up' loans from insurance companies, rather than from the banks.

The growth of the building societies' share of the personal savings market during this period may have been due to a number of factors other than the inhibiting effect of the corset. Share accounts attracted large numbers of small savers and the composite tax rate may have helped the societies. Nevertheless, since the abolition of the SSD scheme, the banks have expanded their lending for house purchase, as well as their share of personal sector savings. Between May 1980 and November 1981, bank lending for house purchase rose from £2.5 billion to £4.7 billion, an annualised rate of growth of 52%. Thus the imposition and removal of the corset may have contributed to these changes in the banks' market share and hence changes in the growth of sterling M_3 in relation to the wider measures of liquidity.

V Conclusions

The SSD scheme was introduced in response to monetary developments in 1973. The scheme was largely effective in inhibiting round tripping and containing the growth of wholesale deposits. During the first, second, and early part of the third corset periods, few SSD penalties were paid, and the scheme does appear to have restrained the aggressiveness with which the banks bid for wholesale deposits. The scheme may also have helped to improve sentiment in the gilt-edged market, thereby influencing the monetary aggregates indirectly.

But the extended use of direct controls raises its own problems. Permanent or semi-permanent controls almost inevitably give rise to domestic and, if allowed, offshore disintermediation. Such controls can compensate to only a limited extent for the weaknesses in the use of conventional instruments of policy—interest rates, debt sales and budgetary adjustments. Temporary controls may be less likely to induce disintermediation, but they suffer from anticipatory behaviour by the banks which distorts the interpretation of the recorded aggregates. Perhaps the greatest danger arises if an ostensibly temporary scheme is retained for an excessively long period because of fears about the consequences of suspending it.

Appendix
Payment of supplementary special deposits

£ millions; *number of banks in italics* (a)

	Total		1st tranche		2nd tranche		3rd tranche			Total		1st tranche		2nd tranche		3rd tranche	
First period									1979 Jan. 17	2	*4*	—	*1*	—	*2*	1	*1*
1974 July 17	6	*14*	—	*2*	—	—	6	*12*	Feb. 21	3	*5*	—	*1*	—	*1*	2	*3*
Aug. 21	1	*7*	—	*2*	—	*1*	1	*4*	Mar. 21	2	*3*	—	*1*	—	—	2	*2*
Sept. 18	2	*5*	—	*1*	—	*1*	2	*3*	Apr. 18	1	*4*	—	*2*	—	—	—	*2*
Oct. 16	1	*6*	—	*1*	—	*1*	1	*4*	May 16	5	*4*	—	*1*	1	*1*	3	*2*
Nov. 20	2	*6*	—	—	—	—	2	*6*	June 20	9	*6*	—	*3*	1	—	7	*3*
Dec. 16	1	*5*	—	*3*	—	—	1	*2*	July 18	2	*6*	2	*5*	—	*1*	—	—
1975 Jan. 15	2	*4*	—	—	—	*3*	2	*1*	Aug. 15	10	*14*	6	*9*	3	*2*	2	*3*
Feb. 19	—	*3*	—	—	—	*1*	—	*2*	Sept. 19	4	*10*	3	*8*	—	*1*	—	*1*
									Oct. 17	1	*12*	1	*10*	—	*2*	—	—
Second period									Nov. 21	3	*8*	—	*4*	—	*1*	3	*3*
1977 May 18	1	*5*	—	*3*	—	*1*	1	*1*	Dec. 17	19	*20*	10	*13*	8	*5*	2	*2*
June 15	—	*5*	—	*4*	—	—	—	*1*	1980 Jan. 16	28	*14*	9	*9*	9	*3*	10	*2*
July 20	1	*4*	—	*2*	—	—	—	*2*	Feb. 20	104	*22*	15	*7*	31	*8*	58	*7*
Third period									Mar. 19	132	*23*	12	*7*	31	*9*	89	*7*
1978 Nov. 15	1	*7*	—	*5*	—	*1*	1	*1*	Apr. 16	216	*27*	14	*6*	31	*13*	171	*8*
Dec. 13	2	*5*	—	*3*	—	*1*	1	*1*	May 21	219	*28*	13	*10*	31	*10*	174	*8*
									June 18	242	*30*	19	*12*	37	*11*	187	*7*
									July 16	456	*47*	27	*19*	63	*17*	366	*11*

(a) For each tranche, the amount of deposits records the *total paid* in that tranche, whereas the number of banks measures those whose *maximum penalty* fell within that tranche.

The debate on methods of monetary control

The difficulties that the authorities had in controlling the monetary aggregates—particularly M3 and sterling M3—in the 1970s led to a public discussion about whether the monetary base should be used as an instrument of control. The Bank made a contribution to this discussion when it published an article *Monetary base control* (page 129) by M D K W Foot, C A E Goodhart and A C Hotson in the June 1979 *Bulletin* (an appendix on the practices of other central banks has not been reprinted here).

Subsequently, in November 1979, the Chancellor of the Exchequer announced in a statement to the House of Commons that he had set in hand a review of methods of controlling the money supply, and that the Bank of England and the Treasury would issue a discussion paper for consultation about possible changes in the methods of control. The Green Paper *Monetary control* was accordingly published in March 1980: Chapter 1 (page 137) describes the means by which the authorities have sought to control the money supply and Chapter 4 discusses various forms of monetary base control.

In the light of the vigorous public debate which followed, the Bank published the authorities' conclusions about techniques of monetary control, outlining proposed changes, in a *Background note on methods of monetary control* (page 148) issued on 24 November 1980.

Monetary base control

This article has been prepared mainly by M.D.K.W. Foot, C.A.E. Goodhart and A.C. Hotson of the Bank's Economic Intelligence Department.

Introduction

1 This article considers whether monetary base control should be the means by which the authorities control the monetary aggregates. We have approached this subject as economists rather than as representatives of the Bank of England, and we seek to contribute to what has hitherto in the United Kingdom been only a limited discussion. Many of the subjects raised in the discussion are candidates for detailed consideration on both a theoretical and a practical level. Moreover, the various proponents of monetary base control often have widely differing proposals in mind, a fact which significantly increases the scope of the analysis required. What follows in this article, therefore, is not intended to be an exhaustive treatment of the subject. In particular, it concentrates on the more theoretical, economic issues and only raises in passing some of the implications of the various proposals for the structure of existing financial markets and for the authorities' present methods of operation.

2 To this end, a brief background for the subject is provided in paragraphs 3–4. The monetary base is then defined (paragraphs 5–8), its historical relevance in the United Kingdom noted (paragraphs 9–12), and its possible theoretical relevance briefly set out (paragraphs 13–21). The various possible forms of control as we understand them are then considered; the implications of strict forms of control are outlined in paragraphs 22–42, and more relaxed versions are discussed in paragraphs 43–50. A brief summary of our views is provided in paragraph 51. There is also an appendix [1] which discusses briefly certain aspects of the financial system in some major countries where the monetary base is rather more familiar than in the United Kingdom.

The background

3 In a number of countries, there are now formal monetary targets. Even where there are not, it is probably much more widely recognised than was the case, say, ten years ago that movements in the stock of money have considerable economic relevance, although the form and extent of this relevance are hotly debated.

4 Among those who believe that 'money matters', there is a group which considers that an appropriate degree of control over the rate of monetary growth can only be obtained by operating primarily to control the rate of growth of the monetary base.[2] To some in this group, current attempts in the United Kingdom to control sterling M_3 are wrongly directed, because the authorities are said to lack the means at present to achieve an adequate degree of short-term control over sterling M_3. The alternative proposed is that the authorities should seek to ensure the desired growth of whichever monetary aggregate they consider most appropriate by operating on the monetary base. Others in the group would go further and suggest that the monetary base—as well as being the means of control—could also be the appropriate target rather than (as in the United Kingdom, France or Western Germany) a broad monetary aggregate such as sterling M_3 or (as in Canada) a narrower monetary aggregate, M_1.

What is the monetary base?

5 In current economic literature, there is a generally accepted concept of 'high-powered money', which is thought of as the sum of the balance-sheet liabilities of the central bank (strictly speaking, the monetary authorities[3]) to the private sector. Thus, anything which leads the central bank to have reduced liabilities to the private sector (for example—and assuming that the Government banks with the central bank, as it does in the United Kingdom—an excess of tax receipts over expenditure, or net sales of government debt) acts to reduce the volume of high-powered money. The phrases 'high-powered money' and 'monetary base' are often used interchangeably. In this article, however, we should like to adopt a more precise terminology and use the phrase 'monetary base' to describe that set of the liabilities of the monetary authorities which they may seek particularly to control.

6 Exactly which liabilities should go into this set is no easy problem. In essence, the issue boils down to asking which set of their liabilities the monetary authorities think that they should control. Among the candidates for inclusion are:

(a) notes and coin in circulation with the public;

(b) notes and coin held by banks (vault cash);

(c) bankers' balances at the Bank of England;[4] and

(d) potential liabilities of the Bank of England, i.e. liabilities incurred as the counterpart to the assets that the Bank may have to assume because of commitments previously given or because of 'automatic' borrowing rights of others (in particular, the lender of last resort facilities to the discount market).

---

[1] Not reproduced here.
[2] There are also those who consider the relevance of the monetary base to be its value as a leading indicator rather than its potential as a control device. This view is considered further in paragraphs 44–6.
[3] For example, in the United Kingdom, the Bank of England issues notes, but coin is issued by a quite separate body (the Royal Mint).
[4] We have deliberately ignored the comparatively small balances held at the Bank of England by the non-bank sector.

7 The definitions actually adopted by those countries where the base is considered relevant vary quite widely (see appendix). In this article, we prefer to begin with a definition that covers just (b) and (c) of the above list, on the view that this pair—or alternatively (c) by itself[1]—might be operationally most relevant in the United Kingdom and also with the hope that this will make the subsequent discussion easier to handle without losing its general relevance. Thus, for example, the size of the base would be greatly increased by the inclusion of (a), notes and coin with the public. But the amount of currency so held is hardly a variable over which the authorities would (or could) seek control. In any case, if the aim is to influence some monetary aggregate consisting primarily of bank deposits, the relevant variable would seem to be that definition of the base—(b) and (c) or (c) alone—directly related to the assets of the banks. Otherwise variations in the non-bank private sector's demand for currency could lead to undesirable fluctuations in the growth of the monetary aggregates.

8 The argument over whether (d) should be included is rather different. Under strict forms of base control, such facilities would not exist and therefore the problem would not arise. However, where such facilities did exist, their inclusion would imply a relationship between the base and the *potential* rather than the actual stock of money. In general, proponents of base control have argued against a definition of this type and, although it has been adopted in certain countries at certain times, it is not considered further here.

The historical relevance of the monetary base in the United Kingdom

9 A banking system as we know it could not have developed had banks not learned how to make loans without collapsing, through want of liquidity, if some depositors wanted their money back. The first line of defence for any bank against such illiquidity was traditionally provided by holding a stock of generally acceptable assets—coin or notes 'behind the counter'. The second consisted of balances with other banks that could be used to obtain additional generally acceptable notes. As the Bank of England became increasingly important as a note issuer and as a 'central bank', it became increasingly convenient to hold Bank of England notes and balances at the Bank.

10 Over time, the liquidity of the banking system came to be increasingly assured by the Bank's extension of lender of last resort facilities to the discount houses (for then banks could safely make secured short-term deposits with the houses and have no doubts about the liquidity of these funds) and also by the extension of markets in liquid financial assets, notably Treasury bills. Thus, when we now think of the liquidity of a single bank, we consider the liquidity provided by the existence of markets on which it can quickly raise new debt or sell existing assets and not just of the level of its holdings of cash and balances at the Bank of England. Similarly, for the liquidity of the banking system as a whole, the relevant point is the preparedness of the central bank to provide unlimited support to the system in times of crisis, not banks' aggregate holdings of cash and bankers' balances.

11 Thus, when it became accepted practice after the Second World War for the London clearing banks to keep a minimum ratio of 8% of cash to deposits,[2] no operational relevance (in the sense of using the Bank's potential control over the supply of cash to restrict the level of bank deposits) was attributed to the ratio; in so far as the requirement had justification, it was prudential. Instead, the authorities were primarily concerned with the level and structure of interest rates, and they were consequently willing to ensure that the clearing banks did not go short of cash.[3] As a result, the clearing banks did not need to hold sizable excess cash reserves, and the recorded ratio was generally very close to 8%.

12 After 1971, even the 8% cash ratio was abolished, but the London clearing banks instead agreed to keep an average of $1\frac{1}{2}$% of their eligible liabilities[4] in the form of non-interest-bearing balances at the Bank.[5] Even more obviously than with the 8% cash ratio, there has been no attempt to use this ratio as a device for imposing a ceiling on the stock of eligible liabilities. As before, the Bank of England has chosen—through its open-market operations and lender of last resort facilities—to concentrate on influencing short-term interest rates, being prepared always to provide funds requested by the banking system but on interest-rate terms of its own choosing.

Why the monetary base may be relevant

13 If banks have to maintain a minimum ratio of cash to deposits and if the central bank exercises sufficiently vigorously its undoubted potential power as 'the' source of cash, then clearly the size of the high-powered money base imposes a ceiling on the level of bank deposits and thus, indirectly, on the stock of money, however defined.

---

[1] The question of whether or not to include banks' holdings of vault cash in the definition of the monetary base raises a number of difficult questions. Since banks with differing kinds of business have differing operational needs to hold vault cash in the normal course of business, the issue of equity as between banks arises. If vault cash were to be excluded from the defined monetary base, however, banks could seek to adjust to their required cash ratio by making otherwise unnecessary transfers between vault cash and bankers' balances at the Bank. Such unnecessary transfers would have implications both for the Bank's ability to control the monetary base tightly and for costs.

[2] See paragraph 351 of the *Report of the Committee on the Working of the Monetary System* (the Radcliffe Committee), Cmnd. 827, (HM Stationery Office, 1959). The ratio could be met by any combination of vault cash and balances at the Bank.

[3] See 'The management of money day by day' in the March 1963 *Bulletin*, page 15. (Reprinted on page 107.)

[4] Broadly, for any bank, these equal sterling deposits excluding those with an original maturity of over two years, plus sterling resources obtained by switching foreign currency into sterling, less the bank's net holdings of claims on the rest of the banking system.

[5] The commitment by the clearing banks in banking month t relates to the level of their eligible liabilities on the make-up day in banking month $t-1$. There is no requirement that the ratio be maintained strictly on a day-to-day basis; daily deviations from the $1\frac{1}{2}$% ratio can be averaged over the banking month and shortfalls or excesses carried forward.

14 More formally and at its simplest, we can write

$$M \equiv C + D \qquad (1)$$

where:

M = the stock of money
C = notes and coin in circulation with the non-bank private sector
D = the deposit liabilities of the banks

and

$$H \equiv R + C \qquad (2)$$

where:

H = the high-powered money base
R = the banks' reserves (say, vault cash plus balances at the Bank of England).

Both (1) and (2) are identities, not behavioural equations, and by simple manipulation they can be made to yield a third identity.

$$M \equiv H \left[\frac{1 + \frac{C}{D}}{\frac{R}{D} + \frac{C}{D}} \right] \qquad (3)$$

15 In other words, *if* the authorities act so as to fix H [1] at some predetermined level, *if* the ratio of currency to deposits is constant and *if* the ratio of banks' reserves to deposits is constant, then the size of M is determined by H. For example, let us assume that:

(a) all banks always maintain 4% of deposits as vault cash to meet immediate operating needs and $1\frac{1}{2}$% in balances at the Bank of England;

(b) this $5\frac{1}{2}$% of deposits constitutes the monetary base and that the banks begin with no excess reserves;

(c) notes and coin in circulation with the public always amount to 15% of deposits; and

(d) the balance sheets of the Exchange Equalisation Account (EEA) and the overseas sector have been omitted and those of the Issue and Banking Departments of the Bank of England consolidated.

16 Let us suppose then that, in a given period, the public sector is a net recipient of one unit from the non-bank private sector (because, say, tax receipts have exceeded government disbursements). The resulting changes in the equilibrium positions of the Bank of England, the banking system and the non-bank private sector are shown in the two halves of the table below.

17 Before the change, the base stood at 5.5 (vault cash 4, bankers' balances 1.5), permitting banks to take deposits of 100. In the final equilibrium position, the base stands at 5.13 (vault cash 3.73, bankers' balances 1.4), again exactly 5.5% of total deposits (93.3). The payment of 1 by the non-bank private sector has actually been accomplished by a fall of 0.9 in the notes they hold, plus a 0.1 reduction in bankers' balances at the Bank; the corresponding gain of course accrues to the public sector, whose deposits at the Bank rise from 5 to 6.

18 For the banking system, however, the process has been altogether more significant, because the decline of 0.37 in the base has necessitated a multiple contraction of deposits of 6.7 (i.e. 0.37 × 100/5.5). Nothing so far in this article has, however, shown how this contraction occurs, and this major question is considered in the next section.

19 The presentation of the determination of the money stock in this fashion has a distinguished academic pedigree, which includes contributions from Phillips, Keynes and Meade.[2] As we have seen, the authorities have not, however, attempted to control H or R. Nor is it the case that the ratio of currency in circulation to deposits necessarily stays constant over time. Obviously this ratio may be affected by technological change (for example the development of credit cards), but also, from a theoretical point of view, there is no obvious reason why the ratio of currency to bank deposits should stay constant over time, at least when the latter are defined broadly to include both transactions *and* savings balances. Finally, there is no reason under the present arrangements why banks'

	Bank of England			Banking sector			Non-bank private sector	
	Liabilities	Assets		Liabilities	Assets		Liabilities	Assets
Position before the change								
Bankers' balances	1.5		Deposits of non-bank private sector	100.0		Deposits with banking sector		100.0
Vault cash in commercial banks	4.0		Capital of banks	10.0		Equity holdings in banks		10.0
			Bankers' balances		1.5	Notes		15.0
Notes in circulation with non-bank private sector	15.0		Vault cash		4.0			
Public sector deposits at Bank of England	5.0		Liquid assets and advances		104.5			
	25.5	25.5		110.0	110.0		125.0	125.0
Position after the change								
Bankers' balances	1.4		Deposits of non-bank private sector	93.3		Deposits with banking sector		93.3
Vault cash in commercial banks	3.73		Capital of banks	10.00		Equity holdings in banks		10.0
			Bankers' balances		1.41	Notes		14.1
Notes in circulation with non-bank private sector	14.1		Vault cash		3.73			
Public sector deposits at Bank of England	6.0		Liquid assets and advances		98.17			
	25.23	25.23		103.3	103.3		117.4	117.4

[1] Earlier, in paragraph 7, it was argued that the authorities should take as their monetary base all or some of the reserves available to the banking system, i.e. R, rather than the total of high-powered money which also includes currency in the hands of the non-bank public, C. The above identity, of course, holds irrespective of how the authorities operate, but focus on the banks' reserve base, R, would reduce the effect on the money stock of fluctuations in the non-bank public's desired cash holdings (the C/D ratio in the above identity).

[2] C. A. Phillips, *Bank Credit*, (New York: Macmillan, 1920); J. M. Keynes, *A treatise on money* (London: Macmillan, 1930); J. E. Meade, 'The Amount of Money and the Banking System', *The Economic Journal*, vol. XLIV (1934), pages 77–83.

reserves of cash and bankers' balances should show a stable relation to any particular monetary aggregate. Only the clearing banks maintain the 1½% ratio, and even that requirement is over a period of time rather than for any particular day and is related to eligible liabilities rather than directly to deposits as recorded in the monetary aggregates.

20 It follows, not surprisingly, that, given present arrangements, there is no close relationship in the United Kingdom between changes in the monetary base and those in any other monetary aggregate. Indeed, to the extent that there has been any causal relationship, it could reasonably be argued that it has run *from* money to the base, rather than the other way round, a causality exemplified by the fact that the 1½% ratio relates to the previous month's eligible liabilities and that the authorities have always chosen to provide, at a price, the base money required. Nor has there been any close relationship between movements in the base and in nominal incomes. Indeed with high-powered money (H) largely consisting of currency in the hands of the public (C), and the latter being demand-determined, (according to our econometric estimates largely in response to current and past changes in consumers' expenditure) the direction of causation runs clearly from nominal income to notes and coin in circulation (C) and high-powered money (H).

21 The relevant question, however, is what would happen if present attitudes and institutional features were changed and the authorities sought to use the base rather than interest rates as a means of controlling the rate of growth of the monetary aggregates. Unfortunately, as noted in the introduction, the answer is related to the form, in particular the time horizon, of the monetary base régime in question. Further complications are added by the existence of a number of other issues that are not of major theoretical relevance in their own right but which represent awkward technical problems to be tackled before at least some forms of base control could be considered in practice.

A strict control of money

22 First we examine the implications of seeking to control the money stock strictly on a short-term basis. Even if it were universally accepted that strict short-term control of the monetary aggregates was undesirable, if not impractical, it would still be useful to consider the implications of strict control as an expositional device in order to clarify the issues. Moreover, there are a number of proponents of strict short-term control of the monetary aggregates, and of these some advocate the use of monetary base control to achieve this end. Of course it is possible to envisage ways in which banks' deposit liabilities might be subject to strict short-term control other than through regulation of the base. Bank deposits could be forced to grow at a pre-determined rate by government fiat, or by the imposition of some form of permanent supplementary special deposits scheme, with penalties on those banks whose deposit liabilities grew too slowly as well as on those whose liabilities grew too fast.

23 Returning to control via the monetary base, the most extreme form of regulation imaginable is one where the operations of the central bank were such as to predetermine the monetary base (for some of the problems involved see paragraphs 37–42) and where the banks were required to achieve their reserve ratio requirement exactly on a daily basis. If short-term control of the monetary base were to be translated into equivalent short-term control of the monetary aggregates, the ability of the banks to vary their actual (free) reserve holdings relative to their required level would have to be limited, for example by penalties applying to both excess and deficient reserves. Examination rapidly suggests that the idea of such tight management is impracticable but, as it throws up a number of points of general relevance to any attempt to control the base over any period, the arguments are worth considering.

24 The most appropriate starting point is perhaps the mechanism by which banks are supposed to adjust to, say, a shortfall of reserves (i.e. the base provided does not permit them to meet their reserve requirements on their existing level of deposits). When considered at all, the mechanism is usually held to be that the banks cut back on lending or sell off marketable assets. However, while this may improve the relative position of one bank, such action only eases the reserve position of the banking system as a whole fractionally, with that fraction depending on the required reserve ratio. Thus *unless the authorities relent and choose to provide more base money,* the only ways that the banks as a whole can overcome their reserve asset shortage are:

(a) to reduce their assets and liabilities by a multiple of the initial shortage of base money;

(b) to attract notes and coin from the public (which would be difficult to do, unless banks were to offer a variable premium for currency, thereby breaking convertibility between currency and deposits); or

(c) if there were lower reserve requirements on time than on sight deposits (as in the United States), to induce customers—by adjusting relative yields—to switch funds from sight to time deposits.

25 To illustrate this essential point, suppose that a bank sells off its Treasury bill holdings. Its balances with the Bank of England will rise, i.e. it will receive more reserve assets; the banks of those who buy the bills will lose an equal amount.[1] Only if the Bank of England steps into the market to buy the bills will the base be increased.

26 A similar conclusion follows with regard to the effect of foreign exchange transactions on the monetary base. As the banks try to improve their individual

---

[1] Provided the non-bank private sector does not purchase Treasury bills with notes and coin, the bank will receive net claims on other banks; its balances at the Bank of England will thus rise and those of other banks fall correspondingly.

position by selling assets, they will force up interest rates. Other things being equal, this will increase the demand for sterling by foreigners who now wish to obtain sterling assets, the rate of interest on which has become more attractive. However, the stock of monetary base will remain unaffected and under the control of the authorities if either the exchange rate is allowed to appreciate freely, or, if this is unacceptable, the inflow of capital is sterilised. A rise in the exchange rate might be forestalled without increasing the monetary base if, when the authorities purchase foreign currencies with sterling and accumulate international reserves in the EEA, they then finance these purchases by the sale of Treasury bills or some other debt instrument which is not included in the definition of the monetary base. Nevertheless, the sale of these debt instruments may raise interest rates further and also maintain monetary tightness, thereby attracting continuing inflows from abroad. This could lead to an unstable situation with persistently rising reserves together with rising domestic interest rates.

27 The same conclusion follows if the banks make what is now the more likely response to reserve pressure of bidding for funds (so-called liability management) by, for example, issuing certificates of deposit. Again, the effect will be to push up interest rates without increasing the base [except in so far as (b) or (c) in paragraph 24 apply]. But, this time, there could be an additional difficulty if the authorities have a broad money aggregate in mind as an intermediate target, in that liability management can have a perverse effect on the adjustment process of the banking system as a whole, since it tends to raise the yield offered on bank deposits relative to the yields on other liquid assets. This could accelerate the interest-rate spiral likely to develop as banks come under reserve pressure and, if rates of interest on bank lending do not keep pace with the rise in market interest rates, actually increase the demand for credit by making it attractive to borrow funds to on-lend in the wholesale money markets.

28 These problems might be mitigated if the reserve requirements on time deposits were lower than those on sight deposits. Then, as interest rates rose—increasing the opportunity cost of holding sight deposits[1]—holders would, over a period of time, switch their funds from sight to time accounts, progressively reducing the banks' overall need for reserves. However, the authorities would presumably only seek to control the monetary aggregates with a differential reserve requirement, in which sight deposits were given a higher weighting than time deposits, if they attached greater importance to the rate of growth of sight deposits than to that of time deposits. In the extreme case where the authorities attached no weight to the rate of growth of time deposits, they could set an M_1 target and only impose reserve requirements on sight deposits. Nevertheless, even with an M_1 target, the speed of adjustment of the non-bank private sector's asset portfolio in response to changes in the differential between sight and time deposit rates might not be fast enough for the banks to be able to meet their reserve requirements at all quickly. As a result, an interest-rate spiral might still emerge.

29 The conclusion of this line of argument is that strict control of the base (which would, of course, imply an end to all the present lender of last resort facilities) would continually threaten frequent and potentially massive movements in interest rates, if not complete instability. Changes in the base would inevitably carry implications for interest rates, and the greater the emphasis on control of the base the less the possibility that the central bank could intervene to ameliorate any interest-rate fluctuations. In the strictest form of control (the day-to-day regulation noted earlier), the problem would, of course, be at its most acute as no adjustment time (e.g. for the banks to curtail their loans to the non-bank public) would be available. Indeed it is highly dubious whether such a system could possibly work, mainly because of the time it would take for markets to adjust to the interest-rate changes induced by the banks in their attempts to meet their reserve requirements. But even for control over longer periods of time, strict control of the base would throw onto financial markets the whole burden of adjustment at present 'shared' by the Bank of England's lender of last resort facilities, its open-market operations, its foreign exchange intervention, and the permitted short-term variability in the level of balances held by the clearing banks at the Bank of England.

Structural adjustments in response to strict control

30 In extreme form, then, base control could imply enormous potential pressure on financial markets. It is a moot point as to how far they would develop to meet the burden. Other reactions would also be likely.[2] We now explore some of these on the assumption that the transitional problems of adjusting to the new system had been overcome.

31 One development might well be the sharp curtailment or disappearance of the overdraft system, indeed the curtailment or disappearance of any exposure, whether by formal or informal commitment, to an obligation to extend loans at some future time. At present, banks extend facilities to customers that in aggregate are roughly only half-used at any time. This is an element of flexibility provided by the banking system which most observers would regard as highly desirable. Even under the present supplementary special deposits scheme, the existence of these facilities may be an embarrassment to a bank, particularly as most empirical work on the demand for bank credit in the United Kingdom suggests that a bank's major defence in such circumstances—to raise the cost of borrowing—may not have a large (and certainly does not have a rapid) effect

---

[1] This assumes that the implicit or explicit return on sight deposits is either constant or at least not quickly responsive to changes in market interest rates.

[2] They would indeed follow from *any* short-term strict control over the money stock.

on the demand for credit.[1] It follows that the stricter the control of money (whatever the form of that control) the more risky it would be for banks to provide overdraft facilities in their present form.

32 A related development likely to occur would be that the banks would come to hold a larger proportion of their portfolio in easily-saleable assets, or, in so far as this was allowed, in excess reserves, correspondingly reducing relatively illiquid lending to the private sector. Similarly the non-bank private sector, being less able to obtain bank facilities, might also seek to hold larger amounts of liquid assets.

33 Such conclusions follow from the fact that the more tightly controlled the banking system the greater the short-term risk of illiquidity for all concerned. In the longer term, when such a system was fully established, it would seem to exhibit a certain inefficiency—with more risk than strictly necessary, balanced by larger liquidity holdings—but otherwise it could conceivably be workable. Such an approach would, however, appear to carry a higher risk of disturbances to the banking system reminiscent in some respects of those in the United Kingdom in the nineteenth century and in the United States before the establishment of the Federal Reserve System. Even under a monetary base control régime, the Bank of England would have to retain the right to use lender of last resort facilities to forestall a banking crisis, and assistance might have to be extended to individual banks more frequently than in the past. In the short run, any sudden change to the new system, with a possibly large but unpredictable increase in the demand for liquid assets in response to the increased risk perceived, would make assessment and management of the overall economic situation more difficult.

34 A third likely development would be the growth of holders of liquid assets not subject to cash ratio requirements, who would arbitrage between short-term liquid assets (such as Treasury bills) and bank deposits,[2] thereby reducing the extent of interest-rate fluctuation. Similarly, the banks might be able, at times of their own choosing, to rearrange some of their on-balance-sheet advances as off-balance-sheet acceptances, so that although they would resell some of their holdings of commercial bills to the non-bank private sector, they would guarantee the ultimate holders of these commercial bills against default by the original issuers. The rapid increase in acceptances almost immediately after the reimposition of the supplementary special deposits scheme in June 1978 suggests that the banks are able to rearrange their portfolios to some extent in this way.

35 Equally, however, such structural developments, resulting in an expansion of near-money liquid assets and an increased elasticity of response in velocity to changes in interest rates, would reduce the significance of a tight control over the money stock and also the monetary base. The financial system evolves continuously to meet the needs of the economy and will, in time, find ways round artificial road blocks.

36 All these developments would be likely to follow from any strict form of base control, though the 'adjustment problem' in each case would be worse, and the speed of the developments faster, the shorter the time horizon over which control was attempted.

Some technical and operational changes required

37 As noted in paragraph 23, day-to-day control of the base is very difficult to envisage. Under present institutional arrangements, there are unforeseen swings into and out of central government balances of up to several hundred million pounds a day, and the first requirement for day-to-day control would be either that the Government moved its business to the commercial banks or that the banking system moved to a next day settlement basis for all transactions. The logic of the first change is that unexpected flows—say from the non-bank private sector to the Government—would then leave bankers' balances at the Bank of England unaffected; at present, as noted earlier, the result of such flows is to alter these balances. The logic of the second change, which in administrative terms at least would constitute a retrograde step, is that the authorities would then have one day's notice of unexpected movements of funds.

38 Even then, however, the authorities would not have any advance warning of shifts in the public's demand for currency, which even on a daily basis can be large. The Bank of England already forecasts the demand for currency on a daily basis, as part of its projection of key factors affecting money markets, and, on occasion, errors here have been of the order of £100 million and are frequently £25-30 million.

39 Further, whatever the length of period over which control of the base is desired, the authorities' predetermined path would have to be set in non-seasonally-adjusted form. As presumably their objective would be to obtain a smooth seasonally-adjusted growth in the base or in some monetary aggregate, they would need to work from a seasonally-adjusted to an unadjusted projection of the base. Given the complexities and uncertainties of the seasonal-adjustment process for financial series, such a procedure could be sensible for, say, quarterly projections, but daily forecasts on such a basis would be subject to very large margins of error. Any attempt to control the banking system strictly on a very short-term basis would, therefore, result in unintended gyrations in the level of deposits.

40 A final difficulty with any form of very short-term control arises out of the question of the appropriate accounting basis for the banks. A lagged accounting

---

[1] Peter Spencer and Colin Mowl, 'The Model of the Domestic Monetary System' part one of *A Financial Sector for the Treasury Model* [Government Economic Service, Working Paper No. 17 (Treasury Working Paper No. 8), December 1978.]

[2] One requirement for such arbitrage to occur is that liability management of the kind described in paragraph 27 did not prevent Treasury bill yields from rising faster in response to reserve asset pressure than the deposit rates offered by banks.

basis is used for the purpose of calculating required reserves in virtually all countries, and is indeed suitable when the purpose of the reserve ratios is to provide a fulcrum for money-market operations to control interest rates. Virtually by definition, however, when the total of required reserves is related to the past level of deposits and where there are no excess reserves at the outset in the system, changes in deposits must cause the authorities to allow changes in bank reserves, and not vice versa, so that monetary base movements can hardly either control, cause or even indicate future movements in bank deposits.

41 One possibility would be to move on to a current accounting basis, with required reserves related to current liabilities. Even in this case, delays in obtaining current information on movements in liabilities (and, depending on the form of the required reserve base, delays also in information on movements of vault cash held at branches), would tend to mean that the banks would simply not be in a position to know what adjustments would be necessary during the course of the day to try to meet their required ratios.

42 It would be more in the spirit of monetary base control, though we do not know of any case where this has been applied, for the reserve ratio to be put on a lead accounting basis, that is to say that the liabilities of a bank at some future time, $t + n$, should be related through a required ratio to its current reserve base at time t. The strictness of the monetary base control régime would then relate to the adjustment time allowed, the averaging procedures adopted and the penalties imposed for non-compliance.

More relaxed versions of monetary base control

43 A number of the operational changes described above could be avoided and the problems of adjustment substantially mitigated with a more relaxed form of base control. Thus, the authorities could perhaps have a desired level for the base over, say, a six-month period but not insist that the base average out exactly at that level and not withdraw the lender of last resort and other facilities which at present avoid sharp short-term instability in financial markets.

44 Indeed at the limit, i.e. with no penalties for failing to meet a particular ratio, in effect with no *required* reserve ratio at all, movements in the monetary base could be regarded primarily as another monetary aggregate, possibly a leading indicator, movements in which could convey information on future developments. (Under present institutional arrangements, as explained earlier, the monetary base in the United Kingdom does *not* act as a useful leading indicator.) However, even with a long run of data, the monetary base series might not come to be a satisfactory leading indicator. Banks might wish to hold additional excess reserves, perhaps as a counterpart to a decline in the demand for bank credit, or an increase in their demand for liquidity. Accordingly, the rate of growth of banks' reserve holdings might not provide a good index of how expansionary the monetary stance was at the time. It has been argued, not least by monetarists, that the attention paid, for example, in the late 1930s by the Federal Reserve Board in the United States to the banking system's excess reserves was misdirected.

45 If the nature of the monetary base series were changed, say with banks required to hold a uniform reserve ratio [1] and a current or lead accounting basis, then it is possible, subject to the comment above, that the series could come to convey more useful information. After such a structural change, however, it would be several years before enough experience, e.g. of seasonal fluctuations, was amassed to enable such movements to be interpreted adequately. Thus, under the changed system banks would most likely have a greater incentive to hold excess cash reserves, depending on the costs involved in holding such excess reserves as against the costs and risks to each bank of finding itself short of cash reserves. It would be some time before any regular pattern of behaviour would be established and discernible.

46 Moreover, the Bank already obtains weekly monetary data from a sample of banks. While this experience is revealing only too clearly the difficulties of interpreting movements in a new series, such weekly data may in time come to provide the authorities with prompt information on monetary developments. Only if the movements in the monetary base should provide a reliable *leading* indicator of monetary developments would the series help the authorities to assess developments.

47 In practice, the phrase 'monetary base control' is not tightly defined; it can range from an attempt to control certain monetary aggregates on a tight day-to-day basis through to a generalised concern with the series as a potentially useful leading indicator, possibly among others, of future monetary developments. Between these two polar positions exists a relatively unexplored territory of gradations from tighter to easier control.

48 The purpose of paragraphs 22–42 is to show that an attempt to use monetary base control rigorously over short periods would be neither desirable nor feasible. The same objections do not hold, at least not to anything like the same extent, to proposals for considerably more relaxed versions of this approach, in which proper and sufficient adjustment time is given to the banking system. Indeed, because it is the rôle of the banking system to absorb and to meet shocks occurring in the demand or supply of money and credit within the economy, the search for tight short-term control of the money stock, for example on a week-by-week basis, would seem to be misguided. This is *not*, however, to

---

[1] As already noted in footnote [1] on page 130, the fact that banks do differing kinds of business and have differing balance-sheet structures makes any approach to 'uniformity' rather difficult in practice.

deny the possibility of improving control techniques for influencing monetary developments over a longer horizon measured, say, in terms of four to six months.

49 In this respect there are perhaps two main ways in which the adoption of a 'relaxed' monetary base system, which did *not* aim to force the banking system into unduly rapid adjustment by imposing penalties on short-term divergences from a required ratio (for example such relaxation could be obtained by some combination of generous averaging procedures, gentle initial penalties or even an absence of a *required* cash ratio) might improve the authorities' control over the system. *First,* if movements in the monetary base did prove to be an informative leading indicator of future developments, it would provide the authorities with information with which to respond more quickly and firmly to diverging monetary trends than they are now able to do. The experience of Switzerland indicates that this may be the case. Indeed, with such a monetary base approach—assuming that it did prove to be a reliable leading indicator—there would perhaps be some presumption that firmer action might be taken more quickly, as the authorities reacted to movements in the monetary base. Nevertheless, against such putative longer-term benefits would have to be set the costs of structural changes involving disturbances and dislocations to well-established arrangements. Moreover, for several years while the system was adjusting to the structural change, it would be virtually impossible for the authorities to glean any worthwhile information from the new series. Furthermore it must be emphasised that the use of the monetary base as an adjunct for improving control over monetary developments is *not* an alternative to varying interest rates for that purpose, but indeed a means of trying to ensure that interest rates vary sufficiently quickly and widely to achieve such greater control.

50 The *second* possible source of benefit from the adoption of monetary base control might occur if such a system entailed or encouraged a change in the structure of financial markets which allowed the authorities to control the volume of debt sales to the non-bank public more closely and effectively; for control of the broad monetary aggregates e.g. sterling M_3, whether with monetary base control or not, must involve sales of sufficient debt by the authorities to offset other factors (for example, the budget deficit) tending to augment monetary growth. Indeed, some proponents of monetary base may see the main advantage of a move in this direction, not in any way as providing any mechanical or 'multiplier' method of monetary control, but rather as a means of forcing or stimulating the growth and development of debt markets, particularly short-term debt markets, in a way that might give the authorities greater control over the total debt sold to the non-bank public in any period. This would, however, be a very round-about way of trying to achieve changes in the structure and nature of such markets, for such changes do not logically require the adoption of a move to monetary base control and could be considered directly on their own merits; some aspects of this latter subject are further discussed in the article on the gilt-edged market on page 86.

51 To summarise: the critics of the authorities' present approach to monetary management often contrast this with what might be obtained if the authorities were instead to adopt monetary base control. One purpose of this article is to show that there are several variants of monetary base control (an imprecise term) and to indicate reasons why *rigid* monetary base control would be unacceptable. More relaxed versions of such a control system might be accompanied by changes in the functioning of certain debt markets, though any such changes should perhaps be considered on their own merits quite separately, and might provide the authorities with additional information to allow prompter and firmer countervailing action. Any such putative benefits would, however, have to be weighed against the costs of making major structural changes in the system.

Monetary control

The following extracts are taken from the Green Paper Cmnd. 7858 published by HMSO in March 1980, and are reproduced with permission of the Controller of Her Majesty's Stationery Office.

CHAPTER 1

THE CONTROL OF THE MONEY SUPPLY

1.1 There are a number of policy instruments available to the authorities in influencing monetary conditions. Of these the main ones are fiscal policy, debt management, administered changes in short term interest rates, direct controls on the financial system and operations in the foreign exchange markets.

1.2 Apart from notes and coin, the £M3 money stock consists of liabilities of the banking system. In considering how the above instruments affect monetary conditions, it is sometimes helpful to examine how a particular control will affect items on the asset side of the banking system balance sheet—the credit counterparts of the money stock. Indeed, by accounting identity, the change in £M3 equals the PSBR *less* sales of public sector debt outside the banking system *plus* the increase in bank lending to the private and overseas sectors *plus* the net external inflow to the private sector *less* the increase in banks' non-deposit liabilities. Useful though this widely known identity is, it must be emphasized that the counterparts are not independent. Policy action on one of them will typically induce changes in the others so that a change in any one rarely has an exactly equal effect on the money supply.

The Main Instruments

1.3 Fiscal policy has a major bearing on the growth of £M3. Tax and expenditure policies are the main means by which the Government affects the PSBR, although those policies also affect the other counterparts of the money stock. For example, a change in taxation of companies can affect their demand for bank loans. A particular change in fiscal policy may have a significantly different effect on £M3 than on the PSBR; the former is usually smaller. It is impossible, however, to forecast the PSBR with precision and therefore very difficult to control it closely. Its size in any period depends on the level of economic activity and the inflation rate as well as the fiscal stance. And over short periods—a year or less—it can fluctuate markedly, even after adjusting for seasonal factors, due to minor variations in the pattern from month to month of Government expenditure and receipts.

1.4 In recent years the PSBR has been large, but substantial sales of gilts and other public sector debt have enabled a high proportion of it to be financed outside the banking system. But sales of gilt-edged stock have also been irregular, and there have been occasions on which the irregularities have accentuated fluctuations in the growth of the money supply. If the money supply starts to grow faster than the target range, investors will expect interest rates to rise and so hold back from buying gilts: this further accelerates the growth of the money supply. On the other hand, there have been other occasions when the authorities have been able to take advantage of the effect of expectations—for example about the PSBR—on the gilts market, to bring about sales which have brought the money supply back under control far more quickly than would have been possible with other instruments.

1.5 In its Quarterly Bulletin for June 1979, the Bank of England considered various suggestions for securing a flow of sales more closely related to the requirements of shorter term monetary control. The Bank has already invited reactions to that paper.

1.6 Short term interest rates have a complex effect on the money supply; they affect all the counterparts but in differing directions, in differing degrees and with varying time profiles. A rise in rates will increase the PSBR through the cost of Government borrowing and affect the timing and amount of tax receipts. It will also affect both the amount and composition of external flows and so the exchange rate. A rise will tend to increase gilt sales both by raising yields and also by affecting expectations about future trends in interest rates. In the short run, however, the effect may be perverse if the rise is viewed as a harbinger of yet higher long term rates. It will also decrease the level of bank lending to the private sector but this is likely to take some months to occur.

1.7 Bank lending to the private sector is determined by a number of factors including the financial position of the company sector, consumer confidence and inflationary expectations, as well as interest rates. It appears to respond only slowly to changes in interest rates. Moreover, the growth of lending exhibits sharp month to month fluctuations in response to normal commercial demand from industrial and other customers. Because of this and the delay before interest rates have their full effects, it is not feasible for the authorities to exercise an exact control over bank lending through interest rates in the short run.

1.8 External flows can exert a powerful influence on domestic monetary conditions, both directly through their impact on monetary growth and indirectly through changes in the exchange rate. Provided that intervention is small or self-balancing so that the exchange rate mainly reflects market forces, the direct effects of external flows on the money supply are likely to be small. However, there is no way in which the domestic money supply can be completely isolated from external flows because even if in total there is no net inflow or outflow, changes in the composition of flows between the various sectors of the economy and abroad will still affect the money supply.

The Efficacy of the Main Instruments

1.9 Using the basic weapons of fiscal policy, gilt-edged funding and short term interest rates, the monetary authorities can achieve the first requisite of control of the money supply—control, say, over a year or more.

1.10 However, there have been substantial swings in the rate of monetary growth, not only from month to month, but also from quarter to quarter. Given both the volatility and short term unpredictability of all the counterparts, it is almost certainly unrealistic to think in terms of a smooth path from month to month. This could only be achieved, if at all, by massive swings in interest rates, and then would probably involve significant switches back and forth between closely substitutable forms of liquidity just inside and just outside the definition of the target.

1.11 Such month to month control is not necessary to achieve the desired restraining impact of monetary growth on the growth of prices and nominal incomes, since that is essentially a medium term relationship. But there would be advantage in shortening the period within which it is possible to exercise control if it were practicable to find ways of doing this. If there were smoother growth of the money supply from quarter to quarter, there would be more complete confidence in the Government's policies, and so expectations could be affected favourably to a greater extent—both in the financial markets and elsewhere in the economy.

Quantitative Controls

1.12 Various forms of quantitative controls have been used, or suggested, to supplement the main instruments of monetary policy. Such controls can be applied either to the assets side of the financial institutions concerned—as with the ceilings on bank lending in the 1960s—or to their liabilities, as in the Supplementary Special Deposits (SSD) scheme. The general pros and cons are, however, the same in either case. A more useful distinction can be drawn between permanent and temporary controls, a point returned to below.

1.13 The main purpose for introducing such controls in this country has been to reduce the need to raise interest rates, at least in the short term, by causing banks to ration their lending. It has generally been recognised that, in time, lending rates would still tend to rise. But controls have more recently been seen as a way of bridging the time-lag before other policies have their effect. They have also, on occasion, provided reassurance to financial markets that the Government is concerned to hold to its monetary policy, thereby helping to end a hiatus in gilt sales. A particular reason behind the form of the SSD scheme was the desire to affect relative interest rates—especially those on bank deposits vis-a-vis other short term assets—to a greater extent than could be achieved through the more general instruments of Minimum Lending Rate (MLR) and open market operations.

1.14 If such a control is effective, it will almost certainly reduce competition within the controlled sector and between that sector and uncontrolled institutions doing similar business. It will involve some resource cost and loss of efficiency. There may also be prudential risks for—almost by definition—uncontrolled forms of business are less likely to be within the ambit of regulation by the monetary authorities.

1.15 If the control becomes permanent, the resource costs and prudential risks may in time be considerable. There is also the danger that funds are disintermediated, that is, business increasingly moves out of the controlled sector. The aggregate most directly affected by the control (£M3 in the case of the SSD scheme) becomes an increasingly distorted measure of the monetary position. This distortion soon becomes apparent, and causes both the statistic and the policy to decline in value.

1.16 If the control is occasional and temporary, resource costs and prudential risks would be much less significant. Distortion of the target aggregate may still occur as exemplified by the build-up of the so-called bill leak since 1978, when the SSD scheme was reintroduced. A different problem arises, however, because the controlled institutions may anticipate the reintroduction of the control and, at the worst, actually precipitate the action they have been expecting. Something of this sort occurred in the first few months of 1978. There is no obvious solution to the problem. A final difficulty with temporary controls is that, if conditions do not improve as quickly as was hoped when the controls were adopted, it becomes difficult to take them off, because of the likelihood of reintermediation and risk of appearing to ease the stance of policy.

1.17 The distortion of monetary indicators by a quantitative control is less misleading if it can be measured. For example, with the SSD scheme, it has at least been possible to monitor the main form of disintermediation hitherto: the bill leak. However, other forms are less easily measurable especially now that

United Kingdom residents are free to transact business abroad in sterling or in foreign currency.

Possible Developments

1.18 Other forms of control—ratio controls of one sort or another—have different purposes. They are designed in part to provide a fulcrum which could allow interest rate changes to be brought about effectively and rapidly to the extent necessary to achieve the monetary target. This is seen as the chief merit in some versions of monetary base control and is considered further in Chapters 4 and 5.

1.19 In the real world, there are no techniques of monetary control which involve no risk at all of disintermediation. But the authorities consider that any new technique must avoid providing a significant incentive to disintermediation. Another consideration is that some changes in methods of monetary control would be so inconsistent with subsequent membership of the exchange rate mechanism of the European Monetary System that they could have to be changed again if the Government decided that the conditions for joining were appropriate.

CHAPTER 4

MONETARY BASE CONTROL

The Concept

4.1 In concept a monetary base scheme is very simple. The banks keep at least a known proportion of their deposits (which, currency in the hands of the public apart, constitute the money supply) in base money[1], however specified, either because there is a mandatory requirement on them to do so or because they can be relied on to do so over a period for prudential reasons. The authorities then either:—

(a) control the amount of base money in existence and so the total growth of the money supply, since the banks' balance sheets cannot exceed a specified multiple of the base;

or (b) use divergences of the base money figure from the desired trend as a trigger for a change in interest rates intended to correct the divergence.

4.2 In the former case, if there is a tendency for the money supply to grow too fast, banks compete in an attempt to secure the base assets which they require to match the growth in deposits. This increases interest rates. This approach therefore is intended to provide a means for the markets to generate the interest rates necessary to bring the rate of growth of the money supply back towards the desired path.

4.3 The latter case is intended to provide for more rapid and automatic adjustments in interest rates than the present discretionary changes since the

---

1. Base money includes bankers deposits at the Central Bank and may also include notes and coin held by either or both the banks and the public.

timing of changes is determined by movements in the base. But the amount of the change would either be discretionary or determined by a scale set in advance by the authorities, rather than by a market process balancing the supply and demand for such a base asset.

4.4 A monetary base scheme in which the extent of interest rate changes is determined by the markets, is directed to both the consideration referred to in paragraph 1.18 above—namely, the timeliness of interest changes and the problem of fixing their amount. (Such systems are referred to below as monetary base control systems). But the variants where only the timing of interest rate changes is determined by changes in the base still face the authorities with the problem of setting the amount either each time or by a predetermined formula. (Such systems might more accurately be described as monetary base indicator systems and are so referred to below).

4.5 The translation of this apparently simple concept into practice raises a number of inter-related problems: as to how the scheme should be specified, as to how the authorities would control the base if the variant was of the first type, and as to how the banks and other financial institutions would behave in the changed environment. There are therefore a large number of potential schemes within the monetary base approach.

Schemes without a Mandatory Requirement

4.6 In one family of monetary base proposals, the bankers' need for base assets stems from their own requirements for operating their business, rather than from a mandatory requirement imposed by the authorities. If such schemes are to control the growth of the money supply by the authorities controlling the size of the base, bankers' requirements for base money must bear a fairly stable relationship over time to their total liabilities. With the present financial structure in the United Kingdom, this is most unlikely to be achieved since, if the present mandatory requirement applying to the London Clearing Banks were removed and not replaced by a more general one, a bank's requirement for cash balances would depend far more on the total level of transactions and type of business than on the size of its balance sheet. For a tolerably stable relationship to exist, it would probably be necessary for the banks' holdings of the base to stem from their need for liquidity rather than for transactions balances. This sort of relationship has been achieved in Switzerland, because balances at the central bank are virtually the only form of domestic primary liquidity[2]. It could only be achieved in this country if there were a major change in the structure of the money markets, including withdrawing the lender of last resort facility. It is this facility which makes a range of money market instruments primary liquidity in the hands of a financial institution. Balances with the Bank of England would then become the only effective form of primary liquidity.

4.7 Even if this were done, and it were practicable to control the base sufficiently closely, it is doubtful whether it would produce a more even growth of the money supply. The banks' liquidity requirements are not absolute and would, in the absence of a mandatory ratio, vary somewhat from time to time: for example, if the banks' primary liquidity ratio moved from 10 per cent to 9 per cent over a period, it would permit the percentage monetary growth to be some 10 percentage points more than the growth of the base over that period.

4.8 It is, of course, true that the authorities' actions to influence the rate of growth of the base would, normally, tend to produce effects which would help

---

2. Primary liquidity consists of those assets which are in all circumstances a ready source of cash to the banking system as a whole.

to control the rate of growth of the money supply itself, at least in the sense that the movement in interest rates would in general be in the right direction. But the interest rate changes so generated could not be relied upon to produce smooth short term monetary growth because of the differing potential short run response of the base and the money stock to changes in interest rates.

4.9 A change to a monetary base system of this type would therefore have significant institutional effects, resulting in a less flexible money market. There would be a period of years before it could be established that there was a predictable relationship between money and the base and there would be no assurance that monetary control would necessarily be better at the end. It is possible that it would be, but there can be no certainty, given the scale of changes in institutional structure required. We therefore conclude, given the known costs and uncertain benefits, that the case for a scheme on this basis has not been made out.

Schemes with a Mandatory Requirement

4.10 A mandatory relationship between the base and deposits could be expressed in three ways:—

(a) lagged accounting—as in the United States—where current base requirements are fixed by reference to deposits in a previous period;

(b) current accounting—as with the RAR requirement—where required base assets relate to the same make-up date as the relevant deposits;

(c) lead accounting where the holding of base assets would put a limit on deposits at some future date.

4.11 The attraction of lead accounting would be that it would give a warning about the immediate future development of the money supply as foreseen by banks. But this would depend on the ability of banks to predict their future balance sheets and then to control them to achieve that forecast. This is difficult for the banks, given:—

(a) uncertainty about calls on facilities—whether overdrafts or term loans;

(b) that the banking system provides residual finance for the Exchequer (including the Exchange Equalisation Account) whose position neither the banks nor the authorities can predict very accurately in the short term.

If, despite these difficulties, the forecasts were to have any value it would be necessary to have penalties for both under and over prediction. But if the penalties were of any significance the banks would protect themselves by artificial adjustment, disintermediation or reintermediation, to ensure that they kept to their forecast: the scale of such artificial adjustment might well be sufficient to cause serious distortions. We therefore consider that a scheme with lead accounting would not meet the requirement that any new system of control should not risk disintermediation on a significant scale.

4.12 Lagged or current accounting requirements run into a somewhat different problem. In the case of a lagged requirement, the total balance sheets of all the banks on one make-up day would determine the holding of monetary base assets they were required to hold on some later date. So, the amount of base assets required on a particular day would be pre-determined by what has already happened, and that amount might not correspond to the level of the base desired by the authorities at that time. The situation with current accounting is similar, since by the time that the banks would know their requirement for base, it would be too late to change it, if the total differed from the level desired by the authorities.

4.13 Several alternative methods have been suggested for bridging the gap between the base desired by the authorities and that needed by the banks to meet their requirements. In broad terms the alternatives are either:—

(i) to provide the banks with the assets they need by lending to the system on a scale of progressively penal rates; or

(ii) to make the requirement less than absolute but with increasing penalties on individual banks for divergences from the norm.

4.14 Under (i), so long as the actual base was above that desired by the authorities, the rate at which the Bank lends would be entirely determined, not by the market, but by the scale which the authorities had laid down. This would be a major determinant of other short term money market rates but the associated change in longer rates would, as now, reflect the markets' response. Under (ii), the market would have a larger role to play, but there would be a risk of significant disintermediation to avoid the penalties on individual banks. Monetary base control systems also encounter the general problem resulting from liability management identified in paragraph 3.3.

4.15 There would also be practical operational difficulties common to all these schemes. The authorities cannot estimate accurately on a day to day basis either the actual base that would be consistent with the (seasonally adjusted) target path for the money supply or the base that the banking system may obtain; or, with current accounting, what the banks would need to match their requirements. This is, in part, because of the large, erratic and unpredictable swings in cash flow on some days.

4.16 These difficulties are such that we doubt whether a monetary base control system with a mandatory requirement to hold base assets would produce the desired results. None of the schemes so far suggested appear to give a reasonable prospect of doing so. Moreover, there would be severe practical difficulties in operating such schemes with any precision. However we would welcome views on whether the difficulties can be surmounted and, if so, by what form of scheme.

Annex A

SHORT TERM INTEREST RATES, RESERVE ASSETS AND SPECIAL DEPOSITS

The Official Influence over Short Term Interest Rates

1. It was noted in para. 3.2 of the main paper that the Bank of England's present influence over short term interest rates is exerted through discretionary changes in MLR, made effective through money market operations conducted through the discount market.

2. In principle, the discount houses' long-standing agreement to underwrite the weekly Treasury Bill tender—whatever the size of the tender—enables the Bank (using forecasts of other cash flows between the banking system and the Bank) to engineer a shortage of cash, week by week, in the money market. Individually banks that are short of cash can either borrow or realise assets in the market, but the overall market shortage can only be relieved by the banking system borrowing from or selling assets to the Bank itself. One form in which

the banking system can obtain such relief at its own initiative is by banks running down cash balances at the Bank: but the scope for this is very limited—only the London Clearing Banks, under present arrangements, maintain cash balances at the Bank of any significant size, and they have agreed to maintain a minimum cash ratio of 1½ per cent of their eligible liabilities on average over each banking month. Apart from this small element of flexibility, the net cash transfer to the Bank has to be financed through the Bank's money market operations which are mainly conducted through the discount market, through the purchase of Treasury Bills, corporation or eligible bank bills or through secured lending, either overnight or for seven days. The form in which, and hence the cost at which, the Bank provides the necessary assistance affects the cost of funds to the discount houses, which will in turn affect both the price that they are prepared to pay for short term assets (most obviously their bid at the subsequent Treasury Bill tender, but also their buying rates for commercial bills, certificates of deposit (CDs), etc.) and the interest rates they are willing to pay for funds borrowed in the market (mostly from commercial banks). Thus the terms on which the Bank is prepared to assist the discount market has a diffused influence on the level of short term interest rates generally.

3. In practice the Bank's influence over short term interest rates is much less mechanical than this would suggest. In the first place, there may be large unanticipated movements of cash between the Bank and the banking system (e.g. through unexpected swings in central government revenue or expenditure, or through official foreign exchange or gilt-edged market transactions)—on a week-by-week as well as a day-by-day basis—which mean that the Bank cannot in the short run be sure that the money market shortage intended will in fact materialise, or that it will not be much larger than anticipated. The resulting pressures on very short term rates can cause them to become quite volatile.

4. But more fundamentally, market interest rates beyond the very short term are often heavily influenced by expectations about the future movement of MLR, which may mean that greater importance is attached to the prospect of capital gains or losses, particularly on longer term money market assets, than to the immediate interest cost to the discount houses of short term funds. In this case, if there is a strong expectation of an early cut in MLR, it may take persistent penal lending to stem a fall in, say, 1-3 month market rates in relation to MLR; or, if an early rise in MLR is expected, even generous help by the Bank to relieve any shortage of funds, or the deliberate creation of easy conditions, may not be enough to induce the houses to hold on to longer term, say, 1-3 month assets, or therefore to prevent the comparable money market rates from rising. Thus in practice the Bank's money market operations are at times intended to influence expectations in a much broader way rather than simply to influence the immediate cost of money to the discount market. Such operations do not depend on the existence of the present RAR.

The Reserve Assets Ratio and Special Deposits Requirements

5. Special Deposits, introduced in 1960, involve those banks subject to the requirement depositing funds with the Bank of England, on an interest-bearing basis, at some specified percentage of their eligible liabilities (ELs)[1]. While the funds are with the Bank, they are not available to the banks, and hence an increase in the rate of call for Special Deposits acts to reduce the liquidity of

---

1. These comprise, in broad terms, sterling deposit liabilities excluding deposits having an original maturity of over two years, plus any sterling resources obtained by switching foreign currencies into sterling. Inter-bank transactions and transactions with the discount market (other than reserve assets) and sterling certificates of deposit (both held and issued) are taken into the calculation of individual banks' liabilities on a net basis, irrespective of term. Adjustments are also made in respect of transit items.

the banking system as a whole. Until September 1971, only the clearing banks were subject to calls for Special Deposits. But since then, the requirement has applied to all banks on the statistical list.

6. Also since September 1971, all listed banks[2] have been requested to hold a minimum of 12½ per cent—on a daily basis—of their ELs in specified reserve assets. Before then, the clearers had maintained voluntary liquidity and cash ratios and the replacement of these by a uniform reserve requirement was seen by the authorities as an integral part of the encouragement of fair competition and of equitable credit control as between banks.

7. Reserve assets are defined broadly as being:—

   (a) balances with the Bank (other than Special and Supplementary Special Deposits).

   (b) money-at-call with listed discount market institutions and brokers;

   (c) Treasury Bills issued by the British and Northern Irish Governments;

   (d) British Government marketable securities (gilts) with less than one year to maturity;

   (e) UK local authority bills eligible for rediscount at the Bank;

   (f) commercial bills eligible for rediscount at the Bank (to a maximum of 2 per cent of eligible liabilities).

This definition of reserve assets adopted in 1971 reflected the Bank's view that no significant change in the structure of the short term sterling markets or its operations therein was required. The choice of definition reflected the authorities' decision not to seek to control strictly the supply of reserve assets, for it included claims on the public sector which could be held by non-banks as well as by banks and also certain claims on the private sector. The lack of control over the supply of reserve assets has not been a particular concern because, as described above, the authorities regard the datum point of control over short-term interest rates as being the 1½ per cent of their ELs kept by the London Clearing Banks at the Bank of England.

8. It was, however, intended that the RAR should be used in conjunction with Special Deposits to mop up any abnormal excess liquid assets in the banking system and, on occasion, to go further than this and to require the banking system to seek to dispose of assets not eligible as reserve assets. It was recognised that this second use might lead to a strong upward influence on, for example, short term interest rates in the inter-bank market and that, under some circumstances, it would be necessary to accompany a call for Special Deposits with an increase in Bank Rate (Minimum Lending Rate from October 1972) so as to bring about the rise in short term interest rates and the consequent fall in prices of marketable short term assets that would be needed to shift debt out of the banking system.

9. In the event, it quickly became apparent that use of joint RAR and Special Deposits requirements presented particular short term difficulties. In the new competitive environment, after September 1971, the inter-bank market became increasingly active, and, when Special Deposts were called late in 1972 and again in July and November 1973, the immediate response of the banking system as a whole was to practice liability management on a much greater scale than had been envisaged in 1971. (In other words, to meet a shortage of reserves engineered by calling Special Deposits, the banks bid for funds in the wholesale money market—increasing their liabilities—with which to obtain more reserve assets,

---

[2]. Certain of the larger finance houses have maintained a similar 10 per cent ratio and been subject to Special Deposits.

rather than reduce their total assets.) Interest rates in such circumstances tended to shift in an unhelpful fashion, with the Treasury Bill rate falling[3] (as the banks competed vigorously to buy additional reserve assets) often in absolute, and always in relative, terms compared to the inter-bank rate which was pushed up as banks bid for funds. As the inter-bank rate rose relative to other rates, the non-bank private sector was encouraged to switch funds into bank deposits and Certificates of Deposit; £M3 rose perversely as a result, in the short term at least. The problem was compounded when institutional rigidities in the system or inhibitions felt by the banks (partly, no doubt, the result of uncertainty as to the authorities' attitude to higher interest rates) made the banks unwilling to pass higher rates on immediately to their customers; this led to a slower rise in the rates on banks' lending than borrowing and consequently provided opportunities for 'round-tripping', namely borrowing from banks to re-lend at a higher interest rate on the money markets. (In the summer of 1973, it is thought that such round-tripping inflated M3 by over 1 per cent in one month). As a result, it became apparent to the authorities that it was better to put up interest rates directly rather than to use Special Deposits to achieve this effect less directly.

10. When the SSD scheme was introduced in December 1973 and on the subsequent occasions when it has been in operation, the effect of the reserve asset requirement in combination with the SSD scheme has been to encourage banks to manage their assets rather than their liabilities. This followed from the fact that the SSD scheme restrained banks' liability management, by imposing an upper bound on the volume of interest-bearing deposits (IBELs) that a bank could take. Thus a bank close to its upper bound and also short of reserve assets tended to find it cheaper to manage its assets (for example, switching from non-reserve to reserve assets) rather than manage its liabilities (which might entail penalties under the SSD scheme). The result was still to put upward pressure on at least some interest rates, as banks sought to sell non-reserve assets and thus pushed their prices down. However, the risk of a jump in inter-bank rates, and thus a perverse short term effect on £M3 was reduced by the operation of the SSD scheme.

11. There were still major limits on what the authorities could achieve, however, not least because of the difficulty of forecasting the likely reserve asset position of the banking system even over short periods of time. This is important because, under the terms of the scheme, the banks can dispose of any excess reserve assets and reduce their IBELs. Further, asset management has frequently taken the form of disintermediation, notably through the bill leak, by which bank lending (and thus £M3 and IBELs) has been kept below what it otherwise would have been, without any significant impact on activity in the economy.

12. The reserve asset ratio has also had the effect of ensuring that banks always hold a significant proportion of their assets in "near-cash"[4]. The total against which the ratio is calculated (ELs) makes little sense in supervisory terms. For example, among other offsets and exclusions, a bank can offset its claims on other banks against its total deposit liabilities in calculating ELs. The Bank

---

3. The introduction of Minimum Lending Rate (MLR) in October 1972 made this a particularly difficult problem. MLR was formally linked to the Treasury Bill rate and, although the authorities had the power to override the formula, they were reluctant to exercise this power except when absolutely necessary. Repeatedly during the first half of 1977, however, the formula had to be overridden as the authorities tried to restrain downward pressure on short term interest rates when a massive volume of funds moved into sterling; while, subsequently, the restoration of short-term interest rates to a level appropriate to domestic monetary policy was achieved through the market-related formula only with considerable difficulties. In May 1978, MLR became fully administered.

4. The reserve ratio was not intended as a prudential control, but it grew out of the liquidity ratio maintained by the clearers until 1971, which did have prudential origins.

of England's proposals for a system designed specifically to meet prudential needs are set out in a separate consultative document. These proposals include:

    (a) that the banking system should normally hold a significant amount of primary liquidity;

    (b) that the assets which the authorities regard as primary liquidity should include certain claims on the private as well as the public sector;

    (c) that the requirement should be specified as a norm—departures from which may be permissable in certain circumstances—rather than as a daily minimum;

13. As the companion document explains, primary liquidity would be provided by cash, and by those assets which the Bank of England is customarily prepared to buy in its open market operations, or which represent claims on institutions in the money market having access to lender of last resort facilities. On strictly prudential grounds, therefore, under the present arrangements for open market operations, the definition should include call money with the discount houses and eligible commercial bills. The proposed list is:—

    (i) cash;

    (ii) balances with the Bank of England;

    (iii) call money with the London discount market;

    (iv) UK and Northern Ireland Treasury Bills;

    (v) bills eligible for re-discount at the Bank of England;

    (vi) British Government securities with less than one year to maturity.

14. The present RAR requirement has little to contribute to the present system of monetary control, especially as and when the SSD scheme is ended. Its limited prudential value would become redundant once specific prudential proposals were adopted.

15. There would, however, remain a need for Special Deposits. It would still be appropriate, as now, to call Special Deposits to absorb excessive liquidity in the banking system as a whole. Further, it would remain true that releases and recalls of Special Deposits could help to smooth out conditions in the money markets and announcements of such moves could help to show the pattern of official policy towards conditions in these markets. For example, the release of Special Deposits would be one option open to the authorities if the liquidity position of the banking system was brought under pressure through, for example, official sales of gilt-edged securities and the authorities thought it appropriate to ease that constraint.

Methods of monetary control

This background note was issued by the Bank on 24 November.

1 Since publication of the Green Paper on Monetary Control[1] the Treasury and the Bank have carried out extensive consultations and discussions on proposals for a change to a system of monetary base control and also on possible improvements to operational techniques within the existing framework.

2 From the consultations on monetary base control, two main types of proposal emerged, with an important distinction drawn between:

(i) non-mandatory systems in which banks are free to choose the amount of cash balances which they hold at the Bank of England; and

(ii) mandatory systems in which banks are required to hold a specified proportion of their liabilities as cash balances at the Bank of England.

3 Present arrangements do not allow firm judgments to be made about the desirability of moving to either kind of base control. In the case of a non-mandatory arrangement, it is not known whether the cash which the banks would choose to hold would be stably related to the money supply or to nominal income over an appropriate period. A mandatory system, on the other hand, particularly if related to a broad monetary aggregate, could prove vulnerable to the diversion of monetary flows outside the controlled area. In addition, and before fully moving to either system, time would be needed for adequate information and experience to be gained about the banks' demand for cash.

4 In this context, the Chancellor has announced in the House of Commons this afternoon that a number of improvements to the present system will be set in hand. These are desirable in their own right but they would also enable more to be learnt about the properties of a monetary base system and would be consistent with further evolution in either of the directions set out in paragraph 2 above.

5 The improvements to be set in hand within the existing framework are as follows:

(i) Once consultations with the banking system regarding adequate holdings of liquid assets have been completed, and appropriate norms agreed, the reserve asset ratio will be abolished. This was foreshadowed in the Green Paper.

(ii) Further consideration will be given to the future of the $1\frac{1}{2}\%$ cash ratio currently applying only to the London clearing banks, with a view to establishing arrangements that would be equitable within the banking system, and that could enable the authorities to monitor the development of the functional demand for cash balances at the Bank of England which could ultimately be associated with a non-mandatory system of monetary base control.

(iii) Discussions will take place with the banks regarding the collection of additional statistics on retail deposits, which would provide further information on monetary conditions and could, if that subsequently seemed appropriate, become the denominator of a cash ratio associated with a mandatory monetary base system.

(iv) Changes will be developed in the Bank of England's methods of intervention in the money market:

(a) It is envisaged that the Bank's intervention will place a greater emphasis on open market operations and less on discount window (lender of last resort) lending. It has been decided that these operations should continue to be conducted in the bill markets rather than through the inter-bank market, and in large part through the existing intermediaries, members of the London Discount Market Association, to whom discount window facilities would remain confined.

(b) Initially, the Bank's operational aim would be to keep very short-term interest rates within an unpublished band which would be determined by the authorities with a view to the achievement of their monetary objectives. The Bank would normally charge a rate on its discount window lending somewhat above comparable market rates but within the unpublished band. At an appropriate stage the Bank might cease to announce a minimum lending rate. These arrangements would allow market factors a greater role in determining the structure of short-term interest rates. It is accepted that this could lead to more flexible, market related, pricing of overdraft facilities.

(c) The Bank's operations would be broadly intended to offset daily cash flows between the Bank and the money markets. The present technique of creating initial shortages in the money markets which the Bank then acts to relieve would be abandoned. There would accordingly no longer be a deliberate over-issue of Treasury bills at the weekly tender.

---

[1] *Monetary Control* (HM Stationery Office, Cmnd. 7858).

6 The Bank will discuss the operational details of these changes with those institutions that will be affected as soon as practicable. It is intended that they will be put into effect next spring.

7 The Bank will also be putting forward proposals for changes in the institutional coverage of credit control and statistical reporting in the light of the Banking Act 1979.

8 Finally, in the light of the above changes, the Bank will examine further the possibilities of broadening the market for short-term central government debt as a means of providing greater flexibility to the government funding programme.

Money market operations since 1981

The Bank's proposals were further explained in two other papers, *Monetary control: next steps* (page 152) issued on 12 March 1981, and *Monetary control—provisions* (extracts reprinted on page 154) issued on 5 August. The reserve assets ratio was abolished and the cash ratio and eligibility arrangements described in these papers were introduced on 20 August 1981. Minimum lending rate, which had fallen into disuse, also ceased to be announced in August 1981, though the Bank said that it might in some circumstances announce in advance the minimum rate which, for a short period ahead, it would apply in any lending to the market. The background to the introduction of these new arrangements, and the means by which the Bank can bring about a change in short-term interest rates, are reviewed more fully in an article *The role of the Bank of England in the money market* (page 156) published in the March 1982 *Bulletin*.

In one important respect these new arrangements did not work as had been foreseen. Because of the unexpected strength of bank lending to the private sector in 1981–82, which persisted even after the sharp rise in interest rates in the autumn of 1981, heavy government funding was needed to restrain the growth of sterling M3. The use of funding policy in this way was explained in the General assessment of the June 1982 *Bulletin*:

It is useful to place last year's experience in the perspective of funding policy more generally. Emphasis has always been placed on financing the public deficit in a non-inflationary way, so as to keep within proper limits the growth of holdings of liquid assets in the economy. The scale on which such financing was required varied with circumstances, and in particular depended on the pressures making for monetary expansion—which include not only the public deficit, but also the scale of bank lending to the private sector. For, other things being equal, an increase in lending by the banks will be reflected in increased deposits—which sales of government debt to the public will reduce. Ensuring an appropriate growth of money may thus at times point to debt sales less than the public deficit; and at other times greater.

It is useful to emphasise that funding operations in fact entail a three-sided exchange of assets—involving the public sector, the non-bank private sector, and the banks. Sales of debt by the Government to the non-bank public are paid for by the latter reducing their bank deposits, and transferring cash from the commercial banks to the Bank of England as the Government's bank. The banks' balances at the Bank of England which are run down to make the transfer are, however, relatively small and close to the operational minimum. If the cash thus lost was not restored through operations by the Bank in the money market, each bank's efforts to make good its cash holdings would cause steep increases in the interest rates paid by the banks for short-term money. This would inevitably bring a general rise in interest rates above the levels needed to achieve the degree of monetary control already decided as appropriate on more general grounds. The sequence is therefore completed, as the third leg of the exchange, by the Bank acquiring assets from the banking system to replenish the banks' balances. Money market operations of this sort are thus a corollary of debt sales when these are high in relation to the borrowing requirement.

In the past, the Bank's money market operations normally took place in Treasury bills. Over recent years, however, holdings of Treasury bills by the banks have been reduced to such a low level that official money market operations have come to be conducted mainly in commercial bills.

High debt sales, together with consequent operations in commercial bills to replenish the cash drain on the banks, are sometimes presented as a process in which the public sector is lending (via the banks) to the private sector, borrowing long term in order to do so. But there is no essential difference between this process and one where money market operations are in Treasury bills. When operations are in commercial bills it is important to remember that the assets acquired by the Bank are claims on the banking system, not on the non-bank private sector, and that the lenders' risk is borne by the banks, not the public sector.

The greater scale of the Bank's money market operations has enlarged the demand for commercial bills. This will have reduced the relative cost to companies of this form of borrowing; and it is sometimes said that it has created profitable opportunities for direct arbitrage. Careful investigation suggests that such opportunities for companies to borrow in this form and invest elsewhere at a higher return have been few, and the potential profitability small (page 165).

These considerations suggest that bank lending is providing a valuable element in facilitating industrial recovery, for which it may not be possible quickly to find substantial alternatives. Though it is not clear how long the rate of bank borrowing will remain at its present level, a relatively high demand for bank finance could therefore continue for the present as the background for monetary policy. On the other hand, there remain strong grounds for avoiding an inflationary growth of liquidity in the hands of the public, and thus for seeking to limit the growth of the broad monetary aggregates. Business demand for outside finance may have passed its peak, and business may well come to be less dependent than recently on bank finance. This would reduce the need for high debt sales in relation to the borrowing requirement. But there are clearly many uncertainties; and the ability to vary the scale of funding remains an essential part of effective monetary policy.

A note describing the consequences of this 'overfunding' for the Bank's money market operations was published in the same issue of the *Bulletin* (reprinted on page 165).

As a result of these developments, the Bank had to undertake, virtually every day, purchases of commercial bills on a much larger scale than had been expected when the arrangements were designed. This made it much more difficult for the Bank, which had become by far the largest operator in the short-term money market, to allow market forces as substantial a role in interest rate determination, as had been intended.

The Bank's reasons for concentrating its money market operations on the bill market are explained in a paper *Bills of exchange: current issues in a historical perspective* (page 166) presented by Mr A L Coleby to a conference on bills of exchange organised by the Institute of Bankers in London on 17 November 1982, to mark the centenary of the Bills of Exchange Act. This paper also reviews experience with the new operational arrangements.

Monetary control: next steps

This paper was issued by the Bank on 12 March 1981.

Introduction

1   The Bank's Background Note of 24 November described a number of improvements to be made to the existing framework of monetary control. Among these improvements were changes in the Bank's methods of intervention in the money markets. The Background Note explained that it was envisaged that the Bank's intervention would place greater emphasis on open-market operations and less on discount window lending; and that it had been decided that these operations should continue to be conducted in the bill markets rather than through the inter-bank market, and in large part through the existing intermediaries, members of the London Discount Market Association, to whom discount window facilities would remain confined.

2   The Background Note also explained that the reserve asset ratio would be abolished, once consultations with the banking system about adequate holdings of liquid assets had been completed. The Bank is setting out in a separate document the basis on which it will now resume discussions on banks' liquidity. That document discusses the need for banks to have regard to the quality of their liquid assets: but, apart from an interim stage, it does not envisage for prudential purposes any across-the-board ratios or norms for bank holdings of primary liquidity. The problem of ensuring an adequate supply of liquid assets for monetary control purposes is discussed below.

3   The Background Note mentioned that further consideration would be given to the future of the $1\frac{1}{2}\%$ cash ratio which is observed by the London clearing banks, and which has served as a fulcrum for money market management while also providing a substantial part of the resources and income which enable the Bank to carry out its general central banking functions. As was foreshadowed in the Green Paper on Monetary Control, presented to Parliament by the Chancellor of the Exchequer last March, it has now been decided to replace this requirement by one whereby recognised banks and licensed deposit-taking institutions, in each case above a minimum size, will be required to hold cash balances on special non-operational, non-interest-bearing, accounts with the Bank. Although the precise basis of calculation remains to be determined, this requirement will apply uniformly and under present arrangements would amount in total to the equivalent of not more than $\frac{1}{2}\%$ of eligible liabilities. The London clearing banks will then maintain on their ordinary accounts with the Bank of England such balances as are necessary for clearing purposes. More generally, recognised banks and licensed deposit-taking institutions who are customers of the Bank will continue to maintain balances on their ordinary accounts at the Bank appropriate to the business conducted over those accounts.

Bill markets

4   As foreshadowed in the Background Note the Bank is now placing greater emphasis in its money market management on operations in bills rather than in discount window lending. The Bank has only very rarely provided funds through the discount window since the end of November despite the fact that on several days there have been substantial cash shortages in the money markets. Handling these shortages through the purchase of bills has been facilitated by the reduction in the reserve asset ratio on 2 January from $12\frac{1}{2}\%$ to 10%, which released for future sale to the Bank substantial amounts of bills previously held, directly or indirectly, as reserve assets. The Bank is also conducting its open market operations in such a way that market factors have a greater effect than previously on bill rates. The Bank has abandoned the practice of quoting prices at which it will buy Treasury or eligible bills of over one month to maturity and now responds to offers of bills for these longer maturities. The market has adapted readily to these changes and the speed and ease with which it has been possible to move is encouraging.

5   The emphasis in the Bank's open market operations on transactions in bills (Treasury bills, local authority bills and commercial bills) means that there will remain a need for bill markets of adequate size and depth to provide the paper in which the Bank's operations will be conducted. But once the reserve asset ratio is abolished, it is not possible to predict with confidence how banks would adjust the amount and composition of their portfolio of high quality liquid assets and what would be the effect of any adjustment on money placed with the discount houses, who are the main market-makers in bills. The banks will of course need to have regard to the Bank's evolving prudential liquidity arrangements but these will permit greater flexibility over the size and composition of high quality liquid assets than the existing reserve asset ratio requirements. It is likely that considerable amounts of funds would be available to the discount houses. The banks would continue to benefit from the fact that the liquidity provided by these funds will be

greater than that provided by some other liquid assets, and from the fact that funds placed with the discount houses are capital certain whereas a holding of bills is not. But there is a possibility that the availability of such funds might in practice, at least at the outset, not suffice to provide a market in bills of the size necessary for the Bank's open market operations. The Bank is concerned to ensure that this situation should not arise.

6 Increased reliance on open market operations in eligible commercial bills will require an adequate supply of these bills. In this connexion the Bank has felt for some time that the present list of eligible names needs to be extended. The present list consists broadly of the London and Scottish clearing banks, the members of the Accepting Houses Committee and the major British Overseas and Commonwealth banks. It dates from a time when the Bank's supervisory arrangements were primarily concerned with British banks. Apart from being a British bank of the requisite standing, the main criterion for inclusion on the list was that the acceptor should have a broadly based and substantial acceptance business which commanded the finest rates in the market.

7 In recent years there have been major changes in the Bank's supervisory arrangements and the number of foreign banks in London has increased. The Bank has concluded that these developments should be recognised in extending the criteria for eligibility.

8 At the same time, the Bank considers that it would be right to link the criteria for eligibility with the arrangements for ensuring an adequate availability of funds to the bill markets. Eligible acceptors have an interest in ensuring that the bill markets function efficiently, which complements the Bank's interest in ensuring that its open market operations can be conducted effectively. The Bank would therefore like to discuss arrangements which would incorporate a link between eligibility and an undertaking to make available, at least initially, secured funds to the discount houses in such a way as to help them fulfil their role as market-makers in those and other bills. The undertaking might be in the form of an agreed average level of funds placed with the discount houses, with a lower minimum level. If it appeared in time that such an undertaking was no longer necessary or the intermediating role of the discount market became less important, the arrangements could, as seen fit, be progressively reduced in scale.

9 During the later stages of the $12\frac{1}{2}\%$ reserve asset ratio the amount of reserve asset call money placed with the discount houses totalled over £$4\frac{1}{2}$ billion. But the Bank judges that an appropriate assured average level of funds made available to the discount houses under the arrangements described above, to enable them to provide a sufficiently broad market in bills, would at present be around £3 billion. It would represent the equivalent of around 5% of eligible liabilities of the major British and foreign banks if they were to participate in the arrangements. Such funds placed with the discount houses would of course be regarded as high quality liquid assets for prudential purposes.

10 On this basis, the Bank will, at its discretion, be willing to extend the criteria for eligibility to other recognised banks which have and maintain a broadly based and substantial acceptance business in the United Kingdom and which can command the finest rates in the market, provided, in the case of foreign-owned banks, that British banks enjoy reciprocal opportunities in their domestic markets. The Bank may wish to set limits on its holdings of any particular name, which will take account of the bank's position in the market. In the case of recognised banks which are branches of overseas banks, such limits will take account also of the bank's current level of sterling business in the United Kingdom in relation to its total business.

The gilt-edged market

11 The Bank is also concerned that there should be an adequate availability of funds to enable the gilt-edged market to continue to function efficiently. The Bank will therefore wish to explore the possibility of similar arrangements being made to ensure that suitably secured funds continue as at present to be made available to the Stock Exchange money brokers (within limits set, as now, by the Bank) and to the gilt-edged jobbers.

Monetary control—provisions

This paper, which was issued by the Bank on 5 August, sets out the new arrangements for monetary control which took effect on 20 August. It includes a list of recognised banks whose acceptances are eligible for discount at the Bank.

Introduction

1   On 24 November 1980, the Bank published a Background Note describing a number of improvements to be made to the existing framework of monetary control.[1] On 12 March this year, in a paper entitled *Monetary control: next steps*,[2] more detailed proposals on a number of the subjects covered in the Background Note were sent to all recognised banks and licensed deposit-takers (LDTs). The present paper sets out the provisions resulting from discussions since then with the various associations, as well as with a number of individual institutions.

The cash ratio

2   A substantial part of the Bank's resources and income in recent years has been provided by the average of $1\frac{1}{2}\%$ of eligible liabilities (ELs) maintained by the London clearing banks in non-interest-bearing accounts at the Bank. This sum has also served as a fulcrum for money market management. The Bank's paper in March proposed that this latter purpose should in future be served by the volume of operational funds which the London clearing banks would retain voluntarily at the Bank for clearing purposes, while the Bank's resources and income should additionally be secured primarily by a uniform requirement on all banks and LDTs to hold non-operational, non-interest-bearing deposits with the Bank. The provisions set out in this section have accordingly been designed to provide, in aggregate, broadly the same amount of non-interest-bearing funds initially as did the previous arrangements with the London clearing banks alone.

3   This non-operational requirement will be $\frac{1}{2}\%$ of an institution's ELs and will apply to institutions covered in paragraph 16(i)–(iii) below having ELs which average £10 million or more in the latest period over which the requirement is calculated. The level of an institution's non-operational balance will be set twice a year in relation to its average ELs in the previous six months.[3]

4   For institutions not on the present statistical list of banks and whose business mainly comprises the provision of fixed-rate finance for periods in excess of one year, the Bank accepts that the introduction of the $\frac{1}{2}\%$ cash ratio may present a special transitional problem. The Bank will be prepared to consider individual representations from such institutions for some temporary alleviation of the requirement. In addition, in recognition of the special conditions in Northern Ireland, the Bank has reduced to $\frac{1}{4}\%$ the cash ratio to be observed by institutions for which Northern Ireland is the principal place of business in the United Kingdom. This concession will apply in respect only of the ELs of their Northern Ireland offices and will run for two years, when it will be reviewed.

Special deposits

8   The special deposits scheme remains in place and will apply to all institutions with ELs of £10 million or more at the latest make-up day for which figures are available.[1] As hitherto, calls will be set as a percentage of ELs. The scheme for differential special deposits[2] has lapsed.

Eligibility

9   As set out in its March paper the Bank has judged applications, by recognised banks wishing their acceptances to become eligible for discount at the Bank, according to the following criteria:

(i)   whether the applicant has and maintains a broadly based and substantial acceptance business in the United Kingdom;

(ii)   whether its acceptances command the finest rates in the market for ineligible bills;

(iii)   whether, in the case of foreign-owned banks, British banks enjoy reciprocal opportunities in the foreign owners' domestic market.

A first list of eligible banks is attached.

10   A bank may apply for eligibility at any time. An eligible bank which wishes to renounce its eligibility is free to do so on giving notice to the Bank.

Undertakings by eligible banks

11   From 20 August 1981, each eligible bank undertakes to maintain secured money with members of the LDMA

---

(1) This Note was reproduced in the December 1980 *Bulletin*, page 428.
(2) This paper was reproduced in the March 1981 *Bulletin*, page 38.
(3) A deposit calculated in, say, May would relate to the monthly average of ELs from November to April inclusive.

(1) Hitherto only banks on the statistical list and finance houses observing a reserve asset ratio have been subject to special deposits.
(2) Details can be found in the March 1973 *Bulletin*, page 52.

and/or secured call money with money brokers and gild-edged jobbers[1]—all at market rates appropriate to the nature of the lending—such that:

(i) the total funds so held normally average 6% of that bank's ELs (as defined in paragraph 5);

(ii) the amount held in the form of secured money with members of the LDMA does not normally fall below 4% of ELs (as defined in paragraph 5) on any day.

12 In relation to the above undertaking, each eligible bank will:

(i) aim to meet the daily average ratio over either six or twelve-month periods (having first notified the Bank of its choice of period), the ratio on any particular day in a banking month being calculated as a proportion of ELs at the last but one make-up day;[2]

(ii) provide monthly returns of its daily figures, which the Bank will use to assess the bank's performance relative to its long-term commitment.

A bank will go below the minimum only in exceptional circumstances and will be ready to explain such action to the Bank when the relevant monthly return is made.

13 The Bank will be prepared to review these undertakings, in consultation with eligible banks and the LDMA, when sufficient experience of the operation of the arrangements has been gained, covering at least a year. The Bank will also be prepared to discuss particular difficulties, as they arise, with any party to the arrangements.

Prudential considerations

14 The Bank has received the assurances required in its paper of 12 March *The liquidity of banks*,[3] and mentioned in the Chancellor's Budget speech, that those institutions in the United Kingdom to whom the reserve asset ratio has applied will discuss with the Bank, in advance, changes in their policies for the management of their liquidity and its composition. The Bank is resuming discussions with the banks on the measurement of liquidity as the basis for continuing supervision.

---

[1] The Bank's concern with the adequate availability of funds for the efficient functioning of the gilt-edged market was noted in *Monetary control: next steps*. There are six recognised money brokers—James Capel & Co., Cazenove & Co., Hoare & Co., Govett (Moneybroking) Ltd, Laurie, Milbank & Co., Rowe & Pitman Money Broking and Sheppards & Chase. Secured call money with these firms has hitherto counted as a reserve asset. The amount of such money which these firms can take will continue to be limited by the Bank.

[2] For example, the relevant ELs figure for each day in banking September will be those as at make-up day in banking July.

[3] This paper was reproduced in the March 1981 *Bulletin*, page 40.

The role of the Bank of England in the money market

As main banker to the Government and ultimate banker to the banking system, the Bank of England is necessarily involved in day-to-day operations in the sterling money market. During the past eighteen months there have been a number of changes to the Bank's operating techniques: the Bank has ceased to announce a minimum lending rate, and its dealing arrangements now permit market forces to influence the structure of short-term interest rates to a greater extent than before. Nevertheless, the authorities continue to hold firm views on the appropriate level of very short-term rates, and seek to keep these within an undisclosed band. The Bank now publishes each day its estimate of the cash position of the money market, and details of its own operations.

After sketching the historical background to these changes, this article describes how the present arrangements evolved, and provides a detailed account of the Bank's daily procedures for deciding what action to take in the money market and for executing it. Finally, these money market arrangements are placed in the context of overall monetary policy.[1]

Introduction

In order to understand the context in which the Bank of England operates, it is important to recognise certain distinctive features of the UK financial framework:

- There is in the United Kingdom a highly centralised banking mechanism for central government receipts and payments: the Bank of England acts as the main banker to the Government, maintaining a major group of official accounts—for example, those of the National Loans Fund, the Consolidated Fund, the Paymaster General (including the Exchange Equalisation Account) and the National Debt Commissioners. Meanwhile, the Issue Department of the Bank is itself part of central government for national accounting purposes.[2] The Government does not hold balances, other than working amounts, with other banks. This centralised system provides the Bank with an up-to-date picture of much of the Government's financial position, and enables it to minimise government balances by employing any surplus cash to reduce the amount of official debt outstanding, thus avoiding unnecessary interest payments by the Government.

- The final daily cash settlements within the banking system, and between the banking system and the Bank (embracing the Government), take place principally across a small number of accounts—those of the London clearing banks—at the Bank. These banks therefore need to hold sufficient balances at the Bank to cover such settlements. The Bank maintains accounts for other customers too—including, for instance, other domestic banks and overseas central banks—but these normally play only a minor part in determining the daily flow of funds between the Bank and the banking system. The clearers' accounts bear the final daily adjustment of the system, as explained in greater detail below.

- There is a facility for same-day settlement in London through what is known as the town clearing. A cheque for more than a certain amount (at present £10,000), drawn on an office of a London clearing bank located within a specified central area of the City of London, may be presented by any other such office at the town clearing for settlement the same day. The settlement takes place after the banks have closed their counters for business, and until it has been completed no participant can be sure of its final cash position for the day.

Because it is banker to the Government and to the clearing banks, the Bank is necessarily involved in the day-to-day transactions between these parties. Government transactions with the rest of the economy are usually several hundred million pounds in each direction each day, and fluctuate widely from day to day. Substantial daily net flows between the banks and the Bank can result. A net flow of funds from the Government is, in the absence of intervention by the Bank, reflected in the accumulation of balances by the clearing banks at the Bank; a net flow to the Government results in a drain on them. Through its operations in the money market,[3] which are mainly conducted through the discount houses as intermediaries (see below), the Bank can offset these flows. The rates of interest at which the Bank deals are likely to have implications for interest rates more generally.

---

[1] This article supersedes much of the article, 'The management of money day by day', in the March 1963 *Bulletin*, but it does not go into the detail of the Bank's internal statistical and accounting procedures: these are incidental to the present article and in any case have not changed much over the years.

[2] The Bank Charter Act 1844 divided the Bank's accounts into those of the Banking Department and the Issue Department. The Issue Department's accounts record the Bank's liabilities in respect of notes issued and the assets which back them. The distinction is not important to the main theme of this article, and is mentioned only when of significance.

[3] The term 'money market' is taken by some to embrace virtually all markets which deal in wholesale sums for same-day settlement, and by others to cover, more narrowly, only those markets where the Bank is itself directly involved. The narrower sense is used in this article.

Historical background

Normally, that part of the Government's borrowing requirement which is not financed by the sale of debt outside the banking system is met by the sale of debt—in particular Treasury bills—to the banking system, which thus acts as the residual source of borrowing for the Government. Historically, holders of Treasury bills valued them for their liquidity, since the Bank generally stood ready to purchase them, at rates in line with, or close to, prevailing market rates, when the banking system was short of cash.

Until the last few years, the UK economy was for a long time managed in a way that provided the banking system with a portfolio of government debt, notably Treasury bills, that was large enough to enable the Bank to offset any daily shortages of cash in the money market by buying Treasury bills, although purchases of local authority bills were commonly made alongside those of Treasury bills. When market shortages were such that the banking system's holdings of Treasury and local authority bills became heavily depleted, the Bank would buy eligible commercial bills—that is, commercial bills accepted by names which made the bills eligible for rediscount at (ie sale to) the Bank—but such conditions seldom persisted for long.[1]

The Bank dealt then, as now, primarily with the discount houses (members of the London Discount Market Association) and only to a strictly limited extent with banks.[2] The discount houses are the principal market-makers in bills. Banks typically hold some liquidity in the form of secured callable or very short-term deposits with the houses,[3] which can be withdrawn or run off to meet cash needs; and they can seek to sell instruments such as Treasury and local authority bills, commercial bills and certificates of deposit to the houses to raise cash. The houses, in turn, may expect to balance their position, if a short one, by selling bills to the Bank—and they alone have been able to borrow from the Bank in the course of the Bank's money market operations: the Bank was at times prepared to lend continuously as part of its regular operations to any house failing to square its book by other means; such lending was against security, for short periods.[4]

These were the chief means by which the Bank relieved cash shortages, although exceptionally it employed other techniques, such as the purchase of gilt-edged stocks from banks for resale to them at a future date. In addition, certain institutions had access, as customers of the Bank, to limited private facilities—such as, in the case of the discount houses and some institutions in the gilt-edged market, for borrowing against security. These facilities provided a necessary but limited safety valve for the individual institutions, but on terms designed to discourage their use in preference to normal market channels. They have never formed part of the Bank's main money market operations and are not covered in the detail of this article.

So far, the description has been in terms of daily shortages of cash in the banking system. On days when there was a surplus, the discount houses generally found themselves with excess cash from the banks, and the Bank would, if it wished to absorb the surplus, offer Treasury bills for sale to the houses; occasionally, the Bank would offer Treasury bills to the banks as well.

The Bank operated in the bill markets at known, pre-determined rates, set for a week at a time by a simple formula based on the rates realised at the regular Treasury bill tender the previous week. When the Bank lent to the discount houses, it was only exceptionally other than at minimum lending rate (MLR)—previously Bank rate. Thus the Bank could deal with the daily imbalances which inevitably occurred in the money market in a way that was neutral to prevailing market rates. This was consistent with a monetary policy that usually aimed for periods of stability in short-term rates, interrupted by discrete adjustments by the authorities.[5]

During this period, the Bank aimed to keep the market at least slightly short of cash from day to day, so as to provide the means to bring about a change in the interest rate structure, if that should be judged necessary. The Bank fixed the quantity of Treasury bills on offer at the weekly tenders so as to assist this aim. All bills on offer were sure to be taken up, because of the discount houses' long-standing agreement (still operative today) to underwrite the tender; but because the successful bidder (and not the Bank) selects the days in the following week on which the bills will be taken up, and because of unpredicted developments among the many other factors that determine the market's position, it was not always possible to establish shortages for each day. In any case, the London clearing banks themselves had some room for manoeuvre: from 1971 to 1981, they agreed to maintain specified average balances on their operational accounts at the Bank,[6] and this averaging procedure meant that these banks could themselves occasionally perform, within bounds, the market's daily adjustment, at little or no cost to themselves. Thus, the

---

(1) Until recent changes in the list, eligible names were mainly restricted to certain British and Commonwealth banks, including the accepting houses. For the purposes of this article, eligible commercial bills and eligible bank bills are therefore treated as synonymous. When the Bank was not purchasing eligible bank bills in its main operations, it regularly bought small sample parcels in order to monitor the bill market (see the December 1961 Bulletin, page 28). Periodically the Bank also made sample purchases of trade bills.

(2) For convenience, the term banks is used in this article to describe banking institutions other than the discount houses. In the context of money market activity the London clearing banks are the most important.

(3) Liquidity in this form has to some extent been obligatory: secured money at call with the houses was a reserve asset under the reserve ratio arrangements which lasted from 1971 to 1981; and, under present arrangements, eligible banks have agreed to hold certain minimum amounts of secured money with the houses.

(4) This has often been described as 'lender of last resort' lending: this is misleading since the lending has often been simply a technical alternative to bill purchases. It has also been described as 'discount-window' lending: this is misleading when considering the detail of money market operations, since discounting is not usually involved and there could be confusion with bill purchases, which are conducted on a discount basis.

(5) There were exceptions to this general description in the period 1972–78 when MLR was for most of the time itself determined by a formula relating it to the Treasury bill tender rate. This procedure was suspended partly for technical reasons (at times of general upward pressure on interest rates, the formula tended to set MLR too low relative to other rates) and partly because the authorities wished to re-establish full control over MLR. In other periods Treasury bill rates did fluctuate relative to MLR, but such divergences were not usually large unless there were strong expectations of a change in MLR.

(6) Each bank agreed to maintain a daily average balance of $1\frac{1}{2}$% of its eligible liabilities.

Bank could not necessarily oblige the market to seek assistance every day; but it could usually rely upon doing so sufficiently quickly to maintain control over the general structure of short-term interest rates.

While these money market operations were the means of implementing interest rate policy from day to day, the principal instruments that reinforced MLR in accomplishing monetary control over a longer period were intended to be the special deposits scheme (which has existed, with modifications, since 1960) and the minimum reserve assets ratio (which applied from 1971 to 1981), together with, on occasions between 1973 and 1980, the supplementary special deposits scheme.[1] Each had direct implications for the money market: a call for special or supplementary special deposits withdrew cash from the banking system, while the reserve ratio arrangements ensured that, continuously, certain of the system's short-term assets were not available to meet cash shortages.

Deficiencies in earlier arrangements and background to recent changes

Certain shortcomings became apparent in the arrangements described above. First, developments such as higher and more variable rates of inflation worldwide and the increased attention given to controlling monetary growth were associated with higher and more volatile interest rates, particularly during the 1970s. If more volatility was inevitable, greater flexibility in the administration of short-term rates seemed appropriate.

Second, the circumstances which had provided the banking system with sufficient holdings of Treasury bills to sell to the Bank on most occasions when cash was short did not persist. Increased attention was given to the control of the stock of money, but a buoyant trend developed in bank lending to the private sector. At least in the short run, unduly rapid monetary growth could most easily be moderated by selling government debt to the non-bank private sector on a larger scale than hitherto in relation to the Government's borrowing requirement.[2] This combination of circumstances created persistent underlying shortages in the money market. The Bank responded in the first instance by reducing the quantity of Treasury bills on offer at the weekly tender. Even so, the Bank still found it necessary to buy Treasury bills—often more than were being issued. Inevitably, the proportion of these in the banking system's portfolio declined[3] and the Bank was then obliged to operate increasingly by purchasing eligible bank bills outright or for future repurchase by the market, or by lending (see box); and it supplemented these techniques during 1980 by providing banks with sale and repurchase arrangements in gilt-edged stocks.

Operations to offset market shortages

The table shows the total value each year of the Bank's operations to offset shortages in the money market by bill purchases and by lending. (Operations to offset surpluses—eg the sale of Treasury bills—are not shown.)

The figures are gross and merely illustrate turnover in the Bank's operations (Issue and Banking Departments). They are not an accurate guide to the relative importance of different operations to balancing the market, because the maturity terms of the operations are not identified. For example, if £1 million is lent to a discount house overnight on each of two consecutive days, a total of £2 million is recorded in the table, whereas only £1 million is recorded if the initial loan is for two days.

Nevertheless, the table illustrates well the increased turnover in commercial bills in the Bank's operations in the last two years, and the relative decline in turnover of Treasury bills.

£ millions

Year beginning 1 March	Treasury bills	Local authority bills	Commercial bills(b)	Lending
1971	5,140	327	114	650
1972	5,245	506	409	1,495
1973	4,216	776	1,503	2,035
1974	5,476	840	437	2,823
1975	9,364	1,125	200	3,868
1976	19,389	1,268	697	29,519
1977	14,740	1,392	47	21,663
1978	16,049	1,509	2,503	9,737
1979	16,337	2,529	3,846	18,217
1980	11,876	2,874	15,863	21,173
1981	3,810	4,349	39,771	4,640

(a) Includes purchases for later resale to the market. Includes purchases by both Issue and Banking Departments.
(b) Almost exclusively eligible bank bills.

Combined holdings of local authority and commercial bills by the Bank (Issue and Banking Departments) reached £4.0 billion at the highest point of the 1981 revenue season (in fact on 16 March), and up to mid-March this year holdings had reached £8 billion on occasion. The greatest amount of assistance given to the market by sale and repurchase agreements in gilt-edged stocks etc with banks (not shown above) was £1.5 billion, in July/August 1980.

Meanwhile, the consultative paper *Monetary control*, issued jointly by HM Treasury and the Bank in March 1980, initiated a major review of methods of controlling the money stock. While leaving many issues open for discussion, the paper firmly concluded that the reserve ratio requirement no longer served a useful function and should therefore end; and that the special deposits scheme should be retained as one means of regulating the liquidity of the banking system. The paper also noted an earlier statement by the Chancellor that the supplementary special deposits scheme should not have a permanent place among the techniques of policy: the scheme ended in the summer of 1980.

In November 1980, the Bank released a Background Note 'Methods of monetary control',[4] which set out, in general terms, certain changes that would be introduced. The Background Note envisaged that the Bank's intervention in

---

(1) For a technical description of these arrangements, see the *Bulletins* for September and December 1971 and for March 1974. For an analysis of how they related to interest rate policy and of the shortcomings that emerged, see the consultative paper *Monetary control* (HM Stationery Office, Cmnd. 7858), in particular Chapters 2 and 3 and Annex A, and also the immediately preceding article in this *Bulletin* (reprinted on page 117).

(2) The sterling money stock could also have been contained if funds had flowed into other currencies as a result of intervention in the foreign exchange market, but, in the period being considered, action of this kind on a substantial scale would have been contrary to prevailing policy on intervention.

(3) For example, the ratio of Treasury bills held by the banking system (excluding the Banking Department of the Bank) to its total sterling assets fell from an average of about 6% in 1975–77 to 1% in 1981.

(4) Reproduced in the December 1980 *Bulletin*, page 428. (See page 148.)

the money market would in future rely less upon direct lending and place greater emphasis than hitherto on open-market operations; intervention should continue to be conducted in the bill markets and not, for instance, in the inter-bank market, and principally through the existing intermediaries, members of the London Discount Market Association, to whom any general lending facilities would remain confined. The Note also indicated that the Bank's initial aim would be to keep very short-term interest rates within an unpublished band, set by the authorities by reference to the general monetary situation. Any lending would normally be at a rate somewhat above comparable market rates, but within the band. The Bank might cease to announce a minimum lending rate. Finally, the Bank would operate with the broad intention of offsetting daily cash flows, in either direction, between the Bank and the money market and would no longer seek to create initial shortages by the deliberate over-issue of Treasury bills.

Behind these proposals lay the desire to introduce a system which, while preserving the Bank's ability to influence short-term rates, would generally permit market forces a greater role in determining their structure. To allow such play for market forces, the system of pre-determined dealing rates had to be abandoned.

The Background Note also promised consideration of the future of the average balance arrangements observed by the London clearing banks (described above), with a view to establishing arrangements more equitable across the banking system as a whole and leaving the clearing banks greater freedom in managing their operational balances at the Bank.

In his Budget speech in March 1981 the Chancellor reported on the progress of the consultations on monetary control. At the same time the Bank issued a further paper, *Monetary control: next steps*.[1] Here, among other matters, the Bank let it be known that it was willing to add to the list of eligible banks (ie those whose commercial bill acceptances it was prepared to buy): the Bank was seeking to broaden the base for its future bill operations and to widen competition. The Bank was prepared to admit any recognised bank as eligible (in addition to those already on the list) which had, in the Bank's judgment, a substantial and broadly-based existing sterling acceptance business in the United Kingdom and which could command the finest rates in the market, provided, in the case of a foreign-owned bank, that British banks could enjoy comparable opportunities in its domestic market. The Bank also wished to explore the possibility of a link between eligibility and an undertaking to make funds available to the discount houses in such a way as to help them fulfil their role as market-makers in bills.

Present arrangements

Following consultations with those concerned, various changes have now been put into effect.[2] The Bank's operating techniques in the money market were changed in stages, beginning in October 1980, and the formal arrangements set out in the Bank's paper *Monetary control—provisions*[3] began to take effect on 20 August 1981. They included an extension of the list of eligible banks;[4] accompanying undertakings by all eligible banks—notably to hold a minimum proportion of their eligible liabilities in secured deposits with the discount houses, in order to underpin the houses' function in the bill markets; the ending of the reserve ratio requirement; and the introduction of the cash ratio scheme, applicable to all institutions in the monetary sector.[5] The purpose of the cash ratio scheme is to provide resources and income to the Bank; it is of no relevance to the day-to-day management of the money market since the deposits placed with the Bank are fixed for some months at a time (the period will be six months when the scheme is fully established). The introduction of the scheme did, however, mean the end of the agreement with the London clearing banks on average balances. These banks are now free to maintain their operational balances at the Bank at whatever level seems appropriate to their clearing needs. To assist the Bank in its daily forecasts of the money market's cash position, the banks advise the Bank of their targets for these balances.

Also with effect from 20 August 1981, the Bank ceased to post a minimum lending rate continuously; but it reserves the right to announce in advance the minimum rate which, for a short period ahead, it will apply in any lending to the discount houses.

Under the new arrangements, the Bank continues to conduct its operations with the market chiefly through transactions in bills with the discount houses. Direct dealings with the banks would involve predominantly the clearing banks, by virtue of their central function in the settlement of daily flows between the banking system and the Bank: in the Bank's view, the resulting concentration of official money market operations on direct dealing between the clearing banks and the Bank would greatly reduce the scope for market forces to determine interest rates.

For the Bank to have a reasonable chance of balancing the market, it is important that the system's overall daily surplus or shortage of cash should be channelled through to the discount houses before the Bank's final operating decisions are taken. Whether this happens is greatly dependent upon the ability of the major banks to estimate accurately and in good time their daily cash position; to do this, they need to know about expected large movements of funds by their customers.

---

(1) Reproduced in the March 1981 *Bulletin*, page 38. (See page 152.)
(2) The evolution of the Bank's techniques in the money markets and the implementation of the new monetary control provisions have been described in successive issues of the *Bulletin*.
(3) Reproduced in the September 1981 *Bulletin*, page 347. (See page 154.)
(4) The Bank also issued guidelines on its practices (regarding, for instance, the types of transaction to which acceptances should relate) when buying eligible bills.
(5) The newly defined monetary sector consists of all recognised banks and licensed deposit-taking institutions, the Banking Department of the Bank of England, the trustee savings banks, the National Girobank, and certain banks in the Channel Islands and the Isle of Man. The cash ratio scheme requires nearly all such institutions above a certain size to hold non-operational, non-interest-bearing deposits with the Bank.

Pre-determined dealing rates having been abandoned, the discount houses compete to sell paper to the Bank,[1] or buy from it when in surplus, through their choice of the rates at which they offer to do business. The Bank can influence interest rates by its reactions to these offers. If the Bank is content with the pattern of rates implied by the offers, it is generally prepared to accept sufficient to balance the market. But if the rates which are offered conflict with the Bank's interest rate objective, all or part of the offers may be rejected; in this case, if the houses are short of funds, they may have a chance to submit further offers (eg if the rejection came at the morning session—see next section), and the Bank again decides which offers to accept.

In addition to, or separately from, any bill operations, the Bank may let the houses know that it is willing to lend, at an interest rate of its own choosing. Such occasions are exceptional, and are in contrast with the earlier arrangements under which the houses could at times borrow continuously. Two examples of when the Bank may decide to lend are:

● When there is an isolated or unexpected shortage—perhaps on a large scale—arising for technical reasons, such as an oversubscription to a new issue of stock by the Government or a half-yearly payment of petroleum revenue tax. In such circumstances the Bank may not wish to relieve the shortage entirely by bill operations, for fear of causing unnecessary distortions to interest rates, and may therefore choose to lend—in which case the rate charged may be close to market rates.

● When the Bank wishes to see very short-term interest rates higher but believes that the discount houses will not offer—or discovers, having invited business, that they have not offered—sufficient paper at high enough rates for the upward adjustment to be effected quickly through bill operations. The Bank may then decline to deal in the bill markets, or may limit its dealings, and thus force those houses that are short of cash to borrow; the Bank then sets a lending rate consistent with the higher level which it is seeking to establish in the market.

The special deposits scheme remains available, with some adjustment of coverage. This scheme enables the Bank to call non-operational deposits, which earn interest at a rate close to the Treasury bill rate, from most institutions above a certain size in the monetary sector, as a means of withdrawing cash from the money market. Administratively, a call for or repayment of special deposits requires a period of notice, so the scheme is best suited to occasions when there is the prospect of a protracted period of surplus cash which the Bank wishes to offset. Once special deposits have been called, their release can be timed to suit the expected pattern of market flows—in particular, to match an expected shortage. Special deposits were last called in December 1979.

Another method, which the Bank used on three occasions during 1981 to remove cash from the market for release at a specific future date, is a special tender for Treasury bills of less than three months' term, set to mature on the desired date.[2]

In the past few months, the Bank has also revived an earlier practice of placing some funds directly into the local authority short-term deposit market. This has been carried out in order to help relieve the extreme pressure on bill resources caused by very large money market shortages.

No other special facilities—such as the purchase and resale agreements in gilt-edged stocks with the banks, the last of which expired in December 1980—have been employed in the mainstream of market management during the past year, although the possibility of their future use cannot be excluded.

Although the Bank does not intend, under the new arrangements, to over-issue Treasury bills in order to create shortages in the money market when none would otherwise exist, it is concerned to preserve the market in Treasury bills. Thus the Bank has continued to offer Treasury bills for tender each week, even though, on occasions, sizable market shortages have been in prospect.

Official operations since the introduction of the new arrangements have, as intended, aimed to maintain very short-term rates in an unpublished band set by the requirements of monetary policy as a whole. The flexibility within this band—and, indeed, the fact that the band can itself be shifted without the direct publicity that used to accompany changes in MLR—generally allows the authorities to alter very short-term interest rates more promptly than before. In determining rates for longer maturities the Bank has normally been content to allow market forces to be the predominant influence, and to follow such rates if it deals in such maturities; but it recognises that its own presence in the market may itself influence market rates.

Daily procedures

The Bank maintains running forecasts of the cash position of the money market—daily for several weeks ahead, and on a weekly or monthly basis over a longer horizon. In effect, these forecasts estimate the likely level of the London clearing banks' operational balances at the Bank, after taking into account all transactions between the Bank (on its own behalf or for customers such as the Government) and the banking system (acting for all other sectors), but before any new official money market intervention by the Bank. By relating these projected balances to the aggregate of the targets which the individual clearing banks view at the start of business each day as the central objective for their closing balances, the Bank produces forecasts of expected surpluses or shortages in the money market. (See the box for an illustration of these and other procedures during a typical day.)

---

(1) The principle is the same whether bills are being offered for outright sale to the Bank, or on a sale and repurchase basis. There are, however, technical differences, which are explained in the next section.
(2) See the September 1981 *Bulletin*, page 332, and the December 1981 *Bulletin*, page 471.

The Bank's money market operations

The figures are illustrative of a typical day on which, prior to any operations by the Bank, there is a market shortage.

The daily arithmetic
The items listed are explained in the main text, in particular in the section 'Daily procedures'.

What is published
The Bank releases information in the course of the day to the main press agencies and by direct input to the Reuter Monitor service.

£ millions

1 Morning estimate of the day's position (before taking account of any official operations that may be in prospect during the day):

Clearing banks' operational balances at Bank, above (+) or below (−) assumed target last night	+ 30	Not usually disclosed
Exchequer receipts (−) net of disbursements (+)	− 210	
Proceeds of net official sales (−) of gilt-edged stocks	− 20	− 220
Net receipts (−) of sterling on Exchange Equalisation Account (EEA)	+ 10	
Increase (−) or decrease (+) in note issue	+ 30	+ 30
Take-up (−) of Treasury bills by market, less maturities in market hands	− 20	
Local authority and commercial bills maturing in the Bank's hands	− 120	− 140
Bills being resold by the Bank to the market	—	—
Repayment (−) to Bank of earlier lending by it	—	—
Other, including other Bank customers	− 10	Not disclosed
	− 310	

1 The following announcement is made at about 9.45 am:

'A shortage of around £300 million is expected today. Among the main factors are:

Exchequer transactions	− 220
Decrease in note issue	+ 30
Bills maturing and take-up of Treasury bills	− 140'

The overall figure is rounded to the nearest 50. The position of bankers' balances is only exceptionally disclosed, while that of other customers is never revealed. 'Exchequer transactions' include in this context the effect of gilt-edged and EEA settlements. Bills being resold to the market would usually be disclosed if significant, as would the repayment of any published lending.

2 At about noon the Exchequer figure is revised to − 190, and that for the note issue to + 40. The revised total is   − 280

2 The revision is not large enough to warrant publication.

3 Soon after midday the Bank purchases bills from the market (see opposite) totalling   + 260

3 Details of these operations are published. Thus, when the operations are complete, the following announcement is made:

'The Bank has undertaken operations, making the following purchases totalling £260 million:

Band 1 Bank bills, £75 million at $13\frac{1}{4}$%

Band 2 Treasury bills, £12 million at $13\frac{5}{16}$%

Band 2 Local authority bills, £18 million at $13\frac{5}{16}-\frac{3}{8}$%

Band 2 Bank bills, £155 million at $13\frac{5}{16}-\frac{7}{16}$% .'

The rates shown for bill purchases are rates of discount.

4 At about 2 pm the Exchequer figure has again been revised, to − 160; and the figure for 'other' items has been revised to + 10. The revised total, before taking account of the operations in (3), is now   − 230

4 The revision is now large enough to justify publication, so the following announcement is made:

'The shortage of around £300 million published this morning has been revised to one of around £250 million, before taking account of today's operations.'

5 If the estimate of − 230 is correct, the bill purchases of 260 will leave the market with a net surplus of 30 on the day. The Bank decides to undertake no further operations.

5 The following announcement is made, at approximately 2.30 pm:

'The Bank has not operated in the money market this afternoon.'

6 When the town clearing has been settled it becomes apparent that the actual Exchequer figure was − 170. Thus the true position for the day was:

Total market shortage	− 240
Bank's operations	+ 260
	+ 20

The clearing banks' operational balances will be 20 above the assumed target overnight.

6 No further announcements are made.

There is inevitably considerable uncertainty in such forecasts. The factors which contribute to the market's position are known with varying degrees of certainty at varying stages in advance. By the morning of a particular day, the picture for that day is usually as follows:

- The Bank has a reasonable estimate, obtained from various government sources, and confirmed in advance in some instances by the receiving or paying banks, of the flows to and from the money market in respect of the various government accounts at the Bank.[1] Some uncertainties remain, however—for example, over the timing of the clearing of expected tax payments—and these may sometimes result in very large swings in the estimate during the day. The picture can never be complete until the outcome of the town clearing is known, which is after the conclusion of normal business.

- The Bank also has a reasonable estimate, based on banks' declared requirements and on past experience of daily and seasonal patterns, of the net change in the circulation of bank notes for the day, which is matched by movements on the clearers' balances at the Bank. The clearing banks may adjust their note movements during the day, so the initial daily estimate is subject to revision.

- The impact of the sterling settlement of any foreign exchange transactions by the Bank, arising from its management of the Exchange Equalisation Account as agent for the Government, is usually known, since most such transactions are settled two business days later.

- Likewise, the impact of official dealings in the gilt-edged market can usually be predicted with reasonable accuracy, since these are normally settled on the next business day after the transaction. New issues are an exception: payment in full or in part is lodged with applications and the extent to which the issues are subscribed, and how much of the payments will be cleared that day, are only known with certainty in the course of the day. Redemptions also create some uncertainty, because it is not possible to predict exactly when recipients will present their redemption warrants.

- The day's take-up of Treasury bills, tendered for the previous week, and maturities of Treasury bills in market hands are known. So too is the value of any local authority or commercial bills maturing in the Bank's portfolio, or of any bills due for resale to the market, which give rise to cash flows from the market to the Bank. Any repayment to the Bank of earlier assistance to the market in the form of lending is also known.

- Other customers of the Bank, such as overseas central banks, assist by giving advance notice, where possible, of likely movements on their accounts.

Morning operations

On the basis of the available information, the Bank makes known to the market, at about 9.45 am, its estimate of the day's position. A figure is given (currently to the nearest £50 million) along with a summary of some main factors. As noted above, many of the factors are subject to revision as the day proceeds. If the overall estimate has changed greatly by noon, the Bank releases a revised figure. The Bank does not base its operational decisions during the day solely on its own estimates of the market's position. It takes account of collective reports on their position from the discount houses, indications of theirs from the major banks, and the state of the market as evidenced by the behaviour of short-term rates. Having considered these factors, together with any particular operational objectives that it has for the day, the Bank decides shortly after midday whether it is then prepared to operate in the money market.

Conventionally, banks withdraw any funds which they require from the discount houses before noon, but they may offer surplus funds to the houses right up to the close of business in the afternoon.[2] So any shortage in the system as a whole can be expected to show in the discount houses' position by noon; indeed, because the banks often make precautionary withdrawals from the houses in the morning which may turn out in part to be surplus to their needs later in the day, the houses tend to report a shortage larger than the Bank's estimate. But an overall surplus is unlikely to show fully at this time.

Thus before lunch the Bank normally acts, if at all, only to relieve a shortage. At this stage, dealings are confined to operations in bills with the discount houses. The Bank, operating through its brokers (Seccombe, Marshall & Campion plc —one of the discount houses), informs the houses that it will consider buying bills—there is usually no distinction at this point between Treasury, local authority and eligible bank bills—in some or all of certain maturity bands.[3] Each house may then offer quantities of the bills to the Bank, specifying a discount rate[4] for each combination of instrument and band which it offers—or, if it so wishes, different rates for separate amounts within each combination. The Bank decides which offers to accept. The decision is often the straightforward one of seeking to buy paper, up to the amount of the shortage as estimated by the Bank, at the best rates offered within each combination of instrument and band in which the Bank chooses to deal. Sometimes, the amount bought may fall well short of the Bank's estimate of the shortage. This may be because the Bank considers some or all of the rates offered to be unacceptably low; more commonly, it may reflect a rather modest amount of offerings, indicating that

---

(1) The flows relate to tax receipts, government spending, transactions in national savings and certificates of tax deposit, etc. These are referred to as 'Exchequer receipts net of disbursements' in the box.

(2) Although banks in the City close their counters at 3.00 pm, they may continue to deal for same-day settlement until the deadline implied by having to present items at the town clearing, which normally closes at 3.50 pm.

(3) Band 1: 1–14 days; band 2: 15–33 days; band 3: 34–63 days; band 4: 64–91 days. All periods are defined in terms of the remaining, not the original, tenor of the bills. The Bank does not usually purchase bills with more than three months remaining to maturity.

(4) Bills are traded on a discount per annum basis. If a bill with a face value of £100,000, due to mature in 91 days, is sold today at a discount rate of 10% per annum, the discount is:

$$£100{,}000 \times \frac{10}{100} \times \frac{91}{365} = £2{,}493.15$$

so that the proceeds are £97,506.85. The true yield (interest rate) to the holder is:

$$\frac{2{,}493.15}{97{,}506.85} \times \frac{365}{91} = 10.26\% \text{ per annum}$$

The true interest rate always exceeds the discount rate, by a greater amount the longer the period to maturity.

the perceived shortage among the discount houses is small in relation to the Bank's estimate, and casting some doubt on the accuracy of that estimate; alternatively, the Bank may have other reasons for believing its estimate to be more than usually uncertain, and may therefore restrict its operations at this session.

An alternative technique is for the Bank to invite the houses to enter into a sale and repurchase agreement in bills. In this case the Bank specifies a terminal date (or dates) for the repurchase by the houses and the rate of discount at which the proceeds of the sale of paper to the Bank will be calculated; the houses then submit offers of bills, each accompanied by the bidding of a rate of interest which the house will pay on those proceeds for the specified period. The Bank responds to the bids in the same way as with outright operations.[1]

This technique is usually chosen so as to enable the market position on future days to be smoothed out—a day of expected surplus could be balanced by choosing it as the repurchase date; or it may be used when the market is particularly reluctant to sell bills of certain maturities to the Bank because of interest rate expectations. Occasionally there may be a policy purpose: for example, switching between techniques may help to prevent a particular rate structure from becoming too firmly entrenched. It may be noted, however, that a repurchase agreement obliges the houses to take back bills at a future date; the houses may therefore be less willing to restock their bill portfolios from the bill market while the obligation exists than they would be if the Bank had bought bills from them outright.

Afternoon operations

The transactions undertaken by the Bank at the morning session are then made public, together with the quantities and rates for each instrument and band.[2] Normally at about 2.00 pm, the Bank will publish any further significant revision to its estimate of the market's position for the day. Once again, the Bank weighs its estimate together with other indicators in deciding whether to invite business with the discount houses, which may be in addition to business transacted at the earlier session. This could involve further operations in bills, in the ways described above. In addition, or instead, the Bank may, as outlined earlier, let it be known that it is willing to lend to the houses. Such lending is against security, at a rate fixed by the Bank, and is generally for a period of up to one week.

If there is a surplus, the Bank usually acts only in the afternoon session to absorb it, for the reasons given above. To do so, the Bank invites the discount houses and the clearing banks to bid for Treasury bills of one or more specified maturities. The Bank does not issue such an invitation unless it is satisfied that an overall surplus exists and that any discount houses still looking for funds have had full opportunity to find them. The inclusion of the banks in the invitation is necessary because they would otherwise be at a substantial disadvantage *vis-à-vis* the houses in finding an outlet for surplus funds. In these operations the Bank again uses its discretion about which bids for Treasury bills to accept, with lower rates being accepted before higher ones for bills of a particular maturity.

The Bank again publishes the details of its market operations in this second session, whether in the bill market or by lending; but any use of the limited private facilities, which continue as before, remains undisclosed.

Because the authorities generally wish to allow market forces the fullest possible scope to influence longer-term interest rates, the Bank prefers, other things being equal, to confine its market operations to paper of as short a maturity as is feasible. This may often mean dealing only in bands 1 and 2, but there are many instances where operations in longer-term paper may be appropriate—for example, if the pattern of future shortages and surpluses in the market indicates that it is desirable to operate over a longer span, or if short-dated paper is scarce in the market, perhaps because of recent official purchases. Even so, the Bank may choose to avoid dealing in longer-term paper in the face of such a scarcity by conducting short-dated purchase and resale deals, thereby mobilising longer paper while dealing only at short rates.

The operations described above are the principal ones undertaken by the Bank, and the daily timetable and procedures are well established. The Bank may, however, alter its arrangements at any time to deal with specific temporary situations or with underlying changes in market structure.

Transactions within the banking system may continue for some time after the Bank has concluded its operations, if any. The inter-bank market in overnight funds may be particularly volatile until dealing is effectively terminated by the need to present items at the town clearing. Only when the outcome of this clearing is known will the net money market position for the day, and the final position of the clearing banks individually at the Bank, be apparent.

The Bank's money market function in the context of overall monetary policy

A point of emphasis in this article has been that the Bank is necessarily involved in the daily operations of the money market, not only as agent for central government finances, but also as the ultimate banker to the banking system. In these roles the Bank cannot avoid involvement in money market operations, and so, either explicitly or implicitly, in the determination of interest rates. The authorities have in fact chosen to continue to exercise substantial influence

---

(1) Any bills of the type and maturity which the Bank is normally willing to purchase in outright deals may be offered for sale and repurchase, provided that they do not mature before the repurchase date. The same rate of discount is used to calculate the proceeds for each bill: this rate is set at least as high as the highest prevailing market rate for any bills that may be used in the transaction; the remainder of the operation involves, in effect, the houses bidding for secured loans. Before October 1980, the method was different: the Bank set a uniform rate of discount at which all bills used in the transaction, regardless of tenor, were sold to it, and subsequently repurchased from it.
(2) See the box for an illustration.

over very short-term interest rates as a positive element of economic policy. The suspension of MLR and the Bank's revised dealing procedures have, however, permitted greater flexibility in the level and structure of rates, and more scope for market forces to influence them. And banks' base rates, which were generally linked to MLR in the past, now tend to move more flexibly in response to market developments. In consequence, the banks may be less vulnerable than before to the form of 'round tripping' whereby a customer exploits interest rate differentials by drawing on a facility related to a bank's base rate and depositing the proceeds in the inter-bank market. The monetary statistics may therefore be less prone to this particular distortion.

The Bank's principal methods of operating in the money market do not have any direct statistical impact on the stock of money, as measured by notes and coin with the public and bank deposits. For example, when the Bank buys eligible bank bills from the market, there is a switch from bills to cash in the assets of the banking system, but no change in deposit liabilities; there is thus only a shift in the statistical counterparts to the money stock, with the Bank taking over, from the rest of the banking system, bill claims on other sectors.[1] Nevertheless, the operations may be designed to influence the stock of money indirectly, through their effect on interest rates. Indeed, the desire to retain a fairly direct influence over interest rates rests on the view that these may have a significant effect on, for example, the demand for money, the demand for credit and the exchange rate, with consequences for the development of the economy more generally.

The money market arrangements now in place provide a framework within which it might be possible to operate some form of monetary base control, although it is not currently being so used. Control of the monetary base implies giving priority to the amount of official money market intervention rather than to the rate at which it is transacted. In its extreme form, where the control is sought over a very short period, the authorities would be obliged to forgo all control over interest rates. As was made clear following the discussions which led to the introduction of the present monetary control arrangements, the repercussions of changing to such a system in the United Kingdom would be uncertain. Nevertheless, the new arrangements may facilitate study of the relationship between monetary base and other economic developments, in particular by allowing the banks freedom to determine, given the prevailing monetary situation, how much of the stock of monetary base they hold, ie their holdings of notes and coin plus their operational balances at the Bank of England.

---

[1] If the Issue Department buys the bills, there is a corresponding decline in holdings of such bills by the monetary sector. But if the bills are bought by the Banking Department—itself part of the monetary sector—there is merely a shift of holdings within that sector.

'Overfunding' and money market operations

In 1976 the authorities introduced a target range for the rate of growth of M_3; from 1977 the target was expressed in terms of sterling M_3. For much of the period since then this aggregate has tended to grow faster than targeted. The main expansionary counterpart to the growth of sterling M_3 has been bank lending in sterling to the private sector. In the fourteen months to mid-April this year (for which the target growth rate for sterling M_3 was 6%–10% per annum, equivalent to an increase of between £5.2 billion and £8.8 billion) lending to the private sector increased by £16.7 billion, and sterling M_3 by £11.4 billion.

In order to mitigate the effect of rapidly rising bank lending to the private sector on the growth of sterling M_3, it has been necessary to sell large amounts of public sector debt to UK non-banks. It is helpful here to define the *net funding position* as net purchases of public sector debt by the UK non-bank private sector *less* the public sector borrowing requirement (PSBR)—both elements seasonally adjusted. When this difference is positive, as was the case in 1977/78 and again in 1981/82, *overfunding* is said to have occurred. (Other definitions of overfunding are possible but this one is most relevant to the control of sterling M_3.)

The table shows that, notwithstanding overfunding in 1977/78 and 1981/82, overall in the last five years there was very modest net underfunding: the PSBR exceeded net purchases of public sector debt by UK non-bank residents by £1/2 billion. In the same period bank lending to the UK private sector rose by around £40 billion.

In the past, a consequence of overfunding has been the repayment of short-term Government borrowing from the banking system by reducing the outstanding total of Treasury bills. More recently, with the banks' holdings of liquid claims on the Government already at a low level, the consequential money market operations following from overfunding have predominantly taken the form of purchases of bank acceptances by the Issue Department of the Bank from the banking system, and the withdrawal by Issue Department of Ways and Means advances to the Government.

Statistically, purchases of bank bills appear as the acquisition by the public sector of claims on the non-bank private sector. This statistical presentation does not, however, imply that in substance the transactions are any different from other forms of money market operations which involve the buying back of public sector debt; their substance is precisely the same. In each case the object of the transaction is solely to relieve the cash shortage which has arisen in the money market as a result of the raising of government finance in another market for the purpose of influencing the rate of growth of the money supply.

The Bank needs to provide cash to the money markets when payments by the banks to the Exchequer exceed the cash flowing in the other direction. The factors giving rise to these flows, and the ways in which the Bank offsets them, were described in detail in the March 1982 *Bulletin*, page 86.

Two of the most important influences on the cash position of the money market—the central government borrowing requirement (CGBR) and government debt sales—are also key elements of the net funding position. A rise in the CGBR will, in many circumstances, entail an increase in the PSBR and, other things being equal, in the banks' cash holdings. On the other hand, official sales of central government debt to UK non-bank residents will reduce the banks' cash holdings.

The link between the net funding position and the net amount of money market operations which are necessary is not a simple one. For example, a rise in the CGBR will not always entail a corresponding increase in the PSBR. Thus a public corporation may borrow from the central government and repay borrowing from banks; this will increase the CGBR but leave the PSBR unchanged, will add to the cash in the money markets (because money has flowed from the Exchequer), but will not affect the net funding position.

Another example is a purchase by UK non-banks of central government debt from banks or from the overseas sector. Other things being equal, this will increase net funding without altering the cash position of the money markets (because no additional cash has gone to the Exchequer). Again, banks or the overseas sector may buy central government debt from the authorities. This causes cash to flow to the Exchequer but does not affect net funding.

Furthermore, net funding is generally calculated in *seasonally adjusted* terms, but the cash position of the money markets inevitably has to be considered in actual terms. At times (such as the main revenue season in January and February) the actual and seasonally adjusted positions differ markedly.

Two other factors may affect the amount of official money market operations needed at any time. An increase in the *note circulation* raises the money market's need for cash, because the banks have to obtain the additional notes from the Bank, which debits the banks' operational balances. Second, transactions by the authorities in the *foreign exchange market* can change the cash position of the money market; a fall in the reserves (as happened during 1981/82) means that the Government is selling foreign currency and acquiring sterling, which reduces the market's sterling cash balances.

The net funding position in any period is only one factor, although often important, in determining the scale of the Bank's money market operations. The table shows that the PSBR was overfunded by £2½ billion in 1981/82; but market operations were required on the much larger scale of some £4¾ billion. The main reasons for the difference were that the CGBR was over £1 billion smaller than the PSBR, the reserves fell and there were net sales of gilt-edged stocks by the banks.

Sterling M_3 and overfunding

Seasonally adjusted

	1977/78	1978/79	1979/80	1980/81	1981/82
	Percentage increases at annual rates				
Target set for sterling M_3(a)	9–13	8–12	7–11	7–11	6–10
	£ billions				
Actual growth in sterling M_3	6.2	5.3	6.4	10.7	10.0
Increase in bank lending to UK private sector	3.7	6.3	9.2	9.2	14.5
PSBR	5.5	9.3	10.5	13.1	8.6
UK non-bank residents' net purchases of public sector debt	6.9	8.4	9.1	11.0	11.1
Net funding (overfunding +, underfunding −)	+1.4	−0.9	−1.4	−2.1	+2.5

(a) The periods for which ranges were published often did not correspond exactly with financial years; for example, a range of 6–10% per annum was published in March 1981 for the period mid-February 1981 to mid-April 1982; this range is shown for 1981/82.

Bills of exchange: current issues in a historical perspective[1]

In the centenary year of the Bills of Exchange Act, this article describes the Bank's longstanding use of bill purchases in its money market operations. Historically the Bank bought bank bills because they were among the best available assets. Their importance as a vehicle for money-market operations was reaffirmed when new arrangements for monetary control were introduced last year. Pursuit of monetary policy objectives has led the Bank to increase very substantially its portfolio of bills over the last two years, and steps have been taken to reverse this trend.

Introduction

The key elements of the Bills of Exchange Act 1882 are familiar to every student of the Institute of Bankers, although it is doubtful whether such familiarity has often bred the response of the judge who once described the Act as 'in truth, a work of art'. But, at least once the examinations have been passed, the student might well see the force of another judge's comment: that the Statute was the 'best-drafted Act of Parliament which was ever passed'. Certainly, there can be few areas of business life where a major statute has survived for a century with only minor amendments and one significant extension.

The success of the Act must owe much to the skill with which the then existing hotch-potch of law on the subject was codified. But that the law was itself so extensive already is an important reminder of just how long bills of exchange had been an integral part of business life. In 1776 Adam Smith could write that 'money is more readily advanced upon them than upon any other species of obligation'. Bills have also long been an integral part of the Bank of England's business life; and the view that commercial bills were a normal and desirable medium for its operations was carried over during the Bank's lengthy transition from private profit-making organisation to a true central bank.

From the 1920s until recently, the Bank's use of the commercial bill market was very limited. The great depression and then the Second World War greatly disrupted trade. The war also vastly increased the volume of short-term government indebtedness, so that from then until the late 1970s, the great bulk of the Bank's open-market operations could be conducted in Treasury bills. To a whole generation, this concentration of official operations on Treasury bills came to be taken so much for granted that anything else seemed somehow improper. In the last few years, however, the Government's monetary policy has greatly reduced the outstanding stock of short-term central government debt and the Bank has turned again to buying claims on the private sector as an indispensable part of its money-market operations. Once more, it has chosen prime bank bills as the instrument for those operations.

This paper explores two main questions. The first concerns the choice of bills as the medium for the Bank's management of the cash available to the banking system. The second is the reason for the size of the Bank's commercial bill holdings having risen so fast and so high. It concludes by examining the implications of the size of those holdings for the monetary control arrangements introduced last year.

[45 & 46 VICT.]   *Bills of Exchange Act*, 1882.   [CH. **61**.]

CHAPTER 61.

An Act to codify the law relating to Bills of Exchange,   A.D. 1882.
Cheques, and Promissory Notes.   [18th August 1882.]

BE it enacted by the Queen's most Excellent Majesty, by and with the advice and consent of the Lords Spiritual and Temporal, and Commons, in this present Parliament assembled, and by the authority of the same, as follows:

PART I.

PRELIMINARY.

1. This Act may be cited as the Bills of Exchange Act, 1882.   *Short title.*

2. In this Act, unless the context otherwise requires,—   *Interpretation of terms.*
   - "Acceptance" means an acceptance completed by delivery or notification.
   - "Action" includes counter claim and set off.
   - "Banker" includes a body of persons whether incorporated or not who carry on the business of banking.
   - "Bankrupt" includes any person whose estate is vested in a trustee or assignee under the law for the time being in force relating to bankruptcy.
   - "Bearer" means the person in possession of a bill or note which is payable to bearer.
   - "Bill" means bill of exchange, and "note" means promissory note.
   - "Delivery" means transfer of possession, actual or constructive, from one person to another.
   - "Holder" means the payee or indorsee of a bill or note who is in possession of it, or the bearer thereof.
   - "Indorsement" means an indorsement completed by delivery.
   - "Issue" means the first delivery of a bill or note, complete in form to a person who takes it as a holder.

[*Public.—61.*]   A 1   1

---

(1) This paper was presented by A L Coleby, Assistant Director of the Bank of England, to a conference on the bill of exchange organised by the Institute of Bankers in London on 17 November 1982.

Why operate in bills?

The monetary arrangements adopted last year retained the historic basis of the Bank's money-market operations, which is that they are conducted in bills, and primarily with members of the London Discount Market Association, which are the only institutions in the banking sector having borrowing facilities at the Bank. Let us trace the origins of these arrangements.

Historically, the Bank bought bills because they were among the best available assets. The principal competitor, believe it or not, was consols. For considerable periods there were no public sector bills competing with bank bills and, among claims on the private sector, the attractions of prime bank bills were considerable. They gave security in depth, in that they bore at least two good 'names', and their creditworthiness had been assessed before they reached the Bank, notably by the acceptor when taking on the commitment. They were also highly marketable, in generally good supply, and available with fairly short maturities, which made them a highly flexible instrument of particular attraction to the Bank at times, such as in the early years of the nineteenth century, when the size of its balance sheet was often volatile. Further, the Bank found that regular purchases were an excellent way of monitoring developments in the bill market which was then of great relative importance.

Given the importance of bill operations to it, the Bank not surprisingly came to have close relations during the nineteenth century with the bill specialists—first, as bill brokers and later as discount houses. Relations with the commercial banks were less close. At least for the first part of the century, the Bank and the joint stock banks regarded each other as commercial rivals, while the latter considered that borrowing from the Bank of England could be construed as a sign of weakness. The Bank for its part came to understand that access to its lending facilities was a valuable privilege. Consequently, it had the problem of how to retain these facilities (and thus underpin confidence in the financial system) without giving the privileged institutions the ability to on-lend more easily or cheaply than those without access to them. The Bank's conclusion was to concentrate its lending facilities on the discount houses because they did not compete with the banks for overdraft or other lending business, or initiate new lending outside the banking sector.

There is now, of course, a much wider range of assets potentially available to the Bank for managing the cash position of the banking system, but the reasons which led us to the present position remain valid. They were strengthened by the presence, among the objectives underlying last year's monetary control arrangements, of the desire to find a market mechanism which would allow much greater scope than before for market influences to play a part in determining short-term interest rates.

The monetary authorities did not intend to abandon taking a view of the level of short-term interest rates likely to be consistent with their wider monetary objectives, expressed as targets for various monetary aggregates. But that view, and the market operations associated with it, were intended to provide no more than a sort of dragging anchor at the very short end of the market. The term structure of rates, out to the three-month point and beyond, was to be fully responsive to market influences; and the outcome of that response was itself to be an important ingredient in the continuous reassessment of the aptness of the official view on the level of very short-term interest rates.

Two conditions were identified as needing to be met for that process to work satisfactorily. The first was that the flow of funds in the money market should not be systematically and heavily out of balance. The Bank's paper in November 1980, it will be recalled, promised not to create unnecessary money-market shortages by the deliberate over-issue of Treasury bills at the weekly tender. I will come back to a discussion of our experience in that respect later on. The second condition was that the operations should be conducted at arm's length from the principal counterparties.

This was an important factor in the decision to continue doing those operations in the bill market. If the Bank operated directly in the inter-bank market, it would inevitably find its operations concentrated on the clearing banks, upon which any cash imbalance is thrown by virtue of their central function in the settlement of daily cash flows. The resolution of the cash imbalance would consequently be likely to involve a small number of, effectively, bilateral deals. It would not be an exercise that allowed any real scope for market influences to bear on the interest rates arrived at for official operations. In the bill market, by contrast, those influences are more widely diffused. It is an asset market, rather than a liability market, in which there are many participants each with potentially different circumstances and expectations.

Creating a flourishing bill market

Having concluded that the bill market was more likely than the inter-bank market to provide the desired mechanism for interest-rate determination, the Bank then had to consider how to ensure that the market was of sufficient depth for the purpose. The former reserve asset ratio requirements had had the effect—increasingly as the supply of Treasury bills declined—of compelling banks to put call money with the discount houses, and there already was a flourishing bill market. We could make no confident predictions what our prospective demands on the market might be. At times they might become substantial, and it seemed right to make arrangements so that there could be significant expansion in the supply of eligible bank bills. In those circumstances, the bill market might be expected to flourish spontaneously. But we also had to have regard for the possibility that, perhaps as a by-product of the economic cycle, there might be times when the Bank's demand for bills would be low. There would then be a risk that the bill market, no longer supported by the reserve asset arrangements, might atrophy, and not be available to meet our needs when they resumed.

From those two considerations emerged two features of the present bill market. Resources to maintain the discount houses' ability to make a market in bills were assured by the introduction of the secured deposit arrangements for eligible banks—at a level initially some two-thirds of those latterly provided through the operation of the reserve asset system. The efficacy of the new arrangements in sustaining the bill market at a time when the Bank is not a buyer has not, of course, yet been put to the test.

Eligibility

Much more tested has been the ability of the system to expand the supply of eligible bills. The principal step which the Bank took to enable that to happen was to enlarge the list of eligible names, which had remained virtually unchanged for two decades and more—a period in which the contribution of foreign banks to banking activity in London had grown apace. The criteria on which additions were to be made to the list were set out by the Bank in March 1981, and had two main elements. The first was the long-standing requirement that a successful applicant must already have built up a good bill business; the second, for foreign-owned banks, was the reciprocity principle.

The Bank's insistence on applicants demonstrating that they already have a broadly-based and substantial acceptance business has seemed odd to some commentators. To build up such a business, while still an ineligible name, in competition with energetic eligible banks, is hardly likely to be very profitable. Is there not a 'chicken and egg' problem? We readily acknowledge that there is a cost, in profits forgone, for a new name to become eligible. But that is deliberate, not accidental. We do not regard eligibility as a matter of status, to be had for the asking if a bank is sufficiently distinguished in its other activities. We see it as directly related to the function of accepting bills, a function to which a successful applicant should be committed once on the list.

The operational need to enlarge the list of eligible banks also provided the occasion to add foreign names to it. Previously, only British banks or those of British origin had appeared. It was timely to recognise the contribution of foreign banks to banking in London by removing any appearance of discrimination. The coming into effect of the Banking Act 1979 had meant that all banks which became recognised, whatever their country of origin, had to satisfy its tests of soundness and management. Nevertheless, it was concluded that eligibility should go only to those foreign banks which could show that UK banks had comparable access to equivalent facilities in their country of origin: the reciprocity principle.

Applying that principle is far from easy, because financial structures differ widely from country to country, and many of our own features are a little unusual. The two key elements that must be found are freedom for UK banks to establish and engage in domestic banking business; and freedom from discrimination, in comparison with domestic banks, in the terms of their access to official facilities for providing liquidity to the banking system. These tests do not go so far as to look for comparable commercial opportunities for UK banks in foreign markets with those available to foreign banks in the United Kingdom. That would be an impossible test to apply.

Aided by the doubling of the number of eligible banks, the supply of eligible bills has grown massively in the past two years, from around £3½ billion in October 1980 to £12¼ billion in October 1982. The growth has been needed in order to supply the Bank's voracious appetite, which has regularly absorbed up to 75 per cent of the available stock. And that leads on to this paper's second main question: why have the Bank's holdings risen so fast and so high?

Why the Bank now holds so many eligible bills

The answer begins with the relationship between monetary targets and bank lending. For much of the period since monetary targets were first published in 1976, bank lending in sterling to the UK private sector has grown considerably faster (in percentage terms) than the target set for money. The contrast was particularly marked in the fourteen months to mid-April 1982, when bank lending rose at an annual rate of 25% against a target for sterling M_3 of 6%–10%.

To help limit the impact on sterling M_3 of such rapid increases in bank lending, the central government has sold large amounts of debt to the UK non-bank private sector. On occasion, as in 1977/78 and 1981/82, this has involved what is sometimes known as 'overfunding': ie, net sales of central government and other public sector debt to the UK non-bank private sector in excess of the public sector borrowing requirement (PSBR). But those occasions were the exception. Over the last five full financial years taken together, debt sales have fallen very modestly short of the PSBR; there has been almost exactly full funding. This contrasts sharply with the previous five financial years (1972/3–1976/7) when the PSBR exceeded debt sales by nearly £14 billion.

Monetary targets and overfunding
£ billions; *seasonally adjusted*

	1972/3 to 1976/7	1977/ 1978	1978/ 1979	1979/ 1980	1980/ 1981	1981/ 1982	1977/8 to 1981/2
CGBR	23.9	4.3	8.4	9.1	13.0	7.6	42.4
Contribution of rest of public sector	10.1	1.1	1.2	1.4	0.6	1.2	5.5
PSBR	34.0	5.4	9.6	10.5	13.6	8.8	47.9
Public sector debt purchased by non-bank residents:							
Central government	15.9	7.0	8.1	8.3	11.5	11.6	46.5
Other public sector	4.4	−0.1	0.4	0.8	−0.5	−0.6	—
Overfunding(a)	−13.7	1.5	−1.1	−1.4	−2.6	2.2	−1.4
Sterling lending to private sector(b)	16.7	3.8	6.3	9.4	8.9	14.9	43.3
Target growth of sterling M_3 maximum(c)	n/a	5.3	5.6	5.8	6.6	7.1	30.4

n/a not applicable.
(a) Public sector debt purchased by non-bank residents *less* the PSBR.
(b) Including Issue Department commercial bills.
(c) Target periods often differed from financial years so these figures are no more than a guide for comparison.

Full funding of the PSBR need not lead inevitably to a large drain of cash from the money market. The outcome depends also on the composition of the PSBR and its financing. In the past five financial years, up to and including 1981/2, the PSBR has exceeded the central government's own borrowing requirement by over £5 billion. In other words, local authorities and public corporations have borrowed over £5 billion from sources other than central government. But their net sales of debt to the private sector were nil. So the funding achieved has involved the central government in over-funding its own needs by more than £4 billion.

Central government's transactions, drawing out a net £4 billion, have been the principal factor affecting the cash position of the money market over the past five years.[1] Other factors, including official transactions in the foreign exchange market, purchases of central government debt by the overseas and banking sectors (which draw cash out of the money market but do not directly affect sterling M_3) and changes in the note circulation have, on balance, aggravated the shortage of cash. This has been particularly so recently. As a result, the banking system—which maintains only a modest level of cash to meet its daily settlement obligations to the authorities—has been persistently short of cash.

Net official money-market operations
£ billions
(Flow of cash to the market, +)

	1977/78	1978/79	1979/80	1980/81	1981/82
Net official purchases of:					
Treasury bills	+0.6	+0.8	−0.1	+1.0	+0.1
Other public sector bills	+0.1	+0.1	+0.1	+0.1	+0.6
Bank bills	—	−0.1	+1.0	+2.2	+4.2
Special deposits	−0.2	+1.2	−0.1	+0.1	—
Other(a)	−0.2	+0.3	+0.5	−0.7	−0.1

(a) Comprises market advances and repurchase agreements on gilt-edged stocks.

This shortage has not been relieved by operations in bank bills alone. Initially, there were special deposits, amounting at their peak in 1976 to £1.8 billion, which could be repaid to the banks. The outstanding stock of Treasury bills was brought down, either by buying them in, or by failing to replace them fully at maturity. But it was increasingly to eligible bank bills that the Bank turned—initially to offset seasonal cash shortages and then on a continuing basis. The peak of such bill holdings in the main 1981 revenue season (March) was £3½ billion, a year or so later £8 billion and, recently, the figure has been around £9½ billion.

An inevitable consequence of such a high level of bill holdings is that the maturing of bills in the Bank's hands is itself the cause of recurring large shortages of cash in the market. The flow of maturities depends also on the average length of the bills in the Bank's portfolio. In the conditions that have prevailed for the past year, of generally optimistic expectations of falling rates, the portfolio has understandably tended to be rather short. In consequence, the Bank's purchases of bank bills (outright and for resale) over the twelve months to end-October were over £87 billion. To illustrate just how dramatic a turnaround this represents from the not so distant past, the corresponding figure for the year to end-February 1978 was £50 *million.* Meanwhile, operations in Treasury and local authority bills, then at a level of £16 billion, had fallen to £7 billion in the latest twelve months.

Implications for the monetary control arrangements

The first thing that has to be said is that the participants in the bill market, acceptors and discount houses together, have done remarkably well to cope so capably with the massive demands we have made of them. Their response speaks well for the resilience of the system we currently have.

On the other hand, it is obvious that the cash shortages just described are a long way from fulfilling the condition of a broadly-balanced market which the interest-rate mechanisms of the new arrangements ideally required. The size of the Bank's operations, day after day, has meant that the dominant influence on bill market rates, dwarfing all others, has been expectations about the rates at which the Bank would be prepared to deal, now or in the near future. We have not been able to avoid becoming a rate setter, and not just for very short bills alone. In the circumstances, it is perhaps as well that the trend of expectations about rates has been so strongly downwards, because at least we have been in no doubt about the direction of market influences.

Also unsatisfactory has been the effect which the sheer size of the Bank's operations in the bill markets has at times had of widening the gap between interest rates on bills and on other forms of private sector finance, making the former relatively cheap.

Consideration of these problems has led to the conclusion that steps should be taken to contain the growth of our bank bill portfolio and, hopefully, to reduce it somewhat. That has involved tackling the principal cause of its recent growth, namely the extent to which other parts of the public sector finance themselves from the banking system. The intention to create a new facility for local authorities at the Public Works Loans Board (PWLB), and for nationalised industries with the National Loans Fund (NLF), was announced by the Chancellor in June.[2] The PWLB facility, offering variable-rate loans which were not previously available, became operational in August, and the NLF facility more recently.

The scope for these facilities to make an impact over time is considerable. Local authorities have around £10 billion of bank borrowing outstanding and public corporation's short-term financing needs could, on occasion, reach £1½ billion. The extent of the use that is made of the new

---
(1) The Bank's operations in the money market are described in the article 'The role of the Bank of England in the money market' on page 86 of the March 1982 *Bulletin.* (Reprinted on page 156.)
(2) See page 353 of the September 1982 *Bulletin.*

facilities is entirely for the borrower to decide, on the basis of their competitiveness, and it may be a little while before we can judge the likely pace of take-up.

In the longer run, the reduction of our portfolio of bills could be assisted by some slowing-down in the rate of bank lending, so that it became no longer necessary to fund the PSBR fully in order to meet monetary objectives. The future course of bank lending is much too hazardous to forecast, but there have been one or two developments recently which could weaken some of the forces of expansion. Particularly welcome have been the signs of revived activity in the corporate bond market, reopening a source of financing for companies which has not been used for a decade.

Conclusions

Given the pressure to which they have been subjected, the new arrangements have worked remarkably well in the past year or so. The participants in the bill market have played an enormous part in enabling the authorities to handle an unprecedented need to inject cash into the system. But the demands we have made on them went well beyond anything we had envisaged at the outset, and this has limited the extent to which we have been able to meet our original objectives, particularly that of allowing greater market influence on the structure of interest rates. Ungrateful though it may seem, we have now turned our hand to steps intended to moderate our demands. To the extent that we succeed in doing so, by one means or another, the system as a whole will benefit.

ECONOMETRIC APPENDIX

Two papers are reprinted in this appendix as examples of econometric work that has influenced the Bank's thinking on monetary policy. Other work of this kind has been published from time to time in the Bank's *Quarterly Bulletin* and in two series of Discussion Papers.

Methods of estimation and fuller details of econometric results were described in technical appendices to these two articles which have not been reprinted here. Lack of space was the main reason. More recent data and developments in methodology have also rendered some of the results out of date, but the particular econometric equations are perhaps of less interest in the context of this book than the insights these papers provide into the way econometrics contributed to the practical policy questions of the time.

The demand for money in the United Kingdom: experience since 1971

A research paper, prepared in the Bank's Economic Section, largely by Graham Hacche.

Introduction and summary

The Economic Section of the Bank has for some time been engaged in the econometric estimation of demand-for-money relationships in the United Kingdom. In a previous paper,[1] Goodhart and Crockett reviewed some published results, and presented their own estimates, based on quarterly data. In a further paper,[2] Price examined more closely the lag structures of the relationships, and presented for the first time equations for the demand for broadly-defined money by the company and personal sectors separately. He concluded from his results that 'equations of the types described provide a sufficiently accurate statistical explanation of past movements in the stock of money to be a useful guide for monetary policy.'

This paper re-examines the findings in the light of more recent experience.

The initial object is to examine the extent to which the behaviour of the money stock since 1971 has diverged from what might have been expected from equations estimated over the preceding period. Thus Section 2 below presents new equations, similar in structure to those previously published but estimated from revised data for the fourth quarter 1963 to the third quarter 1971 (1963 IV – 1971 III), and then compares the forecasts generated by them for 1971 IV – 1974 I with the corresponding actual movements of the money stock. It shows that the demand for money narrowly-defined (M_1) has in only a few quarters been significantly out of line with expectation, and that holdings of broadly-defined money (M_3) by the personal sector were also much as predicted until 1973 I. In contrast, however, companies' holdings and total holdings of M_3, as well as personal holdings after 1973 I, are shown to have grown persistently faster than predicted by the equations.

Section 3 seeks to provide an explanation. It is argued that the introduction during 1971 of the new arrangements for competition and credit control (the new approach) resulted in important changes in the behaviour of the deposit banks which have had the effect of increasing the attractiveness to asset-holders of interest-bearing money in relation to other financial assets. In particular, the deposit banks have for the first time been bidding competitively for large, 'wholesale' deposits in the parallel money markets, and have been issuing certificates of deposit in their own names. In these circumstances, the persistent underprediction of the demand equations for M_3, which appear to fit the preceding period quite well, is not too surprising.

An implication of the argument of Section 3 is that the rate of interest paid on wholesale time deposits and certificates of deposit may have become a significantly more important determinant of the demand for M_3 since 1971. Section 4 attempts to test this hypothesis. It presents a second set of equations, this time based on data taken to the end of 1972, and examines their forecasting performance from 1973 I to 1974 I. It shows that the behaviour of companies' holdings and of total holdings of M_3 since 1971 appears more explicable when, for this period, the interest rate on certificates of deposit (which is probably also representative of rates paid on large time deposits) is included among the explanatory variables of demand. This finding gives some support to the argument of Section 3. Even so, a number of reasons are given why the behaviour of these aggregates during 1972 and 1973 may provide an unreliable guide to their behaviour in the future. Whether the unexpectedly fast growth of personal

[1] C. A. E. Goodhart and A. D. Crockett, 'The importance of money', June 1970 *Bulletin*, page 159.
[2] L. D. D. Price, 'The demand for money in the United Kingdom: a further investigation', March 1972 *Bulletin*, page 43.

sector holdings of M_3 from 1973 I to 1974 I can also be explained by a similar new influence is not examined directly in this paper.

A reviewer of the empirical evidence on the demand for money could write in 1971 that 'there does seem to exist ... a reasonably stable relationship between the demand for cash balances and a few other variables' and could claim that 'the actual quantitative values of the parameters of the functions implied by these observed relationships have remained reasonably steady over time. These parameters have not remained constant, of course, but changes in them have been slow rather than sudden.'[1] This study points to a recent significant, and somewhat sudden, though not surprising shift in certain demand-for-money relationships. At some time in the future there may be more reason for confidence that these relationships have restabilised than there can be at present. But meanwhile, at least, the results reported below encourage caution.

1 Model specification

This first section establishes the general form of the equations estimated. The basic model adopted is one in which — with all variables in natural logarithms — desired money balances in any quarter are a linear function of current and lagged values of appropriate explanatory variables; and in which actual money balances adjust towards desired balances with a lag such that a constant proportion (to be estimated) of any remaining adjustment towards equilibrium is accomplished in each quarter. A variety of possible determinants of desired money holdings is suggested by economic theory. For the purposes of this section, however, attention is restricted to a particular set of three explanatory variables: real income, the price level, and a representative interest rate. Ignoring for present purposes any lags in the desired money stock function the model may be written:[2]

$$\ln M_t^* = a_0 + a_1 \ln Y_t + a_2 \ln P_t + a_3 \ln r_t \qquad (1)$$

$$\ln M_t - \ln M_{t-1} = (1-\gamma)(\ln M_t^* - \ln M_{t-1}) \qquad (2)$$

where

M^* is desired money stock

M is the actual money stock

Y is real income

P is the price level

r is a representative interest rate

$t, t-1$ are time subscripts

$(1-\gamma)$ is the coefficient of adjustment, $0 < \gamma < 1$.

This familiar partial adjustment model yields a single reduced-form equation to be estimated, one of whose arguments is the lagged dependent variable (in this case the lagged money stock):

$$\ln M_t = b_0 + b_1 \ln Y_t + b_2 \ln P_t + b_3 \ln r_t + \gamma \ln M_{t-1} \qquad (3)$$

where

$$b_i \equiv (1-\gamma)a_i, i = 1, 2, 3.$$

Because the variables in this equation are in logarithms, the short-run elasticities of the demand for money with respect to Y, P, and r are given by the respective coefficients b_1, b_2, and b_3, which are to be estimated. However, these coefficients show only the impact effects of changes in the independent variables. The presence of the lagged dependent variable in equation (3) means that the adjustment of the demand for money to a change in an explanatory variable will continue during quarters subsequent to that in which the change occurs. In fact, in the long term the elasticities with respect to Y, P, and r will approach $b_1/(1-\gamma)$, $b_2/(1-\gamma)$, and $b_3/(1-\gamma)$

---

[1] D. E. W. Laidler, introduction to the section on 'The Demand for Money', in *Readings in British Monetary Economics*, edited by H. G. Johnson (Clarendon Press, Oxford, 1972), page 121.

[2] To simplify presentation, stochastic error terms are omitted from equations in this section.

respectively; this is merely to say that after full adjustment, the elasticities are given by the coefficients a_1, a_2, and a_3 of the desired stock equation, (1).

Thus, the log-linear form of equation (3) constrains the elasticities (short-term and long-term) of the demand for money with respect to each explanatory variable to be constant, and in particular, to be independent of the level of the variable. This implicit assumption is convenient and, generally speaking, not implausible. In the case of the interest-rate variable, however, it is perhaps less likely that, for example, a doubling in the rate from 1% to 2% will have the same proportionate effect on the demand for money as will a doubling from 10% to 20%. Therefore equation (3) is amended by entering the interest rate by means of the variable $\ln(1+r)$, rather than by using $\ln r$. This constrains the interest-rate elasticity to vary directly with the rate, so that, for instance, a rise from 10% to only (about) 11·1% has the same proportionate effect on money demanded as a rise from, say, 1% to 2%.[1] Equation (3) is thus amended to:

$$\ln M_t = b_0 + b_1 \ln Y_t + b_2 \ln P_t + b_3 \ln(1+r_t) + \gamma \ln M_{t-1}. \qquad (4)$$

A further amendment of the basic model results from assuming that the long-run price elasticity is unity. This assumption may be justified on three counts. First, and most importantly, it reflects received doctrine: the prediction that real desired money balances will be unaffected by changes in the price level is one of the least disputed in monetary theory. Secondly, when the price elasticity has been freely estimated, in work performed in the Bank and elsewhere, the results have commonly been sufficiently close to unity to support the theory. Thirdly, the high degree of correlation between real income and price means that it is often difficult to know how much credibility can be attached to coefficients of the two variables when freely estimated separately, particularly when the estimated price elasticity is not close to unity. Thus the problem of multicollinearity provides a further rationale for constraining the coefficient of the price variable to its theoretically plausible value.[2]

By constraining the long-run price elasticity in equation (1) to unity, equation (4) becomes

$$\ln M_t = b_0 + b_1 \ln Y_t + (1-\gamma) \ln P_t + b_3 \ln(1+r_t) + \gamma \ln M_{t-1} \qquad (5)$$

which may be rearranged to give

$$\ln(M_t/P_t) = b_0 + b_1 \ln Y_t + b_3 \ln(1+r_t) + \gamma \ln(M_{t-1}/P_t). \qquad (6)$$

Equation (6) is the relationship as estimated; but the results will be presented in the form of equation (5), which makes explicit the value of the short-run price elasticity, $1-\gamma$, of nominal money balances.

The equations were estimated in first differences, using ordinary least squares, but applying the Cochrane-Orcutt transformation to adjust for serial correlation. Notes on the method of estimation are contained in Appendix 1.

2 Estimation period 1963 IV – 1971 III: estimates and forecasting performance

Estimates

Equations were estimated for four monetary aggregates:[3] M_1, M_3, personal sector holdings of M_3 (MP), and company sector holdings of M_3 (MC). (Apart from MP and MC, the remainder of M_3 – about 10% over the estimation period – is held by financial institutions other than banks and by the public sector.) In the case of each aggregate, the equations estimated were of the form of equation (6) above, except that more than

---

[1] This procedure is roughly equivalent to including r [rather than $\ln(r)$] in the equation, since $\ln(1+r) \doteq r$, for small r.
[2] See Appendix 3.
[3] For definitions of these and other data series, see Appendix 2, which also notes some imperfections of the money stock data.

one interest rate and lagged values of the exogenous variables were allowed to enter.[1]

The real-income (or expenditure) variable used for M_1, M_3, and MC was total final expenditure (TFE) at constant prices, and for MP it was personal disposable income (PDI) at constant prices. In each case, the price variable used was the deflator of the appropriate income series. The three-month local authority rate and the yield on 2½% Consolidated Stock (Consol rate) were used to represent, respectively, rates of interest on competing short-term and long-term financial assets; various alternative rates (including equity yields and a euro-dollar rate) were tried, but with less success. Also, for the broad (M_3) aggregates, equations were estimated containing the overnight inter-bank rate and the clearing banks' seven-day deposit rate, as representative of interest paid on time deposits; but the results were unsatisfactory. Thus, no significant 'own rate' influence was found.

For each monetary aggregate, therefore, a number of variant equations were fitted. One 'best' equation for each was then selected by the usual statistical criteria; these are presented in Table A. In Appendix 3 they are compared with the previously published estimates; but some other features of the results are worth noting here.

Table A

Demand-for-money equations 1963 IV – 1971 III[a]

All variables are in natural logarithms

Dependent variable	Constant	Short-run elasticities Y_t	P_t	$1+r^s_t$	$1+r^L_t$	$1+r^L_{t-1}$	M_{t-1}	Standard error of estimate (per cent)	$\bar{R}^2$	D-W[b]	ρ[b]	Long-run elasticities[c] Y	r^s	r^L
M_1	24·574	0·228 (0·158)	0·585	−0·736 (0·317)	−1·568 (0·753)		0·415 (0·134)	1·35	0·49	2·09	−0·6	0·391	−0·081	−0·184
MP	3·912	0·346 (0·086)	0·373			−0·382 (0·392)	0·627 (0·118)	0·78	0·70	2·38	−0·6	0·927		−0·069
MC	24·970	0·319 (0·270)	0·623	−0·657 (0·520)	−1·794 (1·266)		0·377 (0·156)	2·06	0·27	2·15	−0·4	0·511	−0·067	−0·197
M_3	6·725	0·162 (0·123)	0·359	−0·513 (0·199)			0·641 (0·138)	0·95	0·56	2·22	−0·6	0·450	−0·091	

[a] For definitions of the variables, see Appendix 2. Standard errors are shown in brackets beneath the appropriate coefficients.
[b] For the meaning of the Durbin-Watson statistic (D-W) and ρ see Appendix 1.
[c] The long-run price elasticity is constrained to unity in each equation. Long-run interest-rate elasticities are evaluated at the mean interest rates of the estimation period (see footnote [1] on page 176).

First, although all coefficients reported in Table A have the signs expected *a priori*, many are not significantly different from zero.[2] In three of the four equations (MP is the exception) the coefficient of real income in not significant; and neither the MP nor the MC equation contains a significant interest-rate coefficient. These results appear to contrast with many reported elsewhere. They stem essentially from the method of estimation, and in particular from the fact that the equations were estimated in first differences. Estimation in levels would tend to produce more significant coefficients, but it was considered that, owing to the nature of the data, such estimates might be seriously biased (see Appendix 1). The comparatively low coefficients of determination ($\bar{R}^2$) reported in Table A also reflect the method of estimation.[3]

In contrast to the real-income and interest-rate variables, the lagged money stock may be seen to have a coefficient significantly different from zero in each of the four equations. The size of each of these coefficients implies a speed of adjustment towards any desired change in

---

[1] Also, in recent work at the Bank, equations have been estimated containing variables other than the levels of real income, prices, and interest rates. These have included the rate of inflation, and a variable measuring the divergence of the current long-term interest rate from past rates (the latter representing an attempt to identify a Keynesian speculative influence on demand). The results obtained with these other variables were not, however, satisfactory, and are not reported here.

[2] Throughout the paper all significance tests refer to the 5% probability level.

[3] When the equations of Table A were estimated in levels, with no adjustment for serial correlation, all coefficients except one were significant at the 5% level; the exception – r^s in the MC equation – was significant at the 10% level. The lowest $\bar{R}^2$ was 0·71 (MC), the highest 0·98 (MP). The forecasts given by these estimates were, however, more inaccurate than those generated by the estimates reported in Table A, often markedly so, thus indicating that the coefficients estimated in this way were, indeed, biased.

money holdings, which may be seen to be faster for M_1 and MC than for MP and M_3. In fact, the coefficients in the former two equations imply that more than 95% of the desired adjustment to any exogenous change is accomplished after four quarters; the equivalent proportion in the latter two equations is slightly below 85%.

The long-run elasticities implied by the estimated coefficients are shown in the final three columns of the table.[1] While none of these are implausible, it is puzzling that the income elasticity for total M_3 falls below those for the two individual M_3 components, even though these do not account for quite the whole of M_3. It is also perhaps surprising that the income elasticity for M_3, which includes interest-bearing money, is so little greater than that for the more narrowly-defined M_1, with which the idea of economies of scale in the transactions demand for money would probably be more closely associated. Indeed, the fact that all four long-run income elasticities are below unity suggests that the demand for money both narrowly and broadly-defined may have been subject to such economies of scale over the observation period. However, the 95% confidence interval of each estimate includes values above unity, so that the alternative hypothesis that money is a 'luxury good' cannot be rejected on this evidence.

Finally, the standard errors of estimate of the equations are similar to those found generally in investigations of this type. They indicate that the MP and M_3 equations have the best overall fits, while the MC equation appears to be the least well determined.

Forecasting performance 1971 IV – 1974 I

An acid test of the estimated relationships is whether they forecast accurately outside the period over which they were estimated. This sub-section examines the *ex post* 'forecasts' of the equations set out above. Taking appropriate actual values of the exogenous and lagged endogenous variables, the equations were used to predict the quarter-to-quarter movements of each of the four aggregates from 1971 IV to 1974 I. If the equations remained valid, the actual values of the aggregates should lie within (for instance) two standard errors of the corresponding predicted values in (about) 95% of cases (assuming that the error terms are normally distributed).[2] The proportionate forecasting errors were therefore compared with the standard errors of the equations.

The proportionate forecasting error of one of these equations in any quarter is approximately the same as the difference between the actual rate of increase of the appropriate money aggregate and the rate of increase predicted by the equation.[3] Some indication of the results can therefore be obtained from Charts C, E, G, and J, (contained in Appendix 4), which compare actual and expected rates of increase in each quarter. The charts suggest that the results obtained were considerably worse for MC and total M_3 than for M_1 and MP; and a closer examination of the prediction errors quarter by quarter confirms this impression.

The equation for M_3 underpredicted its growth nine times during the ten-quarter forecast period. Each time, except 1973 II, the forecasting error exceeded twice the standard error. Thus in eight quarters out of the ten, there was significant underprediction. The only overprediction was in 1974 I, when the error was not significant, and was indeed the smallest of the period.

The pattern of errors produced by the MC equation was very similar. Thus, underprediction again occurred in nine quarters out of the ten. However, the underprediction in the first two forecast quarters was not significant, although greater than for the M_3 equation. (In fact, in all ten

---

[1] The interest-rate elasticities implied by the coefficients of $\ln(1+r)$ are calculated at the mean interest rates of the estimation period. That is, given that
$$\frac{\partial \ln M}{\partial \ln r} \equiv \frac{r}{1+r} \cdot \frac{\partial \ln M}{\partial \ln (1+r)}$$
the elasticity with respect to r was calculated by multiplying the elasticity with respect to $(1+r)$ by the ratio $r/(1+r)$, evaluated at the mean r of the estimation period.

[2] Owing to the method of estimation, this applies only to forecasts in which actual values of the lagged endogenous variables are used.

[3] The difference between actual and predicted growth rates in period t reduces to $(M_t - \hat{M}_t)/M_{t-1}$ (where $\hat{M}$ is the predicted value of M), whereas the proportionate forecasting error is given by $(M_t - \hat{M}_t)/\hat{M}_t$.

quarters, the prediction errors of the MC equation exceeded those of the M_3 equation; but the standard error of the former is considerably larger too.) As with M_3, the worst results were obtained for 1973 III and 1973 IV: in the first of these the error was over 11%, and was thus more than five times the standard error of the equation. And again, the best results were for 1973 II (a small overprediction) and for 1974 I (a small underprediction).

The equation for M_1 also tended to underpredict: it did so in seven out of the ten quarters. However, five of the seven errors were not significant, and nor were the three overpredictions (1971 IV, 1973 I, and 1973 III). Thus only two of the forecasting errors (1972 II and 1973 II) were over twice the standard error. The worst result was for 1973 II — over three times the standard error.

Over the first six quarters of the forecast period (1971 IV – 1973 I), the MP equation was the best. It too mostly underpredicted (five times out of the six), but only one of the six errors (1972 I) was significant. After 1973 I, however, the performance of the equation deteriorated markedly, with consistent, significant, and increasing underprediction; by 1974 I the prediction error was almost four times the standard error of the equation.

In sum, the success of the equations is evidently limited. The only results which could be called at all satisfactory are those for the M_1 equation, notably the successful prediction of the volatile movements of this aggregate during the last three quarters of the forecast period, and those for the MP equation between 1971 IV and 1973 I, when, with only one exception, the aggregate was each time within 0·75% of the prediction. In contrast, the results for MC and M_3 show quite clearly that the behaviour of these aggregates during 1972 and 1973 cannot be predicted by the demand-for-money relationships estimated from pre-1972 data.[1] The next section seeks to explain this failure.

3 Explaining the failures

There are three possible kinds of explanation for the poor predictions of the MC and M_3 equations:[2]

a the relationships may have been misspecified: for instance, important determining factors may have been omitted, or there may have been misspecification of the lag structures;

b the coefficients in the equations may have been inaccurately estimated or biased, owing to, say, multicollinearity or inadequate adjustment for serial correlation of errors;

c there may have been structural change since the estimation period, so that the behaviour of the relevant aggregates could not have been predicted accurately, even from correctly specified and unbiased estimates. Each of these possibilities may well have something to offer. However, while various economic and econometric arguments might be put forward claiming the importance of the first two possibilities, the third seems particularly applicable.

Thus in May 1971, the Bank issued the consultative document, *Competition and credit control*,[3] and by September the new approach to monetary policy had begun to operate, its aim being to encourage the removal of certain rigidities which had developed in the banking system during the years of ceilings controls on lending and of other restraints on competition and innovation. In particular, the London and Scottish clearing banks' interest-rate agreements were given up; their cash and liquidity ratios were replaced by a 12½% reserve assets ratio applicable to all banks; the special deposits scheme became applicable to all banks; and quantitative ceilings on lending were abandoned. Not surprisingly, these reforms gave rise to important changes in financial markets and in the behaviour of the banks.

[1] Moreover, the forecasts calculated from the equations were 'one step ahead' forecasts only, i.e. the actual value of the lagged dependent variable was used in each period. This is probably a less stringent way of testing the forecasting ability of a model than the alternative method (not used in this paper) whereby the previous period's forecast of the dependent variable is entered.
[2] The subsequent failure of the MP equation will be considered later.
[3] Reprinted in the June 1971 *Bulletin*, page 189.

During the years before 1971, there had been a progressive loss of competitiveness by the clearing banks *vis-à-vis* other banks (owing primarily to the clearers' interest-rate cartel and to their asset-ratio requirements) and a corresponding expansion of the less restricted 'secondary' banking system[1] in relation to the 'deposit' banking system. (The clearing banks as business entities, however, had formed subsidiary companies which operated as secondary banks.) More particularly, with ceilings controls applying to all banks, there had been a loss of competitiveness by the banking system as a whole in relation to other channels of financial intermediation.

It was to be expected therefore that the freeing of the clearers' borrowing and lending rates from their rigid link with Bank rate, the changes in reserve requirements, and the removal of the ceilings on lending would together lead to a reversal of these trends, and thus to a growth in both sides of the banks' balance sheets: after the long spell of 'disintermediation', the new approach would encourage 'reintermediation'.

This is indeed what seems to have happened. The clearing banks were able to adopt more flexible policies for rates on time deposits. Before September 1971, they had paid a standard 2% below Bank rate on deposit accounts. Although this rule has survived in rather more flexible form in the rate still paid for deposits under £10,000,[2] since the advent of the new approach the deposit banks have generally been offering rather higher rates for deposits of medium size (over £10,000 or £25,000), and, more important, they have for the first time bid for large deposits in the parallel money markets. These markets, which had sprung up during the 1960s, and the 'wholesale' deposit business associated with them, thus ceased to be the sole preserve of the secondary banks. For example, soon after the new approach was instituted, the clearing banks for the first time began to issue negotiable certificates of deposit (CDs) in their own names, although a market in these instruments had existed since 1968.[3]

The reforms of 1971 thus, as intended, induced a new competitiveness in the borrowing behaviour of the banks; and it is more than plausible that the new competitiveness of the deposit banks' liabilities in the last three years will have increased the attractiveness of 'money' — if defined sufficiently broadly to include, as with M_3, wholesale time deposits and CDs — relative to other financial assets. Thus, the underprediction of the MC and M_3 equations reported in the previous section may be explicable in terms of this increased attractiveness of interest-earning money balances. This argument would imply that the interest rate on time deposits (and CDs) has become a more significant determinant of the demand for M_3 balances since September 1971. An attempt is made in Section 4 to examine this proposition directly. Meanwhile, it is perhaps worth indicating four pieces of evidence which support the importance in this context of the structural change which occurred with the new approach.

The first of these is the varying degrees of success of the four equations. The equation for M_1, which excludes all time deposits, performed best; the equation for MP, in which no certificates of deposits are included,[4] and in which wholesale time deposits probably form a less important constituent than in MC (or total M_3), came second; and the MC and M_3 equations very clearly came off worst. In fact, perhaps the only feature which is difficult to explain in the context of the structural change is the delay before any significant deterioration appeared in the MP forecasts (although it is in a sense consistent with results presented in Section 2, and elsewhere in this paper, which suggest that the personal sector tends to be relatively slow in adjusting to exogenous changes).

Secondly, the contrast between the growth rates of narrow (M_1) and broad (M_3) money over the period 1971 III and 1974 I, and particularly

[1] Namely, the 'accepting houses, overseas banks, and other UK banks' as in Table 11 of the statistical annex.
[2] The rates paid for deposits under £10,000 since September 1971 have, apart from short-term anomalies, been between 1½% and 2% below the banks' own base rates, subject, since September 1973, to a maximum of 9½%.
[3] See the article 'Sterling certificates of deposit' in the December 1972 *Bulletin*, page 487.
[4] This is not because CDs are not held in the personal sector, but because there is no better information. Sterling CDs issued by banks to the rest of the private sector are attributed to industrial and commercial companies or to other financial institutions.

the exceptionally large increase in companies' broad money holdings, support the proposition that there was an unusually large rise in 'idle', rather than 'active', money balances, attracted by competitive yields in relation to other assets. Seasonally adjusted, M_1 increased by about 20% between 1971 III and 1974 I; M_3 by about 75%; and MC by about 100%.

That there has been an increase in the 'idleness' of the broad money stock may be seen more clearly from Chart B, in which the income velocity of M_3 is plotted against the rate of interest (as represented by the Consol rate[1]) from 1963 I to 1974 I. An increase in interest rates, *ceteris paribus*, should encourage asset-holders to economise on their money balances and so cause the velocity of circulation to rise. Because, over time, movements in velocity will depend upon other factors as well, in particular upon the income elasticity of and time lags in the

Chart A
The income velocity of M_1 and the rate of interest, 1963 I – 1974 I

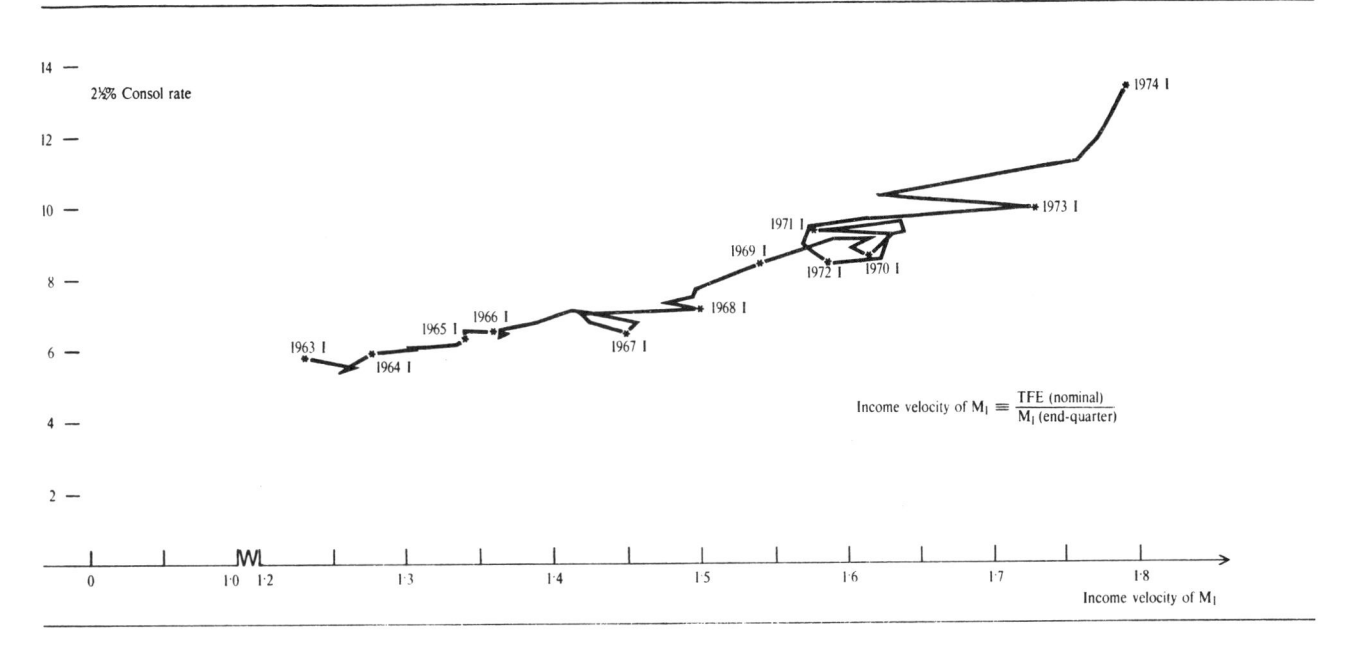

Chart B
The income velocity of M_3 and the rate of interest, 1963 I – 1974 I

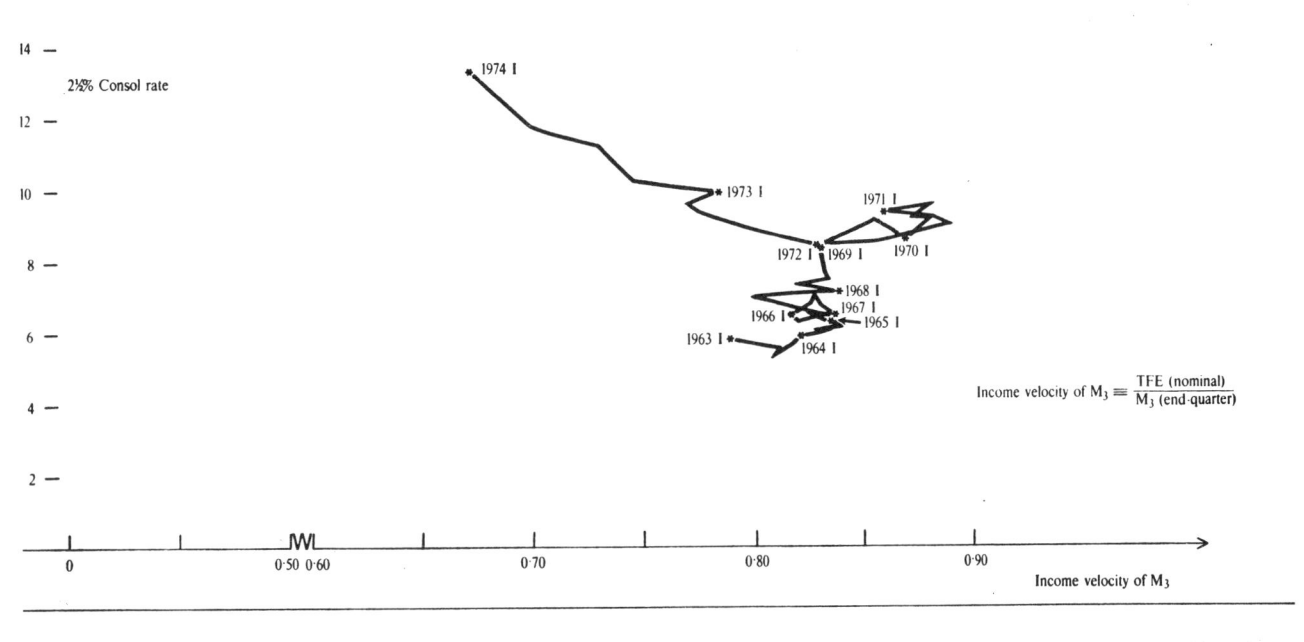

[1] A similar pattern was obtained when the local authority three-month rate was used instead.

demand-for-money function, the *ceteris paribus* qualification is important in the interpretation of Charts A and B.[1] Nevertheless, they show that whereas the income velocity of M_1 (Chart A) has, as would be expected, grown steadily with interest rates, the income velocity of M_3 (Chart B) has fallen markedly since 1971. Indeed, this fall is so different from the pre-1971 experience that the forecasting failure of the M_3 demand equation is hardly surprising. And it is perhaps difficult to see how, during this period of rising interest rates, such a marked increase in the demand for broad money in relation to nominal income could have occurred unless the own rate on money had acquired a new significance in its determination.

Thirdly, the figures of time deposits cannot be satisfactorily disaggregated by rate of interest earned and there is no precise information, therefore, on how much of the increase in time deposits since 1971 has been lodged at competitive money-market rates. However, and this is the third piece of evidence, data relating to banks' issues of CDs are more readily available, and they show the strong expansion in this source of funds to the banks after 1971. In fact, the estimated value of sterling CDs issued by all banks to the rest of the private sector, which was some £420 million, or about 2¼% of M_3, at the end of 1971 III, had risen to £1,470 million, or 5½% of M_3, by the end of 1972.

Fourthly, in Canada, the Bank Act of 1967 introduced reforms in the system of monetary control similar in many respects to the new approach. In particular, the bankers' interest-rate cartel was abolished, and certain restrictions on banks' behaviour — including limitations placed on interest rates — were removed. In the next two years the Canadian monetary aggregates appear to have behaved (in relation to previous experience) in a fashion similar to the UK aggregates since 1971, as the banks expanded more strongly than other financial intermediaries.

This section ends by considering certain ways in which the particular financial and economic environment of 1972 and 1973 may, at various times, have contributed additionally to the rapid expansion of the demand for broad money, given the structural change already discussed.

One such influence, clearly evident on several occasions in these two years, arose from the comparative inflexibility of the banks' base rates in relation to the rates offered by them, in the money market, for deposits. Because of this, sharp increases in money-market rates narrowed the differential between banks' lending rates (determined in relation to base rates) and their (market-determined) borrowing rates; and the margin between 'prime' overdraft rates (1% above base rates) and money-market rates several times became negative. It then became profitable for some bank customers, particularly 'blue chip' companies borrowing at the finest rates, to borrow from the banks merely to redeposit with the banking system. Even when the margin was still positive, so that pure arbitrage or 'round tripping' was not possible, substantial narrowing of the differential doubtless provided a significant incentive to some bank customers to borrow in order to build up their balances of interest-bearing deposits. Thus, customers who feared a return to the pre-1971 system of direct credit controls may well have protected their access to credit by drawing on their overdraft facilities, and accumulated money balances. However, the extent of demand for bank credit and money balances arising from this particular precautionary motive, or indeed for precautionary purposes more generally, is obviously unknown.

At all events, arbitrage inflated the advances and deposits of the banks at various times during 1972 and 1973, and, although this probably had no long-term effect on the growth of the broad monetary aggregates, it certainly produced sharp movements in the short term. The fall in the rates of growth of M_3 and MC during the first quarter of 1974 (see Charts E and G in Appendix 4) probably reflects in part some unwinding of arbitrage. This will have been encouraged by the supplementary deposits

---

[1] Moreover, movements in current interest rates will tend to affect expectations of future rates, and if asset-holders' expectations are extrapolative, movements in the velocity of money may in the short term be 'perversely' related to interest-rate movements. If for example, an increase in interest rates leads to expectations of further increases, the velocity of circulation may fall as asset-holders move out of bonds into capital-certain money.

scheme announced by the Bank in December 1973,[1] and the concurrent announcement by the clearing banks of their intention to adjust their lending rates more rapidly to movements in market rates, specifically in order to curtail arbitrage (although this intention was not, in the event, realised until this July).

Furthermore, the significant rise in the demand for interest-bearing money since 1971 may also suggest an increase in the Keynesian speculative demand for money (already referred to above). Keynes drew attention to the fact that in a model in which money and bonds are the only two financial assets, the demand for money will tend to be high when interest rates are expected to rise. When the more complex array of actual financial assets is allowed for, Keynes' theory becomes a theory of speculative demand for capital-certain assets in general, including, for example, building society shares and deposits, national savings deposits, local authority debt, and so on. Thus, bondholders who expect interest rates to rise will not necessarily switch into 'money' as normally defined; and their choice among capital-certain assets will depend to a high degree upon their relative yields. But the above argument that yields on interest-bearing money have risen in relation to those on other financial assets implies that bondholders will have been more likely than hitherto to switch into assets included in M_3. Two inferences may be drawn from this. The first is that the demand for (broad) money may have become a more unstable function of any set of variables which does not take adequate account of interest-rate expectations (as opposed to existing rates). The second is that when, since 1971, there have been expectations of rising interest rates (and the period has been one of secularly rising nominal rates and growing inflation) then some part of the increases in money holdings may be accounted for by increases in speculative demand which the equations of Section 2 could not easily have predicted.

In sum, there are a number of reasons why the behaviour of the broad monetary aggregates since 1971 — MC and M_3 in particular — is badly predicted by the demand relationships estimated from the period before the new approach, and especially why their growth should have been underpredicted. In this light, the next section examines whether the equations can be improved by taking into account the structural change which is argued to have occurred.[2]

4 Estimation period 1963 IV – 1972 IV: estimates and forecasting performance

Estimates

An implication of this structural change is that the forecasting performance of the equations for broad money could be significantly improved only if the estimation period were extended to take post-1971 behaviour into account. A new observation period was therefore adopted, going to the end of 1972, and thus covering the first five quarters of the new approach, but still leaving five quarters over which to test forecasting performance. The results of the fresh estimations are reproduced in Table B.

[1] March *Bulletin*, page 37.

[2] An alternative 'structural change' explanation for the failure of pre-1971 demand-for-money equations has appealed to some commentators, including M. J. Artis and M. K. Lewis (see their article 'The demand for money: stable or unstable', *The Banker*, Volume 124 Number 577, March 1974, pages 239–47). They assert that the underprediction errors have been due to an excess supply of money in 1972–73: that is, demand equations have not been able to predict the behaviour of the money stock simply because 'we have been off the demand curve'. But this explanation, if closely examined, clearly runs into difficulties. In particular:
a Why did an excess supply apparently not appear for M_1?
b Why did an excess supply not appear for personal sector holdings of M_3 through 1972?
c Why, if there were involuntary holdings of money in the company sector in 1972–73, was companies' demand for bank borrowing so consistently high, and their capital expenditure so consistently less than generally expected?
d Most fundamentally, how did the excess supply arise? Although in recent years, and particularly with the new approach, the authorities have placed a greater emphasis on movements in the monetary aggregates as indicators helping in the formulation of policy, this does not imply that the authorities have used different instruments to achieve their objectives. They do not directly control the money stock, but rather try to influence its development through operations in financial markets which affect the level and structure of interest rates. In this case, it is not clear how an excess of supply over demand could have arisen.

For these and other reasons, a 'shift in the demand curve' appears to provide a more plausible explanation than an excess of supply over demand.

Table B
Demand-for-money equations 1963 IV – 1972 IV[a]
All variables are in natural logarithms

Dependent variable		Constant	Short-run elasticities Y_t	P_t	$1+r^s_t$	$1+r^L_t$	$1+r^L_{t-1}$	$1+r'_t$	M_{t-1}	Standard error of estimate (per cent)	$\bar{R}^2$	D-W[b]	ρ[b]	Long-run elasticities[c] Y	r^s	r^L	r'
M_1		17·504	0·315 (0·153)	0·452	−0·441 (0·293)	−1·324 (0·763)			0·548 (0·127)	1·42	0·48	1·96	−0·6	0·697	−0·062	−0·206	
MP		4·287	0·326 (0·083)	0·301		−0·475 (0·352)			0·699 (0·105)	0·80	0·79	2·43	−0·6	1·081		−0·110	
MC	(1)	12·980	0·334 (0·315)	0·151	−0·105 (0·580)	−1·497 (1·492)			0·849 (0·137)	2·55	0·58	2·21	−0·4	2·206	−0·044	−0·696	
	(2)	−9·303	0·449 (0·268)	0·447		−2·197 (1·100)		3·156 (0·931)	0·553 (0·144)	2·19	0·69	2·40	−0·4	1·003		−0·345	0·568
M_3	(1)	3·833	0·144 (0·137)	−0·013	−0·574 (0·207)				1·013 (0·103)	1·16	0·79	2·25	−0·6	∞	−∞		
	(2)	4·373	0·175 (0·127)	0·176	−0·693 (0·197)			1·173 (0·448)	0·824 (0·119)	1·07	0·82	2·48	−0·6	0·995	−0·248		0·537

[a] For definitions of the variables, see Appendix 2. Standard errors are shown in brackets beneath the appropriate coefficients.
[b] For the meaning of the Durbin-Watson statistic (D-W) and ρ see Appendix I.
[c] The long-run price elasticity is constrained to unity in each equation. For r^s and r^L, elasticities are evaluated at the mean interest rates of the estimation period; for r' they are evaluated at the end of the period.

Two equations are reported for both MC and total M_3. The first in each pair is a re-estimation of the 'best' equation which had been estimated over the shorter observation period (Table A). In each of these the standard error of estimate has risen, and several of the coefficients are less significant. More important, however, in each there has been a marked (and statistically significant) increase in the coefficient of the lagged dependent variable. For MC, this implies a considerably slower speed of adjustment and a marked increase in the long-run elasticities. The implied long-run elasticity with respect to real income, for example, has risen from 0·5 in the previous estimates to 2·2. For the M_3 equation, the results are even more striking, and clearly implausible, for the coefficient of the lagged money stock has risen above unity;[1] but the results for MC suggest that this equation too is misspecified.

None of this is surprising in the light of the argument of the previous section that the interest rate on wholesale money will have attracted certain asset-holders into M_3 balances since the inception of the new approach, and that therefore movements in M_3 could probably no longer be adequately described in terms of demand relationships which did not include an own rate. The next step was to thus estimate equations for MC and M_3 which included an own-rate variable. As noted in Section 2 above, equations containing the clearing banks' seven-day deposit rate and the overnight inter-bank rate had already been estimated over the period ending in 1971 III, without satisfactory results. These experiments were repeated over the new, longer estimation period; but again, the coefficients either had the wrong sign or were not significant, or both. However, the failure to identify a significant own rate over the whole observation period 1963 IV – 1972 IV clearly does not conflict with the hypothesis that the rate on wholesale money became an important influence on the demand for M_3 after the reforms of 1971. To test this hypothesis adequately, various alternative own-rate variables were constructed to reflect the shift in the competitiveness of interest-bearing money.

Four main alternatives were tried. Over the final five quarters, 1971 IV – 1972 IV, each was defined as the three-month CD rate,[2] so as to reflect movements in money-market interest rates (rates paid on large time deposits as well as on CDs) since the new approach. Over the previous period from 1963 II they were defined as follows. Variant A was the clearing banks' seven-day deposit rate (generally Bank rate minus 2%),

[1] This implies that the coefficients in the desired money-stock function, from which (together with the partial adjustment hypothesis) the estimating equation was derived (see above, Section 1), are opposite in sign to those of the equation estimated. That is, the M_3(1) equation of Table B implies a dynamic adjustment process which is unstable, so that no finite long-run (equilibrium) elasticities can be defined.
[2] There is a slight exception in the case of variant C: see below.

Table C
Own-rate variants

Variant	$r_t - r_{t-1}$ 1963 III – 1971 III	1971 IV	1972 I – 1972 IV
A	(deposit rate)$_t - dr_{t-1}$	$CD_t - dr_{t-1}$	$CD_t - CD_{t-1}$
B	Zero	CD_t	$CD_t - CD_{t-1}$
C	Zero	Zero	$CD_t - CD_{t-1}$
D	Zero	$CD_t - dr_{t-1}$	$CD_t - CD_{t-1}$

even though this had not been found significant as a determinant of M_3 balances over this period. Variant B was zero. In this case, there was a danger that the estimates – obtained from first differences – might be biased by the consequent large jump in the first difference in 1971 IV. Variants C and D, therefore, comprised rather arbitrary expedients designed to guard against this danger; each differed from variant B only in the way its first difference in 1971 IV was defined: in variant C, zero was taken, and in variant D it was the CD rate minus the previous quarter's seven-day deposit rate.

The four variants may be compared in Table C, where the first differences of each throughout the period are given. Variants B, C, and D are based on the assumption that until the new approach no own rate was a statistically significant determinant of broad money balances, so that variations in any such own rate could for these purposes be ignored. But all four of the alternatives embody a discontinuity between 1971 III and 1972 I, which is designed to reflect the hypothesis that money-market interest rates became a significant determinant of M_3 balances for the first time towards the end of 1971.[1]

On the basis of the estimations and the forecasting results, variant D was selected.[2] The second MC and M_3 equations in Table B contain this variable (r'); they are the 'best' equations for these aggregates over the new estimation period.

In each of them, the coefficient of the r' variable has the appropriate positive sign, and is significantly different from zero. The long-run elasticity with respect to the own rate, calculated at the end of the estimation period, is in each case greater than 0·5, and therefore comparatively high. The table also shows that these equations have better overall fits than the equations which did not include an own rate. As compared with the earlier estimates, the implied speeds of adjustment in both MC (2) and M_3 (2) are slower, and the long-run income elasticities higher – for the latter, each is now close to 1, whereas previously each was close to 0·5. The long-run elasticities with respect to the competitive interest rates r^s and r^L have also risen quite markedly.

These results give some support to the hypothesis under test. However, the changes which have occurred in the coefficients of the real-income and competitive interest-rate variables imply that the inclusion of the own rate during the period of the new approach has not been sufficient to explain the forecasting errors revealed in Section 2.

Given the successful 'forecasting' performance up to the end of 1972 of the MP equation estimated over the shorter period, it is hardly surprising that the replication of the same equation over the longer estimation period gave satisfactory results (see Table B). Indeed, it again gave the best results of all equations fitted for this aggregate. As compared with the previous estimate, the overall fit is slightly worse; the long-run real-income elasticity has risen slightly from 0·9 to 1·1 (accounted for by an increase in the coefficient of the lagged dependent variable); and both short-run and long-run interest-rate elasticities have also increased slightly. However, none of these changes are statistically significant.

In Section 2, it was found that, taking the whole forecast period into account, the M_1 equation had performed fairly satisfactorily, and that there seemed little reason to conclude that there had been structural change in the determination of the narrow money stock. This inference was given some support when the previous 'best' equation again gave the most satisfactory results over the longer estimation period: this re-estimate is shown in Table B. Like the MP equation, compared with the original estimate, the overall fit is rather worse; and the coefficient of the lagged

---

[1] In earlier work at the Bank, an alternative method was tried of deriving an own-rate variable embodying a similar discontinuity. This variable was defined as the differential between the CD rate and banks' prime lending rates whenever this differential was positive, and zero elsewhere. The variable thus in effect identified when opportunities for pure arbitrage arose, and had the advantage of always taking a zero value naturally, rather than by 'imposition', before the new approach. Although equations were estimated in which this variable was statistically significant, the results imputed an implausibly large proportion of the increase in M_3 during 1972 to arbitrage, and were therefore rejected in favour of the approach reported in the text. However, further research in this direction is probably desirable.

[2] It may be of interest that the only variant whose coefficient was frequently not significant was variant A. It was also not always positive in sign.

money stock has risen, and accounts for an increase in the long-run real-income elasticity from 0·4 to 0·7. However, M_1 remained the least income elastic of the four aggregates.

Forecasting performance 1973 I – 1974 I

As before, the best equations were used to 'forecast' the movements of the four aggregates, this time over the five quarters 1973 I – 1974 I. Actual and predicted growth rates in each quarter are compared in Charts D, F, H, and K in Appendix 4.

Given the forecasting results of the original MP equation, and the similarity to it of the new equation, it is not surprising that little improvement resulted from the extension of the estimation period to the end of 1972. Closer examination confirms the impression obtained by comparing Charts J and K: although in each of the five 'forecast' quarters the error of the new equation was smaller than that of the old, in each of the final three quarters there was again significant underprediction.

The forecasting results of the new M_1 equation, also, were similar to those of the old. Although the extension of the estimation period succeeded in reducing the forecasting errors in three quarters out of the five, there was again significant underprediction in 1973 II. The other four errors were again not significant.

Chart H shows the results for MC. Although the contrast with the old equation (Chart G) is immediately apparent, the success of the new equation, MC (2) of Table B, is in fact rather limited. Overprediction occurred in four quarters out of the five (1973 III being the exception); and in two of these – 1973 I and 1974 I – the errors were significant.

Finally, Chart F, which shows the results for the M_3 (2) equation of Table B, again contrasts markedly with the charted performance of the old equation. In fact two quarters were underpredicted (1973 III and 1973 IV), neither significantly at the 5% level, and three were overpredicted, one significantly (1974 I).

Implications of the results for total M_3, MC and MP

Although the MC and M_3 equations estimated before the introduction of the new approach failed to forecast subsequent behaviour at all accurately, it has been found that equations which fit the data to the end of 1972 quite well may be obtained by inclusion of the CD rate over part of the period. This supports the argument that the own rate on money became a more significant and powerful determinant of the demand for M_3 from the end of 1971 onward.

However, these equations need to be interpreted with even more caution than is usually needed in the interpretation of demand-for-money equations. For the importance of the CD rate to the results may to a large extent be a reflection of the transition to the changed money-market environment, and in particular of adjustment to the growing market in CDs. Also, during the five quarters added in the new estimation period, the attraction of CDs may have been especially great for tax reasons. (The associated tax loophole was blocked by measures in the 1973 Budget.[1])

In short, the fact that the new MC and M_3 equations take into account only five quarters' experience of the new approach may mean that they describe behaviour much of which reflects transitional or other temporary influences. It would therefore be premature to conclude what the characteristics of the demand for broad money will be over any long period. This cautionary note is supported by the limited 'forecasting' success and tendency towards overprediction, especially of the MC equation. Furthermore, it is notable that both the MC and M_3 equations overpredicted in 1974 I, which was the first quarter in which the supplementary deposits scheme was in operation. Although the errors in this quarter cannot be attributed with any certainty to the effects of this

[1] However, 'forecasts' for 1973 II – 1974 I which were based on the hypothesis that the attraction of CDs diminished after 1973 I with the closing of the loophole, were not as good as those discussed above which took no account of a possible tax effect. This is not necessarily surprising, particularly as the CD rate was included to represent the own rate on wholesale money generally, and not only on CDs.

scheme,[1] the central results of this paper imply that it is unwise to be confident in the survival of stable demand-for-money relationships when there are changes in regulations affecting the banks.

Although the behaviour of MP until the beginning of 1973 is explicable in terms of the old relationship, this does not appear to be true for the remainder of the forecast period. An extension of the estimation period beyond the end of 1972 may throw some light on the extent to which the apparent shift in this relationship also can be explained by the addition of an own rate to the list of explanatory variables; but this has not yet been attempted.

Appendix 4

Charts of predicted and actual changes in the monetary aggregates

Chart C
M_1: Estimation period 1963 IV – 1971 III

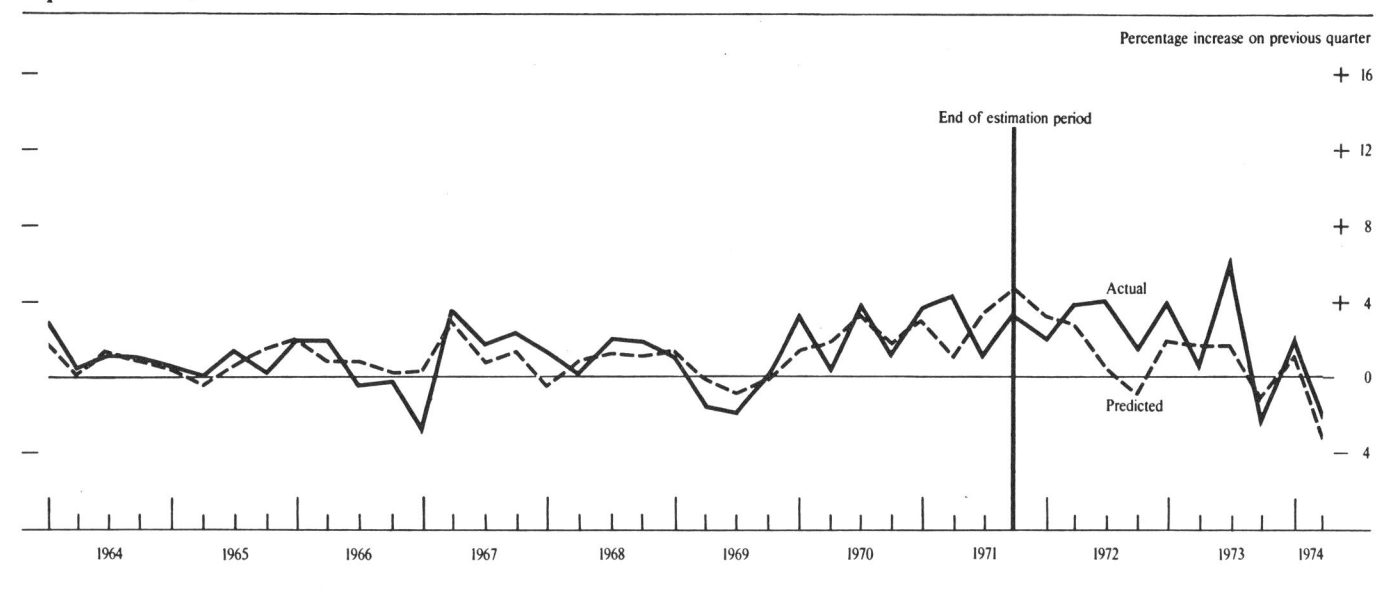

Chart D
M_1: Estimation period 1963 IV – 1972 IV

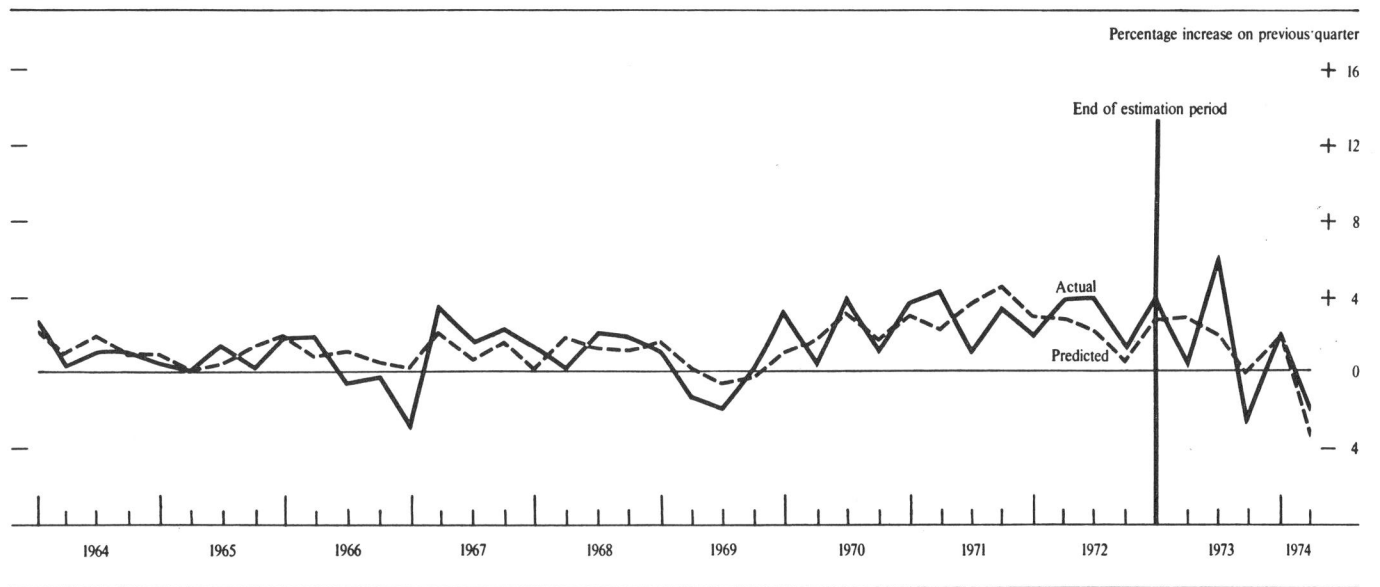

[1] During this quarter there were exceptional influences at work, in particular short-time working in industry and the resulting pressures on company liquidity; and the income and price data used to produce the forecasts for the quarter were tentative preliminary estimates.

Chart E
M_3: Estimation period 1963 IV—1971 III

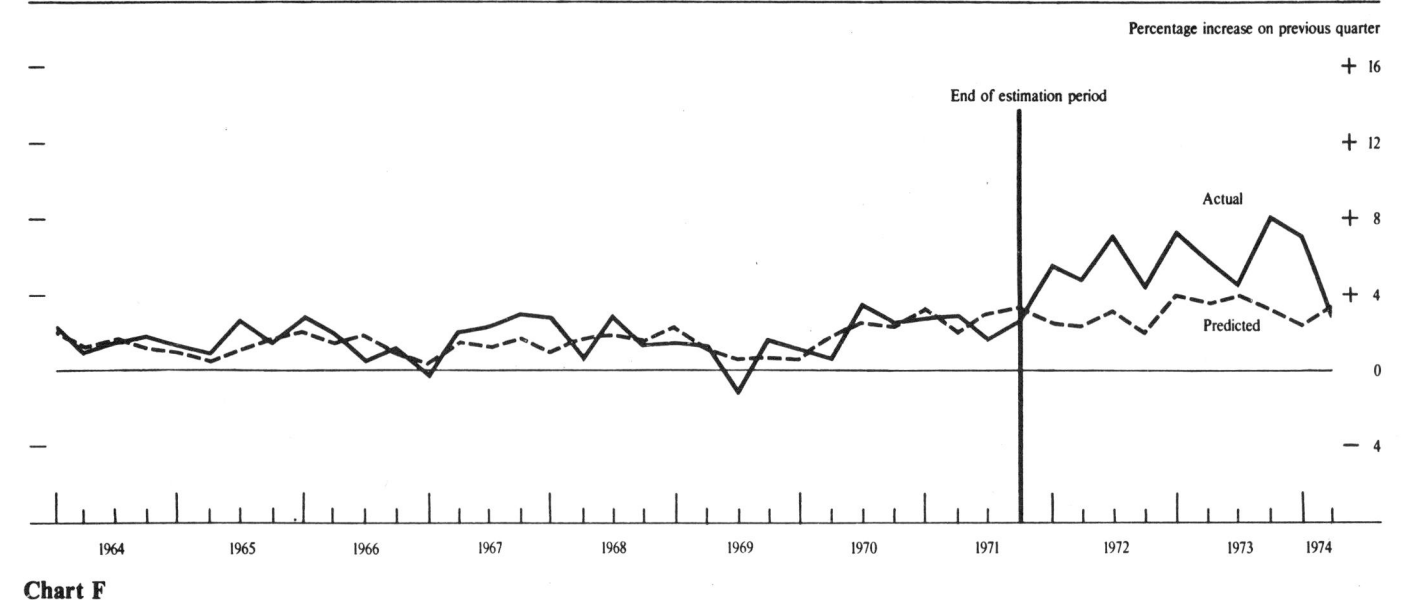

Chart F
M_3: Estimation period 1963 IV—1972 IV

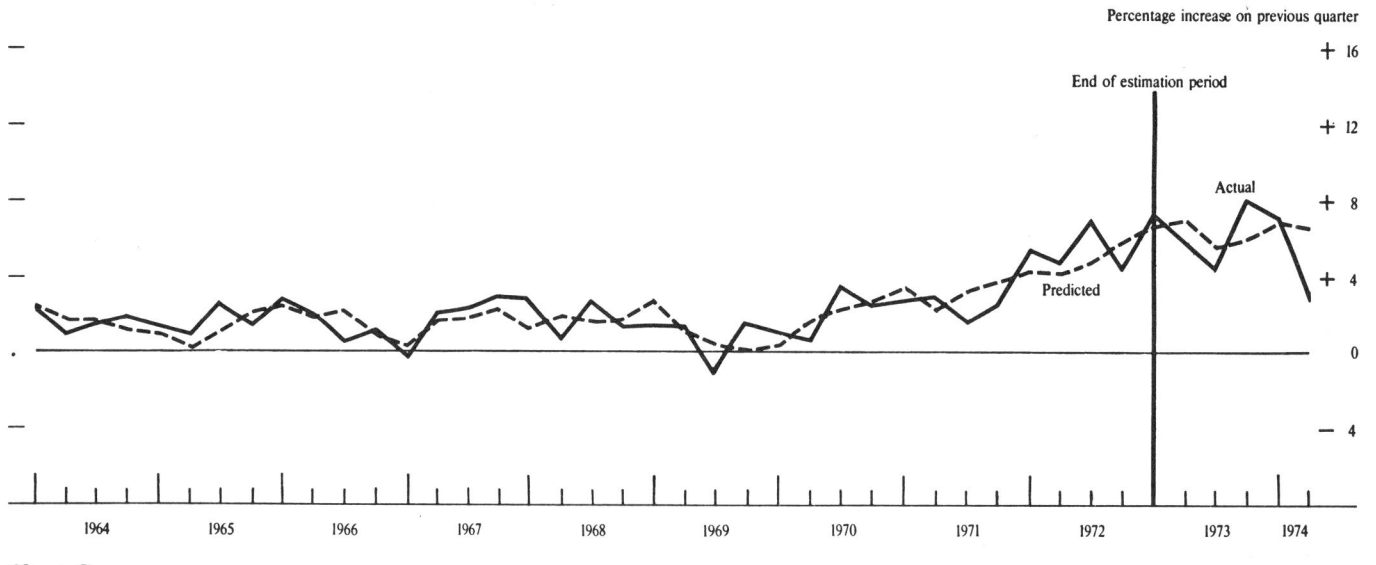

Chart G
MC: Estimation period 1963 IV—1971 III

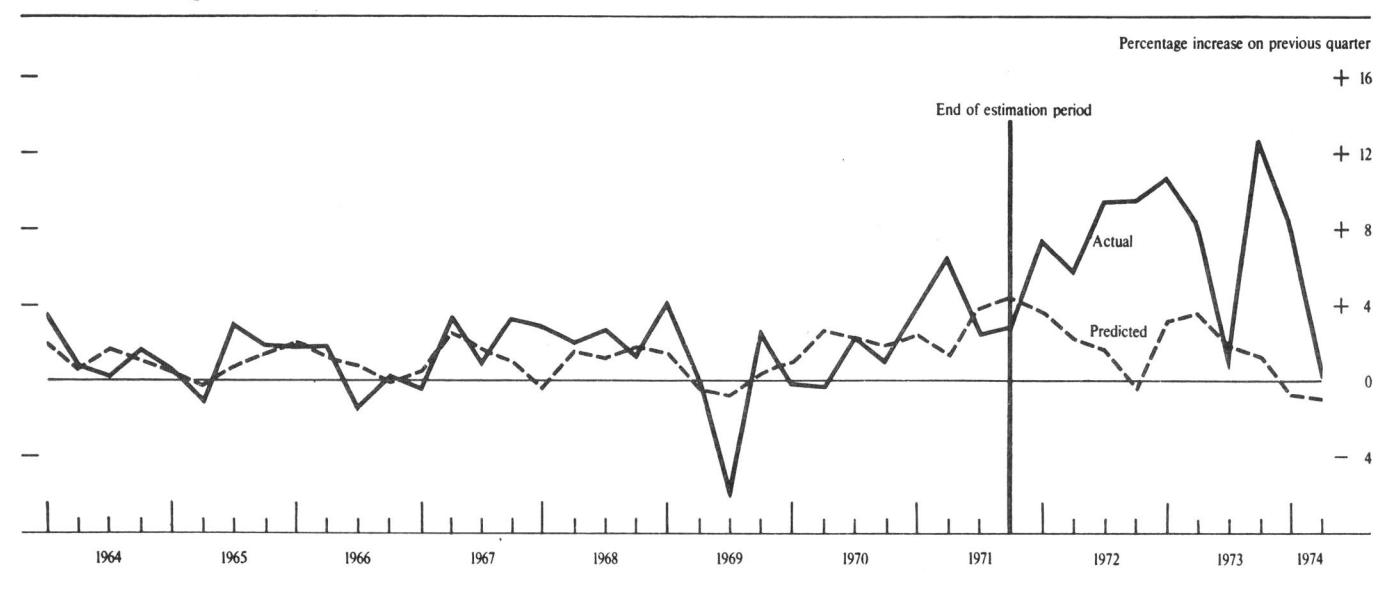

Chart H
MC: Estimation period 1963 IV — 1972 IV

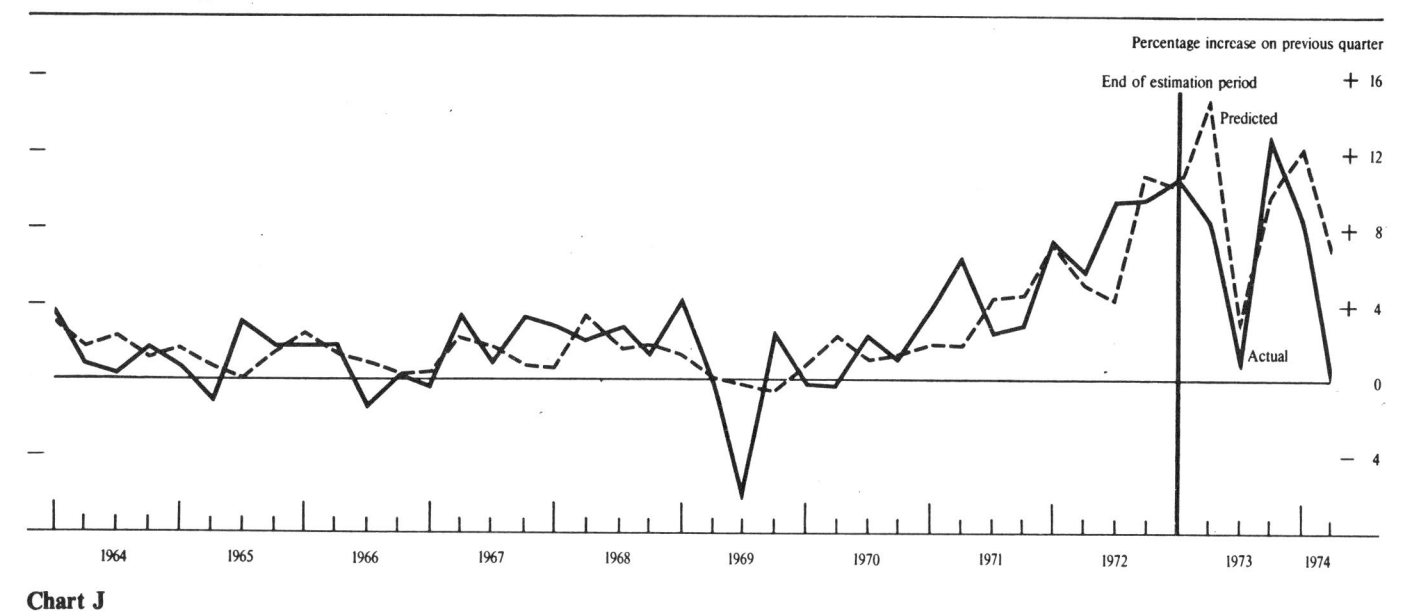

Chart J
MP: Estimation period 1963 IV — 1971 III

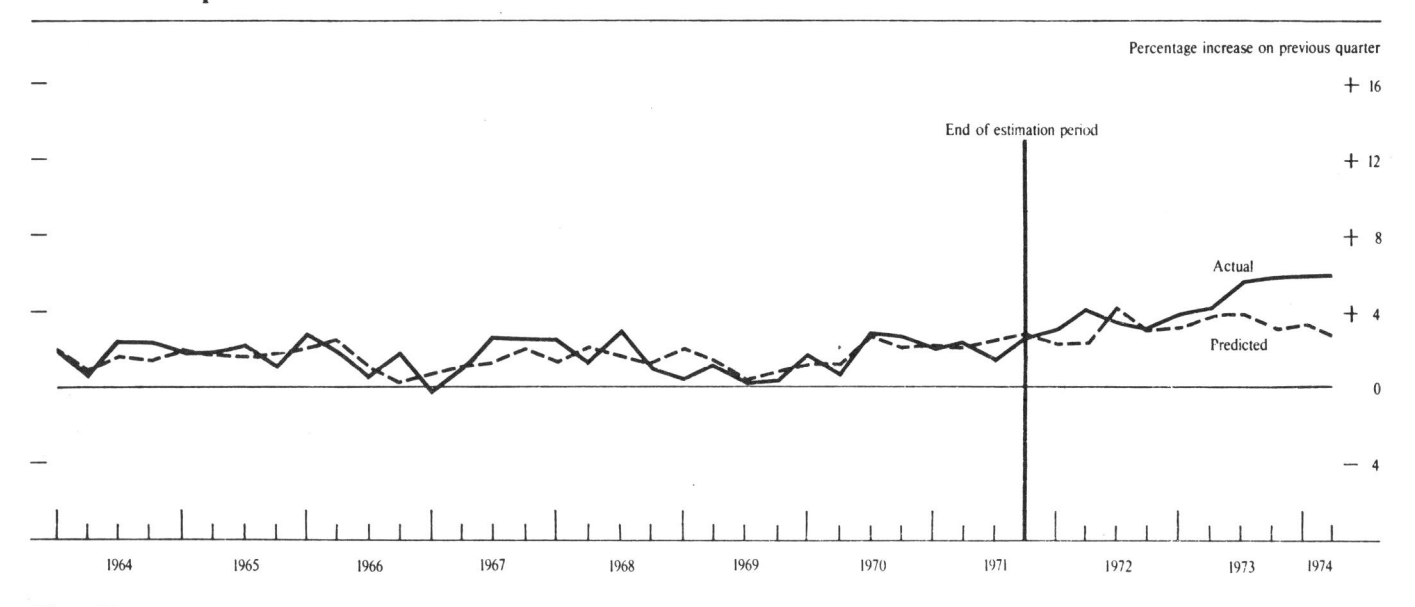

Chart K
MP: Estimation period 1963 IV — 1972 IV

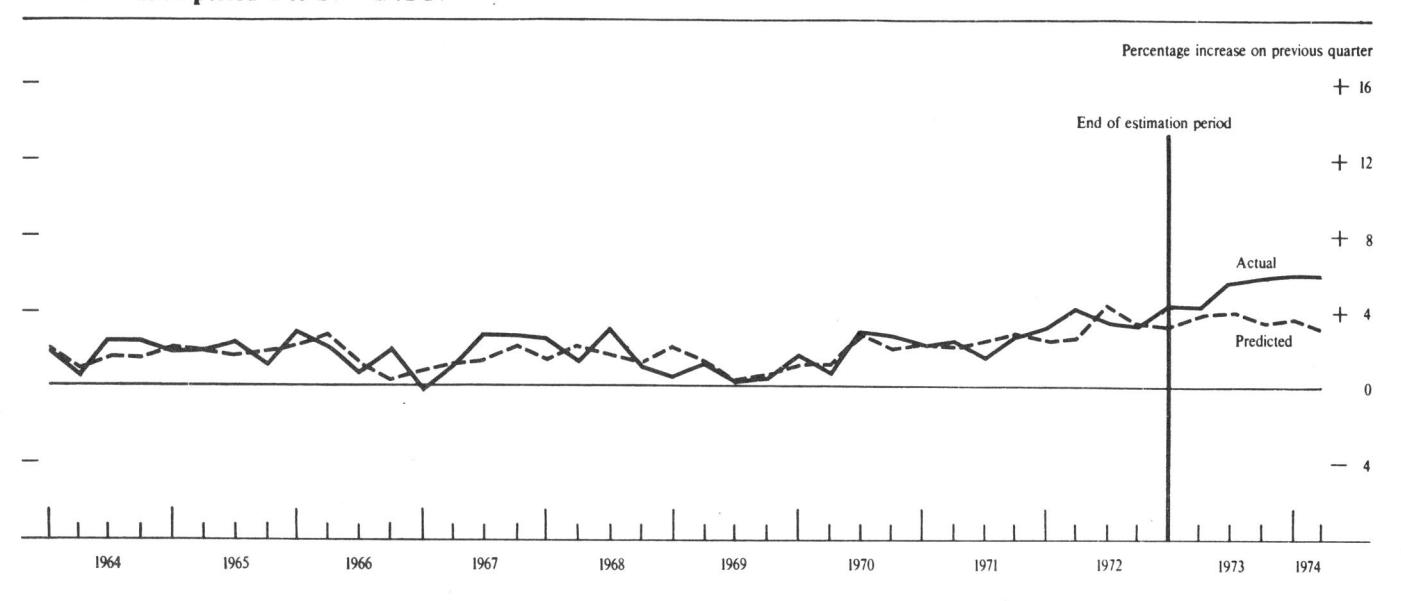

A transactions demand for money

This research article was prepared mainly by R. T. Coghlan of the Bank's Economic Intelligence Department. [1] An earlier version was presented to the Money Study Group in December 1977.

Summary

For as long as economists have been interested in the operation of the economy as a whole, they have been concerned about the existence, or otherwise, of a stable demand for money. That is to say, they have endeavoured to discover what aspects of the economic situation were likely to affect people's desire to hold money balances and what were the time-lags involved between changes in such economic variables and changes in money balances. Economic theory, and indeed commonsense, suggests that changes in, for example, incomes, prices, and interest rates are very likely to lead people to try to increase or reduce their money balances. In recent years, attempts have been made to estimate such relationships statistically, in the form of 'demand-for-money' equations. The practical objectives of such work have been not only to improve the understanding of the financial side of the economy but also to establish an analytical basis for the operation and interpretation of monetary policy.

A good deal of work in this area has been carried out in the United States over the past twenty or thirty years; and it appeared that a stable relationship between various economic variables and money holdings could be established. In this country, work of this type was hampered until the 1960s by the lack of comprehensive statistics for the various definitions of the money supply. Towards the end of the 1960s, however, economists in this country too seemed able to identify a similar stable relationship for the United Kingdom. Three of the Bank's studies were published in earlier issues of the *Bulletin*: June 1970, March 1972 and September 1974.

After about 1972, however, the situation became less clear, apparently because of the institutional changes which followed the introduction of competition and credit control in September 1971. It is now some years since this change, and a longer and more varied run of data is now available. This article describes work which incorporates this additional information and the conclusions which have emerged. It is confined to relationships affecting the narrow definition of the money stock (M_1), which comprises balances held mainly for transactions purposes.

The results indicate that limited data availability probably precluded the earlier studies from actually being able to identify a demand-for-money function which was stable in a strict statistical sense. Moreover, there seems to be evidence that the equations which had previously been estimated were generally too restrictive in the way in which they treated lags between changes in economic variables and the reaction of the money stock to them: in general, most previous studies assumed that such lags in adjustment were the same for all variables determining the demand for money. The results described in this article, however, suggest that there are in fact reasonable grounds for believing that a stable demand relationship for M_1 can be identified, although the pattern of lags involved is more complex than has generally been considered in the past.

Introduction

This article presents some results for the estimation of the demand for money, narrowly defined (M_1). The objective is to determine whether a stable demand relationship can be estimated, paying particular attention to the lag structure. In recent years, attention in this country has been concentrated on the apparent breakdown since about 1972 of all previous estimated demand-for-money functions. The general view seems to have been that reasonably stable relationships had been established up to about 1972 but that they no longer held good. Furthermore, as is made clear below, the 'breakdown' appeared to be independent of the definition of money employed. This article examines the validity and generality of this argument which, if true, would have important repercussions not only for our understanding of financial markets but also on how the impact of monetary policy should be assessed. In fact, the results described in this article suggest, at least as far as M_1 is concerned, that the picture of stability before 1972 and breakdown afterwards is misleading. Although much of the problem with the previous results stemmed from insufficient variability in the data, the results presented in this article suggest that, in general, the lag assumptions imposed have been too restrictive. Adopting a more flexible approach, it is possible to identify a more complex lag structure, which also appears to have remained stable over time.

As a starting point it is argued that there is no general theory of the demand for money which is applicable regardless of the definition of money adopted. We should expect a different behavioural relationship to apply to the demand for M_1 (essentially transactions balances) from that applying to the demand for M_3, where variations are more likely to be caused by changes in portfolio preferences. Furthermore, while there are certain strong theoretical propositions which should be incorporated into any empirical framework, the question of the existence, length and shape of any lags must remain an empirical one. It is the flexible approach to the estimation of lags that distinguishes this study from most others. The estimation results from the tests are summarised below, and set out in detail in Appendix 1. First, however, the existing empirical evidence for the United Kingdom is briefly surveyed to illustrate the background against which this study was undertaken.

Background

At the end of the 1960s, the evidence seemed to suggest that a stable demand for money, as a function of a few variables, had been identified. The general view was probably best stated by Laidler [2] who claimed that, 'this evidence for Britain certainly points to the existence of a stable demand-for-money function in that economy.

---

[1] A number of colleagues in the Bank have contributed to this article; in particular, most of the calculations were carried out by J. M. Hoffman and Miss L. M. Smith. Valuable comments and suggestions have also been provided by economists outside the Bank, notably D. F. Hendry and J. Wise.

[2] D. E. W. Laidler, 'The Influence of Money on Economic Activity—A Survey of some Current Problems', *Monetary Theory and Monetary Policy in the 1970s*, edited by G. Clayton, J. C. Gilbert and R. Sedgwick (Oxford University Press, 1971).

For the United States the evidence is overwhelming, and for Britain it is at the very least highly suggestive'. In September 1971, competition and credit control was introduced and, in the years that followed, the demand-for-money functions which had previously been estimated failed to forecast at all accurately. This was interpreted as meaning that the previously reliable, stable demand functions had broken down. [1] All at once it seemed we had moved from a situation in which the demand for money had been reliably and accurately estimated to a new environment where the money stock no longer exhibited these stable characteristics.

It is important to recognise that the earlier demand-for-money studies in the United Kingdom, upon which the conclusion of stability was based, employed a wide variety of definitions of money, interest rates, income, lag structures and estimation periods.[2] There was very little, if any, concern with the actual definition of money employed. The theoretical basis from which empirical tests were developed, and the interpretation of the results obtained, seemed independent of whether money was defined narrowly or broadly.

Evidence that simple demand functions for both M_1 and M_3 had broken down was provided by Artis and Lewis[3] who reported that, 'the standard demand function simply does not fit the experience of 1971 and 1972', adding that 'the forecasting ability of this equation (in common with alternative equations of the same general character that we tested, whether for M_1 or M_3) is quite good for 1971, but disastrously bad for 1972 and the first two quarters of 1973'. Hacche[4], on the other hand, found that the M_1 equation continued the forecast 'fairly satisfactorily' up to 1973. However, this equation did break down when the period was extended further into the 1970s.

These results have encouraged the belief that there has been a *general* breakdown of all empirical demand-for-money equations in the United Kingdom. The failure to estimate a stable demand function employing single equation techniques, whatever the definition of money employed, had important implications for any attempt to explain recent monetary experience. Artis and Lewis claimed, for example, that, because of the breakdown of M_1 demand functions, this instability could not be fully explained by such new features as the growth of interest-bearing deposits or distortions arising from the CD market.

The equations from which the conclusion of a general breakdown was derived were of the simplest kind, assuming the same length of lag on all variables, and it was important to determine whether they had indeed broken down, or whether the estimates were simply not very stable to begin with. This is particularly necessary since the lag restrictions assumed seem unduly restrictive.

Theory

Most previous work in this country appeared to assume that there was a general theory of the demand for money which was applicable regardless of the actual definition of money employed. This is not the approach adopted in this study. Instead it is assumed that the demand for M_1 balances is predominantly determined by transactions, and to some extent precautionary needs, so that speculative motives for holding money are not expected to be important. Modern theories of a transactions demand for money originated in the work of Baumol[5] and Tobin, [6] who adopted an inventory-theoretic approach which resulted in the so-called 'square-root formula'.[7] Acceptance of this basic approach does not, however, necessarily require acceptance of this formula, as that expectation is dependent upon some rather restrictive assumptions. At the individual level, transaction costs, subjective as well as objective, may be so high, relative to the rate of interest and the level of income/transactions, that this type of active cash management is uneconomic. In that case there would be no interest elasticity, and the demand for money would necessarily rise in line with transactions. An implication of this asymmetry is that aggregation from the individual to the total demand for transactions balances has the effect of increasing the income elasticity and reducing the interest elasticity. Furthermore, once uncertainty about future income and expenditure patterns is allowed for, as is likely to be the case for the large institutional money holders, many different elasticities are obtainable depending upon the specific assumptions made.[8] This approach means that we should expect short rates on closely competing assets to be more relevant than long rates on less liquid assets. It also means that measures of expected capital loss, which portfolio theory suggests should importantly affect the demand for money, will not in this case be relevant. Moreover, the 'income' variable should naturally be selected to represent expected transactions requirements. Taking a broader view of portfolio allocation, we might still expect total wealth to be included in the demand specification. If, however, the inventory-theoretic approach is relevant, then wealth is likely to be of secondary importance, and is assumed, for present purposes, to be reflected in the transactions variable employed.

It is generally assumed that the long-run price elasticity of the demand for money should be unity, on the grounds that economic rationality implies the absence of money illusion. However, although it may seem a reasonable

---

[1] This 'breakdown' refers only to the *estimation* of single equation demand functions, and does not exclude the possibility that a stable, but unidentified, demand function actually exists.
[2] Appendix 3 contains a summary of previous published results.
[3] M. J. Artis and M. K. Lewis, 'The demand for money: stable or unstable?', *The Banker*, March 1974; and 'The Demand for Money in the United Kingdom: 1963–1973', *The Manchester School*, June 1976.
[4] Graham Hacche, 'The demand for money in the United Kingdom: experience since 1971', September 1974 *Bulletin*, page 284.
[5] W. J. Baumol, 'The Transactions Demand for Cash: an Inventory Theoretic Approach', *Quarterly Journal of Economics*, November 1952.
[6] James Tobin, 'The Interest Elasticity of Transactions Demand for Cash', *Review of Economics and Statistics*, August 1956.
[7] This requires the demand elasticities on transactions and the rate of interest (as the opportunity cost of holding transactions balances) to be $+\frac{1}{2}$ and $-\frac{1}{2}$ respectively. There is also expected to be an elasticity of $\frac{1}{2}$ on the 'brokerage fee' (the cost of switching between money and alternative short-term assets). This last influence is generally not measured, under the assumption that the transfer cost remains constant over the estimation period.
[8] A survey of this literature is contained in C. A. E. Goodhart, *Money, Information and Uncertainty*, (Macmillan, London 1975), pages 22–30.

assumption to make, it can be no more than that.[1] We may well expect interest rates to influence the level of investment; that does not relieve us of the necessity to test that assumption.

From an empirical viewpoint, the most important characteristic of M_1 balances is the high probability, firstly, that they have been determined by demand, and, secondly, that simultaneous equation bias is at a minimum; thereby justifying the use of single equation estimation techniques employing M_1 as the dependent variable. M_1 consists of currency and private sector sight deposits with the banking sector, both of which are free from supply constraints.[2] Currency is supplied upon demand, and banks accept all money placed with them on current account, usually without payment of interest. It might be argued that any buffer stocks of liquidity would also be held in the form of money, thereby concealing the true demand relationship. However, if such buffer stocks do exist they would seem more likely to be held in the form of interest-bearing deposits than on current account. As regards the problems of simultaneity, it seems most unlikely that money market interest rates should be determined by the stock of, or change in, M_1 balances. Naturally, if interest rates were varied in an attempt to control M_1, this could introduce simultaneous bias into any attempt to estimate single equation demand functions, but without necessarily changing the underlying relationship. But the authorities have not attempted to control M_1, and single equation estimation seems appropriate to this exercise. This might not be the case when employing other definitions of the money stock.

Most previous demand-for-money studies have included real income only in *per capita* terms, a procedure that proved necessary in order to obtain a significant coefficient. While this might be reasonable for households' money holdings, these are not distinguished separately in the data. Statistics breaking down M_1 balances either between sectors or between interest-bearing and non-interest-bearing deposits have been available only since 1975, and these show that only about two thirds of M_1 balances are held by the personal sector; furthermore this sector includes not only individuals but also unincorporated businesses, non-profit-making bodies and private trusts. Even if we assume households to hold 75% of all personal sector M_1 balances (which is probably on the high side), that still leaves them holding only 50% of total M_1. Deflating aggregate money balances by the number of people, or the number of households, therefore seems to be an arbitrary assumption, and has not been incorporated into this study.

These then are the initial theoretical propositions. Beyond that, the existence and form of any lags must be an empirical question. The existence of lags can be justified in many ways, including the formation of expectations, costs of adjustment, habit preference and lags in the availability of information (or uncertainty about its reliability); they may also simply reflect lags in adjustment in other markets. The actual form of the lag expected is likely to be affected by the rationalisation adopted, and *a priori* there seems little justification for imposing any rigid formula. In fact, most demand-for-money studies have assumed that an identical lag applied to all explanatory variables. The only real attempt to obtain a more illuminating alternative was by Price,[3] who estimated different lags for each of the independent variables. His results were inconclusive (which is probably not surprising given the limited data available at that time), but very interesting. This more flexible approach seems more likely to be correct and it has been generalised in this study. Even if it still turns out that the lags in adjustment are the same for each explanatory variable, at least they will not have been imposed from the outset.

Estimation results

The results from trying to estimate flexible lags are given in Appendix 1, together with estimates from the simple distributed lag models. Simple models refer to those which have imposed *a priori* constraints on the lag weights; the lags have been derived from the standard assumptions of partial adjustment and adaptive expectations, both separately and in combination, and including the implications of imposing various restrictions on long-run parameter values. This represents the approach adopted in the majority of demand-for-money studies in all countries.

There are two main reasons for including the results from estimating equations imposing lag restrictions, even though we have argued in favour of an alternative approach. Firstly, it is within this framework that the argument has been made that a previously stable relationship has broken down. Since the more general approach also gave inconclusive results for the earlier periods dominated by the 1960s, the discovery of a more general relationship for longer periods including the 1970s may be interpreted as a shift in behaviour. It therefore seemed important to establish whether the simpler equations did actually break down. Secondly, given the wide use made of simple distributed lag models, they provide an ideal alternative against which to compare the more flexible approach.[4] Estimating these simple models over a variety of different overlapping data periods[5] does not establish a stable function for the earlier periods. However, as the data period is extended into the second half of the 1970s, the

---

[1] An argument that is often employed to support this assumption is that a change in the scale of measurement, e.g. a conversion of pounds to dollars, would not change real expenditures or the demand for real balances. This is certainly true, but it is not strictly relevant to this argument. What we are concerned with is a continuous updating of uncertain information, not a single discrete change that is universally accepted. Moreover, even if there is some theoretically correct concept of the price-level which would display a unitary elasticity, it is unlikely to correspond to any of the actual data series available.

[2] For a formal discussion of this question see Artis and Lewis.

[3] L. D. D. Price, 'The demand for money in the United Kingdom: a further investigation', March 1972 *Bulletin*, page 43.

[4] In order to estimate separate lags for each of the variables we have attempted to fit a general form of rational distributed lags, and also to estimate freely the individual lag coefficients. Attempts to estimate the weights employing the Almon technique (Shirley Almon, 'The Distributed Lag between Capital Appropriations and Expenditures', *Econometrica*, January 1965) did not prove particularly successful, with small changes in specification capable of producing quite large changes in the lag pattern. Perhaps this should be expected as there does seem to be some evidence, e.g. T. F. Cargill and R. A. Meyer, 'Some Time and Frequency Domain Distributed Lag Estimators: A Comparative Monte Carlo Study', *Econometrica*, November 1974, that the Almon technique is an unreliable method of approximating an unknown lag distribution.

[5] The first period is for 1964(1) to 1970(4), and this is extended by four quarters at a time up to 1976(4). In addition, equations were estimated for 1965(1) to 1976(4), and 1966(1) to 1976(4).

coefficients do become reasonably stable (i.e., they are changed only slightly, if at all, by lengthening or shortening the data period), and also seem economically plausible; in addition, estimates obtained employing quarterly and monthly data are very similar. This evidence could be used to support this approach, employing the argument that the existence of multicollinearity between the explanatory variables concealed the true relationship when the data available were limited to the 1960s and early 1970s. If this argument, in terms of limitations in independent data variation, is the complete explanation, then we would not expect to be able to improve on the best estimates obtained with this model. However, it is also possible that the equations have been mis-specified, and that this provides at least a partial explanation of the results obtained. In either case, it seems difficult to claim that a stable demand function for M_1 had been identified before 1971–72.

This conclusion is supported by the summary of results obtained in previous studies contained in Appendix 3. These results, taken together, do not suggest that stable equations, in any statistical sense, had been identified. A possible reconciliation of the apparent divergence between the earlier claims for stability, and the evidence of empirical studies, may be provided by recognising a qualitative difference in the nature of the evidence. The earlier studies, with only limited data available, obtained equations which had a good statistical fit, and a fairly low interest elasticity. When compared with the more extreme Radcliffian claims of an unstable relationship, and a potentially infinite interest elasticity, it was reasonable to claim that a stable demand function could be estimated. However, when those same equations were examined for internal stability, e.g. by Artis and Lewis, they failed the test. But now the criteria for comparison had changed. Moreover, the traditional M_3 relationship really did seem to break down, and this is likely to have coloured the interpretation of the less obvious evidence for M_1.

Although the evidence would now appear to support the existence of a stable demand-for-money function in the form of the previous simple lag models, the approach still seems too restrictive. In particular, it is unrealistic to impose the requirement that income, prices and interest rates all follow the same lag pattern of adjustment, suggesting that in this respect such equations may have been mis-specified. Rather than accept, or even attempt to 'improve', the statistical performance of these equations, an alternative approach has been adopted: to see if the data itself contained more information on the structure of the relationship, which was being ignored simply because the models that have generally been considered have been too restrictive. Instead of trying to justify very specific, narrowly defined, equations, it would be better to start from a general form and only accept the former if the restrictions they imply on the more general form are found to be satisfied.

This more flexible approach did in fact result in an improvement in explanatory power; see Appendix 1. Furthermore, as might be expected, the resulting lag pattern is quite complex, and is not the same for each of the explanatory variables (see chart). Lags do exist, although they generally seem to be short, and it is easy to see how the simpler distributed lag approximations might provide

Cumulative lag adjustment weights [a]

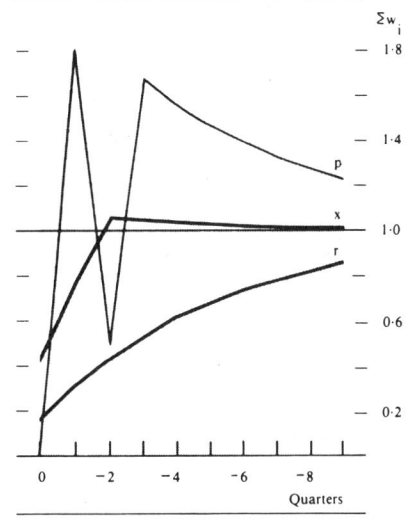

[a] These weights, derived from the general rational distributed lag approach, represent the *proportion* of the total adjustment to the long-run, equilibrium, value of the elasticities, for each of the explanatory variables, completed by the end of each period. The variables are defined in Appendix 1.

an apparently reasonable explanation; *at least so long as no more realistic alternative was considered*. An encouraging feature of these results is that very similar estimates are obtained employing a general rational distributed lag approach and when the individual lag coefficients are freely estimated. This is particularly true of the short-run coefficients (up to a year), although there is some difference in the estimated long-run behaviour.

The evidence clearly indicates a long-run real income elasticity that is very close to unity, with adjustment essentially completed after six months; a price elasticity of approximately 0.75, with no effect in the current quarter, over-adjustment after one quarter and probably completion of the process inside nine months. The total coefficient, and lag pattern, on the rate of interest is less obvious, but is definitely negative. There would seem to be a geometrically declining distributed lag on the rate of interest, although the possibility that the lag is much shorter cannot be excluded. The long-run elasticity is between -0.30 and -0.13, although in either case the value after six months is the same, at about -0.13. Given the transactions approach adopted, a high income elasticity suggests a numerically low interest elasticity. To this extent, the estimates are consistent, although most economists would expect a higher elasticity on prices and, possibly, a lower elasticity on income. This is because there is generally thought to be no money illusion, and some economies of scale in holdings of transactions balances. A number of tentative explanations can be put forward. For example, a possible explanation of the high income elasticity might be that transactions have been growing relative to expenditure so that the coefficient estimate on total final expenditure over-estimates the 'true' coefficient on transactions. Similarly for prices, it could be that as the price level rises the brokerage cost of transferring between money and alternative short-term assets has declined, so that the price term reflects this relationship, and the estimated elasticity is correspondingly reduced. Another possibility is that the deflator employed in estimation is not the same variable as in individual demand functions. This is always a problem with any attempt to find aggregate, composite variables to approximate individual behaviour. Such *ex post* justifications should be treated with extreme caution, and many more possibilities could probably be suggested. The results obtained, and the ease with which plausible explanations can be provided, however, illustrates the necessity to test even such firmly held theoretical propositions as the assumption of a unitary price elasticity.

Comparing the forecast performance of the main equations (Appendix 2) provides support for the conclusions already reached. The equations obtained employing the general approach perform substantially better than the more simple distributed lag models.[1] The forecast performance of these latter equations is in fact considerably worse than might have been expected on the basis of the estimation results obtained.

The stability of the preferred equations, and their *ex ante* forecasting performance, is highly encouraging; these equations correctly predicted the rapid growth of M_1 during 1977 on the basis of forecasts of income, prices and the rate of interest.[2] Any estimated equation must, to some extent, be specific to the period within which it was estimated, and it is therefore encouraging that the equations should have forecast accurately over 1977, which was completely excluded from the estimation period.

The apparent stability of the equations, and their predictive performance is rather better than might originally have been expected, particularly given the recent growth of interest-bearing deposits within the definition of M_1. Further developments in the financial system are quite likely to result in changes in the estimated relationship. It is hoped, however, that such changes will only take place gradually and not result in an abrupt shift in the estimated parameters. The limitations of any formal statistical relationship should be recognised, and there can be no guarantee that these equations will continue to perform as well in the future. However, as decisions have to be made about an uncertain future on the basis of imperfect information, a structural model of this kind should provide a useful guide in clarifying the various options which may exist.

Conclusions

The first point to emphasise is the relatively short lags in the adjustment of M_1 balances that have been estimated. These contrast sharply with the findings of many previous studies. The approach adopted has been not to impose *a priori* lag restrictions, but rather to allow for differing lag patterns on each of the explanatory variables. It is argued that this is a more illuminating approach and, in this case, has resulted in a better understanding of the short-run adjustment process. If there is a strong relationship between certain variables, this is likely to show up in many different forms, as we have seen. It is only in comparison with some alternative that the results can be judged, and very often the range of alternatives considered has been too narrowly defined.[3]

The wide use of distributed lag models in economics means that these results have potentially important implications over quite a broad area. It may be argued, as in this article, that there has been a lack of consistency in the various approaches adopted, but an added problem, which is not restricted to the demand for money, is that most quarterly data series have been compiled only since 1963. There have therefore been only limited data available for econometric testing. Furthermore, the 1960s may well not have been a very representative period, or one likely to yield strong econometric results. These considerations make it difficult to judge parameter stability over time.

There is no real evidence of a breakdown of the demand for M_1 function, as had been suggested, although the possibility of some shift in the relationship cannot be completely ruled out. However, the recent rapid growth in M_1 has at least been consistent with an apparently stable demand for money which is interest elastic, and the outcome has so far closely followed prior forecasts.

Finally, the preferred equations taken together do seem to have identified an adjustment process which is different for each of the explanatory variables, and is both rapid and quite stable. Furthermore, this behaviour could not be adequately captured by simple partial adjustment and adaptive expectations assumptions. It is a conclusion of this study that these simple models should not represent a starting point but only a *possible* outcome of a wider analysis of the data. Taking these results as a base, it should be possible to develop the analysis and obtain further improvements.

---

[1] In addition cusum and cusum of squares tests reveal no evidence of a breakdown of the preferred equations; see R. L. Brown, James Durbin and J. M. Evans, 'Techniques for Testing the Constancy of Regression Relationships over Time', *Journal of the Royal Statistical Society, Series B*, vol. 37, no. 2, 1975.

[2] However, all the forecasts contained in Appendix 2 have been made using actual, published, data on these variables.

[3] A similar argument has recently been proposed by A. S. Courakis, 'Serial Correlation and a Bank of England study of the Demand for Money Function: an Exercise in Measurement Without Theory', *University of Oxford*: mimeo., 1977; and D. F. Hendry and G. E. Mizon, 'Serial Correlation as a Convenient Simplification, Not a Nuisance: a Comment on a study of the Demand for Money by the Bank of England', *London School of Economics*, mimeo., January 1978.

INDEX

Acceptances, *see* Bills, bank
Arbitrage 52, 134, 150, 180
   see also Round tripping

Bank of England 156
   as banker to banking system 163
   as jobber of last resort 87
   Banking Department 109
   Bank of England Act 1946 84
   Issue Department 77, 111
   resources and income 154
   see also Lender of last resort
Bank rate 102, 105, 107, 114, 157
   see also Minimum lending rate
Banks 8, 34, 84
   bankers' balances 107
   cash settlement between 156
   clearing-bank cartel 40
   clearing banks' operational balances 104
   demand for bank credit 118
   deposit banks 33
   lending rates, flexibility of 44
   lending to the private sector 11, 39, 42, 138, 168
   London clearing banks 34
   quantitative controls on 139
   reserves 135
   structural change in banking system 177
   town clearing 156
   see also Competition in banking, Eligible banks, Lending, Liability management, Liquidity of banking system, Reserve asset ratio, Retail deposits, Special deposits, Supplementary special deposits scheme, Wholesale deposits
Bills
   bank 119, 125, 134, 165, 167
   bill leak 119, 125
   bill markets 152, 167
   bill operations 103
   Bills of Exchange Act 166
   commercial 119, 150, 166
   sale and repurchase agreements 163
   trade 119, 125
   see also Treasury bill tender

Cash deposits scheme 12, 85
Cash ratio 34, 105, 148, 154, 159
Central government borrowing requirement 8
Company sector 60
   finance of 70
Competition and Credit Control 2, 31, 52, 83, 114, 115, 119
Competition in banking 3, 32, 43, 52, 115, 178
Convertibility 8
'Corset', *see* Supplementary special deposits scheme
Counterinflationary strategy 72
   see also Incomes policy, Inflation, Medium-term financial strategy, Monetary targets
Credit controls 10, 11, 35, 38, 42, 69, 98
Credit policy 75

Debt management 11, 69, 75, 99
   aims of 79
   see also Funding policy, Gilt-edged stocks, Open market operations
Demand for money 18, 45, 52, 66, 172, 188

   empirical evidence 19, 23, 25, 67
   equation specification 173
   forecasting performance of equations 176, 192
Demand management 46, 53
   see also Keynesian analysis
Direction of investment 94
Discount houses 84, 103, 107, 122, 143, 153, 157, 159, 162, 167
   call money with 110
   undefined assets multiple 122
Domestic credit expansion (DCE) 5, 10, 36, 50, 66

Economic objectives 7, 53
Elasticity of demand for money
   income 176, 191
   interest 18, 174, 189
   see also Demand for money
Eligible banks 153, 154, 159, 168
Eligible liabilities 119, 154
Eurodollar market 34
Eurosterling market 126
Exchange controls 3
   abolition of 69, 125
Exchange rate 55, 73
Exchequer group 107, 110, 156
Expectations 13, 20, 64, 72, 80, 181
External capital flows 37, 55, 59, 138

Finance houses 84
Financial anchor 4
Financial innovation 3
Financial markets 9
Financial statistics 9
Fiscal policy 5, 68, 137
Flow-of-funds accounting 66
Foreign exchange transactions 132, 165
   see also Intervention in foreign exchange market
Funding policy 11, 150

Gilt-edged market 37, 74, 83, 86, 99
   official transactions 11, 37, 40, 47, 77, 116, 137
   uncertainty in 88
   see also Debt management, Open market operations

Gilt-edged stocks
   convertible 89, 101
   demand for 76
   index-linked 96, 101
   issue by auction 101, 102
   jobbers 76, 90, 93, 99, 153
   marketability 76
   minimum price tender 93, 101
   new issues 78
   partly paid 89, 100
   placing of issues 94
   redemptions 78
   sale and repurchase agreements 158, 160
   switching 78
   tender system 92
   tranches 101
   underwriting of issues 94
   variable rate 90, 100
   see also Tap stocks
Government broker 77

Government debt
  short-term instruments 95
  see also Gilt-edged stocks, National savings, Treasury bill tender

Hire purchase controls 12
Housing finance 10, 127

Incomes policy 46, 54, 63, 68
Indexation 96
Inflation 2, 4, 38, 48, 52, 54, 59
  expectations 50
Interest rates 16, 26, 40, 42, 44, 75, 80, 102, 114, 138, 143, 174
  CD rate 184
  ceilings 121
  operations 40
  policy 10, 69
  term structure 167
  unpublished band for short-term 103, 148, 160
Intermediation 3, 60
  disintermediation 69, 119, 125, 139
  reintermediation 52, 126
Intervention in foreign exchange market 37, 68
  see also Foreign exchange transactions
Institutions, long-term investment 94
Issue Department, see Bank of England

Keynesian analysis 15, 67, 181
Keynesian multipliers 27

Lender of last resort 130, 133, 134, 141
Lending
  ceilings 35, 115
  controls 121
  qualitative guidance 116
  see also Banks
Liability management 44, 52, 118, 133, 145
Liquidity of the banking system 130, 141, 147, 155
Liquidity ratio 34, 84, 105
Local authority temporary debt 95

Mais lecture 51
Mansion House speeches 1, 5, 6, 31, 42, 43, 46, 47, 48, 59, 60, 61
Medium-term financial strategy 63, 65, 69
  see also Counterinflationary strategy
Minimum lending rate (MLR) 102, 150, 157
  formula for setting 114
  see also Bank rate
Monetarist analysis 17, 36
Monetary aggregates 2
  choice of 39, 45, 56
  control of 71, 87
  structural change in 67
Monetary base 22, 129
  control 56, 61, 71, 103, 129, 148, 164
  indicator system 135, 141
Monetary control methods 4, 39, 61, 128, 140
Monetary forecasts 56
Monetary growth 43
  credit counterparts 45
Monetary management 56
Monetary multipliers 27
Monetary policy, effects of 13
Monetary strategy, political economy of 65

see also Medium-term financial strategy
Monetary targets 3, 45, 49, 53, 59, 61, 68, 98, 168
  rolling targets 57
Money 14
  at call 119
  definition of 26, 43, 45
  high-powered 129
  illusion 191
  supply as policy instrument 22
  transmission mechanism 15
Money market 35, 84, 102, 105, 107, 134, 156
  afternoon operations 163
  cash shortages 169
  morning operations 162
Multicollinearity 191

National debt
  management of 75
  National Debt Office 77
  see also Gilt-edged stocks
National savings 99

Open market operations 34, 83, 102, 148, 152
  see also Debt management, Gilt-edged market, Money market
Overdraft system 133
Overfunding 70, 150, 165, 168

Parallel markets 35, 125
Personal savings 127
Phillips curve 54
Private-sector liquidity 126
Public sector borrowing
  facilities 169
  requirement (PSBR) 46, 88, 137

Radcliffe Report 1, 5, 7, 16, 36, 51
Reserve asset ratio 40, 102, 115, 119, 120, 122, 144, 148
  see also Competition and Credit Control
Retail deposits 57
Round tripping 119, 120, 164
  see also Arbitrage

Secured deposits arrangements 153, 154, 159, 168
Special deposits 10, 34, 40, 105, 115, 119, 144, 154
  see also Competition and Credit Control
Stock Exchange 99
Supplementary special deposits scheme ('Corset') 3, 44, 52, 60, 117, 146
Sykes Memorial Lecture 83

Tap stocks 78, 100
  pricing of 91
  see also Gilt-edged stocks
Transactions costs 189
Treasury bill tender 108, 157

United States government bond market 92

Velocity 3, 21, 57, 62, 134, 179

Wealth effects 189
Wholesale deposits 119, 178

Yields 20